Global Neoliberalism and Education and its Consequences

Routledge Studies in Education and Neoliberalism

EDITED BY DAVE HILL, *University of Northampton, UK*

1. The Rich World and the Impoverishment of Education
Diminishing Democracy, Equity and
Workers' Rights
Edited by Dave Hill

2. Contesting Neoliberal Education
Public Resistance and
Collective Advance
Edited by Dave Hill

3. Global Neoliberalism and Education and its Consequences
Edited by Dave Hill and Ravi Kumar

4. The Developing World and State Education
Neoliberal Depredation and
Egalitarian Alternatives
Edited by Dave Hill and Ellen Rosskam

Global Neoliberalism
and Education and its
Consequences

Edited by Dave Hill
and Ravi Kumar

Routledge
Taylor & Francis Group
New York   London

First published 2009
by Routledge
270 Madison Ave, New York, NY 10016

Simultaneously published in the UK
by Routledge
2 Park Square, Milton Park, Abingdon, Oxon OX14 4RN

Routledge is an imprint of the Taylor & Francis Group, an informa business

© 2009 Taylor & Francis

Typeset in Sabon by IBT Global.
Printed and bound in the United States of America on acid-free paper by IBT Global.

Library of Congress Cataloging in Publication Data

Global neoliberalism and education and its consequences / edited by Dave Hill
  and Ravi Kumar.
    p. cm. — (Routledge studies in education and neoliberalism ; 3)
    Includes index.
    ISBN 978-0-415-95774-8
    1. Education—Economic aspects. 2. Education and globalization. 3. Neoliberalism. I. Hill, Dave, 1945– II. Kumar, Ravi, 1975–
    LC65.G457 2008
    338.4'337—dc22
    2008009017

ISBN10: 0-415-95774-5
ISBN10: 0-203-89185-6

ISBN13: 978-0-415-95774-8
ISBN13: 978-0-203-89185-8

Contents

Foreword   vii
   NICK GRANT

Acknowledgments   xix

1 Introduction: Neoliberal Capitalism and Education   1
   RAVI KUMAR AND DAVE HILL

2 Neoliberalism and Its Impacts   12
   DAVE HILL AND RAVI KUMAR

3 Neoliberalism, Youth, and the Leasing of Higher Education   30
   HENRY A. GIROUX

4 Higher Education and the Profit Incentive   54
   TRISTAN MCCOWAN

5 Trading Away Human Rights? The GATS and the Right
   to Education: A Legal Perspective   73
   PIERRICK DEVIDAL

6 Education, Inequality, and Neoliberal Capitalism:
   A Classical Marxist Analysis   102
   DAVE HILL, NIGEL M. GREAVES AND ALPESH MAISURIA

7 Brazilian Education, Dependent Capitalism,
   and the World Bank   127
   ROBERTO LEHER

8 World Bank Discourse and Policy on Education and Cultural
   Diversity for Latin America   151
   EDUARDO DOMENECH AND CARLOS MORA-NINCI

9 **The News Media and the Conservative Heritage Foundation: Promoting Education Advocacy at the Expense of Authority** 171
ERIC HAAS

10 **Markets and Education in the Era of Globalized Capitalism** 208
NICO HIRTT

11 **Education in Cuba: Socialism and the Encroachment of Capitalism** 227
CURRY MALOTT

Contributors 245
Index 249

Foreword

Nick Grant

ON DELIGHT AND RESPONSIBILITY

The English young people's author Philip Pullman wrote about the purpose and nature of education in an article for *The Guardian* newspaper of January 22, 2005. His poetic assertion was

> True education flowers at the point when delight falls in
> love with responsibility.

Pullman was concluding a lament on the false methods of teaching literacy that have become common in UK schools, which elevate the grammar of English above the motivations and impact of language use, or why humans want to communicate with each other, and what it is they desire to share observations about. After all, we don't give a baby a dictionary or thesaurus and then await its first essay or lecture!

The social delight in what a person is trying to say to another, and the dialogue it starts, should be the educationalist's starting point. The responsibility to analyze if and how this succeeds, so that we can remember and advance our collective skill, comes next. Learning will happen if we are responsible in this way about the things that delight us.

This is a potent phrase to bear in mind when surveying the global place of education today for students from all parts of the economic spectrum. Much learning is far from delightful. It is often mechanical, pointless, and disenchanting. For some it is an unattainable luxury. For millions it is often simply absent, nonexistent, unknown.

There is also great irresponsibility, exploitation even, in education's funding, administration, and purpose. Like every other commodity education is provided at a price paid often by fees. Increasingly, in the twenty-first century, education takes the form of global *edubusiness* run by *edupreneurs* as part of the investment by capital in service economies.

Increasingly for all parts of the world prepackaged learning materials, imposed curricula, and rigid, micromanaged schemes of work characterize a learning process in both private and public spheres which is passive, lacks dialogue, and intimidates speculative learning and discovery. Progressive notions such as creativity and internationalism are only sanctioned by government in their bastard forms, as necessary elements of global capitalist market competition, not universal hallmarks of humanity.

Teaching becomes mere "delivery" of externally preset activities and "to be driven" is now sufficient to pass for inspiration amongst both teachers and learners. In fact, there's so much 'driving' and 'delivering' going on that teaching could be taken over by each nation's postal service soon!

The learning process becomes almost entirely instrumental, devoted to jumping through forgettable hoops of certification.[1] In this sense the delight is with a student's mere accumulation of credits, not learning for its own, or a socially useful, sake. The producer's delight can be in the profits realizable in a business with a higher global turnover now than the automobile industry.

This global economy can be characterized as, with very few exceptions, one of neoliberalism. From north to south and east to west this system thinks and acts with local and historical variants but core contemporary similarities.

UK evangelists for a free-market approach to education provision such as James Tooley (e.g., Tooley, 2001), whose ideas have certainly contributed to the UK Labour government's shared taste since 1997 with their Conservative predecessors for public-private partnerships, would have us believe that not only can the private sector cater for the world's needs but it can also do so on an equitable basis.

Yet Tooley's simplistic propaganda about a handful of companies from mainly developing world contexts in *The Global Education Industry* barely scratches the surface of world need. According to the Global Campaign for Education (GCE) in 2005:

> . . . over 60 million girls and 40 million boys are still out of school worldwide. The first Millennium Development Goal—equal numbers of girls as boys attending school by 2005—has already been missed, and according to UNICEF, 9 million more girls than boys are left out of school every year. To give every girl and boy a decent primary education by 2015, recent rates of progress need to double in South Asia and quadruple in Africa. (Global Campaign for Education, 2005, p. 3)

The significance of girls' continuing noneducation is that evidence gathered over thirty years shows that educating women is the single most powerful weapon against malnutrition, even more effective than improving food supply. Without universal primary education, the other goals—stopping AIDS, halving the poverty figures, ending hunger and child death, even controlling climate change—won't happen.

For less than 5.5bn dollars more per year, we could provide a quality, free education to every child, and unlock the full power of education to beat poverty. This amounts to less than two and a half days' global military spending. For the price of just one of the cruise missiles dropped on Baghdad, 100 schools could be built in Africa. (Global Campaign for Education, 2005, p. 4)

Whether or not first-world aid is quite the simple solution implied by the GCE here, poorer countries and regions are undeniably in a double bind, having to weather both their historic disadvantages and the contemporary ubiquity of neoliberalism. Nearer home, six million UK adults still cannot read and as many as seventeen million are functionally innumerate.[2]

The issue therefore which motivates this collection of research has been put succinctly as follows:

Capitalism requires increasing numbers of workers, citizens and consumers who willingly do what they are told to do and think what they are told to think. The production of such human capital is the most fundamental role schools play in a capitalist society.

But while its strength is obvious and its overall aims are clear, the on-the-ground nature of this assault is still hard to pin down. (Martell, 2005, p. 5)

The writers in this book examine how neoliberalism actually works in education. The authors trace a general thread across a number of particular global sites to illuminate the turbulent yet recurrent features of learning in a new millennium. How do factors of race, ethnicity, and nationality, or gender and sexuality, impinge on new systems? What happens to minority languages and cultures? How does the rural interact with the urban? Who controls access to or has a voice in managing the new systems? What pay and conditions can the producers, the education workers, expect?

But having started with Philip Pullman's poetic attempt at a working definition of what we might mean by education, we now also need to indulge in "a naming of parts," outlining precisely what we mean by this core term neoliberalism.

DEFINING NEOLIBERALISM

North American geographer David Harvey's *Brief History of Neoliberalism* (2005) defines his subject as:

... in the first instance a theory of political economic practices that
proposes that human well-being can best be advanced by liberating
individual entrepreneurial freedoms and skills within an institutional
framework characterised by strong private property rights, free markets, and free trade. (Harvey, 2005, p. 2)

Harvey is particularly explicit about the relationship between the market
and the state:

The state has to guarantee, for example, the quality and integrity of
money. It must also set up those military, defence, police, and legal
structures and functions required to secure private property rights and
to guarantee, by force if need be, the proper functioning of markets.
Furthermore, if markets do not exist (in areas such as land, water, education, health care, social security, or environmental pollution) then
they must be created, by state action if necessary. But beyond these
tasks the state must not interfere. (Harvey, 2005, p. 2)

Not only have nations with differing political histories embraced neoliberalism from China to New Zealand, South Africa to Sweden, and
Chile to the United States, its apologists also occupy positions of strategic policy influence in the university corridors, media studios, banking
halls, and corporate boardrooms of every metropolis. Key international
finance institutions, such as the International Monetary Fund (IMF), the
World Bank and the World Trade Organization (WTO) are dominated
by its advocates. Indeed, neoliberalism has become "the common-sense
way many of us interpret, live in and understand the world." (Harvey,
2005, p. 3.)

This is not unlike the notion of "common sense" identified by Italian
Marxist Antonio Gramsci, when trying to rationalize the rise of Italian fascism. Indeed, former UK Foreign Minister and current Leader of the House
of Commons Jack Straw personally shopped at London's only socialist
bookshop, Bookmarks, one afternoon late in December 2006—with Min-
isterial bodyguards keeping watch at the door—to pick up volumes of both
Lenin and Gramsci.

Not everyone has followed Straw's career trajectory from student
communist to adult statesman. But a political problem for the remaining
left, in the postglasnost era, has arisen because a rhetoric of liberation
has been carried with such rightward-moving figures to sell a completely
different kettle of fish, usually passed off as a nebulous "Third Way"
politics.

It's not just that Iraq's invasion and occupation are pitched by governments in terms of freedom and democracy, but that the ideology of neoliberalism in education policy is now being touted as the radical solution
to historic underachievement of "deprived" communities. (Like their U.S.

counterparts, UK politicians are not allowed to say "working-class.")
Harvey, noting this language of classlessness in the service of ruling-class
power, questions its sell-by date:

> The widening gap between rhetoric (for the benefit of all) and realiza-
> tion (the benefit of a small ruling class) is now all too visible. (Harvey,
> 2005, pp. 202–203)

This perversion of terminology is not incidental and has had two effects.

First, parochially, it soothes the bile within the body of the UK
Labour Party for those few remaining foot soldiers demanding some
crumbs of domestic comfort to sweeten the bitter fruits of disastrous
foreign policies.

Second, and much more importantly for this global audience, it can
confuse our attempts to understand and identify precisely what level of
neoliberalism we're dealing with, which in turn deters the assembling of
oppositional strategies by elements sceptical of the neoliberal way. For
example, neoliberalism is usually equated with notions of modernity and
excellence, which can imbue its critics with accusations of being old-fash-
ioned and amateurish.

The United Kingdom, largely in the iconic form of Tony Blair, has come
to represent all that is apparently good about neoliberalism. We beg to
differ! Dexter Whitfield's invaluable handbook *New Labour's Attack on
Public Services* highlights 2005 data from the Organisation for Economic
and Co-operative Development (OECD) that show the United Kingdom
enjoying pole position for the "outsourcing" of governmental central services by a modern state; twice as much as France and Italy, more than
Germany and even more, incredibly, than the United States (Whitfield,
2006, p. 34)

UK public servants drown under incessant initiatives with dissembling
titles cascading and overlapping in all branches of our public services. A
new one is on top of us before previous ones have hit the ground. It's a
bedazzling enough picture for those that work daily inside these services;
it must be utterly mystifying to those that don't!

Perhaps the most outrageously misleading notion adored by Labour's
hierarchs is the entity labelled a "Trust." As the preferred funding and
administrative form in the National Health Service and now the British
Broadcasting Corporation it has produced obscene distortions of mis-
match between real needs and efficient services. Consequently there has
never been less popular *trust* in a governmental public sector policy. The
label is now being extended to schools, even though the word itself is
nowhere to be found in the enabling 2006 legislation.

Such inversions of truth and language are almost naturally apparent
from the southern hemisphere. Looking north to neoliberalism's strong-
holds Uruguyan Eduardo Galeano sees clearly that

"Developing countries" is the name that experts use to designate countries trampled by someone else's development. According to the United Nations, developing countries send developed countries ten times as much money through unequal trade and financial relations as they receive through foreign aid.

In international relations, "foreign aid" is what they call the little tax that vice pays virtue. Foreign aid is generally distributed in ways that confirm injustice, rarely in ways that counter it. In 1995, black Africa suffered 75 percent of the world's AIDS cases but received 3 percent of the funds spent by international organisations on AIDS prevention. (Galeano, 2006, p. 37)

This wonderful catalog of neoliberal absurdities, Galeano's *Upside Down: A Primer For a Looking Glass World,* also asks:

In the jungle, do they call the habit of devouring the weakest, the "law of the city"?
   From the point of view of sick people, what's the meaning of a "healthy economy"?
   Weapons sales are good news for the economy. Are they also good news for those who end up dead? (Galeano, 2006, p. 115)

Thus, as the common sense of the twenty-first century, neoliberalism hopes to shape not only the means by which wealth is created and disbursed but also the relations between those creating this wealth. As Harvey notes,

In so far as neoliberalism values market exchange as "an ethic in itself, capable of acting as a guide to all human action, and substituting for all previously held ethical beliefs," it emphasises the significance of contractual relations in the marketplace. It holds that the social good will be maximised by maximising the reach and frequency of market transactions, and it seeks to bring all human action into the domain of the market. (Harvey, 2005, p. 3)

So something as innocent as delight in learning, or the joy of play, can only confront the neoliberal as a challenge or threat, something to commodify, to turn from an intrinsic good into a saleable good, giving it a price before exchanging it for private gain.

   This privatization of value confronts the common wealth of peoples, expressed in terms of their spaces and places, resources and rituals, history and culture in all their signs and meanings, as an alien modernity.

NEOLIBERALISM'S GENESIS

This debasement of language and the prevalence of dog-eat-dog ethics are symptomatic of the neoliberal facts of life, but not their genesis. Harvey does therefore trace for us when, where, and how its predominance was achieved, with a very broad but captivating brush.

Financially key was the "Volcker shock" of 1979, marking a watershed between a period of post–World War II Keynesian orthodoxy (full employment but high inflation) and a period since of monetarist then neoliberal orthodoxy. Paul Volcker was chairman of the U.S. Federal Reserve Bank under President Jimmy Carter. Volcker's move to raise the nominal rate of interest overnight in October triggered a long, deep recession that would put millions out of work, neuter trade unions, initiate the dismantling of welfare states, and put debtor nations on the brink of insolvency.

Politically key were U.S. President Ronald Reagan and UK Prime Minister Margaret Thatcher, who both revelled in tax and budget cuts, deregulation, and confrontation. The key defeat of a strike by U.S. air traffic controllers by Reagan in 1981 and Thatcher's more protracted defeat of UK coal miners by 1985 became testaments to this hegemony. In Britain, energy, transport, and telecommunications industries were asset-stripped and sold off, and media operations were deregulated. The U.S. federal minimum wage, equal to the poverty level in 1980, was 30 percent below that level by 1990. U.S. corporate taxes were reduced dramatically and in 1985 top personal taxes were slashed from 70 percent to 28 percent!

The United Kingdom had already been subject to the infamous IMF squeeze on Chancellor Denis Healey in 1976, when the first retrenchment via funding cuts hit UK public services. By 1980 Thatcher had given banks and building societies new freedoms to lend, not just to nations or regions but also to individuals, producing the politically compromising 1.2 trillion pounds of personal credit card and mortgage repayment debt amongst UK workers in 2006.

This has impacted politically on UK trade unionism, in the sense that individual workers can, subject to increasingly slack credit rating, make a phone call or visit a cash machine rather than seek collective action strategies to improve their pay, thereby cementing Thatcher's legal proscriptions on secondary action[3] and mandatory balloting procedures[4] with the effect that between 1979 and 2006 the percentage of UK workers subject to collective bargaining agreements fell from 78 percent to 33 percent. Tony Blair had assured readers of *The Times* before his first election win on March 31, 1997 that those shackles would remain the most restrictive in the western world.

Also significant to the neoliberal strategy was a new kind of imperialism epitomized by the structural adjustment programs forced on most poor countries via the World Bank or the IMF. These were a kind of arms-length, or, in a different sense, arms-free imperialism. Control and subjugation was effected not by the occupation and repression of aggressor armies but by financial loans from banks, themselves awash with petro-dollars invested by the oil-producing megarich states, on condition that any indigenous state services or nationalized industries were opened up to privatization and control by western—usually North American—businesses.

Whether it is Zambia's copper industry, Tanzania's water supply, Ghana's schools or the continental need for affordable drugs to fight malaria, most of Africa, for example, has been subject to this process since the 1980s, reversing or smashing the political hopes born of the flight by force or consent of traditional Euro-imperialists since the 1960s.

The United States had finessed this strategy in its dealings with Central American nations such as Nicaragua and Cuba in earlier phases of the twentieth century, using local strongmen like Somoza and Batista to run U.S.-friendly political operations whilst keeping the locals quiet. Its fiscal stranglehold on Europe was enshrined with the postwar Marshall Plan, insisting on an easy ride for U.S. products in markets whose infrastructures were systematically restored with dollars and policed by military bases along the Iron Curtain. Any number of client regimes is now in place around the world prepared to do the U.S. president's bidding.

But of direct relevance to this discussion is another aspect of the neoliberal method that Harvey calls "accumulation by dispossession" (Harvey, 2005, pp. 160–165), a typically parasitic rather than regenerative process. That is to say, most fiscal energy within neoliberalism has not actually produced what could be called fresh wealth, but rather a redistribution or revalorisation of existing wealth.

For example, Harvey maintains that the average daily turnover of financial transactions in international markets was worth 2.3 billion dollars in 1983 and 130 billion by 2001. Of a total of 40 trillion dollars for the whole of 2001 Harvey insists that a mere 2 percent—80 billion—were used to support new trade or productive investment. This "churning," the repetitive trade on accounts without adding any real value, spawned phenomena such as hedge funds, which spread bets on the volatility of future stock market commodity prices to the personal accumulation of multimillion dollar riches by financiers. "Fat cats" in City of London finance houses would enjoy a collective bonus in the region of £8.8 billion, with hundreds of individuals pocketing a handy £1 million at the close of 2006—certainly a Christmas to remember for some!

Neoliberal governments and states have played their part in this by opening up new fields for capital accumulation in their own public utilities (water, telecoms, transport, housing, health, pensions, and prisons) and asset-stripping public land, buildings, and amenities whilst deregulating labor rights and environmental protection. Much urban open space is now privately owned and policed.

Such are the priorities that most governments in all areas of economic development will want to justify, sustain, and replicate via their education systems even if the emphasis may be differently balanced or more sophisticated per region, and the real needs much more mundane.

But judged more from a contradictory and child development perspective we might make some global observations.

In Massindi, northern Uganda, finding enough funds to build a robust, hygienic latrine for six hundred students and a dormitory for the girls who have fled the outlying war-torn districts, so that they can be taught in silence in classes of fifty by an occasional teacher, is progress.

In New Orleans, United States, reclaiming any form of public-sector provision would be a triumph right now.

In Nechells, Birmingham, England, getting school class sizes down to twenty-four with well-paid, well-qualified teachers in schools offering good food, plenty of drinking water, and a socially engaging, test-free curriculum to all students, would be progress.

My final comments concern the United Kingdom's new prime minister, Gordon Brown, because these remarks could apply equally to premiers and presidents throughout the world. A defining text to encompass the focus of this book is his speech at the Lord Mayor's Banquet for Bankers and Merchants of the City of London, the "Mansion House speech," made a week before he assumed the premiership of the United Kingdom on June 27, 2007. His opening praise for the success of free market endeavour is followed by a vow to create a UK education system in its honor, where, for instance, every school will have a business partner:

> Only with investment in education can open markets, free trade and flexibility succeed. And the prize is enormous. If we can show people that by equipping themselves for the future they can be the winners not losers in globalisation, beneficiaries of this era of fast moving change, then people will welcome open, flexible, free trade and pro-competition economies as an emancipating force.
>
> If we can become the education nation, great days are ahead of us.
>
> While never the biggest in size, nor the mightiest in military hardware, I believe we are—as the city's success shows—capable of being one of the greatest success stories in the new global economy.
>
> Already strong in this young century, but greater days are ahead of us. Britain the education nation. Britain a world leader for its talents and skills. So tonight, in celebrating the success of the talents, innovations and achievements of the city let us look forward to working together for even greater success in the future.[5]

The glaring contradiction here is liable to be reproduced internationally by current and aspirant politicians of many nations. It sees each state's education system as key to its position in a global league table of economic efficiency. The national good is somehow the international and global good, a sort of globalization in each country. The essentially social and cooperative ethic derived from a natural model of child development, which has informed most educationalists in most countries for centuries, is now challenged by a highly personalized and competitive model of education derived from modern business methodology.

So, this major critique of neoliberalism in schooling and education identifies the types, levers, extents, and impacts of neoliberal policies globally on education workers' rights, conditions and lives; on social class, "race" and gender and other forms of equity, social justice, and access; and on democracy, democratic control, and critical thinking in education.

Writers for this in-depth critical interrogation are a combination of radical academics and labor organization activists.

You, the audience, are expected to comprise students of education, sociology, politics, trade union studies, globalization studies and your teachers, as well as trade unionists and antiglobalisation activists everywhere.

We contend that this is a vital and ground-breaking collection of research in which all readers can find some true delight in learning about learning, but in the service of our common responsibility to make this planet a better place for us all to live on.

NOTES

1. Exemplified by E. Jaeger, "Silencing Teachers in an Era of Scripted Reading," *Rethinking Schools* 20, no. 3 (Spring 2006). www.rethinking-schools.org.
2. Cited by UK Culture, Media and Sport Minister Tessa Jowell in a speech to the Creative Partnerships *Exciting Minds* conference in Manchester on November 27, 2006.
3. Universally better known as "solidarity" or "sympathy action" by union members at nearby sites not necessarily run by the same employer, or other sites run by the same employer, such action was outlawed.
4. Any strike could only now be legal if a new set of bureaucratic steps taking at least a month to complete were adhered to, on pain of employers becoming entitled to seek the sequestration of the relevant union's funds as compensation for illegal or unofficial strikes. Such measures have yet to be repealed since a Labour government came into office in 1997.
5. Full text at: http://www.hm-treasury.gov.uk/newsroom_and_speeches/press/2007/press_68_07.cfm.

REFERENCES

Galeano, E. 1998. *Upside down: A primer for the looking glass world.* New York: Picador.
Global Campaign for Education. 2005. Missing the mark: A school report on rich countries' contribution to universal primary education by 2015. Available with much more useful material at http://www.campaignforeducation.org/resources/resources_latest.php.
Gramsci, A. 1971. *Selections from the prison notebooks.* London: Lawrence and Wishart.

Harvey, D. 2005. *A brief history of neoliberalism*. Oxford: Oxford University Press.

Martell, G. 2006. Introduction to *Education's iron cage and its dismantling in the new global order*. Special edition of *Our Schools/Our Selves* 15, no. 3 (Spring 2006). Contact: ccpa@policyalternatives.ca.

Tooley, J. 2001. *The global education industry. Lessons from private education in developing countries*. 2nd ed. London: Institute for Economic Affairs.

Whitfield, D. 2006. *New Labour's attack on public services*. Nottingham: Spokesman Press.

Acknowledgments

With thanks to my daughter Naomi Hill for her proofing and help and smiles and sunniness in Brighton, England, and to Eleanor Chan of IBT Global in Troy, New York for her proofing and efficiency and greatness to work with, and to Benjamin Holtzman at Routledge in New York for his support and encouragement and patience.

Thanks also to the radical academics, labour movement activists, and leftists and all those exposing and challenging the dominant neoliberal capitalist hegemony, and pointing the way to resistance to national and global economic, social and political injustices and oppression. Not all the writers by any means share my own democratic socialist/ Marxist beliefs and activism—writers in this book come from a variety of left and radical political and ideological traditions and perspectives. But we, in this book, unite in our criticisms of neoliberal Capital, and in our belief at its replacement.

1 Introduction
Neoliberal Capitalism and Education
Ravi Kumar and Dave Hill

THE CONTEXTS OF EDUCATIONAL CHANGE

There is a distinct criticality of the current historical conjuncture. This criticality of our times is characterized by redefinitions of fundamental concepts such as "equality," as neoliberal capital strives to mold discourses to suit its goal. While there is a euphoric façade of rhetoric such as "education for all" on one hand, there is a diminishing role of the state on the other. There is a definitive retreat of the state as a provider of education. This is true of the developed as well as the so-called developing world. This retreat is happening in the face of the global onslaught of private capital, with its insatiable appetite for maximizing surplus accumulation. Hence, we find the gradual destruction of comprehensive schooling in the United Kingdom and severe curtailment of funding for government schools in the United States. Countries like India, riding high on the glory of a booming economy, are no exception to these trends, as the state fails to grant children the right to education despite staggering illiteracy, high dropout rates, and inaccessibility to school facilities. The global march of capital continues relentlessly as opposition is fragmented, weakened, or co-opted. This, however, does not provide capitalism with a smooth path of expansion. It becomes entangled in its own contradictions and the discontent among the masses becomes amply clear in such moments, the case of French working-class assertion being the most recent.

This chapter contextualizes the current anti-egalitarian education system in two ways: (a) the ideological and policy context, and (b) the global/spatial context. The restructuring of the schooling and education systems across the world is part of the ideological and policy offensive by neoliberal capital. The privatization of public services, the capitalization and commodification of humanity, and the global diktats of the agencies of international capital—backed by destabilization of nonconforming governments and, ultimately, the armed cavalries of the United States and its surrogates—have resulted in the near-global (if not universal) establishment of competitive markets in public services such as education. These education markets are marked by selection and exclusion, and are accompanied by and situated within the rampant—indeed, exponential—growth of national and international inequalities.

It is important to look at the big picture. Markets in education, so-called "parental choice" of a diverse range of schools (or, in parts of the globe, the "choice" as to whether to send children to school or not), privatization of schools and other education providers, and the cutting of state subsidies to education and other public services are only a part of the educational and anti-public-welfare strategy of the capitalist class.

National and global capitalisms wish to cut public expenditure and have generally succeeded in doing so. They do this because public services are expensive. Cuts in public expenditure serve to reduce taxes on profits, which in turn increases profits from capital accumulation. Additionally, the capitalist class globally have: (a) a business agenda *for* education that centers on socially producing labor power (people's capacity to labor) for capitalist enterprises; (b) a business agenda *in* education that centers on setting business "free" in education for profit making; and (c) a business agenda for education corporations that allows edubusinesses to profit from national international privatizing activities.

THE CURRENT NEOLIBERAL PROJECT OF GLOBAL CAPITALISM

The fundamental principle of capitalism is the sanctification of private (or corporate) profit based on the extraction of surplus labor (unpaid labor time) as surplus value from the labor power of workers. It is a creed and practice of (racialized and gendered) class exploitation, exploitation by the capitalist class of those who provide the profits through their labor, the national and international working class.[1]

As Raduntz (2007) argues,

> globalisation is not a qualitatively new phenomenon but a tendency which has always been integral to capitalism's growth ... Within the Marxist paradigm there is growing recognition of the relevance of Marx's account expressed in *The Communist Manifesto* that globalisation is the predictable outcome of capitalism's expansionary tendencies evident since its emergence as a viable form of society.[2]

For neoliberals, "profit is God," not the public good. Capitalism is not kind. Plutocrats are not, essentially, philanthropic. In capitalism it is the insatiable demand for profit that is the motor for policy, not public or social or common weal, or good. With great power comes great irresponsibility. Thus privatized utilities such as the railway system, health and education services, and water supplies are run to maximize the shareholders' profits, rather than to provide a public service and sustainable development of third-world national economic integrity and growth. These are not on the agenda of globalizing neoliberal capital.[3]

McMurtry (1999) describes "the pathologization of the market model." He suggested that the so-called "free-market model" is not a free market at all, and that to argue for a "free market" in anything these days is a delusion: the "market model" that we have today is really the system that benefits the "global corporate market." This is a system where the rules are rigged to favor huge multinational and transnational corporations that take over, destroy, or incorporate (hence the "cancer" stage of capitalism) small businesses, innovators, etc. that are potential competitors.

Indeed, it is a system where the rules are flouted by the United States and the European Union (EU), which continue to subsidize, for example, their own agricultural industries, while demanding that states receiving International Monetary Fund (IMF) or World Bank funding throw their markets open (to be devastated by subsidized EU and U.S. imports).[4] Thus, opening education to the market, in the long run, will open it to the corporate giants, in particular Anglo-American-based transnational companies—who will run it in their own interests.

Rikowski (e.g., 2001, 2002a, 2002b, 2008) and others (e.g., Coates, 2001; Robertson, Bonal and Dale, 2002; Mojab, 2001; Pilger, 2002; Devidal, 2004; Hill, 2005a, 2005b, 2006, 2009; Hill and Kumar, 2009; Hill, Macrine and Gabbard, 2008) argue that the World Trade Organisation (WTO) and other "global clubs for the mega-capitalists" are setting up this agenda in education across the globe, primarily through the developing operationalizing and widening sectoral remit of the General Agreement on Trade in Services (GATS).

WHAT NEOLIBERALISM DEMANDS

The difference between classic (laissez-faire) liberalism of mid-nineteenth century Britain and the neoliberalism of today, based on the views of the neoliberal theorist Hayek, is that the former wanted to roll back the state, to let private enterprise make profits relatively unhindered by legislation (e.g., safety at work, trade union rights, minimum wage), and unhindered by the tax costs of a welfare state (e.g. Hayek and Caldwell, 2007).

On the other hand, *neoliberalism* demands a strong state to promote its interests, hence Andrew Gamble's (1988) depiction of the Thatcherite polity as *The free economy and the sStrong state: The politics of Thatcherism*. The strong interventionist state is needed by capital, particularly in the field of education and training—in the field of producing an ideologically compliant but technically and hierarchically skilled workforce. The social production of labor power is crucial for capitalism. It needs to extract as much surplus value as it can from the labor power of workers, as they transform labor capacity into labor in commodity-producing labor processes.

The current globally dominant form of capitalism, neoliberalism, requires the following within national states:

- inflation controlled by interest rates, preferably by an independent central bank,
- budgets balanced and not used to influence demand—or at any rate not to stimulate it,
- private ownership of the means of production, distribution and exchange,

- the provision of a market in goods and services—including private-sector involvement in welfare, social, educational and other state services (such as air traffic control, prisons, policing, pensions, public building works financed by private capital, and railways),
- within education the creation of "opportunity" to acquire the means of education (though not necessarily education itself) and additional cultural capital, through selection,
- relatively untrammeled selling and buying of labor power for a "flexible," poorly regulated labor market, and deregulation of the labor market for labor flexibility (with consequences for education),
- the restructuring of the management of the welfare state on the basis of a corporate managerialist model imported from the world of business (as well as the needs of the economy dictating the principal aims of school education, the world of business is also to supply a model of how it is to be provided and managed),[5]
- suppression of oppositional critical thought and much autonomous thought and education,
- a regime of denigration and humbling of publicly provided services, and
- a regime of cuts in the postwar welfare state, the withdrawal of state subsidies and support, and low public expenditure.

Internationally, neoliberalism requires that

- barriers to international trade and capitalist enterprise be removed,
- there be a "level playing field" for companies of any nationality within all sectors of national economies, and
- trade rules and regulations underpin "free" trade, with a system for penalizing "unfair" trade policies.

This is the theory, anyhow. Of course, rich and powerful countries and trade blocs, such as the USA and the European Union, still manage to circumvent some of these international requirements by, for example, subsidizing their own agricultural production/producers.

THIS BOOK

Within this given situation, when neoliberal capital appears to be an all-pervading phenomenon of capitalist expansion, this volume tries to understand the way it has affected education systems across different countries. The different chapters aim at exploring the consequences of the neoliberal onslaught on education. The chapters, for instance, demonstrate how media are used to manufacture knowledge or how the international financial institutions pressurize the so-called developing countries into accepting the terms and conditions of neoliberal rule. This volume brings together in one place the diverse aspects of neoliberal rule, its working mechanics, and impact on education, through presenting a global perspective.

In **Chapter 2: Neoliberalism and Its Impacts, Dave Hill and Ravi Kumar** show how neoliberal policies both in the United Kingdom and globally have resulted in (i) a loss of equity, economic and social justice; (ii) a loss of democracy and democratic accountability; and (iii) a loss of critical thought.

In **Chapter 3: Neoliberalism, Youth, and the Leasing of Higher Education, Henry A. Giroux** shows how, under the reign of neoliberalism, with its growing commercialization of everyday life, the corporatization and militarization of higher education, the dismantling of the social state, and the increasing privatization of the public sphere, it has become more difficult to address not only the complex nature of social agency and the importance of democratic public spheres, but also the fact that active and critical political agents have to be formed, educated, and socialized into the world of politics. Lacking either a project of hope or a theoretical paradigm for linking learning to social change, existing liberal and conservative political vocabularies appear increasingly powerless with respect to theorizing about the crisis of political agency, class, race, youth, and political pessimism in the face of neoliberal assaults on all aspects of democratic public life. As the vast majority of citizens become detached from public forums that nourish social critique, political agency not only becomes a mockery of itself, it is replaced by market-based choices in which private satisfactions replace social responsibilities and biographic solutions become a substitute for systemic change. As the worldly space of criticism is undercut by the absence of public spheres that encourage the exchange of information, opinion, and criticism, the horizons of a substantive democracy disappear against the growing isolation and depoliticization that marks the loss of a politically guaranteed public realm in which autonomy, political participation, and engaged citizenship make their appearance. With few exceptions, the project of democratizing public goods has fallen into disrepute in the popular imagination as the logic of the market undermines the most basic social solidarities. The consequences include not only a weakened social state, but a growing sense of insecurity, cynicism, and political retreat on the part of the general public. The incessant calls for self-reliance that now dominate public discourse betray an eviscerated and refigured state that does not care for those populations that it considers expendable, especially those who are young, poor, or racially marginalized. The brutality of neoliberalism in its destruction of democratic values, visions, and practices is particularly evident in its view and treatment of young people and higher education. Central to this chapter is a critical interrogation of the inextricable relationship among youth as a social investment, education as a foundation for political agency, and a democratic radical politics as a challenge to neoliberalism and a foundation for rethinking a democratic politics for the twenty-first century.

In **Chapter 4: Higher Education and the Profit Incentive, Tristan McCowan** analyses and critiques the dramatic increase in for-profit institutions (FPIs) of higher education in recent times, both in countries with developed university systems, such as the United States, and in middle-income countries like Brazil, the Philippines, and South Africa. James Tooley and others argue that the profit incentive will ensure that these institutions are cost-effective, providing a high quality of education and enabling an equitable expansion of the system. He identifies seven "virtues" of profit, which will bring positive change in higher education (HE) without the need for state intervention. However, an overview of recent developments in for-profit HE worldwide shows that, while the institutions in question are achieving impressive growth, they are neither contributing to equity nor providing an education of widely recognized quality. The need for profitability is seen to encourage FPIs to offer mainly low-cost courses taught by less-qualified, part-time staff. While little is invested in academic research, substantial resources are allocated to marketing so that demand can be maintained in the face of competition with other institutions. The growth of FPIs is also having an indirect influence on the activities of the public and nonprofit private institutions, and is contributing to a shift in society's understanding of the role of higher education.

In **Chapter 5: Trading Away Human Rights? The GATS and the Right to Education: A Legal Perspective, Pierrick Devidal** reminds us that the right to education is a fundamental human right which also constitutes one of the most precious tools of our societies to face the challenges of the future. In the context of globalization and progressive liberalization of trade, its progressive realization seems to be hindered by the development of the neoliberal agenda promoted by international economic organizations, such as the World Trade Organization (WTO). The birth of the General Agreement on Trade and Services (GATS) and the development of its ever-increasing tentacles have raised serious preoccupation among human rights defenders in general, and education professionals in particular. Indeed, the dynamics of the trade law and the international human rights law regimes appear to be conflicting. This fundamental conflict of norms brings out serious concerns for the protection of the right to education, now *de facto* perceived as a commodity or a service. Nevertheless, international human rights law provides the rules which guarantee the protection of the right to education from the nefarious developments of trade in services. Therefore, because of its superiority and special status the right to education must be protected by states, which bear the obligation to safeguard it from a threatening economic integration. Education is to be taken out of the GATS and of the realm of action of the WTO. The challenges posed by the cross-border internationalization of education can adequately be faced through other mechanisms that would ensure a full implementation of the right to education, while protecting it from being traded away to economic actors which do not have the capacity or the interest to defend it. Therefore, states have to be reminded of their legal obligation to achieve the difficult realization of the right to education through a movement of international public cooperation based on the respect for the most fundamental human-rights principles.

In **Chapter 6: Does Capitalism Inevitably Increase Inequality? Dave Hill, Nigel Greaves and Alpesh Maisuria** explore educational inequality through a theoretical and empirical analysis. They use classical Marxian scholarship and class-based analyses to theorise about the relationship between education and the inequality in society that is an inevitable feature of capitalist society/economy. The relationship between social class and the process of capitalization of education in the United States and the United Kingdom is identified, where neoliberal drivers are working to condition the education sector more tightly to the needs of capital. The empirical evidence is utilized to show how capital accumulation is the principal objective of national and international government policy, and of global capitalist organizations such as the WTO. The key ontological claim of Marxist education theorists is that education serves to complement, regiment and replicate the dominant-subordinate nature of class relations upon which capitalism depends, the labor-capital relation. Through these arguments they show that education services the capitalist economy, helps reproduce the necessary social, political, ideological, and economic conditions for capitalism, and, therefore, reflects and reproduces the organic inequalities of capitalism originating in the relations of production. They also note that education is a site of cultural contestation and resistance. They conclude that, whether in terms of attainment, selection, or life chances, it is inevitable that education systems reflect and express the larger features of capitalist inequality.

In **Chapter 7: Brazilian Education, Dependent Capitalism, and The World Bank, Roberto Leher** examines the changes in Brazilian and Latin American education and suggests that these cannot be exclusively examined from an endogenous educational field perspective. It is essential to relate them to the transformations of the material base and the correlation of forces between social classes inside and outside the country. The starting point of this study analyzes the 1982 debt crisis and the IMF/ World Bank conditions for debt repayment, deepening Brazil's capitalist dependent condition, and Latin America's as well. Public education of quality is no longer strategic in government policies that represent the dominant financial, agricultural and mineral sectors. In the past 25 years an extraordinary expansion of the managerial sector in higher education has occurred. In the same period, public universities have had decreasing resources in spite of the expansion of student registrations. In the perspective of the international capitalist organizations and dominant bourgeois factions, education is understood as an ideological instrument for governing, strongly reducing public spaces of production and socialization of knowledge committed to national problems. Considering the consequences of neoliberal adjustment, it is possible to examine how public education has been defended by antisystemic movements. In Brazil, the Landless Workers Movement (MST) had the first initiative of creating a "popular university," defending education as a political strategy, contributing to articulate several organizations to combat the World Bank's agenda and to defend the public against the private-mercantile.

In **Chapter 8: The World Bank Discourse and Policy on Education and Cultural Diversity for Latin America, Eduardo Domenech** and **Carlos Mora-Ninci** examine the discourse and policy of the World Bank in the field of education regarding cultural diversity, and its relationship with social inequality since the late 1990s. Throughout the past decade, the consequences of implementing policies that include privatization, dismissals of teachers, lowering of real incomes, decentralizing of services, changes in the curriculum towards more accountability, higher standards in the direction of unreachable achievements, and the involvement of banks and private enterprises with the purpose of optimizing profits, together have produced a general widening gap between, on the one hand, an education system for the private schools and elite universities of the very rich; and on the other, the growth of a ripped-off public schools system for the poor. Our analysis suggests that the World Bank discourse and policies in regard to diversity and inequality in education are supported in a technocratic and pragmatic logic founded in a conservative vision of society.

In **Chapter 9: The News Media and the Conservative Heritage Foundation: Promoting Education Advocacy at the Expense of Authority, Eric Haas** emphasizes that since Americans rely on the mass media news as an important source of information on education issues, they indirectly vest news sources with the power to help define the terms of the debate. The mass media news has widely and regularly included think tanks, especially conservative ones, for information and research on education.

This chapter presents data on the scope and presentation of education-related documents and spokespersons from the Heritage Foundation by the news media during 2001. The Heritage Foundation was created to promote conservative values and ideas, and it is one of the largest, most cited, and most influential think tanks of a conservative movement that dominates public policy debate and formation. Emphasizing marketing over research, the Heritage Foundation has aggressively promoted education publications and "experts" with little apparent expertise to policy makers and the news media.

Analysis of news articles shows that news media outlets across the country regularly included the Heritage Foundation as an expert source of information on education in their presentation of education issues, despite the general consensus that they are an advocacy think tank rather than an academic research think tank. Moreover, almost every news item presented the Heritage Foundation in a more favorable scientific light than its actual credentials and practices warranted. This use and presentation by the news media likely increased the Heritage Foundation's influence in promoting conservative education policies like school choice, reductions in education spending, and high-stakes standardized testing.

To the degree that parents and policy makers look to the mass media news for accurate and complete information about schools and education, they did not receive it in the use of Heritage Foundation sources.

In **Chapter 10: Markets and Education in the Era of Globalized Capitalism, Nico Hirtt** notes that since the end of the 1980s, the educational systems of advanced capitalist countries have been submitted to an unceasing flow of criticism and reforms: decentralization, growing school autonomy, program deregulation, more attention to skills and less attention to knowledge, diverse partnerships between education and industry, massive introduction of Information and Communication Technology, and rapid development of private, for-profit education.

These mutations mark a new identity between school and business, namely the transition from the era of "massification" of education to the era of "merchandization" of education. In a context of great economic uncertainty and of growing inequality in the labor market, the educational system is summoned to adapt itself, to sustain more efficiently the economic competition, in a threefold process: first, by educating the workforce; second, by educating and stimulating consumers; and third, by opening itself to the conquest of the markets. As a matter of fact, we have to speak about a threefold "merchandization" that concerns the education system in all its dimensions: curricula, organization, management, and even pedagogic methods.

The present evolution in the education system is taking place at the cost of reduced access to the knowledge and skills required to understand and play a role in today's world. It is precisely those who are most exploited who are being deprived of the intellectual weapons they need to fight for their collective emancipation.

In **Chapter 11: Education in Cuba: Socialism and the Encroachment of Capitalism, Curry Malott** discusses "Cuban education in neoliberal times." He explores the historical development of "socialism" in Cuba, focusing on education, the most important "pillar of the revolution," according to Castro and the Cuban government. Highlighting this point, Castro has frequently noted that "the work of education is perhaps the most important thing the country should do" (Castro, 1997, pp. 4–5, cited in Malott in this volume, and in Malott, 2007) (see also Castro, 2004). Malott situates Cuban education in the context of over fifty years of U.S. terrorism rendering not only their survival, but the social gains in not only education but health care, nothing short of remarkable, by any comparative standards. As the most recent testament of the Cuban government's dedication to the Cuban people, the country's world-renowned social programs have remained solid and growing in the face of neoliberal politics that have forced the nation to reprivatize selected sectors of the economy to support those very programs. Ultimately, Malott challenges us to reflect on what we can learn about fighting capitalism from that tiny island of socialism situated in a sea of capitalism. In the final analysis the complex answer seems to lie within the country's unwavering international solidarity.

NOTES

1. For a debate on, and rebuttal of, the thesis that "class is dead," and/or that the working class has diminished to the point of political insignificance, see Callinicos and Harman (1987); Callinicos (1995); German (1996); Hill (1999); Cole et al. (2001); Hill and Cole (2001); Harman (2002); Hill, Sanders and Hankin (2002). Outside the Marxist tradition, it is clear that many critics of class

analysis (such as Jan Pakulski, 1995) confound class consciousness with the fact of class—and tend to deduce the salience (some would argue, nonexistence) of the latter from the "absence" of the former. The recognition by Marx that class consciousness is not necessarily or directly produced from the material and objective fact of class position enables neo-Marxists to acknowledge the wide range of contemporary influences that may (or may not) inform the subjective consciousness of identity—but in doing so, to retain the crucial reference to the basic economic determinant of social experience.

2. See also Cole (1998, 2004, 2007). It is not our purpose here to discuss contrasting theories of globalization.

3. In the wake of a series of fatal rail disasters it has become readily apparent that public safety has been subordinated to private profit. For example, between 1992 and 1997, the number of people employed in Britain's railways fell from 159,000 to 92,000, while the number of trains increased. "The numbers of workers permanently employed to maintain and renew the infrastructure fell from 31,000 to between 15,000 and 19,000 (Jack, 2001). So Capital downsizes its labor forces to upsize its profits. One result has been an unprecedented series of major fatal train crashes in Britain since the Thatcher government in Britain privatized the railways.

4. See the film *Life and Debt*, about the effect of the World Trade Organisation in effectively destroying the dairy agriculture industry in Jamaica (*http://www. lifeanddebt.org.about*). See also Bircham and Charlton's (2001) *Anti-capitalism: A guide to the movement* and Dee's (2004) *Anti-capitalism: Where now?*

5. The existing management of elite and the undemocratic bureaucracy has been able to develop a management model which gives space to private capital through different concepts such as the public private partnership (PPP). Such a model, while it furthers the interest of private capital, also retains existing structures so that bureaucracy does not endanger its own existence.

REFERENCES

Bircham, E., and J. Charlton. 2001. *Anti capitalism: A guide to the movement.* London: Bookmarks.

Callinicos, A. 1995. *The revolutionary ideas of Karl Marx.* 2nd ed. London: Bookmarks.

Callinicos, A., and C. Harman. 1987. *The changing working class.* London: Bookmarks.

Castro, F. 1997. Editorial. *Granma* (the daily newspaper of the Communist Party of Cuba. Havan, Cuba.

Castro, F. 2004. Speech given by Commander in Chief Fidel Castro Ruz, President of the Republic of Cuba, at the closing session of the Young Communists League 8th Congress, Havana, Cuba. Online at http://www.cuba.cu/gobierno/discursos/2004/ing/f051204i.html.

Coates, B. 2001. GATS. In *Anti-capitalism: A guide to the movement*, ed. E. Bircham and J. Charlton, 27–42. London: Bookmarks.

Cole, M. 1998. Globalization, modernization and competitiveness: A critique of the new labour project in education. *International Studies in Sociology of Education* 8, no 3: 315–332.

———. 2004. New Labour, globalization and social justice: the role of education. In *Critical theories, radical pedagogies and global conflicts*, eds. G. Fischman, P. McLaren, H. Sunker and C. Lankshear, 3–22. Lanham, MD: Rowman and Littlefield.

———. 2007. *Marxism and educational theory: origins and issues.* London: Routledge.

Cole, M., D. Hill, P. McLaren, and G. Rikowski. 2001. *Red chalk: On schooling, capitalism and politics.* Brighton: Institute for Education Policy Studies.

Dee, H. ed. 2004. *Anti-capitalism: Where now?* London: Bookmarks.

Devidal, P. 2004. Trading away human rights: The GATS and the right to education. *Journal for Critical Education Policy Studies* 2, no 2. http://www.jceps.com/?pageID=article&articleID=28.

Gamble, A. 1988. *The free economy and the strong state.* London: Macmillan.

German, L. 1996. *A question of class.* London: Bookmarks.

Harman, C. 2002. The workers of the world. *International Socialism* 96: 3–45.

Hayek, F. A., and B. Caldwell. 2007. *The road to serfdom: Text and documents— The definitive edition* (The Collected Works of F. A. Hayek). Chicago: University of Chicago Press.

Hill, D. 1999. Social class and education. In *An introduction to the study of education,* ed. D. Matheson and I. Grosvenor, 84–102. London: David Fulton.

———. 2005a. Globalisation and its educational discontents: Neoliberalisation and its impacts on education workers' rights pay and conditions. *International Studies in Sociology of Education* 15, no. 3: 257–88.

———. 2005b. State theory and the neoliberal reconstruction of schooling and teacher education. In *Critical theories, radical pedagogies and global conflicts,* ed. G. Fischman, P. McLaren, H. Sünker, and C. Lankshear, 23–51. Boulder, CO: Rowman and Littlefield.

———. 2006. Education services liberalization. In *Winners or Losers? Liberalizing public services,* ed. E. Rosskam, 3–54. Geneva: ILO.

———. 2009. *Contesting neoliberal education: Public resistance and collective advance.* London: Routledge.

Hill, D., and M. Cole. 2001. Social class. In *Schooling and equality: Fact, concept and policy,* ed. D. Hill and M. Cole, 137–159. London: Kogan Page.

Hill, D., and R. Kumar. eds. 2009. *Global neoliberalism and education and its consequences.* New York: Routledge.

Hill, D., S. Macrine, and D. Gabbard. eds. 2008. Capitalist education: *Globalisation and the politics of inequality.* London: Routledge.

Hill, D., M. Sanders, and T. Hankin. 2002. Marxism, class analysis and postmodernism. In *Marxism against postmodernism in educational theory,* ed. D. Hill, P. McLaren, M. Cole, and G. Rikowski, 159–194. Lanham, MD: Lexington Books.

Jack, I. 2001. Breaking point. *The Guardian.* April 3. http://www.guardian.co.uk/politics/2001/apr/03/greenpolitics.hatfield.

Malott, C. 2007. Cuban education in neoliberal times: Socialist revolutionaries and state capitalism. *Journal for Critical Education Policy Studies* 5, no 1. http://www.jceps.com/index.php?pageID=article&articleID=90.

McMurtry, J. 1999. *The cancer stage of capitalism.* London: Pluto Press.

Mojab, S. 2001. New resources for revolutionary critical education. *Convergence* 34, no.1: 118–125. http://www.ieps.org.uk.cwc.net/mojab2002.pdf.

Pakulski, J. 1995. Social movements and class: The decline of the Marxist paradigm. In *Social movements and social classes,* ed. L. Maheu, 55–86. London: Sage.

Pilger, J. 2002. *The new rulers of the world.* New York: Verson.

Raduntz, H. 2007. Comments on a draft of this chapter. (Personal communication: unpublished).

Rikowski, G. 2001. *The battle in Seattle.* London: Tufnell Press.

———. 2002a. *Globalisation and education.* A paper prepared for the House of Lords Select Committee on Economic Affairs, Inquiry into the Global Economy. http://www.ieps.org.uk%20or%20rikowski@tiscali.co.uk.

———. 2002b. *Schools: building for business.* http://www.ieps.org.uk.

———. 2008. Globalization and Education Revisited. *Firgoa: universidade publica.* http://firgoa.usc.es/drupal/node/39090.

Robertson, S., X. Bonal, and R. Dale. 2001. GATS and the education service industry: The politics of scale and global re-territorialization. *Comparative Education Review* 46, no. 2: 472–96.

2   Neoliberalism and Its Impacts

Dave Hill and Ravi Kumar

INTRODUCTION

Neoliberal policies both in the United Kingdom and globally (see Harvey, 2005; Hill, 2005, 2006a, 2009a, b; Hill and Rosskam, 2009; Klein, 2008) have resulted in (a) a loss of equity as well as economic and social justice; (b) a loss of democracy and democratic accountability, and (c) a loss of critical thought. Each of these effects is discussed here.

THE GROWTH OF NATIONAL AND GLOBAL INEQUALITIES

Inequalities both between states and within states have increased dramatically during the era of global neoliberalism. Global capital, in its current neoliberal form in particular, leads to human degradation and inhumanity and increased social class inequalities within states and globally. These effects are increasing (racialized and gendered) social class inequality within states, increasing (racialized and gendered) social class inequality between states. The inequality within societies has acquired new forms. While one finds an increasing class-based polarization at ground level, there is an effort by the ruling classes to substitute for class, as the fundamental defining characteristic of social identity, different social identities such as race and caste. The efforts at rejecting the primacy of class as the primary constituent of social relations are being put forth also by some "celebrated" progressive educationists (such as Apple, e.g. 2006). Sadly enough, progressive working-class movements across the globe also fall prey to such discourses. And ultimately, they facilitate the unhindered march of neoliberal capital and the degradation and capitalization of humanity, including the environmental degradation impact primarily in a social-class-related manner. Those who can afford to buy clean water don't die of thirst or diarrhea.

Kagarlitsky has pointed out that "globalisation does not mean the impotence of the state, but the rejection by the state of its social functions, in favor of repressive ones, and the ending of democratic freedoms" (2001, quoted in Pilger, 2002, p. 5). Many commentators (e.g., Apple, 1993; Hill, 2001a) have discussed the change since the mid-1970s in many advanced capitalist economies from a social democratic/welfare statist/ Keynesian state to a neoliberal state, to what Gamble (1988) has termed *The free economy and the strong state*. The strong state and the repressive apparatuses of the state, have, of course, been dramatically upgraded (in terms of surveillance, control, policing in its various forms) in the wake of September 11, 2001.[1]

According to the UNDP Human Development Report (HDR) 2005 only nine countries (4 percent of the world's population) have reduced the wealth gap between rich and poor, whilst 80 % of the world's population have recorded an increase in wealth inequality. The report states that

> the richest 50 individuals in the world have a combined income greater than that of the poorest 416 million. The 2.5 billion people living on less than $2 a day—40% of the world's population—receive only 5 percent of global income, while 54 percent of global income goes to the richest 10 percent of the world's population. (UNDP, 2005, p. 4)

Writing in May, 2008, Van Auken noted that

> According to the Food and Agriculture Organization (FAO), global food prices have risen by 45 percent in the last nine months alone, with the cost of some basic commodities soaring far higher—wheat by 130 percent and rice by 74 percent over the past year. With 2.5 billion peaple—40 percent of the world's population—living on less than $2 a day, these spiraling food prices confront hundreds of millions with the imminent specter of starvation.

In India, celebrated as an emerging "tiger economy" a recent Government of India report has calculated that 77 percent of Indians live on an income of less that half a dollar per day. This is roughly around 836 million people (Government of India, 2007, p. 6).

The Working Group on Extreme Inequality (2008) (see also Cavanagh and Collins, 2008) in a section headed, Extreme inequality by numbers, displays the following data:

> The top 400 U.S. income-earners in 2005, the *Nation* coverage notes, collected 18 times more income than the top 400 in 1955, and that's *after* adjusting for inflation.

The top one percent of households received 22.9 percent of all pre-tax income in 2006, more than double what that figure was in the 1970s. (The top one percent's share of total income bottomed out at 8.9 percent in 1976.) This is the greatest concentration of income since 1928, when 23.9 percent of all income went to the richest one percent.

The above figures include capital gains, which are strongly affected by the ups and downs of the financial markets. Excluding capital gains, the richest one percent claimed 18.2 percent of all pre-tax income in 1973.) This is the greatest concentration of income, excluding capital gains, since 1929, when the richest one percent received 19.4 percent of such income.

Between 1979 and 2006, the top five percent of American families saw their real incomes increase 87 percent. Over the same period, the lowest-income fifth saw zero increase in real income.

In 1979, the average income of the top 5 percent of families was 11.4 times as large as the average income of the bottom 20 percent. In 2006, the ratio was 21.3 times. In the 2008 tax year, households in the bottom 20 percent will receive $26 due to the Bush tax cuts. Households in the middle 20 percent will receive $784. Households in the top 1 percent will receive $50,495. And households in the top 0.1 percent will receive $266,151.

CEO Pay: In 2006, CEOs of major U.S. companies collected as much money from one day on the job as average workers made over the entire year. These CEOs averaged $10.8 million in total compensation, the equivalent of over 364 times the pay of an average American worker. (Institute for Policy Studies and United for a Fair Economy, Executive Excess 2007, based on data from the Associated Press.)

Meanwhile, *Forbes* magazine estimated that the top 20 private equity and hedge fund managers, on average, took in $657.5 million in 2006, or 22,255 times the pay of the average U.S. worker.

Wages: Between 1972 and 1993, the average hourly wage dropped from $19.32 to $16.20 in 2007 dollars. Since 1993, the average hourly wage has regained only a part of the ground lost, rising to $17.88. Adjusted for inflation, the average wage in 2007 was still lower than it was in 1979.

David Tothkopf, (2008a) has noted

> "The credit crisis is exacerbating the emerging backlash against corporate excess," he wrote. "Elites make billions on markets whether they go up or down and their institutions win government support while the little guy loses his home. Multinational chief executives 30 years ago made 35 times the wages of an everage employee; today it is more than 350 times. The crisis has focused attention on the obscene inequities of this era—the world's 1,100 richest people have almost twice the assets of the poorest 2.5 billion. (See also Rothkopf, 2008b)

It was Karl Marx, more than 140 years ago, who developed the "Theory of Increasing Misery" to explain this inherent feature of capitalist production.

Accumulation of wealth at one pole is, therefore, at the same time accumulation of misery, agony of toil, slavery, ignorance, brutality, mental degradation, at the opposite pole, i.e., on the side of the class that produces its product in the form of capital. (Marx, 1867. See also International Marxist Tendency, 2008).

Markets in Education

Markets have exacerbated existing inequalities. There is considerable data on how poor schools have, by and large, become poorer (in terms of relative education results and in terms of total income) and how rich schools (in the same terms) have become richer. Whitty, Power, and Halpin (1998) examined the effects of the introduction of quasi-markets into education systems in the United States, Sweden, England and Wales, Australia, and New Zealand. Their book is a review of the research evidence. Their conclusion is that one

of the results of marketizing edu
of schools, and/or setting up new
choice of parents and their childr
ized school hierarchies.

In the United Kingdom, for ε
and 1997, the Conservatives est
(children and their parents) by
the local (state, i.e., public) prir
sive school. Thus they introdu
ogy Colleges and Grant Main
from the control of Local (d
firm this creation of a "quas
"parental choice" of schools
anywhere in the country.

Not only that, but the Conservat_
tive, positive discrimination funding for schools. _
were substantially taken out of the hands of the democratically elected _
education authorities (LEAs) by the imposition of per capita funding for
pupils/school students. So students in poor/disadvantaged areas in an LEA
would receive the same per capita funding as "rich kids." Furthermore, this
funding rose or fell according to intake numbers of pupils/students, itself
affected by henceforth compulsorily publicized "league table" performance
according to pupil/student performance at various ages on SATs (Student
Assessment Tasks) and 16+ examination results. (This "equality of treatment" contrasts dramatically with the attempts, prior to the 1988 Education
Reform Act, of many LEAs to secure more "equality of opportunity" by
spending more on those with greatest needs—a power partially restored in
one of its social democratic polices by the New Labour government following its election in 1997).

The result of this "school choice" is that inequalities between schools have
increased because in many cases the "parental choice" of schools has become
the "schools' choice" of the most desirable parents and children—and rejection of others. "Sink schools" have become more "sinklike" as more favored
schools have picked the children they think are likely to be "the cream of
the crop." Where selection exists the sink schools just sink further and the
privileged schools just become more privileged. Teachers in sink schools are
publicly pilloried, and, under "New Labour" the schools are "named and
shamed" as "Failing Schools," and, in some cases either reopened with a new
"superhead" as a "Fresh Start School" (with dismissals of "failing" teachers),
or shut down (see, for example, Whitty, Power, and Halpin, 1998).

These Conservative government policies are classic manifestations of neoliberal, free-market ideology, including the transference of a substantial percentage of funding and of powers away from LEAs to "consumers" (in this
case, schools). "Ostensibly, at least, these represent a "rolling back" of central and local government's influence on what goes on in schools" (Troyna,
1995, p.141).

Conservative government
and remains a mixture of
its neoconservatism is i
1995; cf. Hill, 1997a
involved in promo
cally elected LE
New Labo
ciples and
pettitiven
and b
con
19

Party policy in England and Wales remained
neoliberalism and neoconservatism. An aspect of
s "equiphobia"—fear of equality (Myers in Troyna,
, its hostility to agencies or apparatuses thought to be
ng equality and equal opportunities—such as (democrati-
As (Gamble, 1988; Hill, 1997a, 1999, 2001b).
r's education policy modifies and extends Radical Right prin-
nti-egalitarianism (Hill, 1999, 2001b). Its policy for more *com-
ss* (between schools, between parents, between pupils/students,
tween teachers) and *selection* (by schools and by universities) are a
nuation, indeed, an extension, of most of the structural aspects of the
88 Conservative Education Reform Act, in terms of the macrostructure
and organization of schooling. The Radical Right principle of competition
between schools (which results in an increasing inequality between schools)
and the principle of devolving more and more financial control to schools
through local management of schools are all in keeping with preceding Conservative opposition to comprehensive education and to the powers of LEAs,
as are the ever- increasing provision of new types of school and attacks on
"mixed-ability teaching" and the increased emphasis on the role/rule of capital in education.

New Labour's neoconservatism, echoing that of the Conservatives, also
perpetuates the "strong state" within the "free economy" (i.e., the deregulated, low-taxed, competitive, ultra-capital-friendly economy).

Governments in countries such as Britain, the United States, Australia, and
New Zealand have marketized their school systems. Racialized social class
patterns of inequality have increased. And at the level of university entry,
the (racialized) class-based hierarchicalization of universities is exacerbated
by "top-up fees" for entry to elite universities, pricing the poor out of the system, or at least into the lower divisions of higher education. And, to control
the state apparatuses of education, such marketization is controlled by heavy
systems of surveillance and accountability (Hill and Rosskam, 2009).

Thus, with respect to the United States, Pauline Lipman (2001) notes,

> George W. Bush's "blueprint" to "reform" education, released in Feb-
> ruary 2001 (*No Child Left Behind*) (Bush, 2001), crystallizes key neo-
> liberal, neo-conservative, and business-oriented education policies. The
> main components of Bush's plan are mandatory, high-stakes testing and
> vouchers and other supports for privatizing schools.

Lipman (2001) continues,

> The major aspects of this Agenda and Policy are . . . standards, account-
> ability, and regulation of schools, teachers and students and an explicit
> linkage of corporate interests with educational practices and goals.

Mathison and Ross (2002) detail the many recommended interventions,
both direct (the business agenda *in* education) and indirect (the business

agenda *for* education) by capital in the U.S. environment of corporate take-overs of schools and universities:

> In K–12 schools some examples are school choice plans (voucher systems, charter schools), comprehensive school designs based on business principles (such as economies of scale, standardization, cost efficiency, production line strategies), back to basics curricula, teacher merit pay, and strong systems of accountability. In universities some examples are the demand for common general education and core curricula (often not developed or supported by faculty), demands for common tests of student core knowledge, standardized tests of knowledge and skill for professional areas, promotion of "classic" education, and elimination of "new" content areas such as women's studies, post-modernism, and multiculturalism.

On an international level, diktats by the World Bank, the International Monetary Fund, and other agencies of international capital have actually resulted in the actual disappearance of formerly free nationally funded schooling and other education (and welfare, public utility) services (Hill, 2006a, c). One of the "fast growing economies" in the world, India has principally been doing away with the agenda of equality in education. While the discourse of "choice" has legitimized private education at all levels, those sections which lack purchasing power are being systematically deprived of equal access to good quality education (Kumar, 2006a, Kumar and Paul, 2006). Government schools are the only option left for them.

THE GROWTH OF UNDEMOCRATIC (UN)ACCOUNTABILITY

Within education and other public services business values and interests are increasingly substituted for democratic accountability and the collective voice. This applies at the local level, where, in Britain for example, private companies—national or transnational—variously build, own, run, and govern state schools and other sections of local government educational services (Hatcher and Hirtt, 1999; Hatcher, 2001, 2002; Hirtt, 2008). As Wilson (2002) asked,

> There is an important democratic question here: is it right to allow private providers of educational services based outside Britain (and, I would add, inside Britain, too, indeed, wherever they are based). In the event of abuse or corruption, where and how would those guilty be held to account? . . . Who is the guarantor of "the last resort"? (p. 12)

This antidemocratization applies at national levels, too. As Barry Coates (2001) has pointed out, "GATS locks countries into a system of rules that means it is effectively impossible for governments to change policy, or for voters to elect a new government that has different policies." (p. 28).

In connection with the principle of democratic control, quite interestingly, the discourse on "community participation" and decentralization has been consistently put forth by the World Bank (Kumar, 2006b, pp. 308–13) and by United Nations agencies. However, far from being democratic they ultimately become a top-down approach of governance. Under pressure from such global developmental discourses many states in the so-called third world have factored in what they claim as "democratic accountability" in their state-run educational programs. But it has remained a failure because (a) it runs as a program and not as a permanent concern of the state towards its citizens,[3] and (b) it does not take into consideration the societal politics or economic context of the masses which determine their participation.

THE LOSS OF CRITICAL THOUGHT

The increasing subordination of education, including university education, and its commodification, have been well documented (e.g., Levidow, 2002, Hill, 2001a, 2002, 2004a, b, 2007; Giroux and Myrsiades, 2001; Giroux and Searls Giroux, 2004; Ross and Gibson, 2007; Rikowski, 2007; CFHE, 2003).[4] One aspect is that other than at elite institutions, where the student intake is the wealthiest and most upper-class, there is little scope for critical thought. Scholars have examined, for instance, how the British government has, in effect, expelled most potentially critical aspects of education from the national curriculum, such as sociological and political examination of schooling and education, and questions of social class, "race" and gender for what is now termed *teacher training*, which was formerly called *teacher education*. Across the globe and more so in the newly liberalized economies such as India there is a trend towards looking down upon social sciences on the grounds that they do not produce an employable population. The mantra is of job-oriented courses, which is reflected when many universities and colleges transform their history courses into travel and tourism courses (*The Hindu*, 2004). The change in nomenclature is important both symbolically and in terms of actual accurate descriptiveness of the new, "safe," sanitized and detheorized education and training of new teachers (e.g., Hill, 2001a; 2004a; 2007). Even in those parts of the world where the neoliberal processes were set in motion by the 1990s we find not only that teacher education is transformed into teacher training, but that even the training period has been progressively declining (Sadgopal, 2006; Kumar, 2006c). What can be more disastrous than the systematic degeneration of the role of a teacher to a member of the informalized workforce, which lacks job security and works with a meager salary of as little as twenty-five dollars per month in some of the provinces in India (Leclercq, 2003).

McMurtry (2001) describes the philosophical incompatibility between the demands of capital and the demands of education, inter alia, with respect to critical thought. Governments throughout the world are resolving this incompatibility more and more on terms favorable to capital. One example in England and Wales is the swathe of redundancies/dismissals of teacher educators specializing in the sociology, politics, and contexts of education following the conforming of teacher education and the imposition of a skills-based rigidly monitored national curriculum for teacher training in 1992–1993. One dismissal was, for instance, of one of the authors (Dave Hill) himself. At a stroke, numerous critical teacher educators were removed or displaced. So too were their materials/resources—no longer wanted by the government. Thus, at the College from which I was dismissed, the Centre for Racial Equality, was closed down—its resources no longer required by the new technicist, detheorised, anticritical "teacher training" curriculum (Hill, 1997b, c, 2003). At a more general level, Mathison and Ross (2002) note that

> [the] university's role as an independent institution is increasingly threatened by the interests of corporations in both subtle and obvious ways. "Globalization, "—which Bertell Ollman (2001) defines as "another name for capitalism, but it's capitalism with the gloves off and on a world scale. It is capitalism at a time when all the old restrictions and inhibitions have been or are in the process of being put aside, a supremely self-confident capitalism, one without apparent rivals and therefore without a need to compromise or apologize"—has transformed internal and external relations of university from teaching and research to student aid policies and pouring rights for soft drink manufacturers. Decreased funding for higher education has made universities increasingly susceptible to the influence of big money and threatens the academic freedom and direction of research.

EDUCATION, CLASS, AND CAPITAL

Glenn Rikowski's work, such as *The Battle in Seattle* (2000, 2001, 2007), develops a Marxist analysis based on an analysis of labor power. With respect to education, he suggests that teachers are the most dangerous of workers because they have a special role in shaping, developing and forcing the single commodity on which the whole capitalist system rests: labor power. In the capitalist labor process, labor power is transformed into value-creating labor, and, at a certain point, surplus value—value over and above that represented in the worker's wage—is created. Surplus value is the first form of the existence of capital. It is the lifeblood of capital. Without it, capital could not be transformed into money, on sale of the commodities that incorporate value, and hence the capitalist could not purchase the necessary raw materials, means of production and labor power to set the whole cycle in motion once more. But most importantly for the capitalist is that part of the surplus value that forms his or her profit—and it is this that drives the capitalist on a personal basis. It is this that defines the personal agency of the capitalist!

Teachers are dangerous because they are intimately connected with the social production of labor power, equipping students with skills, competences, abilities, knowledge, and the attitudes and personal qualities that can be expressed and expended in the capitalist labor process. Teachers are guardians of the quality of labor power! This potential, latent power of teachers explains why representatives of the state might have sleepless nights worrying about the role of teachers in ensuring that the laborers of the future delivered to workplaces throughout the national capital *are* of the highest possible quality.[5]

Rikowski suggests that the state needs to control the process for two reasons: first, to try to ensure that this occurs, and second, to try to ensure that modes of pedagogy that are antithetical to labor power production do not and cannot exist. In particular, it becomes clear on this analysis that the capitalist state will seek to destroy any forms of pedagogy that attempt to educate students regarding their real predicament—to create an awareness of themselves as future labor powers and to underpin this awareness with critical insight that seeks to undermine the smooth running of the social production of labor power. This fear entails strict control of teacher education and training, of the curriculum, and of educational research.

CAPITALISM'S EDUCATION AGENDAS

How, in more detail, do education markets fit into the grand plan for schooling and education? What is capitalism's "business plan for education"?

In pursuit of these agendas, new public managerialism—the importation into the old public services of the language and management style of private capital—has replaced the ethic and language and style of public service and duty. Education as a social institution has been subordinated to international market goals, including the language and self-conceptualization of educators themselves (see Mulderrig, 2002; Levidow, 2002). Mulderrig shows how

> education is theoretically positioned in terms of its relationship with the economy and broader state policy (where) an instrumental rationality underlies education policy discourse, manifested in the pervasive rhetoric and values of the market in the representation of educational participants and practices.

She theorizes this

> as an indicator of a general shift towards the commodification of education and the concomitant consumerisation of social actors [within which] discourse plays a significant role in constructing and legitimizing post-welfare learning policy as a key aspect of the ongoing project of globalization.

And the Campaign for the Future of Higher Education slams the commodification of higher education by pointing out that

> students are neither customers nor clients; academics neither facilitators nor a pizza delivery service. Universities are not businesses; producing consumer goods. Knowledge and thought are not commodities, to be

purchased as items of consumption, whether conspicuous or not, or consumed and therefore finished with, whether on the hoof as take-away snacks or in more leisurely fashion. Education is not something which can be "delivered," consumed and crossed off the list. Rather, it is a continuing and reflective process, an essential component of any worthwhile life—the very antithesis of a commodity. (Campaign for the Future of Higher Education, 2003)

Within universities and vocational further education the language of education has been very widely replaced by the language of the market, where lecturers "deliver the product," "operationalize delivery," and "facilitate clients' learning," within a regime of "quality management and enhancement," where students have become "customers" selecting "modules" on a pick 'n' mix basis, where "skill development" at universities has surged in importance to the derogation of the development of critical thought.

Richard Hatcher (2001, 2002, 2006a, 2006b) shows how capital/business has two major aims for schools. The first aim is to ensure that schooling and education engage in ideological and economic reproduction. National education and training policies in the business agenda *for* education are of increasing importance for national capital. In an era of global capital, this is one of the few remaining areas for national state intervention—it is *the* site, suggests Hatcher, where a state can make a difference.

The second aim—the business agenda *in* schools—is for private enterprise, private capitalists, to make money out of it, to make private profit out of it, to control it.

THE CAPITALIST AGENDA *FOR* SCHOOLS

Business wants education fit for business—to make schooling and higher education subordinate to the personality, ideological, and economic requirements of capital, and to make sure schools produce compliant, ideologically indoctrinated, procapitalist, effective workers.

This first agenda constitutes a broad transnational consensus about the set of reforms needed for schools to meet employers' needs in terms of the efficiency with which they produce the future workforce. The business agenda *for* schools is increasingly transnational, generated and disseminated through key organizations of the international economic and political elite such as the Organisation for Economic Co-operation and Development (OECD). In that global context there is a project for education at the European level, which represents the specific agenda of the dominant European economic and political interests. It is expressed in, for example, the various reports of the European Round Table (ERT) of industrialists, a pressure group of forty-five leaders of major European companies from sixteen countries, and it has become the motive force of the education policies of the European Commission and its subsidiary bodies. Monbiot quotes the ERT as saying "the provision of education is a market opportunity and should be treated as such" (ERT, 1998, cited in Monbiot, 2001, p. 331; see also Hatcher and Hirtt, 1999; Hirtt, 2008).

THE CAPITALIST AGENDA *IN* SCHOOLS

Second, business wants to make profits from education and other privatized public services such as water supply and health care.

The work of Molnar (2001, 2005), Monbiot (2000, 2001, 2002), Robertson (Robertson, Bonal, and Dale, 2001) in the United States and in Britain by Rikowski (2001, 2002a, 2002b, 2002c, 2002d, 2003) and Hill (1999, 2006b) highlight another aspect of what national and multinational capital wants from schooling and education—it wants profits through owning and controlling them. Thus privatization of schools and educational services is becoming "big business" (so, too, are libraries—see Ruth Rikowski, 2002). As the weekly radical newsletter *Schnews* exclaims, in an April 2000 article entitled "The Coca-Cola Kids,"

> Education in the West is fast becoming indistinguishable from any other industry. Privatization of education was this week put in the spotlight with the National Union of Teachers threatening strike action not just over performance related pay, but also over big business moving in on the classroom. But what the hell is "Best Value," "Out-sourcing," "Action Zones," and the "Private Finance Initiative"? Shall we peer into the New Labour Dictionary of Gobbledee Gook to find out just what it all means?
>
> How about "Privatization, privatization, privatization." Yes, New Labour is busy selling off everything—they just dress it up in fancy jargon to try and pull the wool over our eyes. Still, why would private companies want to move into education? McDonalds" "operations manual" gives us a clue: "Schools offer excellent opportunities. Not only are they a high traffic (sales) generator, but students are some of the best customers you could have. " And with £38 billion spent on education a year, there's a lot to play for.

Of course, ultimate responsibility within private-company-owned schools and colleges and libraries is not to children, students or the community—it is to the owners and the shareholders.

Such privatization and loss of tax/publicly funded clean water, clinics, and schools results directly in death, disease, and dumbing down (Bircham and Charlton, 2001).[6]

THE CAPITALIST AGENDA INTERNATIONALLY

Rikowski (2002a, 2008) examines the role of the General Agreement on Trade in Services (GATS) and the British government's role in seeking to give British companies the lead in educational privatization internationally. He points out that since February 2000, a whole series of GATS negotiations have taken place. As Matheson (2000) noted,

Backed by the US and UK Governments, the WTO aims to liberalise the service sector further. The immediate impact would be the privatization of some services that have so far been provided by governments. Governments would be obliged to sell off such services as housing, education and water. (p. 9, cited in Rikowski 2002d p. 14)

The drive to privatize public services is powered by a number of forces, but in terms of the GATS the urgency derives from two main considerations. First, home-grown operators need to be nurtured—and quickly—so that when a more powerful GATS process exists U.K. operators in education, health, social services, and libraries can fend off foreign enterprises. This is not just because the Government believes that more of the profits from these privatized public services are likely to remain in the United Kingdom; it is primarily because of the need to "sell" the idea of private companies running schools, hospitals, libraries, and social services to the British public. While French companies might be tolerated for providing electricity or water, the U.K. government perceives there may be more of a problem with American or other nations' companies running schools as profit-making ventures.

Secondly, as Monbiot (2002) indicates, drawing on the work of Hatcher (2001), the government is also mightily concerned that the fledgling U.K. businesses currently taking over our public services can develop rapidly into export earners. This is already happening. For example, the education business Nord Anglia is already exporting its services to Russia and the Ukraine as well as running schools and LEA services in the United Kingdom. Many U.K. universities have franchised operations and a whole raft of deals with other colleges and universities in other countries. U.K. university Schools of Education generate income through consultancies that advise countries like Chile, Poland, and Romania on how to restructure school systems. The government is keen to maximize this export potential across all the public services. The World Trade Organization (WTO) has identified 160 service sectors, and British and U.S. businesses would benefit particularly if the GATS could liberalize trade in services still further by incorporating currently "public" services into their export drives.

In 2000, Britain exported £67 billion worth of services. New education, health, library, and social services business would provide "new opportunities for this export trade to expand massively" (Tibbett, 2001, p. 11). Thus, "international businesses have now seized on service provision as a money-making opportunity" (Matheson, 2000, p. 9). As the WTO Services Division Director David Hartridge said in a speech in 2000, "[GATS] can and will speed up the process of liberalization and reform, and make it irreversible" (Matheson, 2000, p. 9).

The pressure from corporations on the U.S., British and other EU governments to deliver on the GATS is colossal. As Allyson Pollock argues, "[business] sponsors and the Treasury are clear that the future of British business rests on trading in public services on an international scale regardless of the social costs" (Pollock, 2001).

Finally, the leading capitalist powers (the "Quad"—the United States, the EU, Japan, and Canada), driven on by major corporations and business interests, are

> trying to revise GATS so it could be used to overturn almost any legislation governing services from national to local level . . . Particularly under threat from GATS are public services—health care, education, energy, water and sanitation. . . . A revised GATS could give the commercial sector further access and could make existing privatizations effectively irreversible. (Sexton, 2001, p. 1)

This helps explain the British government's determination to push through privatizations, to provide deregulatory frameworks for state services (e.g., the recent Education Bill) and to nurture the growth of indigenous businesses that can virus public sector operations. As yet, there has been no final agreement on the GATS (Education International, 2008) or on its regional variant in the European Union, the Bolkstein Directive (Basketter, 2006; Hill 2006a). Resistance to the GATS is ongoing (Hill, 2009).

NOTES

1. See Hill (2001a) for a discussion of various types of government and state policy: neoconservative, neoliberal, "Third Way," social democratic, socialist, Marxist. See Saltman and Gabbard (2003) and Hill (2001c, 2004a, b, 2006b) for a discussion of the increasing role of the repressive and surveillance state apparatuses in society and in education.

2. See Gillborn and Mirza (2000), Hill, Sanders and Hankin (2002), Joseph Rowntree Foundation, 2007; The Poverty Site, 2007; Gillborn, 2008; Hill, 2009c for recent data on (racialized and gendered) social class inequalities in income, wealth and educational attainment in England and Wales—and how much inequality has increased since 1979 and Althusser, 1971, for the original formulation of these concepts.

3. One needs to differentiate between a program of education and the educational edifice as such. While programs are temporary arrangements to allow spaces for private capital to be created in contemporary times, the educational edifice in the form of government schools is permanent in character, which the neoliberal seeks to destroy.

4. In capitalist society, "well-being" is now equated with "well-having"—we are what we consume. In educational terms our worth is how many years and credits we have accumulated. Indeed, being a student is now a serious game, to build up credits to get a better job. In the United States and in England and Wales today, as in other advanced capitalist states, economic goals of education have sidelined social/societal/community goals, the traditional social democratic goals of education, and have also replaced education/learning for its own sake, the traditional liberal and liberal-progressive goals of education.

5. Perhaps the easiest way of understanding the concept of "national capital" is with respect to Rikowski's definition in terms of *national labour markets*: "the labour-power needs of national capitals refer to those labour-power capacities required for labouring in any labour process throughout the national capital . . . [There] is the drive [to increase] the quality (of labour-power) vis-a-vis other national capitals for gaining a competitive edge" (Rikowski, 2001b, p. 42). This particular definition points towards the national capital (when being viewed in relation to labor power) as the national labor market.

6. This is an important claim, that privatization and loss of tax/publicly funded clean water, clinics, and schools result directly in death, disease, and dumbing down. Many of the chapters in Bircham and Charlton, J. (2001) give examples of this. So, too, with respect to global society, do Cole (2007; George [2004]; Harvey [2005]); Hill (2004b); Hill and Cole (2001); Hill, Sanders, and Hankin (2002); Klein (2001, 2002); Mojab (2001); Monbiot (2000); Navarro, 2007; Pilger (2002).

REFERENCES

Althusser, L. 1971. Ideology and ideological state apparatuses: Notes toward an investigation. In *Lenin and philosophy and other essays*, ed. L. Althusser. New York and London: Monthly Review Press. http://www.marx2mao.com/Other/LPOE70ii.html#s5.

Apple, M. 1993. *Official knowledge: Democratic education in a conservative age.* London: Routledge.

————. 2006. Rhetoric and reality in critical educational studies in the United States. *British Journal of Sociology of Education* 27, no. 5: 679–87.

Basketter, S. 2006. Bolkestein: the monster haunting Europe. *Socialist Worker*, Jan 14, 1983. http://www.socialistworker.co.uk/art.php?id=8072.

Bircham, E., and J. Charlton. 2001. *Anti-capitalism: A guide to the movement.* London: Bookmarks.

Bush, G. W. 2001. *No child left behind.* U.S. Department of Education. http://www.ed.gov/inits/nclb.

Campaign for the Future of Higher Education. 2003. http://www.cfhe.org.uk.

Cavanagh, J. and C. Collins. 2008. The Rich and the Rest of Us. *The Nation*, 11 June. http://www.thenation.com/doc/20080630/cavanagh_collins.

Coates, B. 2001. GATS. In *Anti-capitalism: A guide to the movement*, ed. E. Bircham and J. Charlton, 27–42. London: Bookmarks.

The Coca Cola Kids. 2000. *Schnews 257.* http://www.schnews.org.uk/archive/news257.htm#Top.

Cole, M. 2007. *Marxism and educational theory: Pasts, origins and issues.* London: Routledge.

Education International. 2008. GATS and Globalization: News: "Final Push on Doha?" Brussels: Education International. Online at http://www.ei-ie.org/gats/en/newsshow.php?id=749&theme=gats&country=global.

Gamble, A. 1988. *The free economy and the strong state.* London: Macmillan.

George, S. 2004. *Another world is possible if . . .* London: Verso.

Gillborn, D. 2008. *Racism and education: coincidence or conspiracy?* London: Routledge.

Gillborn, D and H. Mirza. 2000. *Educational Inequality; Mapping race, class and gender—a synthesis of research evidence.* London: Ofsted.

Giroux, H. and S. Searls Giroux. 2004. *Take back higher education.* London: Palgrave MacMillan.

Giroux, H. and K. Myrsiades. 2001. *Beyond the corporate university.* Lanham, MD: Rowman and Littlefield.

Government of India. 2007. *Report on conditions of work and promotion of livelihoods in the unorganised sector.* National Commission for Enterprises in the Unorganised Sector: New Delhi.

Harvey, D. 2005. *A brief history of neoliberalism.* Oxford, England: Oxford University Press.

Hatcher, R. 2001. Getting down to the business: Schooling in the globalised economy. *Education and Social Justice* 3, no. 2: 45–59.

————. 2002. *The Business of education: How business agendas drive labour policies for schools.* London: Socialist Education Association. *http://www.socialisteducation.org.uk.*

————. 2006a. Business sponsorship of schools: For-profit takeover or agents of neoliberal change? *Volumizer,* November 5, 2005. http://journals.aol.co.uk/rikowskigr/Volumizer/entries/651.

————. 2006b. Privatisation and sponsorship: The re-agenting of the school system in England. *Journal of Education Policy* 21, no. 5: 599–619.

Hatcher, R., and N. Hirtt. 1999. The business agenda behind labour's education policy. In *Business, business, business: New Labour's education policy,* eds. M. Allen, C. Benn, C. Chitty, M. Cole, R. Hatcher, N. Hirrt, and G. Rikowski. London: Tufnell Press.

Hill, D. 1997a. Equality and primary schooling: The policy context intentions and effects of the conservative "reforms." In *Equality and the national curriculum in primary schools,* ed. M. Cole, D. Hill and S. Shan, 15–47. London: Cassell.

————. 1997b. Critical research and the dismissal of dissent, *Research Intelligence* 59, 25–26.

————. 1997c. Reflection in initial teacher education. In *Teacher education and training,* Vol. 1 of *Educational dilemmas: Debate and diversity,* ed. K. Watson, S. Modgil, and C. Modgil, 193–208. London: Cassell.

————. 1999. *New Labour and education: Policy, ideology and the third way.* London: Tufnell Press.

————. 2001a. Equality, ideology and education policy. In *Schooling and equality: Fact, concept and policy,* ed. D. Hill and M. Cole, 7–34. London: Kogan Page.

————. 2001b. *The Third Way in Britain: New Labour's neoliberal education policy.* Paper presented at the Conference Marx 111, Universite de Sorbonne/Nanterre, Paris. http://www.ieps.org.uk.

————. 2001c. Education, struggle and the left today: An interview with three UK Marxist educational theorists: Mike Cole, Dave Hill and Glenn Rikowski by Peter McLaren, *International Journal of Education Reform* 10, no. 2: 145–162.

————. 2002. The radical left and education policy: Education for economic and social justice. *Education and Social Justice* 4, no. 3: 41–51.

Hill, D. 2003. second edition. *Brief autobiography of a Bolshie dismissed.* Brighton: Institute for Education Policy Studies. http://www.ieps.org.uk.cwc.net/bolsharticle.pdf.

————. 2004a. Books, banks and bullets: Controlling our minds: The global project of imperialistic and militaristic neoliberalism and its effect on education policy. *Policy Futures* 2, nos. 3–4. http://www.wwwords.co.uk/pfie/content/pdfs/2/issue2_3.asp.

————. 2004b. Educational perversion and global neo-liberalism: a Marxist critique. *Cultural Logic: An Electronic Journal of Marxist Theory and Practice.* http://eserver.org/clogic/2004/2004.html.

————. 2005. Globalisation and its educational discontents: Neoliberalisation and its impacts on education workers' rights pay and conditions. *International Studies in Sociology of Education* 15, no. 3: 257–88.

————. 2006a. Education services liberalisation. In *Winners or losers? Liberalising public services,* ed. E. Rosskam, 3–54. Geneva: International Labour Organisation

————. 2006b. Six theses on class, global capital and resistance by education and other cultural workers. In *Introductory reflections: From re-action to action in contemporary social thought,* ed. O.-P. Moisio and J. Suoranta, 191–218. Jvaskyla, Finland: SoPhi. http://www.sensepublishers.com/catalog/files/90–77874–17–8.pdf.

————. 2006c. Class, capital and education in this neoliberal/ neoconservative period. *Information for Social Change* 23. http://libr.org/isc/issues/ISC23/B1%20Dave%20Hill.pdf.

————. 2006d. *New Labour's education policy.* In *Education studies: Issues and theoretical perspectives,* eds. D. Kassem, E. Mufti and J. Robinson, 73–86. Buckingham: Open University Press.

————. 2007. Critical teacher education, New Labour in Britain and the global project of neoliberal capital. *Policy Futures* 5, no.2.

————. 2008a. ed. *Contesting neoliberal education: Public resistance and collective advance.* London/New York: Routledge.

————. 2008b. ed. *The Rich World and the impoverishment of education: Diminishing democracy, equity and workers' rights.* New York: Routledge.

————. 2008c. *Social class, caste and 'race' in India and Britain: A Marxist analysis critique of caste and of 'race' theory and politics. Radical Notes.* http://radicalnotes.com.

Hill, D., and M. Cole. 2001. Social class. In *Schooling and equality: Fact, concept and policy,* ed. D. Hill and M. Cole, 139–159. London: Kogan Page.

Hill, D., and E. Rosskam, eds. 2009. *The developing world and state education: Neoliberal depredation and egalitarian alternatives.* New York: Routledge.

Hill, D., M. Sanders, and T. Hankin. 2002. Marxism, class analysis and postmodernism. In *Marxism against postmodernism in education theory,* eds. D. Hill, P. McLaren, M. Cole & G. Rikowski, 159–194. Lanham, MD: Lexington.

The Hindu. 2004. Choice-based credit system helpful in meeting demand for jobs. http://www.thehindu.com/2004/02/03/stories/2004020309770400.htm.

Hirrt, N. 2008. Markets and education in the era of globalized capitalism. In *Global neoliberalism and education and its consequences,* ed. D. Hill and R. Kumar, 206–224. New York: Routledge.

International Marxist Tendency. 2008. *In defence of Marxism: World perspectives, Part One,* 6 Feb. International Marxist Tendency. http://www.marxist.com/world-perspectives-2008-draft-one.htm.

Joseph Rowntree Foundation. 2007. *Experiences of poverty and educational disadvantage.* http://www.jrf.org.uk/knowledge/findings/socialpolicy/2123.asp Also http://www.multiverse.ac.uk/ViewArticle2.aspx?ContentId=13682.

Klein, N. 2001. *No logo.* London: Flamingo.

————. 2002. *Fences and windows: Dispatches from the front lines of the global debate.* London: Flamingo.

————. 2008. *The shock doctrine: The rise of disaster capitalism.* London: Picador.

Kumar, R. 2006a. ed. *The crisis of elementary education in India.* New Delhi: Sage Publications.

————. 2006b. Educational deprivation of the marginalized: A village study of Mushar community in Bihar. In *The crisis of elementary education in India,* ed. R. Kumar, 301–42. New Delhi: Sage Publications.

————. 2006c. State, class and critical framework of praxis: The missing link in Indian educational debates. *Journal of Critical Education Policy Studies* 4, no. 2. http://www.jceps.com/index.php?pageID=article&articleID=68.

Kumar, R., and Rama P. 2006. Institutionalising discrimination: Challenges of educating urban poor in neo-liberal era. In *Managing urban poverty,* ed. A. Sabir, 253–89. New Delhi: Council for Social Development and Uppal Publishing House.

Leclercq, F. 2003. *Education policy reforms and the quality of the school system: A field study of primary schools in Madhya Pradesh, India.* Developpement et Insertion Internationale, Document de Travail DT/2003/12. http:// www.dial.prd.fr/dial_publications/PDF/Doc_travail/2003–12.pdf.

Levidow, L. 2002. Marketizing higher education: Neoliberal strategies and counter-strategies. *The Commoner* 3, January. http://www.commoner.org.uk/03levidow.pdf.

Lipman, P. 2001. Bush's education plan, globalization and the politics of race. *Cultural Logic* 4, no. 1. http//clogic.eserver.org/4–1/lipman.html.

Matheson, M. 2000. *Are you being served? WDM in action.* London: World Development Movement.

Mathison, S., and E. W. Ross. 2002. The hegemony of accountability in schools and universities. *Workplace: A Journal for Academic Labor 5*, no. 1. http://www.louisville.edu/journal/workplace/issue5p1/mathison.html.

Marx. K. 1867.*Capital Vol 1: The process of production of capital.* http://www.marxists.org/archive/marx/works/1867-c1/ch25.htm.

McMurtry, J. 2001. "Why is there a war in Afghanistan?" Speech, University of Toronto, Science for Peace Forum and Teach-In, "How Should Canada Respond to Terrorism and War?" http://scienceforpeace.sa.utoronto.ca/Special_Activities/McMurtry_Page.html.

Mojab, S. 2001. New resources for revolutionary critical education. *Convergence 34*, no.1, 118–125. http://www.ieps.org.uk.cwc.net/mojab2002.pdf.

Molnar, A. 2001. *Giving kids the business: The commercialization of America's schools.* 2nd ed. Boulder, CO: Westview.

———. 2005. *School Commercialism: From Democratic Ideal to Market Commodity.* New York: Routledge.

Monbiot, G. 2000. *Captive state: The corporate takeover of Britain.* London: Pan.

———. 2001. How to rule the world: Rich nations should stop running the planet and give way to global democracy. *The Guardian,* July 17, 2001. http://www.guardian.co.uk/globalisation/story/0,7369,522903,00.html.

———. 2002. Public fraud initiative. *The Guardian,* June 19, 2002. http://society.guardian.co.uk//futureforpublicservices/comment/0,8146,739525,00.html.

Mulderrig, J. 2002. *Learning to labour: The discursive construction of social actors in New Labour's education policy.* http://www.jceps.com/index.php?pageID=article&articleID=2.

Navarro, V. 2007. *Neoliberalism, globalization, and inequalities: Consequences for health and quality of life.* Amityville, NY: Baywood.

Ollman, B. 2001. *How to take an exam . . . and remake the world.* Montreal: Black Rose.

Pilger, J. 2002. The new protest movement: Something is stirring among the people. *New Statesman,* November 4, 2002. http://www.zmag.org/content/showarticle.cfm?SectionID=15&ItemID=2579.

Pollock, A. 2001. Private sector lured by £30bn public gold rush, *The Observer (Business),* July 8th, 2001, p. 5.

Rikowski, G. 2000. *That Other Great Class of Commodities: Repositioning Marxist Educational Theory,* BERA Conference Paper, Cardiff University, 7–10 September. http://www.leeds.ac.uk/educol/documents/00001624.htm.

———. 2001. *The battle in Seattle.* London: Tufnell Press.

———. 2002a. *Globalisation and education.* A paper prepared for the House of Lords Select Committee on Economic Affairs, Inquiry into the Global Economy. http://www.ieps.org.uk%20or%20rikowski@tiscali.co.uk.

———. 2002b. *Schools: Building for business.* http://www.ieps.org.uk.

———. 2002c. *Schools: The great GATS buy.* http://www.ieps.org.uk.

———. 2002d. Transfiguration: Globalisation, the World Trade Organisation and the national faces of the GATS. *Information for Social Change* 14: 8–17.

———. 2003. *The suppression and compression of critical space in education today.* Paper presented at University College Northampton.

———. 2006. Education and the politics of human resistance. *Information for Social Change* 23, Summer. http://libr.org/isc/issues/ISC23/B3%20Glenn%20Rikowski.pdf.

———. 2007. *Marxist educational theory unplugged.* A paper prepared for the Fourth Historical Materialism Annual Conference, November 9–11th, School of Oriental & African Studies, University of London. http://www.flowideas.co.uk/?page=articles&sub=Marxist%20Educational%20Theory%20Unplugged

———. 2008. Schools and the GATS Enigma. *Firgoa: Universidade Publica.* Online at http://firgoa.usc.es/drupal/node/4249

Rikowski, R. 2002. *The WTO/GATS agenda for libraries.* http://www.ieps.org.uk.cwc.net/rikowski2002a.pdf.

Robertson, S., X. Bonal, and R. Dale. 2001. GATS and the education service industry: The politics of scale and global re-territorialization. *Comparative Education Review* 46, no. 2: 472–96.

Ross, E. W. and R.Gibson. 2007. *Neoliberalism and education reform.* Cresskill, NJ: Hampton Press.

Rothkopf, D. 2008a. Change is in the air for financial superclass. *Financial Times,* London. May 15. http://www.ft.com/cms/s/0/406952f2-2297-11dd-93a9-000077b07658,dwp_uuid=d355f29c-d238-11db-a7c0-000b5df10621.html.

———. 2008b. *Superclass: The global power elite and the world they are making.* New York: Farrar, Strauss and Giroux.

Sadgopal, A. 2006. Dilution, distortion and diversion: A post-Jomtien reflection on education policy. In *The crisis of elementary education in India,* ed. R. Kumar, 92–136. New Delhi: Sage Publications.

Saltman K. and D. Gabbard. 2003. *Education as enforcement: The militarization and corporatization of schools.* New York: Routledge.

Sexton, S. 2001. Trading health care away? GATS, public services and privatisation. *The Corner House,* Briefing 23. http://www.thecornerhouse.org.uk/pdf/briefing/23gats.pdf.

The Poverty Site. 2007. Educational attainment at Age 16. London: New Policy Institute. http://www.poverty.org.uk/15/index.shtml.

The Working Group on Extreme Inequality. 2008. http://extremeinequality.org/?page_id=8.

Tibbett, S. 2001. It's shocking all over the world. *Tribune* 65, no. 30: 10–11.

Troyna, B. 1995. The local management of schools and racial equality. In *Ethnic relations and schooling,* ed. S. Tomlinson and M. Craft, 140–54. London: Athlone.

United Nations Development Programme. 2005. *Human Development Report (HDR) 2005.* http://hdr.undp.org/en/media/hdr05_overview.pdf

Van Auken, B. 2008. World Global survey reveals growing anger over social inequality. *World Socialist Website,* 20 May. http://www.wsws.org/articles/2008/may2008/ineq-m20.shtml.

Whitty, G., S. Power, and D. Halpin. 1998. *Devolution and choice in education: The school, the state and the market.* Buckingham: Open University Press.

Wilson, C. 2002. Assault on our rights. *Morning Star,* September 12.

3 Neoliberalism, Youth, and the Leasing of Higher Education

Henry A. Giroux

THE SCOURGE OF NEOLIBERALISM

Neoliberalism has evolved into one of the most widespread, antidemocratic tendencies of the new millennium. Its pervasiveness is evident not only in its unparalleled influence on the global economy, but also in its restructuring of "practically every dimension of social life, including the gap between the rich and the poor, the nature of work, the role of big money in politics, the quantity and quality of public services, and the character of family life" (Kotz, 2003, p. 15). Market fundamentalism rather than democratic idealism is now the driving force of economics and politics in most of the world. It is a market ideology driven not just by the accumulation of capital, but also by an ability to reproduce itself as a form of biopolitics reaching into and commodifying all aspects of social and cultural life. Wedded to the belief that "free markets in both commodities and capital contain all that is necessary to deliver freedom and well-being to all" (Harvey, 2003, p. 201), neoliberalism wages an incessant attack on democracy, public goods, the welfare state, and noncommodified values. Neoliberal global capitalism not only escalates class warfare, inequality, and victimization, it also registers a process of human suffering that goes beyond the act of exploitation, and this shift can be seen in the growing process of exclusion. As Zygmunt Bauman (2004) points out:

> [T]he most consequential, dimension of the planetary-wide expansion of [neoliberal capital] has been the slow yet relentless globalization of the production of human waste, or more precisely 'wasted humans'— humans no longer necessary for the completion of the economic cycle and thus impossible to accommodate within a social framework resonant with the capitalist economy. The 'problem of capitalism,' the most blatant and potentially explosive malfunction of the capitalist economy, is shifting in its present planetary stage from exploitation to exclusion. It is exclusion, rather than the exploitation suggested a century and a half ago by Marx, that today underlies the most conspicuous cases of social polarization, of deepening inequality, and of rising volumes of human poverty, misery and humiliation. (pp. 39–40)

Under neoliberalism everything either is for sale or is plundered for profit: public lands are looted by logging companies and corporate ranchers; politicians willingly hand the public's airwaves over to powerful broadcasters and large corporate interests without a dime going into the public trust; the environment is polluted and despoiled in the name of profit making just as the government passes legislation to make it easier for corporations to do so; whatever public services have survived the Reagan-Bush era are gutted in order to lower the taxes of major corporations (or line their pockets through no-bid contracts, as in the infamous case of Halliburton); entire populations, especially those of color and who are poor are considered disposable, schools more closely resemble either jails or high-end shopping malls, depending on their clientele, and teachers are forced to get revenue for their school by hawking everything from hamburgers to pizza parties. The gutting of the social state under neoliberalism is matched by the weakening of interpersonal relations and public life. Atomization is fuelled by a rabid individualism mirrored in an utterly privatized conception of citizenship, competitive and hierarchical structures that shape everyday work relations, and a government-sanctioned culture of fear and insecurity whose organizing pedagogy aims at reducing people's desires and thoughts to obsessively "safeguarding their private lives" (Arendt, 1973, p. 338).

Under neoliberalism, the state now makes a grim alignment with the institutions of finance capital and transnational corporations. Gone are the days when the state "assumed responsibility for a range of social needs" (Steinmetz, 2003, p. 337). Instead, agencies of government now pursue a wide range of "'deregulations,' privatizations, and abdications of responsibility to the market and private philanthropy" (Steinmetz, 2003, p. 337). Deregulation, in turn, promotes "widespread, systematic disinvestment in the nation's basic productive capacity" (Bluestone and Harrison, 1982, p. 6).

As neoliberal policies dominate politics and social life, the breathless rhetoric of the global victory of free-market rationality is invoked to cut public expenditures and undermine those noncommodified public spheres that serve as the repository for critical education, language, and public intervention. Spewed forth by the mass media, right-wing intellectuals, religious fanatics, and politicians, neoliberal ideology, with its merciless emphasis on deregulation and privatization, has found its material expression in an all-out attack on democratic values and social relations—particularly those public spheres where such values are learned and take root. Public services such as health care, child care, public assistance, education, and transportation are now subject to the rules of the market. Health care no longer becomes a measure of the quality of democracy but another market and source of capital accumulation. Social relations between parents and children, doctors and patients, teachers and students are reduced to that of supplier and customer just as the laws of market replace the noncommodified values capable of defending vital public goods and spheres. Forsaking the public good for the private good and hawking the needs of the corporate and private sector as the only source of sound investment, neoliberal ideology produces, legitimates, and exacerbates the existence of persistent poverty, inadequate health care, racial apartheid in the inner cities, and the growing inequalities between the rich and the poor.[1]

In its capacity to dehistoricize and naturalize such sweeping social change, as well as in its aggressive attempts to destroy all of the public spheres necessary for the defense of a genuine democracy, neoliberalism reproduces the conditions for unleashing the most brutalizing forces of capitalism. As social bonds are replaced by unadulterated materialism and narcissism, public concerns are now understood and experienced as utterly private miseries. As the social state is transformed into the corporate/militarized state, politics is now defined in more ample terms and its axis of meaning is inextricably linked to matters of life and death, largely mediated through the prism of disposability, fear, and "security as the sole task and source of [state] legitimacy" (Agamben, 2001). Giorgio Agamben's work, as Jean Comaroff (2007) argues, suggests that "modern government stages itself by dealing directly in the power over life: the power to exclude, to declare exceptions, to strip human existence of civic rights and social value" (p. 208). State violence and totalitarian power, which historically has been deployed against marginalized populations—principally black Americans—have now, at least in the United States, become the rule for the entire population, as life is more ruthlessly regulated and placed in the hands of military and state power. Second, politics can no longer be reduced to participation in elections, access to and distribution of material and cultural resources, or even the regulation and disciplining of the body. On the contrary, politics is increasingly about the power of modern states to impose a state of exception, to condemn entire populations as disposable, and to make life and death the most crucial and relevant objects of political control.[2] As violence, insecurity, and fear empty public life of its democratic possibilities and the warfare state is transformed into a garrison state, life and death lose their distinctive meanings as a measure of what it means to live in a genuine democracy. Instead, life for many people becomes unpredictable, put on short notice, and subject to the vicissitudes of outsourcing, privatization, and a neoliberal Hobbesian ethic in which the losers vastly outnumber the winners. As fear is privatized, shifting from the promise of the state to protect its citizens to the emphasis on the "dangers of personal safety," life replicates art in the form of bad reality television, legitimating the inevitability of social exclusion, which becomes "an unavoidable fate" (Bauman, 2006, pp. 4, 24). Like the consumer goods that flood American society, immigrant workers, refugees, the unemployed, the homeless, the poor, and the disabled are increasingly viewed as utterly expendable, relegated to a frontier zone of invisibility created by a combination of economic inequality, racism, the collapse of social safety nets, and the brutality of a militarized society, all of which "designates and constitutes a production line of human waste or wasted humans" (Bauman, 2004, p. 6).

The aftermath of Hurricane Katrina is deeply instructive about the reign of neoliberalism in the United States and its effects on politics and society. Underlying the tragic and incompetent response to the catastrophe is the way in which the federal government has been gutted by neoliberal ideology, pandering to the rich while eliminating those safety nets essential to delivering the most basic services necessary to providing assistance to the poor, elderly, and sick, as was evident in the government's response to Hurricane Katrina. With few exceptions, the project of democratizing public goods has fallen into disrepute in the popular imagination as the logic of the market undermines the most basic social solidarities. The consequences include not only a weakened social state, but a growing sense of insecurity, cynicism, and political retreat on the part of the general public. The incessant calls for self-reliance that now dominate public discourse betray an eviscerated and refigured state that does not care for those populations that it considers expendable, especially those who are young, poor, or racially marginalized. The brutality of neoliberalism in its destruction of democratic values, visions, and practices is particularly evident in its view of young people and higher education.

YOUTH AND THE POLITICS OF DISPOSABILITY

Under the global reign of neoliberalism, economic growth becomes more important than social justice, and the militarization and commercialization of public space now define what counts as the public sphere. This dystopian recognition points to dire political, social, and economic consequences for young people and the very nature of democracy itself. Democracy increasingly appears damaged, if not fatally wounded, as those who are young, poor, immigrants, or people of color are excluded from the operations of power, the realm of politics, and crucial social provisions. For over a century, Americans have embraced as a defining feature of politics the idea that all levels of government would assume a large measure of responsibility for providing the resources, social provisions, and modes of education that enabled young people to be prepared for a present that would offer them a better future while expanding the meaning and depth of an inclusive democracy. Taking the social contract seriously, American society exhibited a willingness to fight for the rights of children, enacted reforms that invested in their future, and provided the educational conditions necessary for them to be critical citizens. Within such a modernist project, democracy was linked to the well-being of youth, while the status of how a society imagined democracy and its future was contingent on how it viewed its responsibility towards future generations.

But the category of youth did more than affirm modernity's social contract rooted in a conception of the future in which adult commitment was articulated as a vital public service, it also affirmed those vocabularies, values, and social relations central to a politics capable of defending vital institutions as a public good and contributing to the quality of democratic public life. At stake here was the recognition that children constitute a powerful referent for addressing war, poverty, education, and a host of other important social issues. Moreover, as a symbol of the future, children provide an important moral compass to assess what Jacques Derrida calls the promises of a "democracy to come" (2001, p. 253). Such a vocabulary was particularly important for higher education, which often defined and addressed its highest ideals through the recognition that how it educated youth was connected to both the democratic future it hoped for and its claim as an important public sphere.

But just as education has been separated from any viable notion of politics, youth have been separated from the discourse of either the social contract or any ethical notion of what it might mean for society to provide young people with the prospects of a decent and democratic future. Youth increasingly have come to be seen as a problem rather than as a resource for investing in the future. Framed largely as a generation of suspects, they are now treated as either a disposable population, fodder for a barbaric war in Iraq, or defined as the source of most of society's problems. Youth now constitute a crisis that has less to do with improving the future than with denying it. Punishment and fear have replaced compassion and the social investment as the most important modalities mediating the relationship of youth to the larger social order.

No longer "viewed as a privileged sign and embodiment of the future" (Grossberg, 2001, p. 133), youth are now demonized by the popular media and derided by politicians looking for quick-fix solutions to crime. Best-selling authors such as Lt. Col. Dave Grossman and Gloria DeGaentano (1999) argue in their book *Stop Teaching Our Kids to Kill* that young people are more violent than ever before because of what they learn in popular culture, and by default the authors suggest that young people need to be subjected to more extended disciplinary measures. Hollywood movies such as *Kids, Thirteen, Brick,* and *Hard Candy* consistently represent youth as either dangerous, utterly brainless, pathological, or simply without merit. The marketplace only imagines students either as consumers or as billboards to sell sexuality, beauty, music, sports, clothes, and a host of other consumer products. At the same time, in a society deeply troubled by their presence, youth prompt in the public imagination a rhetoric of fear, control, and surveillance as well as laws and policies that fine youth for wearing baggy pants, subject youth to antigang laws that punish them for violating certain dress codes, and offer them schools that implement zero-tolerance policies that are modeled after prisons. In the case of the latter, federal law now provides financial incentives to schools that implement zero-tolerance policies, in spite of their proven racial and class biases; drug-sniffing dogs and cameras have become a common feature in schools, and administrators willingly comply with federal laws that give military recruiters the right to access the names, addresses, and telephone numbers of students in both public schools and higher education. Trust and respect now give way to fear, disdain, and suspicion. Children have fewer rights than almost any other group and fewer institutions protecting these rights.

Instead of providing a decent critical education to poor young people, neoliberals and neoconservatives serve them more standardized tests (Kornblut, 2005, p. 26), enforce abstinence programs instead of sex education, hand out bibles and inculcate right-wing Christian values, and advocate creationism at the expense of reason and freedom.[3] Youth who are poor fare even worse and often find themselves in classes that are overcrowded, lack basic resources, and subject to policies largely designed to warehouse young people rather than educate them with even minimal basic literacy skills. Rather than providing young people with vibrant public spheres, the Bush government offers them a commercialized culture in which consumerism is the only condition of citizenship. But the hard currency of human suffering that has an impact on children can also be seen in some astounding statistics that suggest a profound moral and political contradiction at the heart of one of the richest democracies in the world: over one-third of those in poverty are children, boosting the number of children who are poor to 12.9 million. Similarly, 9.3 million children lack health insurance, and millions lack affordable child care and decent early childhood education; in many states more money is being spent on prison construction than on higher education; and the infant mortality rate in the United States is the highest of any other industrialized nation.

The idea, not to mention the reality, of justice seems dead on arrival as the Bush regime consistently and aggressively attempts to generate retrograde policies that seem intent on increasing corporate power and wasting billions of dollars on a rapacious empire-building agenda. In the name of "free market capitalism," the government increasingly promotes "a predatory culture of open barbarism: the resurgence of open racism, war, imperialism, sexism, religious fundamentalism," (Foster, 2005) and a brutal war against youth marginalized by race and class. Evidence of such an attack can be seen in Laura Flanders's (2005) characterization of Bush's 2006 budget as a hit list targeting teens and kids because it "calls for cuts in emergency medical services for children, cuts in K–12 education funding, cuts in vocational education and the highly successful Head Start Program. There are food-stamp cuts and a five-year freeze on child care. A $41 million college loan program is eliminated. The whole National Youth sports Program which has provided athletics for low income kids is cut, as in cut out." Paul Krugman reinforces the charge calling Bush's budget projections a form of class warfare since he "takes food from the mouths of babes and gives the proceeds to his millionaire friends" (2005, p. A23). In this case, savage cuts in education, nutritional assistance for impoverished mothers, veteran's medical care, and basic scientific research would help fund tax cuts for the inordinately rich. All of this may be good news for those die-hard members of the Christian right, free-market fundamentalists, and power-hungry neoconservatives who are doing everything they can not only to render democracy irrelevant, but also to disempower an entire generation of children whose future is being mortgaged off to the vagaries of corporate power, greed, and religious fundamentalism.

Youth has become one of the most visible symbols onto which class and racial anxieties are projected. The very presence of young people represents the broken promises of capitalism in the age of outsourcing, contract work, deindustrialization, and deregulation. It also regulates a collective fear of the consequences wrought by systemic class inequalities, racism, and a culture of downsizing and deficits that has created a generation of unskilled and displaced youth who have been expelled from shrinking markets, blue-collar jobs, and any viable hope in the future.

Within the degraded economic, political, and cultural geography, youth occupy a "dead zone" in which the spectacle of commodification exists side by side with the imposing threat of the prison-industrial complex and the elimination of basic civil liberties. As market fundamentalism frees itself from political power, it disassociates economics from its social costs and "the political state has become the corporate state" (Hertz, 2001, p. 11). Under such circumstances, the state does not disappear but, as the late Pierre Bourdieu brilliantly reminded us in *Acts of Resistance* (1998) and *The weight of the world: Social suffering in contemporary society* (1999), is refigured as its role in providing social provisions, intervening on behalf of public welfare, and regulating corporate plunder is weakened. The corporate state no longer invests in solving social problems; it now punishes those who are caught in the downward spiral of its economic policies. Punishment, incarceration, control, and surveillance represent the face of the new expanded state. One consequence is that the implied contract between the state and citizens is broken and social guarantees for youth as well as civic obligations to the future vanish from the agenda of public concern. Similarly, as market values supplant civic values, it becomes increasingly difficult "to translate private worries into public issues and, conversely, to discern public issues in private troubles" (Bauman, 1999, p. 2). Alcoholism, homelessness, poverty, and illiteracy, among other issues are seen not as social but as individual problems—matters of character, individual fortitude, and personal responsibility. Ardent consumers and disengaged citizens provide fodder for a growing cynicism and depoliticization of public life at a time when there is an increasing awareness not just of corporate corruption, financial mismanagement, and systemic greed, but also of the recognition that a democracy of critical citizens is being replaced quickly by a democracy of consumers. The desire to protect market freedoms and wage a war against terrorism has, ironically, not only ushered in a culture of fear but has also dealt a lethal blow to civil liberties. At the heart of this contradiction is both the fate of democracy and the civic health and future of a generation of children and young people.

For many young people today, the private sphere has become the only space in which to imagine any sense of hope, pleasure, or possibility. In its place they are increasingly surrounded by a "climate of cultural and linguistic privatization" (Klein, 1999, p. 177), in which culture becomes something you consume and the only kind of speech that is acceptable is that of the fast-paced shopper. The war against youth can, in part, be understood within those central values and practices that characterize a market fundamentalism which emphasizes market forces and profit margins while narrowing the legitimacy of the public sphere by redefining it around the related issues of privatization, deregulation, consumption, and safety. In spite of neoconservative and neoliberal claims that economic growth will cure social ills, the market has no way of dealing with poverty, social inequality, or civil rights issues. It has no vocabulary for addressing respect, compassion, decency, and ethics or, for that matter, what it means to recognize antidemocratic forms of power. These are political issues not merely economic concerns. In contrast, a political system based on democratic principles of inclusiveness and nonrepression can and does provide citizens with the critical tools necessary for them to participate in investing public life with vibrancy while expanding the foundations of freedom and justice.

The current state of youth bears heavily on higher education. Childhood as a core referent for a vibrant democracy and an embrace of social justice appears to be disappearing in a society that not only rejects the promise of youth, but the future itself "as an affective investment" (Grossberg, 2001, p. 133). As higher education is increasingly subject to the rule of market values and corporate power, youth becomes neither a resource of social investment nor a referent for society's obligations to the future. Instead, they become customers, clients, and a source of revenue. Of course, under such circumstances the crisis of youth not only signals a dangerous state of affairs for the future, it also portends a crisis in the very idea of the political and ethical constitution of the social and the possibility of articulating the relevance of democracy itself. In what follows, I want to argue that youth as a political and moral referent does not only refer to young children, but also to those youth who inhabit the institutions of higher learning, poised to become adults by virtue of the knowledge, capacities, and skills they learn as critical citizens, workers, and intellectuals.

HIGHER EDUCATION AS A FRONT OFFICE FOR CORPORATE POWER

Anyone who spends any time on a college campus in the United States these days cannot miss how higher education is changing. Strapped for money and increasingly defined through the language of corporate culture, many universities seem less interested in higher learning than in becoming

licensed storefronts for brand-name corporations—selling off space, buildings, and endowed chairs to rich corporate donors. University bookstores
are now managed by big corporate conglomerates such as Barnes & Noble,
while companies such as Sodexho-Marriott (also a large investor in the
U.S. private prison industry) run a large percentage of college dining halls,
and McDonald's and Starbucks occupy prominent locations on the student
commons. Student identification cards are now adorned with MasterCard
and Visa logos, providing students who may have few assets with an instant
line of credit and an identity as full-time consumers.

In addition, housing, alumni relations, health care, and a vast array of
other services are now being leased out to private interests to manage and
run. One consequence is that spaces on university campuses once marked
as public and noncommodified—places for quiet study or student gather-
ings—now have the appearance of a shopping mall. Commercial logos,
billboards, and advertisements plaster the walls of student centers, dining halls, cafeterias, and bookstores. Administrators at York University in
Toronto solicited a number of corporations to place their logos on univer-
sity-sponsored online courses "for ten thousand dollars per course" (Yates,
2000). Everywhere students turn outside of the university classroom, they
are confronted with vendors and commercial sponsors who are hawking
credit cards, athletic goods, soft drinks, and other commodities that one
associates with the local shopping mall. Universities and colleges compound
this marriage of commercial and educational values by signing exclusive
contracts with Pepsi, Nike, and other contractors, further blurring the distinction between student and consumer. The message to students is clear:
customer satisfaction is offered as a surrogate for learning; "to be a citizen
is to be a consumer, and nothing more. Freedom means freedom to purchase" (Croissant, 2001).

Why should we care? Colleges and universities do not simply produce
knowledge and new perspectives for students; they also play an influential role in shaping their identities, values, and sense of what it means to
become citizens of the world. If colleges and universities are to define themselves as centers of teaching and learning vital to the democratic life of the
nation and globe, they must acknowledge the real danger of becoming mere
adjuncts to big business, or corporate entities in themselves. As Robert
Zemsky warns, "When the market interests totally dominate colleges and
universities, their role as public agencies significantly diminishes—as does
their capacity to provide venues for the testing of new ideas and the agendas for public action" (2003, pp. B7–B9).

And the threat is real. Commercial deals are no longer just a way for
universities to make money. Corporate branding drives the administrative
structure of the university. College presidents are now called chief executive officers and are known less for their intellectual leadership than for
their role as fundraisers and their ability to bridge the world of academe
and business. Gone are the days when university presidents were hired for

their intellectual status and public roles. One example can be found in the hiring of Michael Crow as the president of Arizona State University (ASU) in 2002. Crow, a former vice provost at Columbia University and head of In-Q-Tel Inc., a nonprofit venture capital arm of the Central Intelligence Agency, has attempted with a vengeance to organize ASU along corporate lines. With entrepreneurial types such as Crow now filling the ranks of university presidents, it is not surprising that venture capitalists scour colleges and universities in search of big profits to be made through licensing agreements, the control of intellectual property rights, and investing in university spin-off companies. Deans are likewise often hired from the ranks of the business community and increasingly the intelligence agencies, and evaluated on the basis of their ability to attract external funding and impose business models of leadership and accountability. As Stanley Aronowitz points out in "The new corporate university," increasingly "leaders of higher education wear the badge of corporate servants proudly" (2006, p. 32). And why not, when the notion of market-driven education has the full support of Bush-type Republicans and their corporate allies? Today, scholarship is measured not by the search for truth, rigor, or its social contributions. On the contrary, it is all too willingly defined in support of market needs just as funding for university programs is related to the commodification of ideas and the accumulation of profits. The dean at my former university not only viewed education as a depoliticized discourse, he also completely collapsed the distinction between scholarship and grant-getting by handing out distinguished professorships to academics who secured large grants but did very little in the way of either making important theoretical contributions or publishing widely recognized scholarly work. What is missing from the space of the corporate university is any perspective suggesting that, at the very least, university administrators, academics, students, and others exercise the political, civic, and ethical courage needed to refuse the commercial rewards that would reduce them to becoming simply another brand name, corporate logo, or adjunct to corporate interests.

As the university has increasingly corporatized, the collateral damage mounts, especially with regard to students. As the Bush administration has increasingly pushed for policies that furthered the ongoing corporatization of higher education, students have paid a heavy price. As the Bush administration has cut student aid, plundered public services, and pushed states to the brink of financial disaster, higher education increasingly has become a privilege rather than a right. Many middle- and working-class students have either found it financially impossible to enter college or, because of increased costs, have had to drop out. As the *Chronicle of Higher Education* has reported, young people from poor and disadvantaged families have faced even more difficult hurdles in trying to attain a college education because the Bush administration decided to cut Pell Grants, the nation's largest federal student aid program. In addition, because Congress changed the federal needs-analysis formula, more than

90,000 disadvantaged students were disqualified in 2005 from receiving not only Pell Grants but also state financial aid (Burd, 2005).

As all levels of government reduce their funding to higher education, not only will tuition increase but student loans will gradually replace grants and scholarships. Lacking adequate financial aid, students, especially poor students, will have to finance the high costs of their education through private corporations such as Citibank, Chase Manhattan, Marine Midland, and other lenders. According to the Project on Student Debt (2006), nearly two-thirds of both undergraduate and graduate students at four-year colleges and public universities have student loans. While it makes sense to focus on issues such as the impact of corporate interests on research, the shift in governance from faculty to business-oriented administrators, and the massive increase in adjuncts and casual labor, little has been said about the corporate structuring of student debt and its impact on a sizeable number of people attending higher education. Rather than work their way through college, students now borrow their way to graduation, and in doing so have been collectively labeled by Anya Kamenetz a "generation of debt" (2006, p. 1). As Jeff Williams points out, the average student now graduates with debts that are staggering:

> The average undergraduate student loan debt in 2002 was $18,900. It is more than doubled from 1992, when it was $9,200. Added to this is charge card debt, which averaged $3,000 in 2002 boosting the average total debt to about $22,000. One can reasonably expect, given still accelerating costs, that it is over $30,000 now. Bear in mind that this does not include other private loans or the debt that parents take on to send their children to college. (Neither does it account for "post-baccalaureate loans, "which more than doubled in seven years from $18,572 in 1992–1993 to $38,000 in1999–2000, and have likely doubled again; (2006, p. 53).

Saddled with enormous debts, many students find that their career choices are severely limited to jobs in the corporate workforce that offer them entry-level salaries that make it possible to pay off their loans. Indentured for decades in order to pay off such loans, it becomes difficult for students to consider public service jobs or jobs that offer rewards other than high salaries. One recent survey reported that "two-thirds of law graduates say that debt is a primary factor in keeping them from considering a career in public interest law . . . Other surveys have found that about half of the students who begin law school with stated public interest law commitments go into private practice law upon graduation in large part because of their debt burden" (Tannock, 2006, p. 49).

For many young people caught in the margins of poverty, low-paying jobs, recession, and "jobless recovery," the potential costs of higher education, regardless of its status or availability, will dissuade them from even thinking about attending college. Unfortunately, as state and federal agencies and university systems direct more and more of their resources (such as state tax credits and scholarship programs) toward middle- and upper-income students and away from need-based aid, the growing gap in college enrollments between high-income students (95 percent enrollment rate) and low-income students (75 percent enrollment rate) with comparable academic abilities will widen even further (*New York Times*, 2002, p. A27). In fact, a report by a federal advisory committee claimed that nearly 48 percent of qualified students from low-income families would not be attending college in the fall of 2002 because of rising tuition charges and a shortfall in federal and state grants. The report claimed that "nearly 170,000 of the top high-school graduates from low- and moderate-income families are not enrolling in college this year because they cannot afford to do so" (Burd, 2002). A more recent government report titled *Mortgaging our future: How financial barriers to college undercut America's global competitiveness* (2006) claims that "1.4 million to 2.4 million bachelor's degrees will be lost this decade as financial concerns prevent academically qualified students from the lowest income bracket from attending college" (cited in Porter, 2006, p. A25). And the report suggested that these figures are conservative.

When universities can no longer balance their budget through tuition increases or federal grants, they turn to corporate money and self-branding to balance their budgets. Students become "customers," both of the university's own brand and of corporations who sell to them directly through university deals. Although higher education has never been free of the market, there is a new intimacy between higher education and corporate culture, characterized by what Larry Hanley has called a "new, quickened symbiosis" (2001, p. 103). The result is "not a fundamental or abrupt change perhaps, but still an unmistakable radical reduction of [higher education's] public and critical role" (Miyoshi, 1998, p. 263). What was once the hidden curriculum of many universities—the subordination of higher education to capital—has now become an open and much celebrated policy of both public and private higher education. Increasingly, references to higher education as a valuable commodity or for-profit business have become all too common (Pearlstein, 2003, p. E01). For example, the former president of American University, Milton Greenberg, argues that it is an utterly romanticized assumption to suggest education is *not* a business, and that such romanticism is reinforced by another myth attributed to the romantic age of higher education: namely, "that the substance of teaching, research and learning—protected by academic freedom and professional standards—is not ordinarily subject to profit-and-loss analysis" (2004, p. 11). For Greenberg, education and training for employment appear to be the same thing and as such reinforce the charge that the liberal arts have become useless since they do not translate directly into jobs. Greenberg is utterly indifferent to the increasing commodification of knowledge, secrecy imposed on academics on corporate payrolls, the dismantling of democratic forms of governance, and the increased use of higher education to produce products that can be sold in the market. Not unlike the market fundamentalists or super patriots who either want to privatize higher education or turn it into a bastion of the national security state, Greenberg is blind to the assumption that such forces might pose a grave threat to academic freedom and the function of the university as a democratic public sphere.

If right-wing reforms in higher education continue unchallenged, the consequences will result in a highly undemocratic, bifurcated civic body. In other words, we will have a society in which a highly trained, largely white elite will be allowed to command the techno-information revolution while a low-skilled majority of poor and minority workers will be relegated to filling the McJobs proliferating in the service sector. Moreover, as university leaders increasingly appeal to the corporate world for funding, engage in money-making ventures as a measure of excellence, and ignore that the line between for-profit and not-for-profit institutions of higher education is collapsing, many schools, as educator John Palattela observes, will simply "serve as personnel offices for corporations" and quickly dispense with the historically burdened though important promise of creating democratic mandates for higher education (2001, p. 73).

Of all groups, university and college educators should be the most vocal and militant in challenging the corporatization of education by making clear that at the heart of any form of inclusive democracy is the assumption that learning should be used to expand the public good, create a culture of questioning, and promote democratic social change. Individual and social agency become meaningful as part of the willingness to imagine otherwise, "in order to help us find our way to a more human future" (Chomsky, 2000, p. 34). Under such circumstances, knowledge can be used for amplifying human freedom and promoting social justice, and not simply for creating profits.

If students are now treated as customers, faculty have become a new source of contract labor. The American Council of Education reported in 2002 that "the number of part-time faculty members increased by 79 percent from 1981 to 1999, to more than 400,000 out of a total of one million instructors over all," and that the "biggest growth spurt occurred between 1987 and 1993, when 82 percent of the 120,000 new faculty members hired during that period were for part-time positions" (Walsh, 2002). In fact, more professors are working part-time and at two-year community colleges now than at any other time in the country's recent history. The American Association of University Professors reported in 2004 that "44.5 percent of all faculty are part-time, and non-tenure-track positions of all types account for more than 60 percent of all faculty appointments in American higher education." Creating a permanent underclass of part-time professional workers in higher education is not only demoralizing and exploitative for many faculty who have such jobs but also deskills both part- and full-time faculty by increasing the amount of work they have to do. With less time to prepare, larger class loads, almost no time for research, and excessive grading demands, many adjuncts run the risk of becoming demoralized and ineffective.

One possibility of what the future holds for the corporatizing of higher education can be seen in the example of Rio Salado College in Tempe, Arizona. In a report for the *Chronicle of Higher Education*, Elyse Ashburn observes that the college is the second largest in the Maricopa County Community College District and has a total of 13,314 students (2006, p. A12). And, yet it has "only 33 permanent faculty members, 27 of whom are full-time" (p. A10). Its classes are almost entirely virtual, and it hires close to a thousand part-time instructors scattered across the state. The part-time faculty carry the bulk of the teaching and are paid about $2200 a course. Teaching eight courses, four each semester, calculates to slightly less than $18,000 a year, which amounts to poverty-level wages. The few, privileged full-time faculty earn between $40,000 to $88,000 a year (p. A11). The academic labor force at Rio Salado College in this instance has been, for the most part, entirely casualized with almost no possibility for any of its thousand members landing a full-time position. Linda Thor, the president of the Rio Salado College, often quotes from best-selling business books and "embraces the idea of students as customers" (p. A12). Moreover, consistent with Thor's embrace of corporate principles and efficiency-minded management style, the day-to-day duties of instructors at the college are "simplified by RioLearn, a course-management system designed specifically for the college through a partnership with Dell Inc. and the Microsoft Corporation" (p. A12). Most importantly, this utterly privatized, fragmented, exploitative, and commercialized vision of higher education should not be dismissed as a quirky approach to university administration. In this view, power, time, and decision-making are completely controlled by administrators who view faculty subordination to corporate control either "a thing of nature, and, more to the point, the royal road to academic and financial reward" (Aronowitz, 2006, p. 17). The latter is obvious in the ways in which nonprofit institutions are emulating this model. For instance, the University of Illinois, which has three land-grant nonprofit campuses, plans to launch a whole new college, which would be completely online, operate as a for-profit entity, and consist almost entirely of part-time faculty with no tenured faculty at all. Issues central to university culture such as tenure, academic freedom, and intellectual integrity are dispensed with as faculty governance is now put largely in the hands of administrators, and faculty are reduced to outsourced, casual labor. Allegedly, the rationale for this utterly corporatized approach to education is to make the University of Illinois more competitive, while providing "access to high quality education first and foremost to the people of Illinois" (Jaschik, 2006b). In my view, this educational model with its stripped down version of teaching, its cost-efficiency model of management, and its views of students as customers and faculty as source of cheap labor is exactly what informs the current corporate understanding of the future of higher education. This model represents the face of higher education in the age of global capital and market fundamentalism and is less about education than about training, less about educating students to be informed and responsible citizens of the world than about short-term returns on revenue, all the time providing a pseudo-academic warrant to reduce education to an extension of the corporate world. Clearly, this is a view that needs to be resisted if higher education is to retain any democratic value at all.

At the same time, while compassion and concern for students and teachers wane, universities are eagerly entering into unholy alliances with big corporations. No longer content to make their presence felt on college campuses through the funding of endowed chairs, academic centers, or research about business issues that eventually are used as case studies, companies such as BMW and IBM are taking their involvement with higher education to a new level of involvement. When the German automaker BMW contributed $10 million to Clemson University in 2002 to help develop a $1.5 billion automotive and research center, Clemson gave BMW an extraordinary amount of control over curriculum and hiring procedures. Not only did BMW play a role in developing the curriculum for the automotive graduate engineering school, but it also "drew up profiles of its ideal students; [provided] a list of professors and specialists to interview, and even had approval rights over the school's architectural look" (Browning, 2006, p. C1). In addition, BMW gave Clemson's president a BMW X5 to drive. In spite of Clemson's claims that it retains its independence as a public university despite its close ties with BMW, candidates for the endowed chairs were interviewed by BMW executives and "a network council composed of BMW managers meets monthly to advise Clemson on the curriculum" (p. C6). Thomas Kurfess, the first person hired to fill a BMW endowed professorship, has no reservations about the growing corporatization of higher education, noting that "This is a different model. It is nice to be able to show that it's not just the name beyond the chair . . . [and have] real ties to industry" (Jaschik, 2006a). A lawsuit contesting the contract between BMW and Clemson made public a letter written by a BMW official who stated that "BMW is going to drive the entire campus" (Browning, 2006, p. C6). At least BMW is honest about its intentions and the role it wants to play in shaping Clemson's relationship with industry.

While the cult of professionalism inspires fear and insecurity in academics terrified about maintaining tenure, getting it, or for that matter simply securing a part-time position, university educators also face the harsh lessons of financial deprivation, overburdened workloads, and the loss of power in shaping the governance process. They devote less time to their roles either as well-informed public intellectuals or as "cosmopolitan intellectuals situated in the public sphere" (Aronowitz, 1998,

p. 444). Many faculty live under the constant threat of either being down-sized, punished, or fired and are less concerned about quality research and teaching than about accepting the new rules of corporate-based pro-fessionalism in order to simply survive in the new corporatized academy. Against the current drive to corporatize higher education, commodify curricula, treat students as customers and trainees, and relegate faculty to the status of contract employees, higher education needs to be defended as a public good. Central to such a task is the challenge to resist the univer-sity becoming what literary theorist Bill Readings (1996) in *The univer-sity in ruins* has called a consumer-oriented corporation more concerned about accounting than accountability, and whose mission, defined largely through an appeal to excellence, is comprehended almost exclusively in terms of instrumental efficiency.

BEYOND THE CORPORATE UNIVERSITY

As the power of higher education is reduced in its ability to make corporate power accountable, it becomes more difficult within the logic of the bottom line for faculty, students, and administrators to address pressing social and ethical issues. Ardent consumers and disengaged citizens provide fodder for a growing cynicism and disinvestment in the university as a public good at a time when there is an increasing awareness of corporate corruption, financial mismanagement, and systemic greed, as well as the recognition that a democracy of critical citizens is being quickly replaced by an ersatz democracy of consumers. In the vocabulary of neoliberalism, the public collapses into the personal, and the personal becomes "the only politics there is, the only politics with a tangible referent or emotional valence" (Comaroff and Comaroff, 2000, pp. 305–306). This suggests a perilous turn in American society, one that threatens both our understanding of radical democracy as fundamental to our basic rights and freedoms, and the ways in which we can rethink and reappropriate the meaning, purpose, and future of higher education.

Situated within a broader context of issues concerned with social responsibility, global justice, politics, and the dignity of human life, higher education should be engaged as a public sphere that offers students the opportunity to involve themselves in the deepest problems of society and to acquire the knowledge, skills, and ethical vocabulary necessary for modes of critical dialogue and forms of broadened civic participation. Higher education may be one of the few sites left in which students learn how to mediate critically between democratic values and the demands of corporate power, between identities founded on democratic principles and identities steeped in forms of competitive, atomistic individualism that celebrate self-interest, profit making, and greed. This suggests that higher education be defended through intellectual work that self-consciously recalls the tension between the democratic imperatives and possibilities of public institutions and their everyday realization within a society dominated by market principles. While it is crucial for educators and others to defend higher education as a public good, it is also important to recognize that the crisis of higher education cannot be understood outside of the overall restructuring of social and civic life. The death of the social, the devaluing of political agency, the waning of noncommercial values, and the disappearance of noncommercialized public spaces have to be understood as part of a much broader attack on public entitlements such as health care, welfare, and social security, which are being turned over to market forces and privatized so that "economic transactions can subordinate and in many cases replace political democracy" (Newfield, 2002, p. 314). Against the increasing corporatization of the university and the advance of global capitalism, students must be provided with the pedagogical conditions that enable them to come to terms with their own sense of power and public voice as individual and social agents. In part, this means they should be able to examine and frame critically what they learn in the classroom as part of a broader understanding of what it means to live in a global democracy. Students need to learn how to take responsibility for their own ideas, take intellectual risks, develop a sense of respect for others different from themselves, and learn how to think critically in order to shape the conditions that influence how they participate in a wider democratic culture. At the very least, as Eric Gould has argued, a democratic education must do three things:

> First, it must be an education for democracy, for the greater good of a just society—but it cannot assume that society is, a priori, just. Second, it must argue for its means as well as it ends. It must derive from the history of ideas, from long-standing democratic values and practices which include the ability to argue and critique but also to tolerate ambiguity. And third, it must participate in the democratic social process, displaying not only a moral preference for recognizing the rights of others and accepting them, too, but for encouraging argument and cultural critique. In short, a university education is a democratic education because it mediates liberal democracy and the cultural contradictions of capitalism. (Gould, 2003, p. 225)

But more is needed than defending higher education as a vital sphere in which to develop and nourish the proper balance between democratic values and market fundamentalism, between identities founded on democratic principles and identities steeped in a form of competitive, self-interested individualism that celebrates its own material and ideological advantages. And more is needed than to define the culture of questioning as the most fundamental pedagogical consequence of how we educate young people. Given the current assault on critical educators in light of the tragic events of September 11, 2001 and the conservative backlash against higher education waged by the Bush administration, it is politically crucial that educators at all levels of involvement in the academy create new ways for doing politics by investing in political struggles through a relentless critique of the abuses of authority and power. For instance, the late Pierre Bourdieu wanted scholars to use their skills and knowledge to break out of the microcosm of academia, combine scholarship with commitment, and "enter into sustained and vigorous exchange with the outside world (especially with unions, grassroots organizations, and issue-oriented activist groups) instead of being content with waging the 'political' battles, at once intimate and ultimate, and always a bit unreal, of the scholastic universe" (Bourdieu, 2000, p. 44).

Organizing against the corporate takeover of higher education suggests fighting to protect the jobs of full-time faculty, turning adjunct jobs into full-time positions, expanding benefits to part-time workers, and putting power into the hands of faculty and students. Protecting the jobs of full-time faculty means ensuring that they have the right to academic freedom, are paid a decent wage, and play an important role in governing the university. A weak faculty translates into a faculty without rights or power, one that is governed by fear rather than shared responsibilities and is susceptible to labor-bashing tactics such as increased workloads, contract labor, and the suppression of dissent. Adjunct or part-time educators must be given the opportunity to break the cycle of exploitative labor and within a short period of time be considered for full-time positions with full benefits and the power to influence governance policies. Within the universities and colleges today, power is top-heavy, largely controlled by trustees and administrators and removed from those who actually do the work of the university, namely the faculty, staff, and students. Moreover, the struggle against corporatization must consider addressing the exploitative conditions under which many graduate students work, constituting a de facto army of service workers who are underpaid, overworked, and shorn of any real power or benefits.

The challenge for faculty in higher education is both structural and ideological. On the structural side, faculty, students, and staff need to organize labor movements and unions to challenge the corporatization of the university under neoliberal policies as well as the broader neoliberal polices that bear down on most of the nations of the globe. Universities flush with corporate and military funds have enormous resources that can be mobilized to oppress faculty, exploit staff, and deny the rights of students to a decent education. To fight against such power demands an international labor and student movement capable of exercising enormous power collectively in both influencing and shaping the marriage of academic and economic policies at home and abroad. Such movements must connect to local communities, reach out to national and international organizations, and develop multiple strategies in taking back the universities from the corporations. I want to stress here the need for multiple interventions, extending from taking control of academic departments to organizing larger faculty structures and organizations. At best, faculty and students must unionize whenever they can in order to speak with a collective voice and the power of collective opposition.

Ideologically, faculty must find ways to contribute their knowledge and skills to an understanding of how neoliberal policies, corporate values, market identities, and consumer practices create the conditions for both devaluing critical learning and undermining viable forms of political and social agency. Within the last few years, protests on and off campuses have picked up and spawned a number of student protest groups, including protests against sweatshops and resistance to the increasing militarization of the university. Such movements offer instances of collective resistance to the increasing separation of corporations from traditional politics and public obligations, while rejecting right-wing efforts "to displace political sovereignty with the sovereignty of the market, as if the latter has a mind and morality of its own" (Comaroff and Comaroff, 2000, p. 332). Samuel Weber suggested that what seems to be involved in this process of displacement is "a fundamental and political redefinition of the social value of public services in general, and of universities and education in particular" (quoted in Simon, 2001, p. 47–48). The challenge here is for faculty to learn as much as possible from these student movements about what it means to deepen and expand the struggle for establishing pedagogical approaches and labor movements that can be used to mediate the fundamental tension between the public values of higher education and the commercial values of corporate culture, on the one hand, and fight against the more crucial assaults waged against the welfare state, public services, and public goods, on the other hand. If the forces of corporate culture are to be challenged, educators must consider enlisting the help of diverse communities, interests, foundations, social movements, and other forces to ensure that public institutions of higher learning are adequately funded so that they will not have to rely on corporate sponsorship and advertising revenues.

Engaged academics can learn from such struggles by turning the university into a vibrant critical site of learning and an unconditional site of pedagogical and political resistance. The power of the dominant order does not merely reside in the economic realm or in material relations of power but also in the realm of ideas and culture. This is why intellectuals must take sides, speak out, and engage in the hard work of debunking corporate culture's assault on teaching and learning. They must orient their teaching toward social change, connect learning to public life, link knowledge to the operations of power, and allow issues of human rights and crimes against humanity in their diverse forms to occupy a space of critical and open discussion in the classroom. It also means stepping out of the classroom and working with others to create public spaces where it becomes possible not only to "shift the way people think about the moment, but potentially to energize them to do something differently in that moment" (Guinier and Smith, 2002, pp. 44–45), to link one's critical imagination with the possibility of activism in the public sphere.

It is in the spirit of such a critique and act of resistance that educators need to break with what Pierre Bourdieu has described as a "new faith in the historical inevitability professed by the theorists of [neo] liberalism" in order to "invent new forms of collective political work" capable of confronting the march of corporate power (Bourdieu, 1998, p. 26). This will not be an easy task, but it is a necessary one if democracy is to be won back from the reign of financial markets and the Darwinian values of an unbridled capitalism. Academics can contribute to such a struggle by, among other things, defending higher education for its contribution to the quality of public life, fighting through organized resistance for the crucial role higher education can exercise pedagogically in asserting the primacy of democratic values over commercial interests, and struggling collectively through a powerful union movement to preserve the institutional and ideological conditions necessary to provide both faculty and students with the capacities they need for civic courage and engaged critical citizenship. John Dewey once claimed that "democracy needs to be reborn in each generation and education is its midwife" (quoted in Hollander, 2000). We live at a time when education needs to be reborn if democracy is to survive both in the United States and the world at large. But there is also the obligation that a society has to its young people and the necessity to build institutional structures, values, and power relations that speak to ensuring generations of young people a future that truly addresses the importance of a democratic future. There is more at stake here than a legitimation crisis over how to define the relationship between higher education and the public good, though this problem should not be underestimated. Not acting on that responsibility suggests that higher education is faring poorly in the context of a galloping neoliberalism that sells off public goods and subordinates all noncommodified democratic values to the dictates of the market.

If solutions to the problems facing higher education are to be effective, then they cannot be abstracted from the growing inequality between the rich and the poor that is taking place on a global level. This type of rabid capitalism must be confronted both at home and abroad at multiple levels, including the ideological, cultural, economic, and political. Stuart Tannock is right to insist that "If we are to develop a comprehensive vision of how higher education should serve the public good, we must . . . make sure that when we speak of inequality, we are thinking of it at a worldwide level. And we must, hard as this is to conceptualize, include in our vision of the 'public' and the 'public good' the college- and non-college-educated not just of our own country but across the planet" (2006, p. 50). Part of such a struggle suggests that educators and others organize collectively to oppose the creeping privatization of the university, close the college/non-college wage gap, protect academic freedom, preserve strong tenure contracts, appoint the growing army of part-time academics to full-time tenure-track positions, advocate for engaged scholarship, make critical education central to any understanding of classroom pedagogy, and create an international organization in defense of all forms of education as a public good essential to the very meaning of global democracy. Equally important is the need to transform the fight against militarization and the war in Iraq into a struggle for higher education as a democratic public sphere. One possibility is the demand that higher education be made accessible to every student in this country who wants to pursue such an education. If this government can spend billions of dollars on weapons of war, and a war that has made the world unsafe for democracy, it can surely embrace a redemptive politics by reallocating defense funds for educational needs, providing a combination of grants, scholarships, and no-interest loans to every student in America who qualifies for such aid. Such resistance demands a new political discourse, one that takes power seriously, understands politics as a matter of critique and possibility, reclaims democracy as a progressive and ongoing struggle, and builds social movements to provide a viable politics with organizational force and substance.

For many youth, the future appears to be a repeat of the present, a period not unlike what the singer and songwriter Gil Scott-Herron once called "winter in America." The time for social change has never been so urgent, since the fate of an entire generation of young people is at stake. Educators, parents, and other concerned citizens need to understand more clearly, as the writer Jack Geiger reminds us, how global neoliberalism "distorts individual relationships and magnifies such major social policy issues as poverty, crime, drugs, gangs, welfare, joblessness, and the failure of inner-city schools" (1997, p. 28). In addition, as parents, critical citizens, social activists, cultural workers, and educators we need to reject a growing commercial culture that reduces social values to market relations, limits the obligations of citizenship to the act of consuming, and dismisses economic justice as the product of a bygone era.

The future of higher education is inextricably connected to the future that we make available to the next generation of young people. Finding our way to a more human future means educating a new generation of scholars who not only defend higher education as a democratic public sphere, but who also frame their own agency as both scholars and citizen activists willing to connect their research, teaching and service with broader democratic concerns over equality, justice, and an alternative vision of what the university might be and what society might become under the present circumstances, it is time to remind ourselves that collective problems deserve collective solutions and that what is at risk is not only a generation of young people now considered to be generation of suspects, but the very promise of democracy itself.

NOTES

1. For detailed discussion on these aspects see Henwood (2003); Phillips (2003); and Krugman (2003).
2. Some of the most important work on disposability can be found in the scholarship of Zygmunt Bauman. See, especially, Bauman (2004).
3. I have taken up this critique in great detail in Giroux (2004).

REFERENCES

Agamben, G. 2001. On security and terror. Trans. Soenke Zehle. *Frankfurter Allegemeine Zeitung,* September 20. http://www.egs.edu/faculty/agamben/agamben-on-security-and-terror.html.
American Association of University Professors. 2004. Contingent faculty appointments. *AAUP Bulletin,* September 29. http://www.aaup.org/Issues/part-time/.
Arendt, H. 1973. *Origins of totalitarianism.* New York: Harvest.
Aronowitz, S. 2006. Higher education in everyday life. In *Deconstructing Derrida,* ed. P. P. Trifonas and M. A. Peters, 104–17). New York: Palgrave.
———. 1998. The new corporate university. *Dollars and Sense,* March/April: 32–35.
Ashburn, E. 2006. The few, the proud, the professors. *Chronicle of Higher Education,* October 6: A10–A12.
Bauman, Z. 1999. *In search of politics.* Stanford: Stanford University Press.
———. 2004. *Wasted lives.* London: Polity.
———. 2006. *Liquid fear.* London: Polity.
Bluestone, B., and B. Harrison. (1982.) *The deindustrialization of America: Plant closings, community abandonment and the dismantling of basic industry.* New York: Basic.
Bourdieu, P. 1998. *Acts of resistance: Against the tyranny of the market.* New York: The New Press.
———. 2000. For a scholarship with commitment. In *Profession 2000,* ed. Modern Language Association, 40–45. New York: Modern Language Association.
Bourdieu, P., Sayed, A., Christen, R., Champagne, P., Balazs, G., Wacquant, L., Borgois, P. and Lenoir, R. 1999. *The weight of the world: Social suffering in contemporary society.* Trans. Priscilla Pankhurst Ferguson. Stanford: Stanford University Press.
Browning, L. 2006. BMW's custom-made university. *New York Times,* August 29.
Burd, S. 2002. Lack of aid will keep 170,000 qualified, needy students out of college this year, report warns. *Chronicle of Higher Education,* June 27. http://chronicle.com/daily/2002/06/2002062701n.html.
———. 2005. Changes in federal formula means thousands may lose student aid. *Chronicle of Higher Education,* January 7. http://chronicle.com/free/v51/i18/18a00101.htm.
Chomsky, N. 2000. Paths taken, tasks ahead. In *Profession 2000,* ed. Modern Language Association, 32–39. New York: Modern Language Association.
Comaroff, J. 2007. Beyond bare life: AIDS, (bio)politics, and the neoliberal order. *Public Culture* 19, no.1: 197–219.
Comaroff, J., and J. L. Comaroff. 2000. Millennial capitalism: First thoughts on a second coming. *Public Culture* 12, no.2: 291–343.
Croissant, J. L. 2001. Can this campus be bought. *Academe,* September–October. http://www.aaup.org/publications/Academe01SO/so01cro.html.

Derrida, J. 2001. The future of the profession or the unconditional university. In *Derrida down under*, ed. L. Simmons and H. Worth, 233–247. Auckland, New Zealand: Dunmarra.

Flanders, L. 2005. Bush's hit list: Teens and kids. *Common Dreams News Center*, February 13. http://www.commondreams.org/views05/0213–11.htm.

Foster, J. B. 2005. The End of Rational Capitalism. *Monthly Review*, March 2005. www.monthlyreview.org/0305jbf.htm (accessed January 10, 2006)

Geiger, J. 1997. The real world of race. *The Nation*, December 1: 27–29.

Giroux, H. A. 2004. *The abandoned generation*. New York: Palgrave.

Gould, E. 2003. *The university in a corporate culture*. New Haven: Yale University Press.

Greenberg, M. 2004. A university is not a business (and other fantasies). *Educause* 29, no.2: 10–16.

Grossberg, L. 2001. Why does neo-liberalism hate kids? The war on youth and the culture of politics. *The Review of Education/Pedagogy/Cultural Studies* 23, no. 2: 111–36.

Grossman, D., and Gloria DeGaentano. 1999. *Stop teaching our kids to kill*. New York: Crown.

Guinier, L., and A. D. Smith. 2002. A conversation between Lani Guinier and Anna Deavere Smith: "Rethinking power, rethinking theatre." *Theater* 31, no. 3: 31–45.

Hanley, L. 2001. Conference roundtable. *Found Object* 10, Spring:103.

Harvey, D. 2003. *The new imperialism*. New York: Oxford University Press.

Henwood, D. 2003. *After the new economy*. New York: The New Press.

Hertz, N. 2001. *The silent takeover: Global capitalism and the death of democracy*. New York: The Free Press.

Hollander, E. L. 2000. The engaged university. *Academe*, July/August. http://www.aaup.org/publications/Academe/2000/00ja/JA00Holl.htm.

Jaschik, S. 2006a. BMW professors. *Inside Higher Education*, August 25. http://insidehighered.com/news/2006/08/25/clemson.

———. 2006b. The new State U. *Inside Higher Education*, August. http://insidehighered.com/news/2006/08/31/illinois.

Kamenetz, A. 2006. *Generation of debt*. New York: Riverside.

Klein, N. 1999. *No logo*. New York: Picador.

Kornblut, A. E. 2005. Bush urges rigorous high school testing. *New York Times*, January 13.

Kotz, D. 2003. Neoliberalism and the U.S. economic expansion of the '90s. *Monthly Review* 54, no.11: 15–33.

Krugman, P. 2003. *The great unraveling: Losing our way in the new century*. New York: W.W. Norton.

Krugman, P. 2005. Bush's class-war budget. *New York Times*, February 11.

Miyoshi, M. 1998. "Globalization," culture, and the university. In *The Cultures of Globalization*, ed. Fredric Jameson and Masao Miyoshi, 247–70. Durham: Duke University Press.

Newfield, C. 2002. Democratic passions: Reconstructing individual agency. In *Materializing democracy*, ed. R. Castronovo and D. Nelson, 314–344. Durham: Duke University Press.

New York Times. 2002. Pricing the poor out of college. March 27.

Palattella, J. 2001. Ivory towers in the marketplace. *Dissent*, Summer: 70–73.

Pearlstein, S. 2003. The lesson colleges need to learn. *Washington Post*, December 17.

Phillips, K. 2003. *Wealth and democracy: A political history of the American rich*. New York: Broadway.

Porter, J. R. 2006. Financial strains keep millions out of college, panel says. *Chronicle of Higher Education*, September 22.

Project on Student Debt. 2006. *Quick facts about student debt*. April 4. http:// projectonstudentdebt.org/files/File/Debt_Facts_and_Sources_4_4_06.pdf. (accessed December 28, 2006).

Readings, B. 1996. *The university in ruins*. Cambridge, MA: Harvard University Press.

Simon, R. 2001. The university: A place to think? In *Beyond the corporate university*, ed. H. A. Giroux and K. Myrsiades, 45–56. Lanham, Md: Rowman and Littlefield.

Steinmetz, G. 2003. The state of emergency and the revival of American imperialism: Toward an authoritarian post-Fordism. *Public Culture* 15, no. 2: 323–45.

Tannock, S. 2006. Higher education, inequality, and the public good. *Dissent*, Spring: 45–52.

Walsh, S. 2002. Study finds significant increase in number of part-time and non-tenure-track professors. *Chronicle of Higher Education*, October 29. http:// chronicle.com/daily/2002/10/2002102904n.htm.

Williams, J. J. 2006. Debt education: Bad for the young, bad for America. *Dissent*, Summer: 53–59.

Yates, M. D. 2000. Us versus them: Laboring in the academic factory. *Monthly Review* 51, no. 8. http://www.monthlyreview.org/100yates.htm.

Zemsky, R. 2003. Have we lost the "Public" in higher education? *Chronicle of Higher Education*, May 30.

4 Higher Education and the Profit Incentive

Tristan McCowan

INTRODUCTION

Despite the reforms of the last twenty years, education systems worldwide do not yet resemble the competitive markets in which most commodities are traded. Proponents of markets and privatization in education tend to advocate a system in which some state intervention is necessary, whether this be direct funding of schools (as in the UK quasi-market), indirect funding through vouchers, or simply quality assurance and regulation. Markets are frequently justified on the basis of parents' or students' rights to choice, or by the greater efficiency and quality ensured through competition. Privatization is also at times promoted as a means of reducing the state monopoly and achieving greater academic freedom, as was alleged in the case of Buckingham University (Geiger, 1986).

Tooley's (1996; 1998; 1999; 2000) defence of markets in education, however, goes much further. Rather than balancing the business values necessary for efficiency with interventions to ensure quality and equity, he advocates an open market with very minimal state control, seeing the profit motive to be intrinsically beneficial for education. He summarizes his arguments as the "seven virtues of the profit motive," based on his observations of education companies around the world. These are:

1. The desire for expansion
2. The necessity for quality control
3. Brand names solve the information problem
4. The necessity of research and development
5. Proper rewards for, and utilization of, teachers
6. Attracting investment and cost-effectiveness
7. Concern for student destinations (Tooley 2000, pp. 197–200)

Tooley's ideas have achieved considerable diffusion and have been adopted by organizations such as the International Finance Corporation and the Institute of Economic Affairs. The importance of his work is that it provides an intellectual justification for the expansion of the private sector in education. Companies, and the organizations supporting their interests, are keen to have academic support in order to convince governments to reduce regulations and allow access to the lucrative education market. For this reason it is vital to assess the validity of Tooley's claims. If his argument—which is a *moral* and not simply a *pragmatic* one—were to gain widespread credibility, it would have serious consequences for the ability of states to defend their public education systems, and for the notions of equality of opportunity and democratic control on which the systems in principle rest.

This chapter will examine Tooley's arguments in relation to higher education (HE). This is an area of great relevance, since the public and traditional private sectors in many countries have shown themselves ill-equipped to meet the fast-growing demand for university places, creating opportunities for new forms of provision. For-profit institutions (FPIs) in some middle-income countries have brought a rapid increase in tertiary enrollment, and in the Unites States have provided opportunities for those who would have difficulty attending a traditional campus-based institution. Studies such as those of Chipman (2002), Steier (2003) and Sinclair (2003) argue that high levels of access to HE will only be possible with profit-making institutions. However, it remains to be seen whether the recent increase in enrollment in FPIs has been matched by desirable levels of quality, and whether they can ensure an equitable expansion in the long term.

This chapter argues that Tooley's position is not supported by the current experiences of for-profit education around the world. Rather than focusing exclusively on the philosophical basis of his argument, which has had ample attention elsewhere (e.g. Ranson, 1993; Winch, 1996; Brighouse, 1998, 2000), it will provide some examples of the ways for-profit institutions function in practice in relation to the proposed seven virtues. The generation of profit through subsidiary activities or joint ventures has also become a common practice in public universities: this study, however, will focus on private for-profit institutions.

THE GROWTH OF FOR-PROFIT HIGHER EDUCATION

While private-sector involvement in education has traditionally been non-profit, and often dominated by religious groups, there has recently been an increase in for-profit activity. Some of the forms in which profit-making manifests itself, such as catering services, have a minor influence on the nature of the institution; others, such as textbook publishing and on-site advertising, can have a strong effect on curriculum and student experiences. Recently, however, there has been an increase in profit-making activity at the level of the institution itself or its managing body. In some countries, such as Russia, this type of profit-making is still officially illegal, but many others have passed legislation allowing the entry of companies into the education market, and in some cases have actively promoted it (Maas, 2001; McCowan, forthcoming; Tooley, 2000). In the United Kingdom there have been experiments with the contracting out of management of state schools to companies, a process that is gaining momentum in the USA. A number of these companies, such as Edison, have gained prominence on the stock market, and education is increasingly seen as an investment opportunity offering significant returns.

However, the areas which have been most conducive to the development of fully private (i.e. private financing and private management) for-profit education have been the preschool and postsecondary levels. This chapter will address developments in the latter. While in Europe this is still in its early stages, the United States has a well-established sector and the growth is even more dramatic in countries with less-developed HE systems. This process is likely to accelerate if the General Agreement for Trade in Services (GATS) is enforced in relation to public education systems (Kelk & Worth, 2002). Many public institutions—such as the London School of Economics—are also developing for-profit wings (Bok, 2003).

For-profit postsecondary education in the United States has its origins in the correspondence education boom at the start of the twentieth century (Noble, 2001). Then, as now, the new providers were met with a degree of suspicion by the general public—fueled by a number of scandals concerning recruitment strategies—and with resistance (as well as a certain amount of imitation) by the traditional educational establishments. Their success, however, was guaranteed by the desire of working adults to better their career prospects without having to undertake a conventional degree.

The current growth of the FPIs in the United States is based on the same target population, but as well as distance education (now through the Internet), there are physical institutions, albeit with organizational structures radically different from those of the traditional campus. They range from large, publicly traded companies to "single-campus mom-and-pop proprietary schools that serve an extremely narrow niche" (Borrego, 2002). Despite still having a low share of overall enrollments (approximately 3 percent for degree courses), the growth of the sector has been phenomenal. The number of degree-granting FPIs increased from 165 to 721 between 1981 and 1999, and enrollments rose almost 48 percent between 1996 and 2000, compared to 5.7 percent in the traditional sector. There has been a further 21 percent increase in enrollment between 2002 and 2003. Approximately 11 percent of institutions offering four-year and 30 percent of those offering two-year degrees are in the for-profit sector, and FPIs control 41 percent of the online distance-learning market. It is also becoming an increasingly attractive area for investors: for-profit HE gave a 108 percent return from 1999–2001. Vulnerable nonprofit institutions are at increasing risk of being taken over by education businesses (Blumenstyk, 2003b; Borrego and Blumenstyk, 2001; Kelly, 2001; Kinser and Levy 2005; Morey, 2001; Phillips, 2003).

The largest of the new generation of FPIs is the University of Phoenix, whose enrollment grew by 163 percent between 1998 and 2003, reaching a total of nearly 200,000 students. It is run by the Apollo Group, whose stock market valuation of £6.7 billion is equal to the endowment fortune of Yale, the second richest university in the country (Phillips, 2003).

Phoenix has a distinctive educational approach. Like the old correspondence courses, it targets working adults, providing courses that are closely linked to the workplace, with accelerated completion, campuses in convenient locations, and new approaches to teaching staff and curriculum. The *Phoenix model* is outlined in the 1997 publication, *For-Profit Higher Education: Developing a World-Class Workforce,* written by the university's founder, John Sperling, and its president, Robert Tucker. They lead the battle to pressure the U.S. federal and state governments into relaxing regulations, allowing FPIs to compete for grants on an equal footing with nonprofit institutions and to operate freely throughout the country. In 1996, Apollo succeeded in pressuring Pennsylvania into revoking its ban on for-profit universities (Morey, 2001).

FPIs became eligible for federal and state student financial aid in the 1970s, but scandals in the 1990s concerning the aggressive recruitment of students eligible for aid had brought a certain amount of distrust from central government (Burd, 2003; Morey, 2001). Life became considerably easier, however, under the Bush administration, which has been "lavishing the institutions with praise" (Burd, 2003). Sally Stroup, chief Washington lobbyist for the Apollo group, was appointed in October 2001 as assistant secretary for postsecondary education at the Department for Education.

Europe's HE systems, with their stronger state control, have been more resistant to the entry of FPIs, but there are signs of change. While the Buckingham experiment in the United Kingdom has not led to a wave of privatization (the institution is, in any event, nonprofit), Germany has opened the door to for-profit HE with the establishment of Hanseatic University (Chapman, 2003). Portugal, already with a third of its students in private institutions, is a prime target for education companies, as is central and eastern Europe, as demand for business qualifications for the new capitalist economies increases.

The highest proportions of students enrolled in FPIs, however, can be found in the low- and middle-income countries (LMICs), particularly in Asia, but also in parts of Latin America and Africa. Arguably the most successful education company outside the United States is India's National Institute for Information Technology (NIIT), which has a large network of postsecondary IT training centres, as well as educational software production, giving it an annual turnover of US$73 million with some 500,000 students. While it plays a complementary role to the main universities, and might not be said to mount a direct challenge, it is growing in power—both in financial terms and on account of the necessity of its qualifications on the job market. South Africa has the most established FPIs in the African continent, including the company Educor, which has an annual turnover of US$26 million and some 300,000 students (Tooley, 2001).

While low-income countries do not as a general rule have sufficient numbers of affluent students to support many private universities, prospects in middle-income countries are very good. Due to the generally poor coverage of the existing HE systems and the lack of regulation, FPIs can enter the mainstream degree-awarding market (as well as the mature student, vocational, or distance markets) and have great potential for expansion. The Philippines has the most established for-profit sector in Asia, accounting for over 47 percent of the total enrollment and 66 percent of institutions (Philippines Commission on Higher Education, 2003), but there are also growing sectors in Jordan, Malaysia, Vietnam, China, Thailand, and Indonesia (Levy, 2002; Maas, 2001). Approximately 44 percent of all HE institutions in Brazil are for-profit, and the sector is growing throughout Latin America, despite the traditionally strong state control (Instituto Nacional de Estudos e Pesquisas Educacionais Anísios Teixeira, 2003). A new law in Peru, for example, allowed the Peruvian University of Applied Sciences (UPC) to become a for-profit corporation (Maas, 2001). This expansion has some financial backing from the International Finance Corporation, and the support of the World Bank as a whole.

However, while the traditional religious or philanthropic universities form a clearly distinct group, the difference between for-profit and nonprofit status in the new institutions is not always obvious. Australia's Bond University, established in 1989, is officially nonprofit, but still speaks proudly of its annual "profits," and is promoting a rapid overseas expansion, principally in South Africa (Bond University, 2004). This is particularly true in LMICs: many companies in Brazil, for example, are registered as nonprofit for the purposes of securing grants and tax breaks, but effectively function as businesses, aiming for aggressive expansion, and siphoning off what are effectively profits to associated foundations (Davies, 2002). This is the case with UNIP and Estácio de Sá, the two largest universities in the country (Instituto Nacional de Estudos e Pesquisas Educacionais Anísios Teixeira, 2003) (the latter, in fact, eventually made an official conversion to for-profit status in 2004).

There is no doubting the growing presence of FPIs around the world, or their financial viability. Yet their justification from an educational perspective is far from clear. The seven arguments provided by Tooley will, therefore, be considered in order to assess the extent to which the dramatic growth of these institutions is a positive development in HE.

FIRST VIRTUE: THE DESIRE FOR EXPANSION

One of the most depressing spectacles in the current educational setup is of an excellent state school in a deprived area—and there are a few—

with a long waiting list. The school has a successful formula, strong and dynamic leadership, but it doesn't occur to anyone to do other than turn poor parents away. (Tooley 2000, p. 197)

Tooley's first point is that we can only provide good schools for all if those that are successful are allowed to expand, and have an incentive to do so, as do businesses in other areas. (Tooley is here writing with reference to schools in the United Kingdom, but his arguments are intended to apply to all levels and locations). He argues furthermore that without the profit incentive, investors will be unlikely to risk taking over failing institutions or starting from scratch in disadvantaged areas.

An initial observation can be made at this point. Businesses in other areas do expand when they are successful, but this does not mean that they automatically make themselves available to all. Many people would like a Mercedes car, but the company does not expand so as to provide for everybody. In many cases not expanding may be an essential strategy for maintaining the exclusivity, and therefore the value, of one's product. This is likely to occur in education, where goods are *positional,* in that one's qualifications are valued in relation to the qualifications held by others in society. Moreover, some institutions consider that their educational effectiveness can be guaranteed only by maintaining their small size.

Having said this, it is likely that some successful institutions and courses will indeed expand. In the case of the HE companies, this occurs both through establishing new institutions and through taking over existing ones. In 2001, there were a number of large-scale takeovers in the United States: Argosy Education Group was acquired by rival Education Management Corporation (EDMC), Career Education bought EduTrek International, and Sylvan Learning Systems acquired a 41 percent stake in Walden University (Borrego and Blumenstyk, 2001; Jacobson, 2001). In 2003, Career Choices was absorbed by Corinthian Colleges, as was the Canadian CDI Education Corporation, and EDMC bought up a further eighteen smaller institutions (Blumenstyk & Farrell, 2003).

The concentration has been so intense that by 2002 only eight companies accounted for more than 62 percent of all the revenues generated by FPIs in the United States (Gallagher et al., 2002) In addition, the University of Phoenix has sold its curricular and organizational model to twenty-four other universities in exchange for a percentage of their revenues (Sperling and Tucker, 1997). Tooley may argue that this is evidence of the market's ability to promote the expansion of high-quality institutions, but it does appear to work against the other great battle cries of the free-marketeers, namely, choice and diversity.

Expansion of enrollment is particularly important in countries with low coverage at the HE level, and is frequently used by governments and the World Bank as a justification for private sector growth. However, the expansion of FPIs has a number of consequences that may counteract the benefits of increased enrollment. First, problems arise when the expansion in question occurs across national borders. When institutions from powerful countries enter the markets of LMICs there will inevitably be some threat to the latter's sovereignty and autonomy, and to the ability of their education systems to serve the needs of the wider society. Industrialized countries like the United States owe much of their power and prosperity to the use of universities to promote the interests of the state, particularly in terms of military and scientific research. There is evidence that the expansion of education companies from Organisation for Economic Co-operation and Development (OECD) countries will be increasingly located in the developing world. Apollo entered the Brazilian market through a partnership with the Pitágoras Group (McCowan, 2004). Sylvan Learning Systems operates in nine countries, and ITT Educational Services and Apollo Group both entered the Chinese HE market in 2003 (Blumenstyk, 2003b). These universities are very popular with local students aiming to impress future employers with the prestige of a foreign-accredited degree. This phenomenon is not, however, confined to private FPIs: a number of public universities are also pursuing aggressive profit-making ventures abroad.

There are a few examples of companies from middle-income countries entering the markets of the wealthy countries: in addition to its prolific activities in Asia and Africa, NIIT has opened centers in the United States and United Kingdom, and Educor has bought a stake in Canada's International Business Schools (International Finance Corporation, 1999; Tooley, 2000). However, these examples are rare, and the situation is unlikely to change given the conditions of global trade and the hierarchy of educational prestige. (What is the likelihood that North Americans or Europeans will enroll in an offshore campus of a Bangladeshi or Nigerian university?)

South Africa has attempted to limit the number of degree courses being offered by overseas providers, arguing that they are making profits using public resources, through state-subsidised local staff and facilities (MacGregor, 2000). Most countries try to impose some restrictions like these, but the ability of governments to act in the interests of their own people, already weak in the face of powerful multinationals, may be weakened further by international trade agreements (Kelk and Worth, 2002).

SECOND VIRTUE: THE NECESSITY FOR QUALITY CONTROL

Tooley's argument for the second virtue is the cornerstone of his argument for markets in general:

> The schools or colleges have as their *raison d'être* the provision of quality educational services. If they don't do this, they'll go out of business. (Tooley 2000, p. 198)

Quality control, according to Tooley, is best ensured by market forces, since the education companies will only be profitable if the education provided is of high quality and therefore in high demand. Neither altruism, nor even an interest in education, is necessary: survival in the marketplace depends on high standards. Not even the limited government regulation evident in areas such as food and transport is seen to be required. The quality control provided by government through its standardized tests is seen to reflect political rather than educational concerns, and to be "mired in subjectivity and waffle" (p. 198).

It is beyond the scope of this chapter to assess the fairness of Tooley's criticisms of current government quality control in the United Kingdom. In any event, even if his view of the current practice of nationalized assessments and targets is justified, this is a specific case and cannot lead to a rejection of government intervention in principle. The question is whether the free market system can itself ensure high quality for all.

Following from the first virtue, expansion is only a good in itself if the institution in question is of a high quality. However, there are cases where demand is high even in the absence of educational quality, often due to skillful branding and advertising (discussed in the context of the third virtue) or to lack of choice. In Brazil, a number of institutions that are widely regarded to be of dubious quality, such as Estácio de Sá and UniverCidade (sic.), have achieved phenomenal growth simply because for many there is no alternative—whether geographical or financial (McCowan, 2004; forthcoming). The implication of Tooley's thesis is that the high demand for McDonald's and Burger King foods is proof of their quality. Yet demand is related not only to quality but also to price, therefore making high quality in many cases available only to the rich.

> Many FPIs argue that they are pioneers of a new form of HE which is better suited to the contemporary world. However, their distinctive conception is largely determined by constraints of expenditure. Sperling and Tucker (1997) state, "Traditional institutions require a full-time faculty, usually tenured with PhDs, library buildings, labs, dorms, student unions and athletic facilities, none of which is required by working adults" (p. 58).

It is true that working adults will probably not require dormitories, and may not require student unions and athletic facilities, yet it is less easy to see why they would not want libraries, laboratories or full-time lecturers with PhDs. The point is that it is impossible for Phoenix to pay for these things *and* be profitable. Just because fee-paying students will choose to forfeit certain facilities (such as libraries and labs) in order to keep down the costs of their education, it does not follow that these are not important in education or indeed not desired by the students. Once again, demand does not guarantee quality.

NIIT's conception of quality is expressed by the president of the company's U.S. wing:

> First, the company views its training business as a manufacturing business. The student is the raw material, and the training process is well defined, certified under ISO9001. The instructors are like machinists. At the end of it there is the finished product, a certified student. (International Finance Corporation, 1999, p, 47)

The pedagogical dangers of this type of approach hardly need stating.

Tooley overlooks another important point regarding demand for education. For the individual, schooling is desirable both in terms of educational development and in terms of the final diploma, which is necessary for future employment and other opportunities. However, these two are not necessarily coexistent: it is possible to obtain a diploma that is accepted on the job market without having an education of high quality. This is particularly likely in LMICs if the diploma in question has the prestige of an overseas institution. It may be argued that an individual has the right to choose to obtain a diploma without high educational quality, but that ignores both the interests of other people in society (everyone has an interest that doctors, engineers, teachers, electricians, and so forth have had a high quality of education) and the longer-term interests of the individual.

Teacher education is a high growth area for FPIs, both at the undergraduate and graduate levels, and in the United States is largely dominated by Sylvan (Blumenstyk, 2003a). Prospective teachers are increasingly drawn to those courses "that are quick and easy," according to Beverly Young, director of teacher education programs at California State University (quoted in Blumenstyk, 2003a). Autonomy from public control in this area has serious consequences, since the training received has an impact not only on the individual teachers but also on the thousands of children that they will teach.

Dr. Hans Karle, president of the World Federation for Medical Education, observing that the number of medical schools worldwide had grown from 1,300 to 2,000 in the previous eight years, expressed concern that the quality of medical education has suffered, stating that a growing number are "businesses to attract students who cannot get into medical schools in their own countries," and that while "some of these schools are badly needed . . . others are simply moneymaking ventures"(quoted in the *Chronicle of Higher Education,* September 26, 2003).

Many FPIs, worried about litigation by students dissatisfied with the quality of the institutions or the value of their qualifications, have introduced arbitration clauses to protect themselves. According to Farrell (2003c), these clauses in the United States "are being used by the institutions to take advantage of uninformed students and to avoid being held accountable for the quality of the product they provide."

In the instance of bankruptcies and failures of FPIs there are serious implications for students engaged in degrees, and for past graduates whose qualifications are in danger of losing their value. These eventualities seem more than possible: there have been failures such as the online education initiatives Fathom and Pensare (Bok, 2003), while the United States company Career Education Corporation stands accused of deceiving investors about its financial performance and of forging student records so as to pass its audit (Blumenstyk and Farrell, 2004).

THIRD VIRTUE: BRAND NAMES SOLVE
THE INFORMATION PROBLEM

The third virtue is strongly linked to the second. Branding is seen by Tooley as a means by which the public can be sure it is choosing education of a high quality. An argument frequently given against markets in education is that "consumers" will suffer from a lack of information about the institutions in question and their relative qualities. This, according to Tooley, can be solved by brands:

> I know nothing about lap-top computers, for example, but I was able to buy one of the highest quality without anyone taking advantage of my ignorance. How? I bought into a *brand name*. We know that the company's reputation is absolutely paramount and that the company knows that *some* of its customers are informed and can't take the risks that I am not one of these. (Tooley, 2000, p. 198; emphasis in original)

Reputation may indeed be an incentive for ensuring that quality is made *consistent* (although, as stated before, the *level* of quality will usually be linked to price). However, the success of a brand is not solely dependent on the quality of the product. Inherent in the very idea of brand promotion is that it is the brand itself (Nike, Starbucks), and the lifestyle images associated with it, that is desired by the consumer, rather than simply the product (a good running shoe, a cup of coffee). Resources are spent therefore on improving the quality of the brand, and not that of the product—Tooley (2001) recommends allocating 10 percent of the education company's total expenditure, but it could be more. (According to Noble [2001], the for-profit correspondence courses in the first half of the twentieth century spent 50–80 percent of revenues from tuition fees on advertising and recruitment.)

> Private HE institutions in southern Brazil spend an average of over US$400 a year in advertising for every new student enrolled, equivalent to about three months' fees (Braga, 2002). This is money that is being spent not on educational quality, but on convincing prospective students of the quality of the institution. As the incentive for FPIs is profit, and

not education, aims are achieved when there is demand for the courses, whether that demand is based on a real or a perceived quality.

As well as by advertising in the media, successful branding is achieved by visibility of outlets: Klein (2000) shows that the branding benefits for Starbucks make it worthwhile to establish new high-street stores even if they are individually loss making. FPIs tend to have their campuses in locations that are both accessible to customers and visible for the general public. Phoenix, for example, has branches in shopping malls; Estácio de Sá has one in a theme park just outside Rio de Janeiro.

In addition to the tenuous link between branding and product quality, the expansion of a brand will inevitably result in homogenization and standardization. Tooley's argument here seems to rest on an identification of standardization and quality. True, a standardized product will not be subject to *varying* quality, but that does not mean it will have *high* quality.

FOURTH VIRTUE: THE NECESSITY OF RESEARCH AND DEVELOPMENT

The fourth virtue is bold in that it challenges the widespread assumption that FPIs conduct little research. Again Tooley argues that competition makes it essential for companies to carry out these activities effectively. However, he is referring not to publicly beneficial research, but to that which contributes to the profitability of the individual institution or company.

Tooley makes a second point, stating that "Another virtue of the profit motive is that the market will ensure that such research-based best practice gets copied by others, and hence disseminated to all" (p. 199). It is true that "effective" methods will be adopted by other companies where possible, but Tooley surely overestimates the ease with which companies have access to each other's research. The same competition that will give incentive to improvement will also encourage companies to prevent competitors having access to the secrets of their success.

The fact is that FPIs in the United States and elsewhere have been successful partly because they do *not* invest in research. Nonprofit universities find it increasingly difficult "to compete with institutions like the University of Phoenix and Walden, which place less emphasis on costly endeavors like research" (Blumenstyk, 2003a). As well as limiting the ability of nonprofit institutions to carry out research in the public interest, this could have a negative effect on the quality of the educational experience of students, who will no longer benefit from exposure to the environment of academic research.

Evidence from Brazil also challenges Tooley's claims. FPIs here conduct little research, with the exception of the development of their own teaching materials, the rights to which are jealously guarded. The head of the Estácio de

Sá chain has described academic research as "pompous uselessness" (Folha Dirigida, 2001). UNIP/Objetivo—frequently praised by Tooley—invests as much as 8 percent of its annual receipts on research into high-technology didactic materials, which, as well as establishing a successful and exclusive brand of educational resources, brings benefits to the owner João Carlos di Genio's large media empire. The wider research carried out by the group is usually linked to di Genio's many business interests, such as cattle breeding (he is said to own the most expensive cow in the world), and in establishing patents on Amazonian plants (Parajara, 2003).

NIIT is described by Tooley (2000) as being "the most notable example of R&D" (p. 199). However, while 5 percent of its turnover is spent on developing commercial educational applications, only 0.7 percent is spent on noncommercial research, and even this is in part "justified in terms of brand promotion" (p.199). Teixeira and Amaral (2001), in their overview of new private institutions, see moving away from research in all its forms as a worldwide trend.

FIFTH VIRTUE: PROPER REWARDS FOR, AND UTILIZATION OF, TEACHERS

The fifth virtue extols the benefits of for-profit education in releasing teachers from fixed salaries and limited contact with students. Tooley exploits the ambiguities of the word "proper" here: while at first glance it would seem to indicate that teachers would be paid more, in reality he means "proper" as in "what they deserve"—in other words, that only "good" teachers would be paid well.

> Imagine if the same principle applied in other communication businesses—we would have the odd spectacle of a Jeremy Paxman limited to broadcasting to a tiny audience on a local hospital radio, say, or writing only for the *Malvern College Times*. (Tooley 2000, p. 199)

Tooley laments that gifted teachers can only benefit a few hundred people a week due to an "egalitarian straightjacket," and that with profit incentives, their services would be made available to thousands. This view seems to confuse the concepts of *teaching* and *communication*. Of course, a gifted teacher or lecturer can *reach* thousands of people a day, as they currently do through books, articles and the Internet. Yet, that does not mean they can *teach* thousands of people a day, unless that teaching is going to have no element of personal contact, no asking and answering of questions, feedback, assessment, and so forth.

FPIs do reward "successful" teachers, using performance-related pay, with some lecturers receiving higher salaries—or, alternatively, facing dismissal—on the basis of their students' test scores and other output evaluations (Borrego, 2002). However, FPIs almost universally have highly centralized curricula with few possibilities for significant input from teachers. In addition, they make a separation between teaching and research, with lecturers not themselves required to undertake any significant research activities (Morey, 2001).

The following are instances of this "proper utilization" of teachers. The curriculum development team of Phoenix University, for example,

> guid[e] Phoenix's instructors in exactly what to teach and how to teach it. . . . Some education experts say that approach values uniformity over creativity. But Phoenix officials defend their methods, arguing that the process ensures consistent quality across a broad spectrum of teaching skills. . . . The review process is designed to operate "almost for the lowest common denominator" of instructional ability. . . . (Farrell, 2003b)

NIIT are also committed to "supporting" their academic staff:

> Each course tutor is given a batch file, which describes in meticulous detail all the courses to be taught, the sub-units, the material to be covered, and the time taken on each section—this even prescribes how long must be taken over each overhead transparency! (Tooley, 2000, p. 117)

Tooley's exclamation mark here is of admiration, not disbelief. C. N. Madhusudan of NIIT states:

> [NIIT's] instructors are the production managers. Traditional universities are very person-specific, person-driven, where the instructor has a tremendous role to play in the outcome. NIIT has tried to reduce this role by restructuring the methodology of education, and by transforming the process of training into a product. (International Finance Corporation, 1999, p. 47)

FPIs also have a greater proportion of part-time staff than do nonprofit or public institutions, a feature that may make for financial efficiency but is unlikely to enhance academic quality. Phoenix has only 140 of its approximately seven thousand lecturers on a full-time contract (Morey, 2001). They also tend to have lower qualifications, and are not in general required to have a PhD. Similar trends are seen in Brazil and elsewhere (Instituto Nacional de Estudos e Pesquisas Educacionais Anísios Teixeira, 2003). Gonzalez (1999) relates the high returns on for-profit HE in the Philippines to the very high workload and low salaries of teaching staff.

SIXTH VIRTUE: ATTRACTING INVESTMENT AND COST-EFFECTIVENESS

Two points are made here: first, that the profit incentive brings badly needed capital to education, and second, that profitability requires institutions to run efficiently, while in the present system "there is little encouragement to deliver educational services more cheaply" (Tooley, 2000, p. 199).

It is possible that FPIs are more efficient than traditional institutions, and that a desire to make profit may indeed encourage a less wasteful used of resources. However, most direct comparisons are misleading, since the lower costs of FPIs are typically the result of lower expenditure on research, academic staff, libraries, and other features widely believed to be of value in education. While a course at Phoenix and one at the University of California at Berkeley both lead to a "degree, " that does not make it possible to compare their expenditure per student on equal terms. Claims for the efficiency of private universities in Brazil, for example, do not take into account public institutions' expenditure on university hospitals, staff pensions, and community services (Davies, 2002).

Another important factor is that large universities function on the basis of cross-subsidization, where expensive courses like engineering or medicine are run alongside cheaper ones like law or business studies. FPIs naturally choose to run only those courses which are most cost-effective, thereby poaching a disproportionate number of students from the cheaper courses (Phillips, 2003; Teixeira and Amaral, 2001). Other institutions thereby face increasing costs per student, meaning a loss of enrollment for the private nonprofits, and for the public sector further accusations of inefficiency.

An example of the cost-saving activities of FPIs is given by NIIT:

> *Carry-home-PC* is a solution to the question: how do you minimize student's [sic] presence inside your facility? . . . Similarly, the company created the computer drome, like an aerodrome, where a huge number of computing facilities are crammed under one roof (International Finance Corporation, 1999, p. 48).

There is unlikely to be consensus that dissuading students from frequenting the educational institution or cramming them together are cost-saving strategies which are justified from an educational perspective.

At the same time as struggling to keep expenditure on students as low as possible, FPIs find it necessary to provide their executives with handsome rewards. In 2000, DeVry's top two executives were earning $1.1 million a year, with average pay for chief executive officers in for-profit HE companies at $568,000, excluding major sources of income such as stock options. John Sperling of Apollo made about $10.7 million with the sale of 250,000 shares in one week in July 2001. He owns a total number of over 18 million shares in the company (Borrego, 2001).

SEVENTH VIRTUE: CONCERN FOR STUDENT DESTINATIONS

Tooley's final argument for the profit incentive is that it will encourage institutions to equip students for subsequent employment, both through providing them with the necessary links with businesses and by running recruitment agencies. Tooley elsewhere in the book and in *The global education industry* (2001) gives a number of examples of education companies which have bought agencies of this sort.

While these factors are certainly a bonus for the individuals involved, and will make the institutions desirable to prospective students, it does not seem a valid principle around which to organize an educational system. After all, social networks function in the elite "public" (private) schools of the United Kingdom which facilitate acquisition of high-level jobs, but this can hardly be used as a justification for the private sector in education.

There might be worrying implications for equality of opportunity. With education companies controlling not only provision of qualifications but also job recruitment, their power would rise significantly, leaving young people increasingly dependent on a private education that only some will be able to afford.

As well as easing the passage between university and work, FPIs are concerned to provide students with the types of skills that will help them in the workplace. In fact this is the primary justification given by Sperling and Tucker (1997) and other defenders of for-profit education. Their criticisms of traditional universities have some justification, no doubt, at least in terms of catering for the working adults around which Phoenix orients itself. Yet why should this make necessary a *for-profit* institution? The unusual logic of their argument can be summarized as follows:

1. Traditional universities are not good.
2. For-profit institutions are not traditional universities.
3. Therefore, for-profit institutions are good.

It is not clear why the solution is for-profit status, or why the flexible hours, easy access, and accelerated and work-based study that are advocated could not just as easily be provided in a public institution (as can be seen to some extent in the case of Birkbeck or the Open University in the United Kingdom). Markets in general, it is argued, being based around demand, are more responsive to individuals needs, but—as discussed in previous sections—this cannot be the only principle on which to organize an educational system, since education has societal as well as individual consequences. The only other argument given for for-profit status by Sperling and Tucker (1997) is that it is less of a burden on the taxpayer: like many defenses of for-profit HE it is an argument relating to the economic advantages of a free-market economy, and not to the educational advantages of a marketized education system.

Student destinations, after all, are not only those of employment. Research carried out by Persell and Wenglinsky (2004), using longitudinal data from the United States National Center for Education Statistics, found that students of FPIs had lower levels of civic engagement than other students when controlling for differences not related to their attendance at the institution. Antonio Flores, President of the Hispanic Association of Colleges and Universities of the USA—which does not allow for-profit institutions to join—states:

> These for-profits tend to zero in on skills and training necessary to get jobs, and not so much on developing their students as engaged citizens . . . And we believe that institutions that are only concerned with the private benefit of education to the individual are really dismissing half the value of education, which is for the individual to add to society as an informed citizen. (Farrell, 2003a)

CONCLUSION

Representatives of FPIs worldwide often show a righteous indignation at opposition to their commercial activities. This is well expressed by the former president of the University of the East, in the Philippines:

> We are sick and tired of being told that profits are evil, that we should not make a profit at all as if we could operate meaningfully at a loss, as if suffering a loss would make us better schools. (Geiger, 1986, p. 63)

Clearly it is not better that a for-profit educational institution runs at a loss. The question, however, is whether it should be for-profit in the first place, and the onus is on these institutions to show the benefits of the profit incentive, both in raising the quality of the education provided, and making that education available to all.

This chapter is not intended as a defense of the traditional universities or of current government policy. Tooley's criticisms in this respect may be well justified, but that is not in itself a justification of for-profit or even private HE. Arguments in favor of for-profit education are based on the idea that while the "bottom line" of an education company is profit, this is not harmful to the educational quality of the institutions, and indeed can be positively beneficial. Tooley calls this "the virtue of the seven virtues"

(p. 200). Nevertheless, the above examples show a number of ways in which the requirements of profitability are having a negative effect on the nature of the education provided. It is important to note that this is not so much a characteristic of the *private* sector as a whole, but specifically of the *for-profit* subsector based on the business model.

Newton (2002) argues that the FPIs pose little threat to the established HE system in the United States since they are limited to a particular segment of the market in which traditional universities do not operate. There is evidence, however, that this may be changing, as companies like Apollo start to move into the market for young undergraduate students (Blumenstyk, 2004). This view also underestimates the ability of the growing for-profit universities to influence society's beliefs about the nature and purpose of HE. As the for-profit sector expands and promotes its message, HE increasingly becomes valued only in so far as it brings some tangible material benefit to the individual. Education that provides more general benefits to the individual—in terms of critical, intellectual, aesthetic and emotional abilities that are hard to quantify—is being increasingly sidelined, as is education that brings benefits to society as a whole. This process will increase as the political and economic power of the for-profit sector grows, and the public and nonprofit sectors, through ideological commitment or financial necessity, remodel themselves in the same image.

REFERENCES

Blumenstyk, G. 2003a. Companies' graduate programs challenge colleges of education. *Chronicle of Higher Education*, September 5.
———. 2003b. For-profit colleges: Growth at home and abroad. *Chronicle of Higher Education*, December 19.
———.2004. Biggest for-profit education company makes a bid for the youth market. *Chronicle of Higher Education*, April 23.
Blumenstyk, G., and E. F. Farrell. 2003. In for-profit higher education, buying binge heats up. *Chronicle of Higher Education*, July 11.
———. 2004. A season of purchases and lawsuits for for-profit colleges. *Chronicle of Higher Education*, January 9.
Bok, D. 2003. *Universities in the marketplace: The commercialization of higher education*. Princeton: Princeton University Press.
Bond University. 2004. *Bond University*. http://www.bond.edu.au (accessed January 8, 2004).
Borrego, A. M. 2001. Stock options sweeten packages for executives in for-profit higher education. *Chronicle of Higher Education*, November 9.
———. 2002. For-profit, for students. *Chronicle of Higher Education*, June 28.
Borrego, A. M., and G. Blumenstyk. 2001. As Wall Street took a dive, higher-education stocks rebounded. *Chronicle of Higher Education*, May 11.
Braga, R. 2002. *Estratégias de combate a inadimplência*. Vitória: Hoper Comunicação e Marketing Educacional.
Brighouse, H. 1998. Why should states fund schools? *British Journal of Educational Studies* 46, no. 2: 138–52.
———. 2000. *School choice and social justice*. Oxford: Oxford University Press.

Burd, S. 2003. For-profit colleges want a little respect. *Chronicle of Higher Education*, September 5.

Chapman, C. 2003. For-profit saviour for flagging system. *Times Higher Education Supplement*, December 5.

Chipman, L. 2002. Affording universal higher education. *Higher Education Quarterly* 56, no. 2: 126–42.

Chronicle of Higher Education. 2003. For-profit medical schools proliferating globally. September 26.

Davies, N. 2002. Mecanismos de financiamento: a privatização dos recursos públicos. In *O Empresariamento da Educação*, ed. L. M. W. Neves, 151–176. São Paulo: Xamã.

Farrell, E. F. 2003a. For-profit colleges see rising minority enrollments. *Chronicle of Higher Education*, May 30.

———. 2003b. Phoenix's unusual way of crafting courses. *Chronicle of Higher Education*, February 14.

———. 2003c. Signer beware. *Chronicle of Higher Education*, April 18.

Folha Dirigida. 2001. Entrevista polêmica: "Pesquisa é uma inutilidade pomposa." October 15.

Gallagher, S., J. McVety, A. Newman, and E. Trask. 2002. *Learning markets and opportunities 2002: Market growth slows to 2.6 percent*. Boston: Eduventures.

Geiger, R. L. 1986). *Private sectors in higher education: Structure, function and change in eight countries*. Ann Arbor: University of Michigan.

Gonzalez, A. 1999. Private higher education in the Philippines: Private domination in a developing country. In *Private Prometheus: Private higher education and development in the 21st century*, ed. P. Altbach, 101–112. London: Greenwood Press.

Instituto Nacional de Estudos e Pesquisas Educacionais Anísios Teixeira. 2003. *Censo da Educação Superior 2002*. Brasília: Instituto Nacional de Estudos e Pesquisas Educacionais Anísios Teixeira.

International Finance Corporation. 1999. Investment opportunities in private education in developing countries. Proceedings of the International Conference, Washington, D.C., June 2–3.

Jacobson, J. 2001. Argosy acquired by for-profit rival. *Chronicle of Higher Education*, July 20.

Kelk, S., and J. Worth. 2002. *Trading it away: How GATS threatens UK higher education*. Oxford: People and Planet.

Kelly, K. F. 2001. *Meeting needs and making profits: The rise of for-profit degree-granting institutions*. Denver: Education Commission of the States.

Kinser, K., and D. C. Levy. 2005. *The for-profit sector: U.S. patterns and international echoes in higher education*. Working paper no. 5. Albany, N.Y.: Program for Research on Higher Education.

Klein, N. 2000. *No Logo: No space, no choice, no jobs: Taking aim at the brand bullies*. New York: Picador.

Levy, D. C. 2002. South Africa and the for-profit/public institutional interface. *International Higher Education* 29.

Maas, J. v. L. 2001. Investing in private higher education in developing countries: Recent experiences of the International Finance Corporation. *Economic Affairs*, September: 30–37.

MacGregor, K. 2000. SA to close for-profit courses. *Times Higher Education Supplement*, February 25.

McCowan, T. 2004. The growth of private higher education in Brazil: Implications for equity and quality. *Journal of Education Policy* 19, no. 4: 453–472.

————. Forthcoming. Expansion without equity: An analysis of current policy on access to higher education in Brazil. *Higher Education.*

Morey, A. 2001. The growth of for-profit higher education. *Journal of Teacher Education* 52, no. 4: 300–311.

Newton, R. R. 2002. For-profit and traditional institutions: A comparison. *International Higher Education* 27.

Noble, D. F. 2001. *Digital diploma mills: The automation of higher education.* New York: Monthly Review Press.

Parajara, F. 2003. A Equação Di Genio. *Istoe.* May 14.

Persell, C. H., and H. Wenglinsky. 2004. For-profit post-secondary education and civic engagement. *Higher Education* 47: 337–59.

Philippines Commission on Higher Education. 2003. *Higher education system: Overview.* http://www.ched.gov.ph/statistics/index.html (accessed December 20, 2003).

Phillips, S. 2003. The startling rise of "pseudo universities." *Times Higher Education Supplement,* November 28.

Ranson, S. 1993. Markets or democracy for education. *British Journal of Educational Studies* 41, no. 4: 333–52.

Sinclair, M. 2003. Three futures for university provision: The social justice market, capitalism and private for-profit universities. *Journal of Higher Education Policy and Management* 25, no. 2: 161–71.

Sperling, J. and R. N. Tucker. 1997. *For-profit higher education: Developing a world class work force.* New Brunswick: Transaction Publishers.

Steier, F. A. 2003. The changing nexus: Tertiary education institutions, the marketplace and the state. *Higher Education Quarterly* 57, no. 2: 158–80.

Teixeira, P., and A. Amaral. 2001. Private higher education and diversity: An exploratory survey. *Higher Education Quarterly* 55, no. 4: 359–95.

Tooley, J. 1996. *Education without the state.* London: Institute of Economic Affairs.

————. 1998. The "neo-liberal" critique of state intervention in education: A reply to Winch. *Journal of Philosophy of Education* 32, no. 2: 267–81.

————. 1999. Should the private sector profit from education? The seven virtues of highly effective markets. *Educational Notes* no. 31. London: Libertarian Alliance.

————. 2000. *Reclaiming education.* London: Cassell.

————. 2001. *The global education industry: Lessons from private education in developing countries.* 2nd ed. London: Institute of Economic Affairs.

Winch, C. 1996. *Quality and education.* Oxford: Blackwell.

5 Trading Away Human Rights?

The GATS and the Right to Education: A Legal Perspective

Pierrick Devidal

INTRODUCTION

"Education is a fundamental right, set forth in the Universal Declaration of Human Rights and the International Human Rights Covenants, which have force in international law. To pursue the aim of education for all is therefore an obligation for States." (Matsuura, 2002, n.p.)

"Everyone is entitled to a social and international order in which the rights and freedoms set forth in this Declaration can be fully realized." (Universal Declaration of Human Rights, art. 28)

The right to education is one of the most important rights of the "second generation" of human rights.[1] It is an essential condition to the full enjoyment of every other economic, social, cultural, and also civil and political rights. Educational systems and programs are the object of the right to education. They have become a part of the globalization process, and have been influenced by deregulation and liberalization. The internationalization of education has created a very important market, with great commercial potential, that has attracted the interest of many private investors and multinational corporations.[2] Education has become a service, a sector submitted to increasing international trade and its rules.

The development of trade in educational services is nevertheless constrained by the existence of national legislations and regulations corresponding to the implementation of states' duty to protect the right to education under international law. Like in other sectors of services, corporations and private suppliers of educational services have pushed for the liberalization of the sector and the limitation of national regulations that prevent the development of free trade. The birth of the World Trade Organization (WTO) in 1994 has given trade diplomats and corporate lobbyists the opportunity to create an international instrument for the regulation of the liberalization of trade in services: the General Agreement on Trade in Services (GATS). As of today, the GATS is still in construction and its scope of application has not yet been defined.

Nevertheless, educational services are already subject to negotiations, under the pressure of important lobbies.

The recent popular movements of opposition have emphasized the limits of the liberalization process. They have also demonstrated that the WTO has suffered from an important democratic deficit (Esty, 2001, p.1), and that an important part of the public opposes, or at least questions, the extension of its mandate. Popular demonstrations have criticized the effect of the WTO policies on fundamental sectors of our lives, like health and education. The relevance of these movements has certainly been affected by their disparity and relative incoherence. However, they have highlighted the existence of serious concerns regarding the current liberalization process and the democratic decline that seems to go along with it.[3]

This chapter is divided into two parts. The first part is an introduction to the legal basis of the GATS and of the right to education. It is largely descriptive and is designed for readers having no background on the subject. Knowledgeable readers can directly skip to the second part of the chapter, which analyzes the conflict between the trade and the human rights regimes. Part 2 will evaluate the potential effects of the GATS on the right to education and demonstrate the fundamental conflict between the notions of "educational service" and "right to education." The final part will introduce perspectives on the evolution of education under the GATS, and call for a radical change in international educational policies.

PART ONE: THE LEGAL BASIS OF INTERNATIONAL TRADE IN SERVICES AND OF THE RIGHT TO EDUCATION

The Gats: A Progressive and Perpetual Liberalization of Trade in Services

Origins, Evolution

The GATS was a major achievement of the 1986–1994 Uruguay Round. The negotiations reforming the 1947 General Agreement of Tariffs and Trade (GATT) and creating the WTO had not only succeeded in transforming a technical tool into a major international organization regulating trade, but also in widening considerably the scope of international trade regulations by including services and intellectual property rights in its mandate (World Trade Organization, 1994, n.p.). The GATS was a real success because it constituted the very first multilateral agreement concerning international trade in services. Its success also lays in its wide scope, *rationae personae* and *materiae*. Indeed, the GATS is binding on the 144 WTO members, as a part of the "package deal" agreements. Moreover, it potentially covers all service sectors, with the exception of air transportation and services supplied by the government (GATS, art. 1). The emergence of an international instrument regulating trade in services corresponds to the ever-increasing importance of this sector, amplified by the development of globalization in transport and communications technologies.

The success of the GATS is now seriously threatened by the general failure of the 1999 Seattle negotiations, and the 2003 Cancùn meeting (*The Economist*, 2003, p. 11). Nevertheless, the spiral of ever-greater liberalization of trade in services[4] seemed to have overcome the public constraints. Indeed, since February 25, 2000, the GATS has been reactivated through the Millennium Round of negotiations, entitled *GATS 2000*. The failure to reach consensus does not stop the negotiations. The Millennium Round was reinforced by the adoption of negotiation guidelines and procedures at the Doha Conference in November 2001. Currently the member states are submitting their proposals regarding the expansion of the GATS's material scope to the Council for Trade in Services, which is responsible for the supervision of the negotiations (GATS, art. XXIV). They should have been completed by January 2005.

Nature, Aims, Objectives

The GATS is a general international agreement aimed "to establish a multilateral framework of principles and rules for trade in services with a view to the expansion of such trade under conditions of transparency and progressive liberalization and as a mean of promoting the economic growth of all trading partners and the development of developing countries" (GATS, Preamble). Thus, the GATS has a hybrid nature: it is both a framework convention and a regulatory treaty. It imposes general obligations on its members, and dictates measures to adopt for the liberalization of trade in services. It also obliges member states to adopt a constructive approach and engage in a "built-in" system of continuous negotiations, for an ever-higher liberalization of trade.

As every other WTO agreement, the objectives of the GATS rules are to remove barriers to trade, to "regulate the deregulation" of the international trading system, and to ensure the enforcement of the sacrosanct nondiscrimination principle. Indeed, the principle of non-discrimination between national and non-national suppliers is fundamental to the WTO scheme and consists in two subprinciples: the "most-favored nation" and the "national treatment" rules. The WTO principle of nondiscrimination is different from the nondiscrimination standard of human rights law because it is trade-oriented (United Nations High Commissioner for Human Rights, 2002, par. 59). It is aimed at the development of *free* trade, not *fair* trade. This fundamental difference is at the core of the conflict between the two regimes and will be dealt with later.

The GATS is legally enforceable through the general WTO system and therefore benefits from the effectiveness of the WTO's machinery. However, also because it is part of the WTO, the GATS suffers from severe criticisms. It has been described as highly complicated, opaque, and uncontrollable.

Moreover, it is governed by an organization that is constantly attacked for its bureaucratic nature and lack of transparency and democratic control.

Structure of the GATS

The GATS operates on three levels: the main rules and obligations generally applicable, the individual schedules of member states' specific commitments to market access and national treatment, and annexes dealing with rules for each specific sector of service (World Trade Organization, 1999, n.p.).

The Main Rules and Obligations: A "Top-Down" Approach

The main rules and obligations of the GATS apply to the 144 WTO members and to all services covered by the agreement (GATS, Part II). They are composed of the most-favoured nations (MFN) clause, the transparency principles, and the dispute settlement system.

The MFN clause creates an obligation for all members to treat their trading partners equally. Article II of the GATS states that "with respect to any measure covered by this agreement, each member shall accord immediately and unconditionally to services and service suppliers of any other member treatment no less favourable than that it accords to like services and services suppliers of any other country." This rule forms an integral part of the WTO nondiscrimination principle and is quite simple in practice. Indeed, it obliges a member state to apply any decision or measure regulating trade, positive or negative, equally to all its partners. The MFN clause does not prevent a state that does not open its market to benefit from the equal treatment rule in other countries' markets, and therefore creates a risk for "free-riders" (Association of Universities and Colleges of Canada, 2001, p. 4). The MFN principle can be subject to exceptions. Indeed, as prior commercial agreements preceded the GATS, the MFN rule had to be adjusted to the existence of previous contradictory "preferential commitments" (Association of Universities and Colleges of Canada, 2001, p. 4). However, these exemptions are challenged at each negotiation round and must be of atemporary nature (GATS, art. XX).

The *transparency rule* is part of the general principles applicable to the GATS (GATS, art. IV). It is a general obligation to act in good faith, which requires member states to maintain transparent relations with the other WTO members and the WTO Secretariat. The obligation consists in maintaining communications, providing accurate trade-related information, and publishing and communicating legislations, regulations and measures within the scope of the GATS. The Dispute Settlement machinery of the WTO applies to the GATS (GATS, art. XXIII), according to its own Dispute Settlement Understanding (hereinafter DSU). General exceptions are also available within the GATS system (GATS, art. XIV). These exceptions have originally been interpreted restrictively under other agreements, but are now subject of a more constructive approach (under GATT), notably by the Appellate Body (World Trade Organization Appellate Body, 1996/1998, n.p.).

Individual Schedules of Specific Commitments: The "Bottom-Up" Approach

The GATS specifies for each member state the extent to which market access and national treatment are granted for specific sectors. It is considered a "bottom-up" system, which reflects the gradualist nature of the GATS (World Trade Organization Secretariat, 1999, n.p.). Under this part of the GATS, each member state makes specific commitments concerning each service sector covered by the agreement.[5] Each country possesses its own schedule of commitments in relation to market access and national treatment for each specific sector. The "bottom-up" approach is relatively exceptional, because in other international trade agreements, the opposite approach is usually adopted: every sector is covered, unless specifically excluded. Some kind of flexibility was necessary to allow states to "tailor their commitments" to these objectives (Association of Universities and Colleges of Canada, 2001, p. 5).

In the GATS, commitments in services are classified by the mode of supply: *cross-border supply,* in which the service is provided while the provider and the consumer do not leave their country; *consumption abroad,* where the consumer travels to obtain a service abroad; *commercial presence,* where the supplier provides the service abroad through agencies or subsidiaries; and *presence of a natural person,* where a person from one country supply a service in another country.

The commitments on market access define the conditions that a state wishes to impose on foreign suppliers of services in a particular sector. The access to a specific sector of service can be totally denied, unrestricted or conditioned, as long as the conditions are applied without discrimination to all other member states.[6] The commitments on national treatment define the terms and conditions that will be applicable to domestic and foreign "like" service suppliers within the country without discriminations. The individual schedule permits evaluation of the degree to which the national market will be open, and which rules will be applicable. The application of the national treatment principle can be complicated because it supposes a clear distinction between domestic and foreign "like" services, which may not always be easy considering that the text of the GATS does not provide any indication. Therefore, as the United Nations High Commissioner for Human Rights has asked, "would, for example, a not-for-profit education service provider be like a for-profit education provider?" (United Nations High Commissioner for Human Rights, 2002, par. 24).

Thus, the GATS provide enough flexibility to allow every country to shape its commitments, limit its obligations and is "the most flexible agreement in the WTO system" (European Commission, 2004). However, it should be noted that this flexibility is very relative. Indeed, the progressive nature of the GATS implies that every limitation will be renegotiated and progressively restricted.

Moreover, "where commitments are made, the government undertakes not to introduce new restrictions," (United Nations High Commissioner for Human Rights, 2002, par. 25) unless it provides adequate compensation to countries affected by the modifications.

The Negotiating Process

The GATS has a "built-in" agenda and is, in theory, promised to an ever-greater scope of application. The process functions on the basis of a "request-offer" process and the bargaining process is reciprocal, but not symmetrical. The negotiations process is therefore favorable to big economic powers, which possess more "carrots and sticks" than their partners, and are more likely to see their offers accepted.

The permanent negotiation process has created pressure groups and informal agreements that tend to favor the interests of strong service providers which are inclined to develop "top-down" negotiating techniques, "horizontal negotiating modalities," and "formula approaches" that accelerate the liberalization process (Association of Universities and Colleges of Canada, 2001, p. 6).

If the liberalization of services can have positive effects on the protection of human rights, this nevertheless implies certain safeguard mechanisms that the GATS does not seem to have. The GATS permit constructive flexibility, but no restrictive flexibility. For instance, if an undertaken commitment becomes threatening for the maintenance of an adequate educational system, it can only be withdrawn by ensuring adequate compensations to affected parties (WTO Secretariat, 1999, n.p.). This principle is necessary for the legal security of the system and for the protection of every party to the agreement. However, it is highly complex (Association of Universities and Colleges of Canada, 2001, p. 29) and restricts considerably the ability of the state to take necessary measures to restore a potentially damaged system (von Kopp, 2002, p. 4).

The Right to Education: A Progressive and Dynamic Empowerment of Human Rights

Origins, Sources

The right to education was originally considered an economic and social right, a right of the "second generation" (Dailler and Pellet, 1999, pp. 641–42). It was a product of communist ideas on human rights, but has rapidly been accepted as a more fundamental right, irrespectively of its socialist origin, and has finally been codified in the Universal Declaration of Human Rights (art. 26). The moral and legal value of the right to education has then been reaffirmed and amplified through several codifications in the major modern human rights instruments, but also in soft-law mechanisms, guidelines and codes of conduct.[7] However, it is Article 13 of the International Covenant on Economic, Social and Cultural Rights (ICESCR) that is "the most wide ranging and comprehensive article on the right to education in international human rights law" (United Nations Committee on Economic, Social and Cultural Rights, 1999, par. 2). It states that

> the States Parties to the [. . .] Covenant recognize the right of everyone to education. States agree that education shall be directed to the full development of the human personality and the sense of its dignity, and shall strengthen the respect for human rights and fundamental freedoms. They further agree that education shall enable all persons to participate effectively in a free society, promote understanding, tolerance and friendship among all nations and all racial, ethnic or religious groups, and further the activities of the United Nations for the maintenance of peace. (United Nations General Assembly, 1966, n.p.).

Article 13 is the longest provision of the ICESCR. Some have argued that it is so widely accepted and recognized that it has become a norm of international customary law (Hodson, 1998, pp. 39–40).

Nature, Evolution

The right to education is an "empowerment right" because it is "both a human right in itself and an indispensable means of realizing other human rights" (United Nations Committee on Economic, Social and Cultural Rights, 1999, par. 1). Education is not only an economic, cultural or social right, it is a rather more global concept that reflects "the indivisibility and interdependence" of human rights (United Nations Committee on Economic, Social and Cultural Rights, 1999, par. 2). Indeed, the right to education is considered "the best financial investment States can make," (United Nations Committee on Economic, Social and Cultural Rights, 1999, par. 1) because it allows individuals to evolve in their society, participate in the political and economic life of their community, struggle against poverty or oppression[8] and most importantly benefit from the "joys and rewards of human existence" (United Nations Committee on Economic, Social and Cultural Rights, 1999, par. 1). Education is aimed at enabling children to develop their personalities and abilities to face the challenge of life. Education "goes far beyond schooling [and] embrace[s] the broad range of life experiences and learning processes which enable children, individually and collectively [. . .] to live a full and satisfying life within society" (United Nations Committee on the Rights of the Child, 2001, par. 2). The right to education is a thus a fundamental right, a tool that makes the realization of political, civil, economic, cultural and social rights possible.

The dominance of the western conception of human rights, emphasizing the protection of civil and political rights, has hindered the emergence of the right to education as a fundamental right. Because of its socialist origins, it was not until the decline and the fall of the communist bloc after the Cold

War that the right to education was the object of "serious efforts for the international implementation."[9] However, through the development of the modern corpus of international human rights law, and especially through the activities of United Nations human rights bodies, the significance of the right to education has been more widely accepted. Unfortunately, there has been no materialization of these theoretical legal successes. Indeed, as noted by the United Nations Special Rapporteur, "the right to education has been marked by retrogression rather than progressive realization as required by the [ICESCR]" (United Nations Committee on Economic, Social and Cultural Rights, 1998, par. 1).

The right to education is of universal application; it is a right to education *for all*. Nevertheless, "the precise and appropriate application of the [right] will depend upon the conditions prevailing in a particular State party" (United Nations Committee on Economic, Social and Cultural Rights, 1999, par. 6). Like other human rights, the right to education is dependent on states' behaviors and policies. However, more than other rights, the right to education is highly dependent on the *action* of states, not only on their *reaction*. The right to education cannot simply be "*exercised*" or "*enjoyed*." It is not a right "*of*" education, it is a right "*to*" education. Thus, the individual is the recipient of the right, and the state is the bearer of a duty to provide this right. The respect for the right to receive education is measured on several "interrelated and essential features": availability, accessibility, acceptability, and adaptability.[10]

The general characteristics of the right to receive education are "common to education in all its forms and at all levels." Indeed, the right to education is a permanent but gradual right, which is exercised throughout the successive steps of life. To each step corresponds a particular level of education.[11]

The enforcement of the normative content of the right to education is dependent on the existence of certain mechanisms and principles that safeguard the integrity of the right and preserve its "essential features." An educational strategy is necessary to ensure that the "system of schools at all level" (ICESCR, art.13.2) functions efficiently and allows the right to education to be available, accessible, acceptables and adaptable. The strategy developed must provide a system of fellowship that reduce the chances of de facto discrimination against disadvantaged groups, and ensure the improvement, or limit the deterioration, of material conditions of teaching (United Nations Committee on Economic, Social and Cultural Rights, 1999, par. 27).

The right to educational freedom allows the conciliation of the right of the child, the duties of the state, and the rights of the parents. The educational programs provided by the state must not interfere with the cultural and religious rights of the child, and the general system must allow parents to choose "schools, other than those established by the public authorities" as long as they "conform to such minimum educational standards as may be laid down by the state" (ICESCR, art.13.3).

The principle of nondiscrimination and equal treatment requires states to adopt any measure necessary to eliminate discrimination in practice. This principle can justify certain discriminatory measures, or affirmative actions, by which a state would favor a group of persons, which would otherwise be in an unequal situation (United Nations Committee on Economic, Social and Cultural Rights, 1999, par. 32).

The principle of academic freedom and institutional autonomy applies to the right to higher education more particularly. It protects the creativity and freedom of expression of teaching staff, and requires a certain degree of autonomy for the management of the institution. These principles have to be protected by states, which have a positive obligation to do so under international law.

Positive Obligations, Active Duties for States

Article 2 of the ICESCR requires states to "take steps, individually and through international assistance and cooperation, especially economic and technical, to the maximum of its available resources, with a view to achieving progressively the full realization of the [covenant] by all appropriate means." The right to education is progressive and subject to a progressive implementation by states, which have a specific and continuing obligation "to move as expeditiously and effectively as possible" towards its full realization (United Nations Committee on Economic, Social and Cultural Rights, 1990, par. 9). Therefore, states do not only have an obligation of conduct, but also an obligation of result.[12]

The state is subject to three kinds of obligation (Eide, 1989, p.14): to *respect,* by not interfering with the enjoyment of the right; to *protect,* by ensuring that third parties do not interfere with the enjoyment of the right; and to *fulfill,* by providing the necessary conditions to the enjoyment of the right (United Nations Committee on Economic, Social and Cultural Rights, 1999, par. 48).

The positive nature of states' obligations is also marked by the duty to cooperate with other states in the fulfilment of their obligations. In combination with Article 2 of the ICESCR, Article 13 creates an obligation of solidarity that requires states to cooperate for the full realization of the right to education at the international level (United Nations Committee on Economic, Social and Cultural Rights, 1999, par. 48). Additionally, states have a duty of precaution. They must ensure "that their actions as members of international organizations, including international financial institutions, take due account of the right to education" (United Nations Committee on Economic, Social and Cultural Rights, 1999, par. 56), and do not interfere with their ability to perform their obligations. Consequently, at the supranational level, the obligation to consider, respect, and protect the right to education also applies to international organizations. States are not relieved of their duty to ensure the right to education by transferring part of their power or sovereignty to an international organization. This latter duty of precaution is particularly at stake with the development of the GATS, which poses serious threats for the protection of the right to education.

PART TWO: THE CONFLICT BETWEEN
TRADE AND HUMAN RIGHTS LAW

The process of globalization also affects education. Expanded personal mobility and worldwide expansion of new information and communications technologies have transformed the world of education into a huge commercial market.

Cross-border supply of education from one country to another via telecommunications, and especially through the Internet, is developing rapidly. It allows a better access to education for communities and regions that do not have sufficient infrastructures, and therefore could contribute to the realization of the goal of international cooperation in the progressive realization of the right to education. However, this would imply that the groups in need of international assistance have access to the adequate technology, and it is very unlikely that this will be the case if they cannot, primarily, afford efficient educational programs (United Nations High Commissioner for Human Rights, 2002, par. 41).

Consumption of education abroad is probably the most common example of the international development of education. Indeed, more and more students are leaving their country to study abroad. This opening of the education system could seem highly favorable to the right to education. However, the risk of the development of "dual market structures" is significant, and there is a chance that the difference between "schools for rich" and "schools for poor" would increase. Indeed, "the education curriculum might direct itself more to satisfying the needs of paying foreign students than nonpaying local students, and nationals might suffer" (United Nations High Commissioner for Human Rights, 2002, par. 42).

The development of *foreign direct investment* in the area of education could also contribute to the elevation of educational infrastructures in countries where government resources are insufficient. However, this would lead to a privatization of the education system that might impair the government's ability to fulfil its duty to provide the right to education.

The *international movement of educational service suppliers* could be highly valuable to the development of education expertise worldwide. However, it is also endangered by creating the possibility of a "brain drain," in contradiction with essential elements of the right to education (United Nations High Commissioner for Human Rights, 2002, par. 47).

Thus, the liberalization of trade in educational services can have varied impacts on the developments of the right to education, and therefore needs to be controlled. Indeed, some have even come to the conclusion that "the key question from a human rights perspective is not whether liberalization does or does not promote human rights; rather, it is how to determine the right form and pace of liberalization to ensure the protection of human rights and how to reverse policies that are unsuccessful" (United Nations High Commissioner for Human Rights, 2002, par. 50). The problem is that it is very doubtful that the GATS is the appropriate instrument to ensure this essential task of reconciliation between the development of an education market and the protection of the right to education. In fact, the agenda of the GATS is materially and theoretically incompatible with the agenda of the realization of the right to education according to international human rights law.

Education and the Gats: Transforming Human Rights into Services

Education and the GATS: An Ambiguous Relationship

As we have noted above, the GATS is still a work in progress, an instrument in construction. Therefore, its scope and effects remain largely unknown. Unpredictability is the consequence of the absence of definition of the scope of the agreement. It also results from the ambiguity within the original text. This is especially true with respect to education.

Potentially, the scope of the GATS is quite vast. Indeed, it could eventually covers all kind of measures taken by every state party at all levels of government, affecting trade in all services. However, a significant restriction exists: services provided "in the exercise of governmental authority" are not covered by the GATS principles (GATS, art.1). This exception originally corresponded to the necessity for governments to be free from interference in their ability to supply public services that usually are the materialization of their duty to provide economic and social rights, including the right to education. Nevertheless, this exception is likely to be meaningless in practice. First, international law exceptions are always interpreted restrictively.[13] Second, there is an exception to the exception that is likely to nullify any practical effects. Indeed, public services provided by governments on a commercial basis, or in competition with private service suppliers, are excluded from the scope of the exception (GATS, art. I.3). There is no clear indication of what commercial competition really means in terms of public services. Even though "the ambiguity surrounding article I.3. has been noted in much of the literature about GATS" there has been no "clear resolution" of the problem (Nielson, 2004).

Modern states have a tendency to rationalize public expenditures and decentralize their powers. These trends, added to the liberalization of the economy, have provoked governments to limit their role in the deliverance of public services. Therefore, in practice, very few services provided "in the exercise of governmental authority" actually remain a strict monopoly of public authorities. The private sector has largely infiltrated the domain of public services, and this is also true for education. Thus, it is very likely that education will not be considered a service covered by the "governmental services" exception (Larsen, Martin and Morris, 2002, p. 3). Under the GATS's definition, education is a commercial activity, and not a public service supplied in the pure exercise of governmental authority (Education International/Public Services International, 1999). Indeed, the ambiguity of the GATS's scope creates suspicion, partly because the strategy demonstrates that education is seen as a commodity, and not as a right.

Education as a Commodity

The general nature of the GATS and its "built-in" spiral tend to imply that every exception to the GATS is of a temporary nature. What is not covered by the agreement today could be included tomorrow. This is especially relevant if one considers the structure of the individual commitments schedules. Indeed, the sector of education is divided into five subsectors.[14] Specific scheduled commitments are usually undertaken by subsectors, or even sub-subsectors, as states are free to use additional distinctions (Association of Universities and Colleges of Canada, 2001, par. 25–26). Moreover, the structures of domestic educational markets are in constant evolution and, therefore, definitions of "educational service" under GATS are subject to changes (World Trade Organization Council for Trade in Services, 1998, par. 4). The dissolution of education into activities and subsectors reveals the economic approach adopted by the GATS negotiations. It also indicates that the built-in agenda might, little by little, subsector by subsector, cover every educational activity.

The use of business vocabulary, development strategies, and management techniques reveals the commercial strategy that is leading the GATS negotiations.[15] This strategy can conflict with the concept of education as a public good as

> there is a problem in thinking about trade in services, particularly public services. To be traded, a thing has to be a specific commodity on which a price can be put. Most of us don't think of social services or education in that way. We tend to think of them as social and cultural relations with a general overall cost, but not as segmented economic units. (Kuehn, 2004, p.1).

Indeed, under the GATS, the risk of transforming human rights into services exists because "the market is the dominant force in policy" (Nielson, 2004). Some professionals feel that

> (e)ducation is treated purely as a commercial, tradable commodity. There is no recognition of its role as a means of nation-building; a local storehouse of knowledge; the vehicle to transmit culture and language; the prerequisite for a vibrant democracy and a contest of ideas; a source of innovation and change, a desirable activity per se. (Kelsey, 1999, par. 2).

The large majority of professionals, teachers, professors, and students' unions have publicly denounced the utilization of education as a commercial product and their opposition movement certainly demonstrates the legitimacy of opposing a trade-oriented definition of education.[16] This concern is shared by organizations of the "civil society," which have already proclaimed in an official declaration that "education is a right, not a commodity" (European Social Forum, 2002).

WTO: "A Trade's, Trade's World"

This problem clearly results from the trade-oriented nature of the politics of law at the WTO. Within the WTO, "decisions taken reflect primarily the voice of the main trading nations," and at the national level,

> domestic trade policy formation is marked by similar inequalities in terms of who is inside the process and who is kept outside . . . For example, the power departments—commerce and finance—are likely to be there, but you will seldom find the weaker environmental or social policy departments. We also see the representation of major commercial interests in national trade policy and investments decisions. (Mehra, 2001, p. 81).

While civil society groups struggle to have access to the political debate, influential commercial lobbies and "invisible economic actors" are manipulating national policy making to use human rights as tradable commodities. As Barnhizer (2001) points out,

> they can use their global power to manipulate national policy-making, to influence both corrupt and honest political leaders, and move their resources and bases of activity freely if they see better deals elsewhere or are resisted in their efforts to gain concessions . . . The very concept of democracy is threatened by the scale on which such enormously powerful and unaccountable economic leviathans operate and by the equivalent scale of institutions such as . . . the World Trade Organization." (p. 5)

This uncertainty concerning the relation between the GATS and education is emphasized by the opacity of the negotiations. Negotiations on the development of GATS are lead by states, which make proposals, requests, and offers. However, final decisions and commitments are the result of secret negotiations held at the headquarters of the WTO in Geneva, behind closed doors (Jennar, 2000). This lack of transparency is a problem that applies to the WTO system in general. It creates an issue of democratic control that is particularly a matter of concern with respect to important public goods like education. Thus,

> the system operates outside the ability of any nation's citizens to control. They [trade negotiators] take decisions, create policies, and implement actions that have never been agreed to by the citizens of a particular nation . . . The result is that the mechanisms of citizen participation and political control over decisions that impact their lives in the most fundamental ways are becoming increasingly remote." (Barnhizer, 2001, p. 5).

Indeed, there is no review mechanism of the negotiations between trade diplomats and corporate lobbyists who "make the deals" in Geneva. Moreover,
these negotiators lack *real* legitimacy, because they are not subject to any form
of public scrutiny. Indeed, if their *official* legitimacy is not in question, as they
are appointed by democratically elected governments on the basis of their professional and technical competences in the area of international trade, they
suffer a lack of democratic legitimacy that results from the very nature of the
WTO negotiations process. As Habbard and Giraud (1999) have argued, "as
it stands, the WTO remains a private club, devoid of any serious democratic
checks and balances." This later is so intrinsically opaque that

> negotiations are power-driven and all sorts of trade-offs are permissible:
> even trade offs that national officials have not mandated or national par-
> liaments made aware. (. . .) This is the crux of the problem. In essence
> the negotiating process is fundamentally undemocratic. Both parliamen-
> tary and citizens' groups need to be engaged in the determination of na-
> tional trade priorities and policies *before* things reach the negotiation
> stage. (Mehra, 2001, p. 76, emphasis added)

Consequently, nothing prevents the negotiators from defining the exceptions
narrowly, and the sectors covered by the agreement extensively. A large number of critics have proposed institutional and fundamental reforms of the
WTO in order to increase democratic control over the policy-making process. However, because of the trade-oriented nature of the WTO system, it is
unlikely that these reforms would suffice.

Reforms?

Some have argued that, given the inevitability of the WTO, it would be possible to ensure the protection of human rights by reforming its system. They
have proposed procedural and institutional reforms in order to increase the
legitimacy and transparency of the WTO policies. The requirements of prior
human rights impact assessments,[17] the intervention of NGO's and representatives of the civil society in the political debate and the creation of national
public forums would certainly help to increase the weak legitimacy of the
WTO (Mehra, 2001, p. 83), which remains one of the less publicly known
international organizations. However, beside their benefit for the public information, these reforms would let important human rights, such as education,
into the realm of action of the WTO.

At the institutional level, the involvement of United Nations agencies and
bodies in trade policy making has been defended as a solution for the political isolationism of the WTO (Mehra, 2001, p. 83). The collaboration at the
interagency level is an excellent way to prevent the conflict between trade
and human rights policies. Nevertheless, considering the lack of binding and
negotiating powers of human rights bodies, it is unlikely that they would be
able to significantly influence the policy-making process, where, as we have

seen, commercial interests are the driving forces. To put it simply, education must be taken out of the realm of action of the WTO, which has neither the legitimacy, the expertise, nor the competence to deal with such an important human right. Indeed,

> the Agreement Establishing the WTO is not a constitutional instrument in the sense of constituting a political or social community, and its mandate and objectives are narrowly focused around the goal of "expanding the production of and trade in goods and services." Despite the expansion of the original GATT mandate into areas such as the services industries and intellectual property rights, and proposals to expand its role to cover the enforcement of regimes at the national level which are favourable to international foreign investment, the basic structure of the Organization has remained unchanged. It is an institution which is dominated by producers, and in which the economic, social, cultural, political and various other interests of a great many people are not, in practice, represented. Its institutional structure, its processes and the outcomes it sanctions are far from what would be required of a body to which significant human rights authority could be entrusted. (Alston, 2002, p. 30)

This conclusion does not equal a blank check on education for United Nations bodies. The United Nations Educational, Scientific, and Cultural Organization (UNESCO) and the Committee for Economic, Social and Cultural Rights have the appropriate expertise and savoir faire with regard to education. However, as WTO supporters could argue, they should not have a monopoly on the protection of human rights vis-à-vis nefarious trade policies. These organs suffers a lack of coherence and efficiency, notably due to the highly politicized nature of the decision-making process. They should remain in charge of initiating human rights policies and controlling their application by states, as well as by financial and trade organizations. They also need to achieve better support for other forms of international collaboration in the field of education, by integrating institutionally the participation of education stakeholders more efficiently. The international community as a whole is responsible for the creation of a more efficient human rights regime, in which the supremacy of human dignity over trade must be ensured, to prevent conflicts of norms.

Free Trade and Education: A Fundamental Conflict

Regulating Deregulation, Removing Barriers to Trade

As stated in its Preamble, the goal of the GATS is the liberalization of trade in services. In practice, it consists in the application of liberal economic theories in trade of services: restricting governmental intervention and reliance on the "invisible hand" to regulate the market. "GATS is based on the principle of free competition, which says that freedom of trade is the best guarantee for the highest possible quality at the lowest possible cost" (Oosterlinck, 2002, p.1). In sum, the GATS aims at reducing national intervention and "increasing the decrease" of regulation from the WTO, because as Zutchi (2001) puts it, "liberalization does not mean de-regulation, on the contrary, further liberalization requires an appropriate regulatory framework to sustain it."

In the area of education, there are many "nontariff barriers" to the development of international trade.[18] Indeed, every measure taken by public authorities, at all levels of governance, can constitute a barrier to trade. "For example, requirements for specific local content in courses; or for the presence of a certain number of local staff on the governing board [of a school]; or for teaching in the local language could all be challenged as a 'disguised trade restriction'" (Kelsey, 1999, par. 7). In any case, every measure "affecting trade" will come under the scrutiny and checks of the GATS, whether it is a barrier or not (WTO Panel, 1997). The ability of governments to use their power to regulate the educational system is therefore under greater scrutiny, and must comply with rules that are enforceable through one of the most efficient systems of international law.

However, it should be recalled that the commitments undertaken by states under GATS are voluntary. Only states can decide which sector or service they want to submit to the GATS's rules. The WTO is only the forum where states express their will, and it could be argued that education can remain outside the scope of the GATS, if states so decide. Indeed, many have decided to keep their educational systems, or at least parts of them, outside the negotiations.[19] However, in the practical sense, states do not have absolute control over the level of their commitments. The bargaining process of the continuous negotiations forum has created a lot of pressures that states are simply not always able to resist, depending on their economic force.[20] The result of the request/offer process and the development of horizontal formulas restricts considerably the margin that states have in maneuvering of states in their ability to control the expansion of the GATS's scope. States might have to make important sacrifices in order to secure the protection of certain fundamental economic interests. Their ability to control the degree of engagement is impaired by the dynamic nature of the GATS in always requiring further commitments. Moreover, the nature of the GATS and the "rollback rule" (Association of Universities and Colleges of Canada, 2001, par. 37) also implies that the ability of future governments to choose their own policies is restricted. Indeed, "once a government has promised to reduce restrictions on foreign education providers, a future government cannot reimpose such measures or new measures that would have a similar effect without breaching the agreement" (Kelsey, 1999, par. 9). Consequently, "limitations are not cast in stone" (Nielson, 2004)[112] and the progressive trade-offs resulting from the negotiating process are a permanent threat to the weak safeguard rules already existing.

Nevertheless, the GATS recognizes the right of states to derogate from their commitments and legislate or to take measures in areas of legitimate public policy.[21] First, the general exceptions provisions allow governments to take derogatory measures when necessary to protect, inter alia, public morals. A wide interpretation of the notion of public morals could imply the possibility for the government to take derogatory measures necessary to protect the educational system, that contribute significantly to the emergence and protection of public morals. However, considering the restrictive interpretation that is usually given to these general exceptions, it is very unlikely that article XIV of the GATS constitutes an efficient safeguard for education. Indeed, within "regulatory globalization," utility dominates rights.[22]

Realizing Trade and Education: Dynamisms in Conflict

The problem is that the possibility for government to regulate service activities is considerably reduced by the GATS. Governments' measures that affect trade in services are subject to a strict necessity test that will apply to a wide range of domestic regulations. In fact, "no government measure 'affecting trade in services,' whatever its aim—environmental protection, consumer protection, enforcing labour standards, promoting fair competition, ensuring universal service, or any other goal—is, in principle, beyond GATS scrutiny" (Sinclair, 2000, p. 3). Therefore, under the GATS, certain public policies aimed at the promotion of social or educational objectives would be prohibited because they "affect trade" and are not strictly necessary to the maintenance of the educational system. The real issue is that the GATS has operated a transfer of democratic governmental authority from the state to the WTO. Indeed, the burden of proof lies on the government. If a governmental measure is challenged in the WTO system, the government will have to demonstrate that the measures are strictly necessary, and that they do not constitute a barrier to trade.[23] Then, "the delicate responsibility for balancing the public interest with commercial considerations" would be transferred "from elected governments representatives to appointed tribunals or WTO panels" (Sinclair, 2000, p. 7).

This transfer of authority would not be so controversial if it did not negatively affect human rights. Indeed, the GATS could be considered a waiver by states of their right to regulate. However, with respect to human rights, and with the right to education in particular, states do not have a right, but a *duty* to regulate. As we have seen, the right to education implies that states must ensure the quality of the school system, respect for the essential features of education, and the progressive realization of a free education. Under international human rights law, states are required to take any necessary steps to protect individuals from any interference in the enjoyment of their right to receive education. Yet the measures necessary to ensure availability, adaptability, acceptability, and quality are the same measures that constitute barriers to trade under the GATS. If GATS wants to remove these barriers to trade in education services, it also needs to remove the power of governments to regulate in this area. However, under international law, states cannot abandon their duty to regulate and protect the right to education by transferring their powers to an international organization. Fundamentally, the right to education implies a dynamic of increasing intervention by the state until the right to education is fully realized. Under GATS, the dynamic is of a decreasing role of states in the regulation of education.

The capacity of the state to control the educational system is already impaired. Budget cuts and rationalization of public administration have induced certain states to generally reduce their expenditures in education programs (Van Damme, 2001, p. 3). Other states are also constrained to strict structural adjustment rules by international monetary institutions. The need for educational development and investments exists. Therefore, the necessity for external intervention will increase. Private and corporate interests will intervene in the education market to compensate for the defection of public authorities. They will provide funding and apply development strategies to education programs. However, this economic approach seems quite irreconcilable with the nature of the right to education. Indeed, "the raison d'être of economic and social rights is to act as correctives to the free market. Governments have human rights obligations because primary education should not be treated as a commodity" (United Nations Committee on Economic, Social and Cultural Rights, 1998, par. 7). Education is a global concept, a tool for the realization of broad and essential social objectives. When education becomes too centered on its relation with the economy, as it would be under the GATS, it is inevitable that there will be a distortion of these social objectives. The GATS's rationale of free competition equals the increase of private investment in education. This trend does not follow human-rights requirements. Indeed, investments are dependents on the evolution of the market and profits. Education programs would therefore be limited to the possibilities offered on the market, which seems irreconcilable with the obligation of governments to develop the possibilities of education progressively.[24]

Conflicting Norms

Another problem is the very definition of what constitutes discrimination. Indeed, the concept of nondiscrimination is a fundamental principle of international law. However, it is a very broad concept that includes a wide range of applications. The ideas of nondiscrimination that are embodied in human-rights law and in the GATS are significantly different, if not completely conflicting (Mehra, 2001, pp. 78–79). Under GATS, nondiscrimination consists in the national treatment of foreign like service suppliers and the application of the MFN clause. Under human-rights law, discrimination on grounds of race, color, sex, language, religion, political opinion, birth, or national or social origin is strictly prohibited. However, "importantly, the human rights principle does not envisage according equal treatment to everyone in all cases, but rather supports affirmative action in the interests of promoting the human rights of the poor and vulnerable" (United Nations High Commissioner for Human Rights, 2002, par. 59). Thus, if a government decides to provide public subsidies for a certain class of vulnerable people in order to promote their access to the right of education, it will act in conformity with the principle of nondiscrimination under human-rights law, but would violate it under GATS law. The issue of "nondiscrimination versus affirmative action" is central to the conflict between the human rights and the trade regimes (Mehra, 2001, pp. 78–79).

The GATS makes no "attempt to discriminate between subsidies. [But] subsidies can be good or bad. Good subsidies are those which enable . . . affirmative action measures, bad subsidies are those that perpetuate harmful social practices," such as development of dual market structures in education. The central issue is that under GATS "both good and bad subsidies are attacked by the WTO without discrimination . . . Finally, the human rights principle of nondiscrimination is in conflict with the trade principle of nondiscrimination. The human rights principle refers to individuals and groups, the trade principle to nations and firms" (Mehra, 2001, p. 80). This conflict should be resolved in the favor of human-rights law, under which the notion of nondiscrimination has acquired the status of a peremptory norm of international law (United Nations High Commissioner for Human Rights, 2002, par. 59). However, given the closed nature of the WTO legal system and its trade orientation, it is very likely that if such a case arose under the WTO dispute settlement system, it is the GATS interpretation of the nondiscrimination principle that would be favored.

Conflicting Theories, Conflicting Regimes

The WTO has been presented as a specific field of international law (Kuyper, 1994, p. 227), or even a self-contained regime, immune from the interference of general rules of international law.[25] These arguments are inspired from the functionalist and utilitarianism "normative underpinnings of trade law" (Garcia, 2001, p. 88). Indeed, the "efficiency model" (Dunoff, 1998, p. 347) of trade law is "exclusively concerned with the twin values of economic efficiency and welfare" (Garcia, 2001, p. 88). Therefore, in the international trade regulatory framework, the objective of an ever-freer trade dominates every other nontrade considerations, because it is allegedly a crucial "precondition for the enjoyment of . . . human rights." Consequently, human rights are subject to an economic vision, that integrate them as essential economic instruments to the "proper functioning of economic and political markets," and a perfect tool to legitimize liberal economics (Petersmann, 2000a, p. 1365).

In this context, if a conflict of norms arises within the jurisdiction of the WTO, it is an economic methodology of utilitarianism that will be applied in the resolution of the dispute. Indeed, "dispute resolution is not simply a mechanism for neutral application of legislated rules but is itself a mechanism of legislation and of governance" and therefore, "dispute resolution tribunals function in part as agents of legislatures" (Trachman, 1999, p. 336). "On this view, an act will be judged morally right if its consequences for the aggregate of individual utility . . . [Therefore] the trade institution will follow its own normative approach, which commits it to sacrificing human rights protection when doing so would yield a greater aggregate satisfaction of human preferences" (Garcia, 2001, pp. 89–91). In fact, the functionalist vision of human rights adopted by the WTO clearly appears in the application of the necessity test when evaluating the legality of an article-XIV-based exception to the GATS's rules. The necessity test is the ultimate safeguard for nontrade-oriented measures within the WTO dispute resolution system. It functions as a simple "trade-off device" that balances the weight of economic welfare versus human rights and allows the "trade [of] any amount of human rights impairment in exchange for a greater amount of trade welfare benefit" (Garcia, 2001, pp. 89–91). This adjudication mechanism is in total contradiction with the theories and principles forming the basis of human-rights law.

In the human-rights regime, human rights are perceived as a philosophical and legal manifestation of human dignity (Alston, 2002, p. 5), a "transcendental standard of justice" based on "the non-utilitarian liberalism of Locke and Kant" (Garcia, 2001, p. 88). The justification of human rights is based on moral and philosophical principles that integrate human dignity as a supreme objective, detached from any utilitarian cost-benefits analysis. "The normative arguments advanced for the protection of human rights are deontological: they focus on principles about how people are to be treated, regardless of the consequences" (Garcia, 2001, p. 88). Consequently, in case of conflict of norms, the deontological approach of the human rights regime would favor human rights claims over trade rules, because they "ordinarily trump utility, social policy, and other moral or political grounds for action" (Donnelly, 1989, p. 10). If a conflict of norms between GATS's rules and the protection of the right to education arose within the human rights regime, the right to education would be protected against the negative effect of trade measures, because human rights are trumping values in conflicts of norms. Considering that "it is a fundamental feature of the landscape of global social policy in the late 20th century that no one institution has the effective jurisdiction to create and adjudicate norms in all aspects of social concern" (Garcia, 2001, p. 96), it appears that the human-rights regime and the trade regime will remain two different subsystems of international law, with their own normative underpinnings and judicial system. On the one hand, the human-rights regime suffers from a critical lack of efficiency that partially results from the political and diplomatic nature of the United Nations human-rights bodies. The United Nations' judicial mechanisms for the enforcement of protection of human rights are weak, fragmented, and "sadly deficient" (Robertson, 1981, p. 350), because they are part of an "authoritarian" and "state-centred system" (Petersmann, 2002a, p. 291). On the other hand, the trade regime is characterized by one of the most efficient enforcement mechanisms of the international system (Petersmann, 2000b, p. 25).

Naturally, trade lawyers have argued that the most appropriate solution to prevent conflicts of norms between trade and human-rights law would be to integrate the protection of human rights within the mandate of international economic organizations such as the WTO (Petersmann, 2002b, p. 621). It has also been argued that the inclusion of human-rights exceptions within the WTO agreements (Ball, 2000, pp. 76–79), the amendment of the necessity test with the proportionality test (Garcia, 2001, p. 100) or other extra safeguards would allow human rights to benefit from the trade-enforcement mechanisms and to be protected from excessive economic utilitarianism. However, the fundamental inadequacies between the competences of trade lawyers and the necessary expertise necessary for the implementation and enforcement of human rights, added to the liberal-utilitarian philosophy of trade institutions, demonstrates that it is evident that the WTO is not the appropriate forum for the adjudication of conflicts of norms between trade and human-rights law.

The international trade regime should not be granted powers over the creation and adjudication of human-rights policies because it is based on and functions according to paradigms, principles, and rules that are in contradiction with fundamental human-rights principles and theories. The solution is to prevent the outbreak of conflicts of norms a priori, and to ensure that the realization of human rights is given the political and legal superiority that it deserves.

CONCLUSION, EVALUATIONS, AND PERSPECTIVES

The GATS is a very important instrument, necessary for regulating the development of international trade in services, inevitable in the age of globalization. However, it is still a work in progress, an "untested process" (Nielson, 2004, p. 91) and there appear to be many ambiguities regarding its scope and effects, especially with respect to human rights. It is possible (although unlikely if the WTO system remains opaque and closed) that the implementation of the GATS principles and rules would have positive effects on the protection and development of particular human rights. Nevertheless, when facing important uncertainties on the costs and benefits of a system in construction, the reasonable approach is always *prevention rather than cure*. Therefore, considering the incompatibility of the trade and human-rights agenda with regard to education, it appears necessary to stop the current negotiations on trade in educational services under the Doha Round and ensure a priori that its development will not affect the protection and promotion of human rights.

The present negotiations are defining the fate of education under the GATS. Indeed, they will delineate the starting point of the GATS's coverage of the educational sector, which can only increase in the future. The recent proposals of the main GATS proponents (the United States, the European Union, Japan, Canada, New Zealand, and Australia) seem to indicate that at least the sector of higher education will be included in the GATS (Nielson, 2004, p. 91). Higher education is particularly in the sight of the trade diplomats and corporate lobbyists negotiating in Geneva because it is a developing sector that has considerable commercial potential. These developments are a matter of extreme concern because they tend to create a trade model for education. This will lead to the transformation of the right to education into a commodity, a commercial service that would be subject to a free market, rather than to rules of international human rights law.

The increasing and uncontrolled liberalization of trade is a danger for education. The privatization of the educational sector would prevent the realization of the objective of a progressive free education for all, by the introduction of fees that would create a dual market, where the best programs will be accessible only to the richest groups of individuals, in contradiction with the principle of availability and nondiscrimination. Moreover, the privatization of the education system under the GATS implies a progressive withdrawal of governmental authority and regulation. This would leave the educational sector in the hands of private and corporate interests that would favor economic over social interests. It would also considerably reduce the ability of states to ensure the quality of education and fulfill their obligation under human-rights law by transferring their powers to an organization that does not have the expertise or the capacity to ensure the protection of the right to education, in conformity with international law. Additionally the democratic deficit from which the WTO suffers is supplementary evidence that an important public good like education cannot be traded away without ensuring that sufficient safeguards and mechanisms will allow the protection of the essential features of this fundamental right. The strong opposition movement raised by education stakeholders demonstrate the urgent need for action.

The GATS is a necessary instrument for the regulation of trade in a limited number of commercial services. However, it is not necessary to education. Indeed, there are other mechanisms of internationalization and globalization than the GATS that would be more adapted to the nature of the educational sector.[26] "Nonprofit internationalization" (Kelsey, 1999,+ p. 89) mechanisms already exist in the context of governmental and international public cooperation. They have allowed significant progress in the development of international education systems that function in conformity with the interests of our societies and in conformity with the principles of international human rights law.[27]

In sum, "we are in fact demanding no more than governments should respect and fulfil their obligations under international human rights law— binding obligations they have voluntarily undertaken" (Nowak, 1991, p. 425). Therefore, education must be kept out of the GATS's scope of regulations. The current negotiations on trade in educational services must be stopped and governments must ensure that their commitments under the GATS will not affect their ability to perform their duty to protect and realize the right to education. Education is too important to our societies to be endangered and traded away without any safeguards. The GATS needs to be transformed to ensure that fundamental public services like education, health, and culture are definitively prevented from being subjected to trade rules and policies; that it would protect the right of governments to exercise their right and duty to regulate for the promotion of quality and social objectives that are interdependent with the right to education; that human- rights assessments of trade policies are undertaken to ensure that the implementation and interpretation of the GATS are compatible with human-rights law; and that democracy and transparency are promoted to ensure the viability of an efficient and constructive dialog on the promotion of human rights through international cooperation.

NOTES

1. Economic, social, and cultural rights are rights of the so-called "second generation," in contrast with civil and political rights (right of the first generation), which appeared first chronologically, because of the domination of western countries' liberal conception of human rights on the codification of international law. They are also contrasted with the rights of the "third generation," which intend to link human rights with the socioeconomical context of their realization (right to development, right to a clean environment . . .). The main difference between rights of the first and the second generation concerns the position of the individual vis-à-vis the state. In the former, the state has a duty not to interfere with the enjoyment of civil and political rights by the individual, whereas it should provide the necessary structures for the enjoyment of economic, social and cultural rights by the individual for the later (Dailler and Pellet, 1999, pp. 641–42).
2. An example of this trend is the creation of a "World Education Market" in Vancouver, Canada, in May, 2000. For OECD countries, "export revenue in education services amounted to an estimated minimum of US$30 billion in 1999, not much less than the financial services sector" (Larsen and Vincent-Lancrin, 2003, p. 2).
3. As Mehra argues, "Citizens' concerns have moved from focusing almost exclusively on the role of the state in respecting, promoting, protecting and fulfilling human rights, to focusing on the supra-national, multilateral bodies and non state actors such as transnational corporations." (Mehra, 2001, p. 76).
4. Indeed, art. XIX of the GATS states that "members shall enter into successive rounds of negotiations . . . with a view to achieving a progressively higher level of liberalization" (World Trade Organization, 1994).
5. Business, communication, construction and related engineering, distribution, education, environment, finance, health and social related services, tourism and travel, transport and others (World Trade Organization Secretariat, 1999).
6. Market access can be limited with respect to the number of service suppliers, the total value of service transactions, the total quantity of service output, the number of natural persons in a particular service, the participation of foreign capital or the legal nature of suppliers (World Trade Organization Secretariat, 1999).
7. As such, the right to education is codified in the Convention on the Rights of the Child (art. 28), the United Nations Convention on the Elimination of All Form of Racial Discrimination (art. 3), the Convention on the Elimination of All Forms of Discrimination against Women (art.1 0), the European Convention on the safeguard of Human Rights and Fundamental Freedoms, First Protocol, art. 2 (Council of Europe, General Assembly, 1950), the African Charter on Human and Peoples' Rights, art.17 (African Union, 1981), the American Convention of Human Rights (Additional Protocol, art. 17), the World Declaration on Education for All (art. 1).
8. In 1787, Thomas Jefferson wrote that "to educate and inform the whole mass of people is the most legitimate engine of government" because it would enable the people to "see that it is in their interest to preserve peace and order" (Jefferson, 1787).
9. However, it should be recalled that "although Socialist States had been on the forefront to put economic, social and cultural rights on the same level as civil

and political rights, in the late seventies and early eighties it was them who resisted every initiative to strengthen this extremely weak implementation mechanism" (Nowak, 1991, p. 419).

10. Availability: the right to education must be made available. States have a duty to ensure that a sufficient quantity of educational facilities and programs are available within their territories. The qualitative requirement concerning what is considered as an "available" institution "depends upon numerous factors, including the developmental context within which they operate." Accessibility: the available educational institutions must be physically and economically accessible to everyone, without discrimination. Therefore, it has to be affordable to all (including most vulnerable groups), and situated in safe and "reasonably convenient" geographical areas. Acceptability: "(t)he State must ensure that the form and substance of education, including curricula and teaching methods are acceptable to students and, where appropriate, parents." The right to education must be provided in conformity with the social and cultural context of the recipient of the right, and of appropriate quality and relevance. Adaptability: the State must ensure sufficient flexibility in its educational programs, so that education is adaptable to the social and cultural variables of society (United Nations Committee on Economic, Social and Cultural Rights, 1999, par. 6).

11. The right to primary education has the particularity of being a compulsory right that every individual must receive. Therefore, it must be made absolutely universal and "available free to all." The right to secondary education varies among countries, but should generally prepare students for vocational and further educational opportunities. It "shall be made generally available an accessible to all by every appropriate means, and in particular by the progressive introduction of free education." Therefore, although free primary education is the primary objective, it does not relieve the state of its obligation to adopt any appropriate measure to develop free secondary education that will be available to everyone without discrimination. The right to higher education is not universal, because it depends on the capacity of individuals. Access to higher education will be conditioned to expertise and relevant experience of candidates, but must be generally available to everyone with the same capacity, "and in particular with the progressive introduction of free education." The right to fundamental education is a safety right, by which State must ensure that individuals who have not completed their primary education nevertheless receive sufficient education to satisfy their "basic learning needs." The right to fundamental education is of universal application, and "extends to children, youth and adults, including older persons" (United Nations Committee on Economic, Social and Cultural Rights, 1999, par. 8).

12. As Nowak argues, "an obligation of conduct points to a certain action or measure the State should adopt. An obligation of result is less concerned with the choice of the line of action taken, but more concerned with the results the State should achieve" (Nowak, 1991, p. 422).

13. "International law has a special interpretive principle for the interpretation of exceptions. This rule is expressed in Latin as *exceptio est strictissimae applicationis* which means exceptions to treaty obligations are construed restrictively. Similarly, within the decisions of the GATT and the WTO, exceptions to trade obligations have been narrowly interpreted" (Association of Universities and Colleges of Canada, 2001, par. 31).

14. Primary education, secondary education, higher education, adult education, and other education services (World Trade Organization Council for Trade in Services, 1998, par. 3).

15. According to Nielson, "in trade language, nations are 'importers' or 'exporters' and education is delivered through 'modes.' Many in higher education are

uneasy with this trade language, but that discomfort does not signify opposition to cross-border education, rather, it indicates anxiety about whether the future of cross-border education will be dominated by a trade model or a model that emphasizes higher education's enduring contribution to the public good of all nations" (Nielson, 2004).

16. As an example a large number of education professional unions have declared that "as stakeholders in education, we have reached the conclusion that it is inappropriate for education systems to be regulated within the GATS framework. Education is of such critical importance to the social, cultural and economic development of society that it should not be subjected to the binding rules of an international treaty that prioritizes trade liberalization over other goals . . ." (GATSwatch, 2003).

17. According to the United Nations, "a procedural approach can become an effective method of challenging disregard of human rights in macroeconomic policies through a requirement that a human rights impact assessment be carried out before such policies are developed and implemented" (United Nations Committee on Economic, Social and Cultural Rights, 1998, par. 10).

18. As Frase and O'Sullivan explain, "because services are not object, barriers to trading services are referred to as non-tariff barriers" (Frase and O'Sullivan, 1999, p. 2). These barriers consist in immigration requirements, foreign currency control measures, credit and credential recognitions, monopoly on national licenses, limits on foreign direct investment, nationality requirements, needed tests, restriction on foreign recruitments, or national subsidies rules. (WTO Council for Trade in Services, 1998, par. 30).

19. Documents concerning the negotiations and new proposals on education are available at http://www.wto.org/english/tratop_e/serv_e/s_propnewnegs_e.htm.

20. As the Association of Universities and Colleges of Canada explains, "countries are increasingly coming under pressures to open their education market to foreign services providers. Moreover, much of this pressure is coming from three of the Quadrilateral governments—the United States, the European Union, Japan and Canada—the countries with most influence at the WTO" (Association of Universities and Colleges of Canada, 2001, par. 37).

21. The GATS Preamble recognizes, inter alia, " . . . the right of members to regulate and to introduce new regulations, on the supply of services within their territories in order to meet national policy objectives . . ."

22. As Garcia highlights, "finally, availability of the public morals . . . exceptions depends upon whether article XX would be interpreted as available for 'outward-oriented' measures designed to influence the human rights policies of another jurisdiction, which existing GATT jurisprudence calls into question" (Garcia, 2001, p. 85).

23. Sinclair explains that "governments would be compelled to demonstrate, first, that nondiscriminatory regulations were 'necessary' to achieve a WTO-sanctioned legitimate objective and, secondly, that no less commercially restrictive alternative measure was possible" (Sinclair, 2000, p. 7).

24. As the United Nations Special Rapporteur on the Right to Education points out, "a definition of education as 'efficient production of human capital' may well be cited as an argument for such investment but excludes the concept of education embodied in human rights law and classifies it in 'externalities.' The increasing change of terminology from 'primary' to 'basic' education might imply the lowering of the child's right to education, both quantitatively and qualitatively. As it is well known, the effects of such innovations are likely to be discriminatory unless specific policies are in place to prevent this" (United Nations Committee on Economic, Social and Cultural Rights, 1998, par. 14).

25. A self-contained regime is a system "embracing, in principle, a full (exhaustive and definite) set of secondary rules . . . intended to exclude more or less totally the application of the general legal consequences of wrongful acts" (Simma, 1985, p. 111).
26. For example, "properly understood globalization presents new opportunities to address human rights problems. It represents expanded capabilities for human rights cooperation among governments, as well as among far-flung non-governmental organization. It allows the enhanced flow of information and technology needed to identify and respond to human rights threats" (Barnhizer, 2001, p.7).
27. For example, see The Bologna Joint Declaration of the European Ministers of Education of June 19, 1999. available at http://www.unige.ch/cre/activities/ Bologna%20forum/Bologne1999/bologna%20declaration.htm.

REFERENCES

African Union. 1981. *African charter on human and peoples' rights.* Organization of African Unity Doc. CAB/LEG/67/3 rev. 5. Reprinted in *International Legal Material* 21: 58. http://www.africa-union.org/official_documents/Treaties_%20 Conventions_%20Protocols/Banjul%20Charter.pdf.

Alston, P. 2002. Resisting the merger and acquisition of human rights by trade law: A reply to Petersmann. *European Journal of International Law* 14: 30.

Association of Universities and Colleges of Canada. 2001. *Canadian higher education and the GATS.* AUCC background paper 2001/07. http://www.aucc.ca/_pdf/ english/reports/2001/gats_07_e.pdf.

Ball, S. 2000. International free trade agreements and human rights: Reinterpreting Article XX of the GATT. *Minnesota Journal of Global Trade* 10: 62.

Barnhizer, D. 2001. Human rights strategies for investigation and "shaming," resisting globalization rhetoric, and education. In *Effective strategies for protecting human rights: Prevention and intervention, trade and education,* ed. D. Barhnizer, 75. Aldershot: Ashgate.

Council of Europe, General Assembly. 1950. European convention on the safeguard of human rights and fundamental freedoms. http://conventions.coe.int/Treaty/en/ Treaties/Html/005.htm

Council of Europe. 1952. *European Convention on the safeguard of Human Rights and Fundamental Freedoms, First protocol.* March 20. http://www. echr.coe.int/NR/rdonlyres/D5CC24A7-DC13–4318-B457–5C9014916D7A/0/ englishAnglais.pdf

Dailler, P., and A. Pellet. 1999. *Droit international public.* 6th ed. Paris: LGDJ.

Donnelly, J. 1989. *Universal human rights in theory and practice.* New York: Cornell University Press.

Dunoff, J. L. 1998. Rethinking international trade. *University of Pennsylvania Journal of International Economic Law* 19: 347.

Education International (EI)/Public Services International (PSI). 1999. *The WTO and the millennium round: What is at stake for public education?* Education International/Public Services International. http://www.world-psi.org/TemplateEn. cfm?Section=About_PSI&Template=/ContentManagement/ContentDisplay. cfm&ContentID=13758

Eide, A. 1989. Right to adequate food as a human right. *United Nations Human Rights Study Series 1;* 14. New York: United Nations Human Rights Center, United Nations Publications.

Esty, D. C. 2001. Beyond the club model. In *Efficiency, equity and legitimacy: The multilateral trading system at the millennium,* ed. R. B. Porter, P. Sauve, A.

Subramarian, and A. B. Zampetti. Washington DC: Harvard University Center for Business and Government, Brookings Institution Press. http://www.gets.org/gets/library/listcontent.

European Social Forum. 2002. *Principles of guidance of the Education Group Charter of the European Social Forum*. Florence. http://www.fse-esf.org/spip.php?rubrique73.

European Union Commission. 2004. Trade in services, in *Trade Issues*, Europa. http://www.europe.eu.int/comm/trade/issues/sectoral/services/index_en.htm.

European Union, European Parliament. 1989. Declaration of the European Parliament of fundamental rights and freedoms. Doc. A2–3/89. *Official Journal of the European Communities No C 120/51*. May 16. http://www.europarl.europa.eu/omk/omnsapir.so/pv2?PRG=CALDOC&FILE=001025&LANGUE=EN&TPV=PROV&LASTCHAP=12&SDOCTA=7&TXTLST=1&Type_Doc=FIRST&POS=1.

Frase, P. and B. O'Sullivan. 1999. *The future of education under the WTO*. Movement for Democracy and Education. http://www.omc-pour-les-nuls.chez-alice.fr.

Garcia, F. J. 2001. Protecting the human rights principle in a globalizing economy. In *Effective strategies for protecting human rights: Prevention and intervention, trade and education*, ed. D. Barhnizer. Aldershot: Ashgate.

GATSwatch. 2003. *Get education out of the GATS*. Joint Declaration. http://www.choike.org/nuevo_eng/informes/1169.html.

Habbard, A-C., and M. Giraud. 1999. *The World Trade organisation and human rights*. Position paper. Paris: Federation Internationale des Droits de l'Homme.

Hodson, D. 1998. *The human rights to education*. London: Dartmouth Pub. Co.

Jefferson, T. 1787. *Letter to James Madison*, December 20. In The Complete Jefferson (1943): 120–23. Cited by Louis B. Sohn, The World Bank and the right to education, in *Liber Amicorum Ibrahim F.I. Shihata*, ed. S. Schlemmer-Schulte and T. Ko-Yung, 740. Kluwer: Leiden.

Jennar, R. 2000. GATS: Six reasons to fear the precise threats on education. *L'Humanité*, October 12.

Kelsey, J. 1999. *Ten reasons why the GATS is bad for public education*. Association of University Staff of New Zealand. http://www.aare.edu.au/aer/online/30030f.pdf

Kuehn, L. 2004. *Globalization, trade agreements and education: Trade deals prevent governments from protecting education*. British Colombia Teachers' Federation. http://www.gatswatch.org/education.html

Kuyper, P. J. 1994. The law of GATT as a special field of international law. *Netherlands Yearbook of International Law 25*: 227. The Hague: T.M.C. Asser Press.

Larsen, K., J. Martin, and R. Morris. 2002. *Trade in educational services: Trends and emerging issues*. Working paper. Organisation for Economic Co-operation and Development. www.oecd:org/dataoecd/54/44/2538356.pdf.

Larsen, K., and S. Vincent-Lancrin. 2003. Can trade in international education work? *OECD Observer*, March. www.oecdobserver.org/news/fullstory.php/aid/872/The_learning_business.html.

Matsuura K. 2002. 21st century debate on education for all. In *Education for all: The unfulfilled promise*, ed. United Nations Education, Scientific and Cultural Organization. http//:weekly.ahram.org.eg/2002/605/op11.htm.

Mehra, M. 2001. The intersection of trade and human rights. In *Effective strategies for protecting human rights: Prevention and intervention, trade and education*, ed. D. Barhnizer, 78–79. Aldershot: Ashgate.

Nielson, J. 2004. A quick guide to the state of play in the GATS negotiations. In *U.S. update on GATS: January 2004*, ed. American Council on Education. http://www.acenet.edu/AM/Template.cfm?Section=Intl&TEMPLATE=/CM/ContentDisplay.cfm&CONTENTID=22812.

Nowak, M. 1991. The right to education: Its meaning, significance and limitations. *Netherlands Quarterly of Human Rights* 4: 418. . The Hague: Kluwer Law International.

Organization of American States. 1988. *American Convention of Human Rights, First Protocol*. O.A.S. Treaty Series No 69. Washington, DC: Organization of American States. http://www1.umn.edu/humanrts/oasinstr/zoas10pe.htm

Oosterlinck, A. 2002. *Trade in educational perspectives: A European perspective*. Spreekversie, May 23. Washington, D.C. http://www.oecd.org/datao-ecd/36/39/2750393.pdf

Petersmann, E. U. 2000a. From "negative" to positive integration in the WTO: Time for mainstreaming human rights into WTO law? *Common Market Law Review* 33: 1363.

———. 2000b. The WTO constitution and human rights. *Journal of International Economic Law* 3: 25.

———. 2002a. Constitutionalism, international law and "we the peoples of the United Nations." In *Tradition and Weltoffenheit des Rechts: Festschrift für Helmut Steinberger*, ed. H.-J. Cremer, 291. Springer, Berlin.

———. 2002b. Time for a United Nations "global compact" for integrating human rights into the law of worldwide organizations: Lessons from European integration. *European Journal of International Law* 13: 621.

Robertson, A. H. 1981. The implementation system: International measures. In *The International Bill of Rights*, ed. Louis Henkin, 350. New York: Columbia University press.

Simma, B. 1985. Self-contained regimes. *Netherlands yearbook of international law* 16, 111. The Hague: T.M.C Asser Press.

Sinclair, S. 2000. *How the World Trade Organization's new "services" negotiations threaten democracy*. Ottawa: Canadian Center for Policy Alternatives.

The Economist. 2003. Cancun's charming outcome. *The Economist*, 368 (8342): 14. London. September 20.

Trachman, J. P. 1999. The domain of WTO dispute resolution. *Harvard International Law Journal*, 40: 336. Harvard Law School, Cambridge: Publications Center.

United Nations Committee on Economic, Social and Cultural Rights. 1990. General Comment N°3 on the nature of the obligations of the parties. United Nations Document E/C.12/1991/23, p. 9. http://www.unhchr.ch/tbs/doc.nsf/0/4ceb75c549 2497d9802566d500516036?Opendocument.

United Nations Committee on Economic, Social and Cultural Rights, 20th Session. 1999. General Comment N°11 on the plans of action for primary education, United Nations Document E/C.12/1999/4, p. 2. http://www.unhchr.ch/tbs/doc. nsf/(symbol)/E.C.12.1999.4.En?OpenDocument.

United Nations Committee on Economic, Social and Cultural Rights. Background Paper submitted by the Special Rapporteur on the right to education, United Nations Document E/C.12/1998/18, p. 1. http://www.un.org/documents/ecosoc/docs/1999/e1999–22.htm.

United Nations Commission for Human Rights, Sub-Commission on the Promotion and protection of Human Rights, 54th Session. 2002. Economic, social and cultural rights, liberalization of trade in services and human rights. Report of the High Commissioner on human rights, United Nations Document E/CN.4/Sub.2/2002/9, 2002: 59. June 25. http://www.unhchr.ch/huridocda/huridoca.nsf/(Symbol)/E.CN.4.Sub.2.2002.9.En?Opendocument.

United Nations Committee on the Rights of the Child. 2001. *General Comment N°1 on the Aims of Education*, United Nations Document CRC/GC/2001/1. http://www.unhchr.ch/tbs/doc.nsf/(symbol)/CRC.GC.2001.1.En?OpenDocument.

United Nations General Assembly. 1966. International Covenant on Economic, Social and Cultural Rights, General Assembly Resolution 1514, United Nations Document A/6316. Reprinted in *International Legal Material* 6: 360. 1999. Washington: American Society of International Law Publications.

————. 1981. General Assembly Resolution 34/180. United Nations Convention on the Elimination of All Forms of Discrimination Against Women. Sept. 3. http://www.un.org/womenwatch/daw/cedaw.

————. 1984. General assembly resolution 2106 A (XX). *United Nations Treaty Series 85*: 1465. United Nations Convention on the Elimination of All Form of Racial Discrimination. New York: United Nations Publications.

————. 1989. Convention on the Rights of the Child. General Assembly Resolution 44/25, Annex, United Nations Document A/44/25/49, 1989. revised in United Nations Document A/Res./44/25/Corr.1, 1990. Reprinted in *International legal material* 28: 1457. 1989. Washington: American Society of International Law Publications.

Van Damme, D. 2001. *Higher education in the age of globalization: The need for a new regulatory framework for recognition, quality assurance and accreditation.* Introductory Paper for the UNESCO Experts Meeting, p. 3. Paris. http://www. unesco.org/education/studyingabroad/highlights/global_forum/presentations/ vandamme_pp.ppt.

Von Kopp, B. 2002. Education Transformation and GATS, New Paradigms in government and administration. Contribution to the International Symposium "Transformation of Education in Comparative Perspective. January 24–26. University of Erfurt, and Bundeswehr University of Hamburg, Berlin. http://www.dipf.de/ publikationen/veroeff2002_print.pdf.

World Trade Organization. 1994. General agreement on trade in services. Reprinted 1999, in *International Legal Material*, 33: 1125. Washington: American Society of International Law Publications.

World Trade Organization, Appellate Body Report. 1996. *United States—standards for reformulated and conventional gasoline*, (WT/DS2). May 20. http://www. internationaltraderelations.com/WTO.Gasoline%20(AB%201996).htm

————. 1998. *United States- Import Prohibition of Certain Shrimp and Shrimp Products*, (WT/DS58/AB/R). October 12. http://www.sice.oas.org/DISPUTE/ wto/58abr.asp

World Trade Organization Panel. 1997. *European Communities—regime for the importation, sale and distribution of bananas: Complaint by the United States.* Report of the panel. WT/DS27/R/USA (1997). http://www.sice.oas.org/DISPUTE/ wto/banecar.asp.

World Trade Organization Secretariat Council for Trade in Services. 1998. *Education services, background note by the secretariat*, WTO, S/C/W/49, p. 3. September 23. http://www.wto.org/english/tratop_e/serv_e/w49.doc.

————. 1999. *The GATS: Objectives, coverage and disciplines.* http://www.wto.org/ english/tratop_e/serv_e/gatsqa_e.htm.

Zutchi, B. K. 2001. WTO Symposium on Issues Confronting the World Trade System. July 6–7. Geneva: World Trade Organization Headquarters. http://www.wto.org/ english/forums_e/ngo_e/ngo_symp_2001_e.htm.

6 Education, Inequality and Neoliberal Capitalism

A Classical Marxist Analysis

Dave Hill, Nigel M. Greaves and Alpesh Maisuria

INTRODUCTION

This chapter examines the relationship between capitalism and educational inequality. From a Marxist perspective, inequality is a long-term and inevitable consequence of the capitalist system. Education does not stand alone and remote from the practices and thought processes of society in general. It both reflects and supports the social inequalities of capitalist culture. The "education industry" is a significant state apparatus in the reproduction and replication of the capitalist social form necessary for the continuation of "surplus value" extraction and economic inequality. Hence, Marxists argue that there are material linkages between educational inequality, exploitation, and capitalist inequalities in general. This has been brought into much sharper relief during the current reactionary phase of neoliberal capitalism in such countries as Thatcherite/post-Thatcherite Britain and Reaganite/post-Reaganite United States.

The question as to whether the development of a capitalist society inevitably increases inequality in education will be explored in two ways. In Section 1, the enquiry is addressed through the lens of Marxist theoretical analysis. Capitalism is a particular economic form driven by a relentless profit motive in which exploitation and inequality—for example of income, of life chances—are inbuilt features. This section will explain why, therefore, we might expect to find evidence for a relationship between education and class inequality. In Section 2, the question of capitalism and inequality is investigated by drawing, inter alia, on recent empirical research and the near-universal agreement among a wide range of national, international, and comparative studies examining the impacts of neoliberal capitalist policies for education (such as preprivatization, privatization, commercialization, commodification, and marketization of schools and universities).

The conclusion attempts a synthesis of the empirical and theoretical concerns of the chapter. As confirmation of the key substantive concern of Marxist education theorists, a distinct correlation between capitalist economic inequality and educational inequality is revealed. Our analysis is that this relationship is causal and reciprocal. Capitalism causes and increases economic and education inequalities, which then, in turn, become functional to capitalist production and culture. This effect is evident in the long term. Short-term snapshots of certain instances and conjunctures do not tend to reveal the full historical picture. (For a discussion of "termism," long- and short-term policy and their impacts, see Hill, 2001, 2005a).

SECTION 1: MARXIST ANALYSIS OF THE RELATIONSHIP BETWEEN CAPITAL AND EDUCATION—A CONCEPTUAL APPROACH

Renaissance of Marxist Education Theory

In the past several decades and in opposition to escalating capitalist class practices that increase exploitation of the many by the few in order to raise the rate of profit, works from Richard Brosio (1994), Kevin Harris (1994), Teresa Ebert (1996), Ebert and Masazavardeh (2007) and Michael Neary (1997) have signaled a renewed period of development and experimentation in Marxist educational research, theory, and radical pedagogy—one that puts the focus on the classical Marxist understanding of class as a binary relation to the means of production and as a social relation that decisively shapes social practices. Works in this vein are Paula Allman (1999, 2001); Richard Brosio (2000); Peter McLaren (2000, 2005a, 2005b); McLaren and Farahmandpur (2005); Bertell Ollman (2001); Carmel Borg, John Buttigieg, and Peter Mayo (2002); and Dave Hill et al. (2002). There is renewed interest in theorizing and researching issues of class, gender, and race in education from within "orthodox" Marxism, that understanding of Marxism that bases its critiques on a theorization of class as a binary and determinant relation (see Kelsh, 1998, see Hill, 1999, 2006a, b; Hill and Cole, 2001; Kelsh and Hill, 2006; Kumar, 2006, 2008, Ebert and Masazavardeh, 2007, 2008; Kelsh, Hill and Macrine, 2009). Furthermore, many are developing Marxist binary class analysis to address an increasing range of education policy issues and theoretical concerns, such as lifelong learning, mentoring, the learning society, social justice, globalization, educational marketization, the business takeover of education (see Glenn Rikowski, 2001, 2002, 2003, 2005, 2008; Kenneth Saltman and David Gabbard, 2003; and Saltman, 2005) and public services related to education, such as libraries (Ruth Rikowski, 2005).

There are, of course, many (neo-)Marxists who reject class as a binary relation that decisively shapes social practices. These theorists understand class as Max Weber theorized it: as myriad cultural strata that are effects rather than causes of social inequity. Weberian class, however, cannot explain inequity; it can only describe it. As descriptive rather than explanatory, (neo-) Weberian formulations of class cannot serve as a reliable guide to praxis. Against the epistemological instability caused by the insertion of pluralist, nonessentialist (such as postmodernist) and Weberian-type schemata into leftist theoretical frameworks, an insertion that displaces the explanatory Marxist concept of class, a vigorous contestation has developed over the concept of class (Rikowski, 2001; Kelsh and Hill, 2006; Ebert and Zavarzadeh, 2007, 2008; Kelsh, Hill and Macrine, 2009), one in which this chapter participates.

Kelsh and Hill (2006), Paraskeva (2006), and Farahmandpur (2004) take as an example of "revisionist left" writers who reject class as a binary relation the work of Michael W. Apple. Apple writes prolifically and influentially among left educators against neoliberal and neoconservative ideological and political hegemony in the United States. His analysis and political objective are that there is, and should be, an alliance of political interests in which the tryptych of social class, "race," and gender have equal importance as both explanatory and as organizing principles (e.g., Apple, 2001, 2005, 2006). The introduction of extraclass determinants of social inequality follows a Weberian-derived notion of class as a tool of classification useful only to describe *strata* of people, as they appear at the level of culture and in terms of status derived from various possessions, economic, political, or cultural.

However, as a tool of *class* categorization, Weberian-derived classifications of social strata cannot provide reliable knowledge to guide transformative praxis—that is, they cannot serve as a reliable guide to action that aims to replace capitalism with socialism (a system whereby the means of production, distribution, and exchange, are collectively, rather than privately, owned). In Weberian classifications, there is no objective capitalist class, and no objective working class, just myriad strata. Similar assumptions surface in anti-essentialist, postmodernist approaches (for a critique, see Hill, 2001, 2005a; Hill, Sanders, and Hankin, 2002; McLaren and Scatamburlo D'Annibale, 2004). Such classification systems substituted for Marxist class theory fuel the ideological notion that "class is dead" (Pakulski and Waters, 1996).

It is interesting, and rarely remarked upon, that arguments about "the death of class" are not advanced regarding the capitalist class. Despite their horizontal and vertical cleavages (Dumenil and Levy, 2004), the capitalist class appears to know very well who they are. Nobody is denying capitalist class consciousness. They are rich. They are powerful. And they are transnational as well as national. They exercise (contested) control over the lives of worker-laborers and worker-subjects.

Marxists agree that class is not the only form of oppression in contemporary society, yet it is also a fact that class is central to the social relations of production and essential for producing and reproducing the cultural and economic activities of humans under a capitalist mode of production. Whereas the abolition of racism and sexism does not guarantee the abolition of capitalist social relations of production, the abolition of class inequalities, by definition, denotes the abolition of capitalism. As Marx argues in *Wage-Labour and Capital* (1933), "capital . . . *without wage-labour, ceases to be capital*" (p. 46).

Hickey, for example, points to the functionality of various oppressions in dividing the working class and securing the reproduction of capital; these oppressions construct social conflict between men and women, or black and white, or skilled and unskilled, thereby tending to mask the conflict between capital and labor (Hickey, 2006, p. 196). While Apple's "parallellist," or equivalence, model of exploitation (equivalence of exploitation based on "race," class and gender, and his "tryptarch" (or tripartite) model of inequality produces valuable data and insights into aspects of gender oppression and "race" oppression in capitalist United States, such analyses serve, as Hickey (2006), Gimenez (2001), Hill (2006a, b, 2009a, b) and Kelsh and Hill (2006) suggest, to occlude the class-capital relation, the class struggle, and to obscure the essential and defining nature of capitalism, the labor-capital relation and its attendant class conflict. With respect to one aspect of structural inequalities reproduced within the educational system in England and Wales, specifically, educational attainment, Gillborn and Mirza (2000), themselves using the "official" (British government census classification) Weberian-derived categorizations of social strata, show very clearly that it is the difference between social strata that is the fundamental and stark feature of the educational system, rather than "race" or gender. While this would seem to suggest the usefulness of Weberian-based understandings of class, our point is that this is a descriptive understanding of inequity, not an explanatory one, and that only a binary understanding of class can explain inequity and thus point to what must be done to restructure society so that inequity is not built into it.

In sum, there is a recognized need among Marxists, first, to restate the epistemic foundation of Marxism; and, in so doing, second, to reclaim the reliable, because objective, strand of the left-wing critique of capitalist education practices and their ideological justification though a class-based ontology (Kelsh and Hill, 2006).

Restating Class

For Marxists, class is not an arbitrary or abstract concept. Rather, it is a verifiable feature of certain human life processes. According to *The German Ideology*, written by Marx and Engels in 1845–1856, human society passed through different productive epochs and in each there were opposing groups of people defined according to the objectively different relationships they had to the means and products of material production. That is, in every epoch, economic practices structure human society into "classes" with diametrically opposed interests rooted in relations of ownership to the means of production. These relations of ownership to the means of production constitute what Marx calls the "relations of production" and this is an arena of perpetual tension and struggle (1977, p. 179). The relations of production always develop the "forces of production" (factories, workplaces, plant, equipment and tools, and knowledge of their use), and the relations together with the forces constitute the specific "mode of production" or "economic base" (Marx, 1977, pp. 161, 168). This productive "infrastructure" forms the organizational rationale and dynamic for society in general and these are reflected in the social institutions (e.g., the state) that spring up and become established in accordance with the needs of the existing productive relations.

The relations of production under capitalism always aim at raising the rate of profit for the capitalist class; indeed, crises always arise for the capitalist class in the form of a fall in the rate of profit. The aim of raising the rate of profit always exerts pressure for changes, shifts in the relations of production (such as outsourcing) that lower, for example, the cost of labor. The institutions which attempt to guard the existing relations of production from crises (principally the state) work, precisely and contradictorily, to obstruct the unfettered development of the forces of production, to which those forces tend, by maintaining the existing relations of production. These fetter development insofar as the relations constrain development to the aim of raising the rate of extraction of surplus value. Eventually, the pressure of contradictions rooted in the class contradiction becomes too great, development of the forces of production too restricted by the existing relations of production, and the mode of production increasingly becomes open to transformation. At the point of revolutionary transformation, new social and political institutions develop, ones that ensure new relations of production capable of enabling the free development of the material forces of production because they are not based on a class binary. *The German Ideology* constitutes Marx's attempt to depart from the metaphysical abstraction of the Hegelian idealist method and locate the motor of historical change in living, human society and its sensuous processes.

For later thinkers, such as Lenin, the significance of Marx's transformation of dialectics is the identification of the concept of "class struggle" as the essential historical dynamic. In any era, and most certainly in the capitalist, society is locked in conflict, since the needs of a certain group in the productive process are always subordinated to another. Marxists hold that this social conflict cannot be truly reconciled with the source of its economic causation, and that this perpetual tension is the seedbed of revolution.

The capitalist era is both typical of human history and at the same time unique. It is typical in that its production techniques involve the exploitation of one human being by another, but it is unique in history in terms of its advancing this principle to unprecedented levels of efficiency and ruthlessness. For Marx, writing in the Preface to *A Critique of Political Economy* of 1859 (known simply as the "*Preface*"), the capitalist era marks the zenith of class struggle in history and human exploitation cannot be taken further (1977, p. 390). The only redeeming feature of capitalism is its assembling its own social antithesis in the "proletariat" or "working class," which is destined to rise up against the bourgeoisie (profiteering or "ruling class") and abolish class and exploitation and thus bring "the prehistory of human society to a close" (1977, p. 390).

What, though, do Marxists mean by capitalist "exploitation"? In the first volume of *Capital*, Marx argues that workers are the primary producers of wealth due to the expenditure of their labor in the production of commodities. However, the relationship between the owners of the means of production (the employers) and the workers is fundamentally exploitative since the full value of the workers' labor power is never reflected in the wages they receive. The difference between the value of the labor expenditure and the sum the worker receives for it is known as "surplus value," and this is pocketed by the employer as profit.

Marx saw surplus value as the distinguishing characteristic and ultimate source of class and class conflict within the capitalist system (Cuneo, 1982, p. 378). However, for Marx, surplus value is not merely an undesirable side effect of the capitalist economy; it is its motive force and the entire system would readily collapse without it. Technically, while surplus value extraction is not wholly unique, historically, to capitalist systems, all capitalist systems are characterized by it. Marx is thus able to offer a "scientific" and objective definition of class in the capitalist epoch based on which side of the social equation of surplus value one stands and to show, moreover, that this economic arrangement is the fundamental source of all human inequality.

Class is therefore absolutely central to Marxist ontology. Ultimately, it is economically induced and it conditions and permeates all social reality in capitalist systems. Marxists therefore critique postmodern and poststructural arguments that class is, or ever can be, "constructed extra-economically," or equally that it can be "deconstructed politically"—an epistemic position which has underwritten in the previous two decades numerous so-called "death of class" theories—arguably the most significant of which are Laclau and Mouffe (1985) and Laclau (1996).

Capital, Immiseration, Education and Ideology

Marx's views on education, rarely expressed, tend toward an articulation of its "commodifying" properties in relation to both teachers and pupils. In other words, education is assessed according to its practical or "use value" for capital. Marx writes:

> [i]f we may take an example from outside the sphere of production of material objects, a schoolmaster is a productive labourer, when, in addition to belabouring the heads of his scholars, he works like a horse to enrich the school proprietor. That the latter has laid out his capital in a teaching factory, instead of in a sausage factory, does not alter the relation. (Marx, 1867, p. 477)

As a "sausage factory" in itself, the school is unlikely to hold out much prospect that pupils could be geared for anything other than the interests of capital. Marx (together with the Marxist "reproduction theorists" of the mid-late twentieth century and currently, such as Harris, 1979, 1982, 1984, 1994; Hill, 1989, 1993, 2001, 2004, 2005a, 2006b, 2007; Sarup, 1978, 1984) would certainly have scoffed at the humanist notion that education is geared to the interests of the child, although "resistance theorists" (such as Willis, 1997; Giroux, 1983a, b, 1998; Giroux and McLaren, 1986, 1989) and critical pedagogues such as Giroux, Freire, Shor, and McLaren assert the possibilities for teachers and students challenging the capitalist system within schools, engaging in liberatory and transformative education (e.g. Freire, 1998; Shor, 1992; Shor and Freire, 1997). However, as far as capital is concerned, education is merely instrumental in providing and setting a pupil's future "use value" in production. The importance of this is that there is no other standard to which to aspire, other than that defined by capital, for the purposes of capital.

More subtly perhaps, though no less crucially, education has a role in conditioning and institutionalizing children not only for exploitation at work but toward an acceptance of their future life conditions and expectations. This is as true of the supposedly broad liberal arts education of today in the United States, or the purportedly "broad" national curriculum for schools in England, as of more obviously utilitarian vocational models such as Soviet technical and vocational schooling. In any case, Marxists seek the explanation of this phenomenon in the processes of what Marx in the *Preface* called the "superstructure" (1977, p. 389).

The dynamics of production permeate all other activities in society such that there arises a vast complementary superstructure on the level of human thought or "ideology." The superstructure—consisting of all those elements widely understood as "culture" and "politics"—becomes simultaneously a product and necessary agency of the economic base. It is the cauldron in which thoughts, opinions, biases, and outlooks—rooted in and expressing class positions and interests—are formulated and exchanged and become, due to the power and control exerted by the ruling class, broadly supportive of existing economic practices. In other words, the superstructure, because it is conditioned by the binary class relations of production that constitute the base, reproduces in the ideological field class differentials by either (re)presenting these as legitimate somehow; as "natural" (simply the way things are); or by covering up and disguising the original source of class inequality.

The superstructure has, therefore, a vital concrete function. In a negative sense, it protects the dominant economic group by deflecting and disguising the adverse sensations of production. For example, during the period in which Marx and Engels wrote, Europe was rife with social criticism. The literary works of Charles Dickens (1812–1870) in England and Victor Hugo (1802–1885) in France are replete with moral outrage. However, much of it tended to reflect disgust that the major privileges of liberal philosophy, such as "individual empowerment," "self-ownership," and so forth, were contradicted by the extant material conditions of the poorest members of society. In other words, such liberal social critics tended to assume that the liberal revolutions, those that had accompanied transitions to capitalist modes of production throughout Europe, were incomplete or that their highest ideals had been subsequently betrayed somehow.

In fact, many nineteenth-century social critics exposed a fundamental internal paradox of liberal philosophy. On the one hand, freedom is sacrosanct and there should be minimal interference in individual choice and behavior; on the other hand, the activation and preservation of freedom requires social intervention or "big government." We find this theme, for example, in the political theories of the philosophic radicals Jeremy Bentham (1748–1832) and James Mill (1773–1836) who, along with their fellow critics in literature, assumed that what was required to meet dire social need was in effect more liberalism or indeed the "right kind."

Marx, however, raises the stakes of social criticism beyond liberalism, an ideology which he believed had largely run its course. For Marx, what was required was socialism but this was not so much an "idea" as an entirely new social form in which capitalist economic practices and corresponding state support had been swept away by proletarian revolution.

Marx believed he had every reason to be confident. In *The Communist Manifesto* and elsewhere, and derived in part from his earlier humanist writings on alienation, Marx saw the increasing "immiseration" of the workers as a vital revolutionary factor. From a series of articles written in 1849 for the journal *Neue Rheinische Zeitung* and later in the first volumes of *Capital*, Marx's idea of immiseration is that as capitalism develops its cost in human terms would increase proportionately. Workers are singularly vulnerable since their only resource is their labor power, and they are dependent for their subsistence on selling this power to someone else, as we have seen, always for less (exchange value) than its true value. The workers have, therefore, limited material resources and ability to control the processes of capitalism and its long-term tendencies to drive workers' wages down.

In effect, the workers shoulder the cost of an inherently unstable system. For example, the uptake of labor by capital periodically falls short of labor availability. This leads to unemployment, the creation of a ("raced" and gendered) reserve army of labor, and competition for jobs. Sometimes the reserve army is over the border in maquiladoras; sometimes far away in colonies and neocolonies; sometimes through the importation of formerly subject peoples into the colonial/imperial "motherland;" sometimes through the simple "free movement" of labor, as in the newly enlarged European Union; and sometimes through bringing more women laborers into the paid economy. On the other hand, the downward pressure on wages relates directly to downward pressure on commodity prices—labor being a commodity itself.

Subject to stiff market competition, capitalists act on labor as an immediate and malleable factor in the pricing of the commodity. Capitalists are compelled to reduce their overhead costs and are ever-vigilant in their bid to gain an advantage over their competitors. Many variables are beyond the capacity of the capitalist to control, such as the price of raw commodities which, Marx assumed, will be roughly the same for all capitalists, but this is not necessarily the case for the variable labor. Here, the capitalist exerts some measure of control. Indeed, the demands of competition result in the general trend for downward pressure on labor costs.

Of course, this pressure clashes fundamentally with the interests of those whose sole means of subsistence is their labor power. The capitalist's ability to compete will therefore depend upon the self-organization and interest-recognition of a given labor force. For Marx, such recognition was not inevitable. For Marx, people would certainly recognize their needs, but owing to ideological forces, they would likely *not* attribute their need to capitalist class practices; indeed they would likely attribute it elsewhere—to a drought, for example, or a war, or, whatever the capitalist class ideologues were offering as "reasons" for immiseration. This is why Marxists must engage in ideology critique—critique that shows the class interestedness of dominant ideas. Some persons certainly would recognize that their needs were not being met owing to capitalist class practices. These would be, for example, the "small section of the ruling class [that] cuts itself adrift, and joins the revolutionary class, the class that holds the future in its hands," those who "have raised themselves to the level of comprehending theoretically the historical movement as a whole" (Marx and Engels, 1985, p. 91). And they might be others. There would have to be some, since if (as Marxist theory argues) ideas are a reflection of the binary class relations of the base, there would have to be ideas that represent the workers, not just the capitalists. Indeed, this is the basis for resistance theory—hegemony leaks! So, while recognition of need was inevitable, *how* one would understand that need, its causes, would vary according to the dominant ideas in circulation and the "gaps" in them, and whether there were sufficient numbers of educated persons who would break from the ruling ideas because they were educated enough to "see" the arc of history.

It would prove difficult to disguise from *all* the workers and *all* of the ruling class the source of workers' misery and alienation. However, the growth of superstructures in terms of democratic enfranchisement, "bourgeois democracy," trade unionism, and welfare states resulted in what Marxists dub the "embourgeoisement" of the working class or what Marshall (1990, p. 31) calls the pressure for "upward mobility." Rose (1960) considered, for example, how the Conservative Party in Britain was able to command a broad appeal and concluded that an important factor was the increasing association of workers with the values of the middle class. Similar, analysis can be made of other advanced capitalist countries such as the United States, France, and Germany. Embourgeoisement results, subjectively, if not objectively, in a blurring of the distinction between classes and the deradicalisation of the workers. Patently, this effect is attributable to the superstructure which reflects the interests of the dominant class but only because the dominant class owns the means of production and has the money (congealed and stolen labor power) to flood culture with its ideas.

Analysis of the role of the superstructure in the process of deradicalisation was initiated in large part by the Italian Marxist Antonio Gramsci (1891–1937). He argued from a fascist prison cell in the 1930s that the superstructure has a constructive (rather than exclusively negative) dimension—emphasizing an aspect of Marxist theory that had always been at its core but which, owing to the historical material conditions of the time Marx and Engels made their key arguments, remained deemphasized in their works, as Engels was later to argue (Engels, letter to Joseph Bloch, 1890). Therefore, Marxists should take the initiative and become more positively engaged in the life of the superstructure. It is, he wrote, "the terrain on which men move, acquire consciousness of their position, struggle, etc" (Gramsci, 1971, p. 377). As a consequence, the idea of education in Gramsci's thinking is similar to his views on ideology. Education in the widest sense is a vital tool for the advancement of civilization to a necessary level to meet with productive need. For Gramsci, ideology becomes a force for the advancement of the interests of one class over another by its presenting its viewpoints as fair, moral, just, and so forth—as just "plain common sense." Gramsci called this force "hegemony" and it represents a particular account of reality which promotes both its own advancement throughout society and the suppression of rival accounts. Of course, equally, Gramsci offers the prospect of turning the tables on the capitalist class by encouraging the proletariat to throw off its ideological subordination and to cultivate its own version of reality as the first stage in revolutionary preparation (Greaves, 2005). This is the classic task of Marxist and communist educators, to transform the working class from an objective "class in itself," into a "class for itself"—a class with class consciousness, aware of its political project to replace capitalism.

Gramsci (1971) perceived that in capitalist systems the task of permeating society with a particular version of reality is given over to the capitalist's "chiefs of staff," or dominant "intellectuals," that is, rather than capitalists themselves. School is, therefore, an obvious locus of intellectual recruitment and hegemonic exchange. As Gramsci puts it, "(s)chool is the instrument through which intellectuals of various levels are elaborated" (p. 10) "(and part of an) overall framework of a policy for forming modern intellectual cadres" (p. 26). First, children learn at school the prevailing mores of society and adopt the conditions of "good citizenship." Second, children are selected for a future role in production either as producers themselves or as the intellectual legitimizing agents of productive logic in the superstructure.

Gramsci's ideas on the pedagogic and reproducing nature of the superstructure have been influential within the Marxist tradition. They are explored by Louis Althusser (1971) and Bowles and Gintis (1972, 1976, 1988). For Althusser, the needs of capital are reproduced ideologically by replicating capitalist practices and conditions at multiple social levels. Children are structuralized by education because the education system is part of a state apparatus that *cannot do otherwise* than work in the interests of capital. A state contrived in accordance with the dictates of a given economic form cannot be brought to perform in ways that are at odds with its structural character. One effect of this is that educational systems of capitalist societies become inherently hierarchical and elitist.

This process prepares the student for passive acceptance of the inequalities in expectation and reward that will be faced in the world of capitalist production. Indeed, education is preparation for future market evaluation and the process of commodification through which capitalism assesses human value and worth. Bowles and Gintis (1988) track this analysis. They write:

> (t)he hierarchical order of the school system, admirably geared towards preparing students for their future positions in the hierarchy of production, limits the development of those personal capacities . . . and reinforces social inequality by legitimating of students to inherently unequal "slots" in the social hierarchy. (1988, p. 18)

Bowles and Gintis (1988) recognise that over and above the interest of the child and the free development of its faculties lies a "hidden curriculum." Education transmits a curriculum to students that is conditioned to the needs of both the forces of production (skills, techniques, know-how) and the relations of production (class, class differentials, inequality). In catering to the needs of the productive forces and the acquisition of skill, the curriculum is open in the sense that the purpose of education is fully apparent. However, Bowles and Gintis (1972) argue that a hidden message is smuggled into education alongside the dissemination of vocational know-how that serves to justify social relations.

> The school is a bureaucratic order, with hierarchical authority, rule orientation, stratification by "ability" as well as by age, role differentiation by sex (physical education) . . . etc., and a system of external incentives (marks, promises of promotion, and threat of failure) much like pay and status in the sphere of work. (p. 87)

Section 1 has offered a synopsis of the Marxist analysis of education and its a priori assumptions on education in capitalist systems. We now turn to provide supporting empirical data.

SECTION 2: CAPITAL AND EDUCATION—AN EMPIRICAL ANALYSIS

Turning the Screw—Neoliberalism and Fiscal Inequality

The introduction and extension of neoliberal social policies in Britain, the United States after the New Right reactionary movements of the 1980s, and more globally (notably in Chile under Pinochet and elsewhere in Latin

America under an assortment of generals and "big business" control) offers fertile ground for Marxist analysis since economic inequality and class division has sharpened markedly (Dumenil and Levy, 2004; Harvey, 2005; Global Policy Forum, 2006). The immiseration of the worker that super-structures and state activities had done much to ameliorate since Marx's time might be making a comeback (Brennan, 2003; Glyn, 2006).

And so, with the economic gains of the thirty-year postwar "boom," from the 1940s to the 1970s, when (in advanced capitalist countries) real wages of the working classes and standards of living improved, (as did the "social wage" welfare and social benefits) the theory of immiseration went into decline. However, following the hidden economic depression of the 1970s ("hidden" because it was compensated for in the West by the large-scale drafting of women into the workforce), Marx's theory of immisera-tion has regained validity. Since 1970, especially in the case of the United States, real wages have fallen dramatically. However, real family income has remained relatively stable as women entered the workforce. Families have the same amount of money to spend as before, but a lot more hours are being worked. Recent research (Dumenil and Levy, 2004; Harvey, 2005; Hill, 2004, 2005b; Hill et al., 2006) testifies that the "class war from above" is in full swing, characterized by the increase in the rate of extraction of surplus value, in advanced capitalist and in developing coun-tries—with the rich getting richer, the poor poorer, and workers and trade union rights and liberties under attack.

Currently there is a "race to the bottom" in which worldwide wages and conditions of labor are being held down by neoliberal national and global policies such as the structural readjustment programs of the World Bank and the International Monetary Fund, and the "liberalization" of trade agenda of the World Bank's General Agreement of Trade in Services (GATS) (Rikowski, 2002, 2003; Hill, 2005b; Hill et al., 2006). Together with competition from the substantially lower-wage economies such as India and China, we see Marx's rising rate of exploitation reemerging, a century and a half after he first predicted it (Glynn, 2006). In justifying the intensification of labor, the ideological state apparatuses such as edu-cation and the media, and of the repressive state apparatuses of the laws, army, and police (Althusser, 1971, Hill, 2004)—play a full role in trying to "manage" citizens and workers into accepting the "common sense" of an individualistic, consumerist, and hierarchically stratified society.

Dumenil and Levy (2004) highlight the increasing inequality in the United States. Those in the highest tax bracket are paying tax at a tax rate around half that of the 1920s, whereas the current tax rate for those in the lowest tax bracket are more than double of what it was then. In a forerunner of George W. Bush's "trillion-dollar tax giveaway to the rich," Reagan cut the top rate of personal tax from 70 percent to 28 percent. The results can be seen most starkly in the remuneration packages of chief executive officers (CEOs), whose income soared by 25 percent in 2005 to $17.9 million, with six CEOs accumulating between USD$100–$280 million that year (Strass and Hansen, 2006). This compares with the average worker in the United States gaining a meagre 3.1 percent increase, which is below inflation. Real-term wages are in decline and the wealth of the nation is being transferred to the few in the capitalist oligarchy class (Strass and Hansen, 2006). In addition, both the U.S. administration and the British government have also dramatically cut taxes on businesses and multinational corporations, inflating profits.

Similarly, in Britain, the working class is paying more tax. The richest groups are paying a smaller proportion of their income in taxes in comparison to 1949 and to the late 1970s. These dates were both in the closing stages, at the end of two periods, of what might be termed "Old Labour," or social democratic governments (in ideological contradistinction to the primarily neoliberal policies of "New Labour"). As a percentage of income, middle and high earners in Britain pay less tax in 2003 than at any time for thirty years. It is the poorest, the lowest paid (one-third of the population is paid below the EU decency threshold of the minimum wage), who are paying more despite the economy having doubled since the 1950s (Toynbee, 2003). In comparison with the late 1970s, the "fat cats" are now paying around half as much tax (income tax and insurance contribution rate). These people are paying less income tax and national insurance as a percentage of their earned income than in 1949. "As a percentage of income, middle and high earners pay less tax now than at any time in the past thirty years" (Johnson and Lynch, 2004), In contrast, the average tax rate for "the low paid" is roughly double that of the early 1970s—and nearly twice as much as in 1949 (Johnson and Lynch, 2004). The subtitle for Johnson and Lynch's article is, appropriately, "sponging off the poor."

The encroachment of capital into state/public education has intensified because of a decline in the rate of capital accumulation. New markets outside of the traditional private sector domain were needed (Hursh and Martina, 2003), especially to take advantage of economies of scale. In order to accommodate the business imperative, the U.S. and British governments opened up, and continue to liberalize, the public-sector services, including education.

In Britain, New Labour's neoliberalizing policies aimed at deregulating educational provisions are potentially paving the way for the private sector to gain a stranglehold on state services (Hill, 2006c). The private sector is involved in almost every element of the British education services, with activities ranging from selling services to educational institutions, to managing and owning schools and other facilities. Education ancillary services such as cleaning, catering, security, and reprographics have been outsourced to private-sector companies. On a national scale, functions such as inspection, student fees and loans handling, and record keeping are increasingly run by private corporations rather than by the Local Education Authority (LEA) or the national government. And the current preprivatization of state schooling in England and Wales (Rikowski, 2005) could well see a system of publicly funded, privately controlled schooling.

The "Sausage Factory" in Action: Standardization and Centralization of Education

It should not be thought that the struggle between classes, in part played out in education, can be eradicated by state provision and such measures as standardized national curricula. For Marxists, the state can never be neutral while serving a capitalist economy, even though it can be used as a site of struggle and can effect reforms. State involvement in education represents the attempt at regulation, harmonization, and rationalization. The standardizing and centralizing powers of the state allow for a practical and ideological correlation between national educational provision and national economic need. The state turns the interests of capital into national educational strategies. Of course, the rhetoric of government policies, such as that of No Child Left Behind in the United States and the rhetoric of the Blair government in its 2006 Education Bill for England and Wales, do not solely advance a vocational or human capital rationale. (However, is it remarkable how demoted or absent, relative to the 1960s, are rationales based on liberal-progressivist child-centered ideology, or social democratic redistributionist ideology). There are other rationales, such as political competitive vote-winning considerations. There is also the legitimacy question. In societies such as Britain, the United States, and other liberal democratic polities, where economic inequality is high and growing, upward mobility between social classes has to be seen to be attainable—the message is "work hard and you'll be rewarded." If these messages permeate the masses who do not enjoy much of the spoils, then they are more likely to tolerate the riches that few enjoy within that society. However, if these meritocratic messages of attainable riches and advancement through a meritocratic education system are not widely accepted, then this poses legitimacy—and political survival problems—for political and economic elites.

As part of a strategic state objective, education is driven by the need and desire of capital for capital accumulation. Currently, in advanced capitalist countries education has a particular, distinctive economic and business orientation: it seeks a specialist workforce, whether by a dual-track system such as in Germany, or through supposedly single-track, more "comprehensive" systems, as in the United States. Both types of system, as well as hybrid types, are specialized in that they are designed to train or educate for the purposes of capital. In both types students are differentially and hierarchically trained and/or educated (Hirtt, 2004) to maximize economic return in the development of a "knowledge economy." In the worldwide division of labor other education systems, and the economies they serve, have different functions. In some historic-geographical spaces these include the production of raw materials and/or low-skilled factory assembly work, together with supervisory capacity. This has the effect of stratifying children into crude (gendered and "raced") class strata categories. One result is the failure to provide a holistic educational experience aiming to enrich pupils' personal development and talents.

The state allows for and encourages, therefore, the harmonizing and standardizing of education provision toward the needs of capital. As McNeil (2000) observes, state standardization and centralization nevertheless replicates capitalist social relations in that it "creates inequities, widening the gap between the quality of education for poor and minority youth and that of more privileged students" (p. 3).

The state is a key agency for the defense of extant relations of production. Hence, Marxists would point to the antiradicalizing effect of education through the smothering of creativity, imagination, and critical thought. By this is meant radical political creativity, imagination, and political thought. Rikowski (2001) suggests that the state needs to control the social production of labor power for two reasons. First, to try to ensure that the social production of labor power—equipping students with skills, competences—occurs. Second, to try to ensure that modes of pedagogy that are antithetical to labor-power production *do not and cannot exist*. In particular, it becomes clear, on this analysis, that the capitalist state will seek to destroy any forms of pedagogy *that attempt to educate students regarding their real predicament—to create an awareness of themselves as future labor powers and to underpin this awareness with critical insight that seeks to undermine the smooth running of the social production of labor power.* This fear entails strict control, for example, of the curriculum for teacher education and training, of schooling, and of educational research. Hill (2003, 2004, 2007) argues that neoliberal capital and governments stifle critical thought—by compressing and repressing critical space in education today, with capital and neoliberal ideology and policy seeking to neutralize and destroy potential pockets of resistance to global corporate expansion and neoliberal capital.

A historic example of this is the smothering and incorporation of independent working-class educational provision (such as in nineteenth-century Germany and Britain). National "homogenization" given over to "task-related knowledge" approaches of capitalized education systems (Kimbell and Perry, 2001; Maisuria, 2005) is a destructive, as well as in some respects constructive, process, because it creates robotic people less able to *think* beyond the scope of their function in society. Creativity, imagination, and critical thought are, of course, valued within education systems, but primarily insofar as they are constrained within a capitalist framework, focused on the development of relatively compliant human capital. A restrictive educational experience limits cognitive emancipation and empowerment by limiting human horizons to the requirements of capital.

Of course, there are some differences between capitalist countries. Social democratic countries have a low Gini coefficient—i.e., relatively lower levels of inequality resulting from decades of social democratic rule and reforms. This is exemplified by Sweden, a country with a large state, impressive welfarist policies, and nationalized public services. Sweden's levels of inequality has barely increased (from a relatively low baseline) according to the GINI coefficient index (Hopkin and Blyth, 2004). In addition, Sweden in the twenty-first century enjoys significantly more equality than the United Kingdom did thirty years ago (*ibid.*). However, whether social democratic, redistributionist governments will continue to limit the intrusion of capitalist interests into state provision, against the backdrop of increasingly globalized neoliberalism, remains to be seen. Where "the balance of class forces," the class struggle, is sufficiently strong—with millions pouring onto the streets in defense of their pensions, public utilities, and services, and labor rights, then neoliberal capital can be thwarted. And, with a rise in class consciousness nationally and globally, be replaced.

Choice and Inequality

In the United Kingdom, while in government from 1979 to 1997, the Conservatives established a competitive market for consumers (children and their parents) by setting up new types of schools in addition to the local (state, i.e., public) primary school or the local secondary comprehensive school.

Empirical evidence by Hoxby (2000, 2003a, 2003b) shows that the result of this "school choice" is that inequalities between schools increased because in many cases the "parental choice" of schools has become the "schools' choice" of the most desirable parents and children—and rejection of others. In the United Kingdom, parental social class and income is the most important factor affecting educational attainment (Galindo-Rueda and Vignoles, 2003).

Choice means that so-called "sink schools" have become more "sinklike" as more favored schools have picked the children they think are likely to be successful. Where selection exists the sink schools just sink further and the privileged schools just become more privileged (this is particularly pertinent in England and Wales, in the wake of the 2006 Education Bill by the New Labour government, which proposes to permit increased selection "by aptitude" in schools). The Association of Teachers and Lecturers lambastes marketization in education: "The trouble with choice is that those least able to choose find that, if the market rules, it tends to prioritise those customers which do not take up too much of its resources" (Bousted, 2006).

Teachers in these "ghetto schools for the underclass" are publicly pilloried, and, under New Labour the schools "named and shamed" as "Failing Schools," and, in some cases either reopened with a new "superhead" as a "Fresh Start School" (with dismissals of "failing" teachers), or shut down (see, for example, Hill, 1997; Whitty, Power and Halpin, 1998). Similar policies and effects are seen in the United States as a result of the No Child Left Behind legislation of the American congress (Hursh, 2003).

Hierarchical differentiation is the consequence of experiments with choice. This is so of the tripartite system in the United States—private, suburban, and urban schooling—and in Britain, with the tripartite system of private fee-paying schools, schools (such as Academies) opted out of Local Authority/school district control, and working-class local council and authority schools. Further differentiation is spurred on by the publication of various test results such as SATS.

Differentiation is being formally replicated in higher education (Machin and Vignoles, 2006). This is easily understood in the United States, where elite universities charge student fees many times those of lower-status universities. In the United States university fees are assessed on a need/income basis for each student, with many poor and needs-based students paying little or nothing for fees at institutions like Harvard or Yale. This has, however led to comments such as "in order to attend an expensive university, one has to be either very rich, or very poor." Overall, the correlation between size of fees and size of working-class attendance at universities in the United States is marked. In the United Kingdom, the turn-of-the-millennium differentiation between Oxbridge and the elite "Russell Group" of universities, the other "old" universities, the "new" (i.e., ex-Polytechnic) universities, and the institutes/colleges of higher education is formalized. It is widely expected that elitist universities will be permitted to charge higher fees. (Until 2006 all universities in Britain charged the same fees, indeed, until the late 1990s the government paid all fees for all citizens). Now there is the further development of a ("racialized") class-based hierarchicalization of university entry, essentially pricing the poor out of the system, or at least into the lower divisions of higher education.

Research by the Centre for Economics of Education at the London School of Economics found that "poorer students are [in 2006] more likely to go to higher education than they were in the past, [however] the likelihood of them doing so relative to their richer peers is actually lower than it was the case in earlier decades" (Machin & Vignoles, 2006, p.14).

Markets have exacerbated existing inequalities in education. There is considerable data, most notably by Whitty, Power, and Halpin (1998) and Machin and Vignoles (2006), on how poor schools have become poorer (in terms of relative education results, retention of students, and in terms of total income) and how elitist rich schools (in the same terms) have become richer through marketization in the United States, Sweden, England and Wales, Australia, and New Zealand.

In order to foresee the future, there is some worth in looking at diktats and structural readjustment programs of the World Bank, the International Monetary Fund, and other agencies of international capital, "often push highly controversial economic policy reforms on poor countries, like trade liberalization and privatisation of essential services" (Eurodad, 2006; see also Schugurensky and Davidson-Harden, 2003; Hill, 2005b; Hill et al. 2006; Rosskam, 2006; and Tomasevski, 2006a, 2006b). The 2006 Eurodad report continues,

Our research found that 18 out of the 20 poor countries we assessed had privatization related conditions attached to their development finance from the World Bank or IMF. And the number of "aggregate" privatisation-related conditions that the World Bank and IMF impose on developing countries has risen between 2002 and 2006. For many countries privatisation-related conditions make up a substantial part of their overall conditions from the World Bank and IMF. (p. 3)

Increasing the role of the private sector (including *for*-profit) organizations at primary, secondary, and tertiary levels creates unequal access to schooling based on social class, despite compensatory measures, such as subsidies, intended to limit the stratifying effects of capitalization. Private schools cherry-pick, or "cream off" the children of wealthier families who are more equipped to succeed at school, leaving the public school system to admit more challenging students with greater needs. Furthermore, state schools generally have fewer resources than private schools, and therefore need the "investments" from pupils from wealthier backgrounds to replenish books, furniture, and materials.

Ironically, but not unexpectedly, the World Bank's corporate lending arm, the International Finance Corporation (IFC) (2001), has claimed that fee-paying educational institutions can "improve" equity:

[p]rivate education can indirectly benefit the lowest socio-economic groups by attracting families who can afford some level of fee away from the public system, thereby increasing capacity and per student spending for the students who remain in the public system. Similarly, the emergence of private tertiary institutions allows governments to reduce funding in such institutions and instead to invest in lower levels of education, thus improving distributive efficiency. (p. 5)

The idea that the siphoning off "education investments" from wealthier pupils away from the public system actually increases equity is based on a highly contestable argument. Reimers (2000) notes that

[t]he poor have less access to preschool, secondary, and tertiary education; they also attend schools of lower quality where they are socially segregated. Poor parents have fewer resources to support the education of their children, and they have less financial, cultural, and social capital to transmit. Only policies that explicitly address inequality, with a major redistributive purpose, therefore, could make education an equalizing force in social opportunity. (p. 55)

Indeed, principles of universal access, for example, as enshrined in international covenants such as the United Nations Convention on Economic, Social and Cultural Rights, reflect a quite different notion of educational equity than that based on "choice" promoted by the World Bank and the IFC (Schugurensky and Davidson-Harden, 2003) and subscribed to by successive governments in the United States and Britain. The arguments about inequality in this section are succinctly articulated by a Council's Director of Education in the northeast of England:

> Everything is to be done to keep middle England happy, to give them their choice of school—so they don't have to pay for private schools—to guarantee them the places that other children ought to have and, worst of all, to give their schools the powers to keep out those other children they don't want their own children to mix with. (Mitchell, 2006)

CONCLUSION: HOW CAPITALISM (EXAGGERATED BY NEOLIBERALISM) INEVITABLY INCREASES EDUCATIONAL INEQUALITY

In Section 1, it was suggested that class should remain central to the leftist critique of capitalist education systems and that Karl Marx and subsequent Marxist thinkers possess the epistemic and explanatory upper hand over pluralist, Weberian, and deconstructionist (such as postmodernist) accounts of society.

Section 2 reinforced the theoretical claim that education is functional to capitalism in two essential ways. Firstly, education imposes division amongst children in preparation for the stratification of labor within the labor process. Suitably selected for tasks in production, the child is then educated and skilled to the level deemed suitable by capital for work. The child's individual needs are, despite the best will and effort of many teachers, deemed secondary to the needs of production by capital and the governments funded and supported by capital. Secondly, education conditions the child for a career of exploitation, inequality and differentials, conformity, and passivity. For the majority, education, despite the best will and efforts of many teachers, lowers expectation, and confines and fragments outlooks into myriad specialist skills that block the attainment of the bigger life picture. In short, education prepares and cultivates future workers to become both useful and productive and obedient and docile.

Section 2 located empirically the actual linkage between the capitalist economy and educational outcome by examining neoliberal policy, the role of the state, and the effect of the commodification of education by its increasing exposure to market ethics and practices. The evidence tended to support the Marxist claim that in capitalism a sector such as education is tightly controlled in the interests of capital, despite the resistant and counter-hegemonic efforts of students, teachers and communities.

Education is embedded in class relations and reflects, reinforces, and replicates the tendency of capital to produce and reproduce inequality.

Capital leads to capitalization of education, and the principal capitalist objective then is to accumulate value and surplus value in order to make profits. Capitalism is indifferent to the obvious inequalities, disadvantage, and discrimination it perpetuates, for it the end (profit making) justifies the means. The upshot is clear, then: in the long term and in macropolitical terms, capitalism does indeed lead to increasing education inequality.

In many countries, capitalism has been fairly successfully regulated, the Gini coefficient, depicting levels of inequality in the distribution of education in the labor force, diminished. But when the crunch of declining capital accumulation arrives, then capitalists do not abolish themselves. They turn to Nazism or Fascism, or to a permanent "war on terror," taking away rights of protest and dissent. Or, as in the United Kingdom, the party that was formerly the party of the working class, the Labour Party, that did, through most of the twentieth century, pursue social democratic policies along with procapitalist policies, has become transformed, under "New Labour," into another capitalist party, no longer even with a mass working class membership, adopting neoliberal policies that lead to greater inequalities.

The inequalities documented in this chapter can be eradicated. Working-class consciousness and class struggles can and do resist. This can be through resistance by parliamentary reformist means, for example, in the social democratic states of northwest Europe. These are not socialist, in the sense that socialism wishes to replace capitalism. Social democrats, however, wish to make capitalism more benign. Social democracy is a contradictory form of resistance to capital—or at least to its wider and wilder depredations—and educational inequalities. Social Democrats seek to advance workers' rights and to reduce inequality—but also to maintain capitalism. As Rosa Luxemburg (1899/1970) explained, the core aim of the revisionist left is the "bettering of the situation of the workers and . . . the conservation of the middle classes" (p. 60).

In contrast to social democracy, socialist forms of resistance to capitalism take either revolutionary means (as seen in Russia, Cuba, and China) or evolutionary means, such as through the parliamentary/democratic processes as witnessed in Nicaragua in the 1980s or Venezuela under Hugo Chavez. Both are responses to the increasing inequalities under capitalism. Both are responses to the choice offered by Rosa Luxemburg, the choice between (capitalist) barbarism on the one hand, or, on the other, socialism.

ACKNOWLEDGEMENT

We would like to thank Deborah Kelsh for her comments on this chapter.

REFERENCES

Allman, P. 1999. *Revolutionary social transformation: Democratic hopes, political possibilities and critical education.* Westport: Bergin & Garvey.
———. 2001. *Critical education against global capitalism: Karl Marx and revolutionary critical education.* Westport: Bergin & Garvey.
Althusser, L. 1971. Ideology and ideological state apparatuses: Notes towards an investigation. In *Lenin and philosophy and other essays*, 127–86. New York: Monthly Review Press.
Apple, M. 2001. *Educating the 'right' way: Markets, standards, God, and inequality.* New York and London: Routledge/Falmer.
Apple, M. 2005. Audit cultures, commodification, and class and race strategies in education. Policy Futures in Education 3, no. 4: 379–399. http://www.wwwords.co.uk/pdf/viewpdf.asp?j=pfie&vol=3&issue=4&year=2005&article=6_Apple_PFIE_3_4_web&id=86.140.234.166
Apple, M. 2006. Review Essay: Rhetoric and reality in critical educational studies in the United States, *British Journal of Sociology of Education* 27(5): 679–687. November.
Borg, C., J. Buttigieg, and P. Mayo, eds. 2002. *Gramsci and education.* Lanham, MD: Rowman & Littlefield.
Bousted, M. 2006. Education reforms will condemn millions of children to "ghetto schools," warns ATL's general secretary. Association of Teachers and Lecturers. https://www.atl.org.uk/atl_en/news/conferences/ATL_2006/reports/mary_bousted.asp.
Bowles, S., and H. Gintis. 1972. IQ and the social class system. *Social Policy* 3, no. 4.
———. 1976. *Schooling in capitalist America: Educational reform and the contradictions of economic life.* New York: Basic Books.
———. 1988. Schooling in capitalist America: Reply to our critics. In *Bowles and Gintis revisited: Correspondence and contradiction in educational theory*, ed. M. Cole. London: Falmer Press.
Brennan, T. 2003. *Globalization and its terrors.* London: Routledge.
Brosio, R. 1994. *A radical democratic critique of capitalist education.* New York: Peter Lang.
———. 2000. *Philosophical scaffolding for the construction of critical democratic education.* New York: Peter Lang.
Cuneo, C. J. 1982. Class struggle and measurement of the rate of surplus value. *Canadian Review of Sociology and Anthropology* 19, no. 3: 377–426.
Dumenil, G., and D. Levy. 2004. *Capital resurgent: Roots of the neoliberal revolution.* London: Harvard University Press.
Ebert, T. 1996. *Ludic feminism and after: Postmodernism, desire, and labor in late capitalism.* Ann Arbor: The University of Michigan Press.
Ebert, T., and M. Masazavardeh. 2007. *Class in Culture.* Boulder, Colorado: Paradigm Publishers.
Ebert, T. and Zavarzadeh, M. 2007. Daily lessons on Class. *The Red Critique: Marxist Theory and Critique of the Contemporary*, 12. Online at http://www.redcritique.org/WinterSpring2007/dailylessonsonclass.htm.
Engels, F. 1890/1987. Letter to Bloch. In *Reader in Marxist philosophy.* eds. H. Selsam & H. Martel, 204–206. New York: International Publishers.
Eurodad. 2006. World Bank and IMF conditionality: A development injustice. http://www.eurodad.org/uploadstore/cms/docs/Eurodad_World_Bank_and_IMF_Conditionality_ReportFinal.pdf.
Farahmandpur, R. 2004. Essay review: A Marxist critique of Michael Apple's neo-Marxist approach to educational reform. Journal of Critical Education Policy Studies 2, no.1. http://www.jceps.com/index.php?pageID=article&articleID=24
Freire, P. 1998. *Teachers as cultural workers.* Boulder, CO: Westview Press.

Galindo-Rueda, F., and A. Vignoles. 2003. *Class ridden or meritocratic?* London: London School of Economics, Centre for the Economics of Education.

Gillborn, D., and H. Mirza. 2000. *Educational inequality; Mapping race, class and gender: A synthesis of research evidence.* London: Ofsted.

Gimenez, M. 2001. Marxism and class, gender and race: Rethinking the trilogy. *Race, Gender & Class* 8, no. 2: 23–33.

Giroux, H. 1983a. Theories of reproduction and resistance in the new sociology of education: A critical analysis. *Harvard Education Review* 55, no. 3: 257–93.

Giroux, H. 1983b. *Theory and resistance in education: A pedagogy for the opposition.* London: Heinemann.

Giroux, H. 1988. *Teachers as intellectuals: Toward a critical pedagogy of learning.* Granby, MA: Bergin and Garvey.

Giroux, H. & P. McLaren. 1986. Teacher education and the politics of engagement: The case for democratic schooling. *Harvard Education Review,* 56 no. 3, 213–238.

Giroux, H. & P. McLaren. 1989. *Critical pedagogy, the state and cultural struggle.* New York: State University of New York Press.

Global Policy Forum. 2006. Inequality of wealth and income distribution. http://www.globalpolicy.org/socecon/inequal/indexinq.htm.

Glyn, A. 2006. Marx's reserve army of labour is about to go global. *The Guardian.* April 5. London.

Gramsci, A. 1971. *Selections from the prison notebooks,* ed. and trans. Q. Hoare and G. N. Smith. London: Lawrence & Wishart.

Greaves, N. M. 2005. In search of the "real Gramsci": A historicist reappraisal of a Marxist revolutionary. Unpublished doctoral dissertation, University of Northampton, UK.

Harris, K. 1979. *Education and knowledge* London: Routledge & Kegan Paul.

Harris, K. 1982. *Teachers and Classes: A Marxist Analysis.* London: Routledge and Kegan Paul.

Harris, K. 1984. Two contrasting theories. *Education With Production,* 3 no. 1, 13–33.

Harris, K. 1994. *Teachers: Constructing the future.* London: Falmer Press.

Harvey, D. 2005. *A brief history of neoliberalism.* Oxford, England: Oxford University Press.

Hickey, T. 2006. Social class. In *Education, equality and human rights,* 2nd ed., ed. M. Cole. London: Routledge Falmer.

Hill, D. 1989. *Charge of the right brigade: The radical right's assault on teacher education.* Brighton: Institute for Education Policy Studies. http://www.ieps.org.uk.cwc.net/hill1989.pdf

———. 1993. Review of Post-modern education: Politics, culture, and social criticism, by S Aronowitz and H. Giroux. *Journal of Education Policy* 8(1): 97–99 (1991). Minneapolis: University of Minnesota Press.

———. 1997. Equality and primary schooling: The policy context intentions and effects of the conservative "reforms." In *Equality and the national curriculum in primary,* ed. M. Cole, D. Hill, and S. Shan. London: Cassell.

———. 1999. Social class and education. In *An introduction to the study of education,* ed. D. Matheson and I. Grosvenor. London: David Fulton.

———. 2001. State theory and the neo-liberal reconstruction of schooling and teacher education: A structuralist neo-Marxist critique of postmodernist, quasi-postmodernist, and culturalist neo-Marxist theory. *The British Journal of Sociology of Education* 22, no. 1: 137–57.

———. 2003. Global neo-liberalism, the deformation of education and resistance. *Journal for Critical Education Policy Studies* 1, no. 1. http://www.jceps.com/index.php?pageID=article&articleID=7.

————. 2004. Books, banks and bullets: Controlling our minds: The global project of imperialistic and militaristic neo-liberalism and its effect on education policy. *Policy Futures* 2, nos. 3–4. http://www.wwwords.co.uk/pfi e/content/pdfs/2/issue2_3.asp.

————. 2005a. State theory and the neoliberal reconstruction of schooling and teacher education. In *Critical theories, radical pedagogies and global conflicts*, ed. G. Fischman, P. McLaren, H. Sünker, and C. Lankshear. Boulder, CO: Rowman and Littlefield.

————. 2005b. Globalisation and its educational discontents: Neoliberalisation and its impacts on education workers' rights, pay, and conditions. *International Studies in the Sociology of Education* 15, no. 3: 257–88.

————. 2006. New Labour's education policy. In *Education studies: Issues and critical perspectives*, ed. D. Kassem, E. Mufti, and J. Robinson. Buckingham: Open University Press.

————. 2006a. Class, Neoliberal Global Capital, Education and Resistance. *Social Change* 36, no. 3: 47–76. New Delhi, India: The Council for Social Development.

————. 2006b. Class, capital and education in this neoliberal/ neoconservative period. *Information for Social Change*, 23. http://libr.org/isc/issues/ISC23/B1%20 Dave%20Hill.pdf.

————. 2007. Critical teacher education, New Labour, and the global project of neo-liberal capital. *Policy Futures* 5, no. 2. http://www.wwwords.co.uk/pfi e/content/ pdfs/5/issue5_2.asp.

———— . 2008a. 'Race', class and neoliberal capital in urban contexts: Resistance and egalitarian education. In *an international examination of urban education: The destructive path of neoliberalism*, eds. C. Mallot and B. Porfilio. Rotterdam, Netherlands: Sense Publishers.

————. 2008b. Education, class and capital in the epoch of neo-liberal globalisation. In *marxism and education: renewing dialogues: Volume 1—opening the dialogue*, eds. A. Green and G. Rikowski. London: Palgrave Macmillan.

Hill, D., K. Anijar-Appleton, A. Davidson-Harden, B. Fawcett, D. Gabbard, J. Gindin, L. Kuehn, C. Lewis, A. Mukhtar, R. Pardinaz-Solis, B. Quiros, D.Schugurensky, H. Smaller, and B. Templer. 2006. Education services liberalization. In *Winners or losers? Liberalizing public services*, ed. E. Rosskam. Geneva: International Labour Organisation.

Hill, D., and M. Cole. 2001. Social class. In *Schooling and equality: Fact, concept and policy*, eds. D. Hill and M. Cole. London: Kogan Page.

Hill, D., P. McLaren, M. Cole, and G. Rikowski. 2002. *Marxism against postmodernism in educational theory*. Lanham, MD: Lexington Books.

Hill, D., M. Sanders, and T. Hankin. 2002. Marxism, class analysis and postmodernism. In *Marxism Against Postmodernism in Education Theory*, ed. D. Hill, P. McLaren, M. Cole, and G. Rikowski, 159–94. Lanham, MD: Lexington Books.

Hirtt, N. 2004. Three axes of merchandisation. *European Educational Research Journal* 3, no. 2: 442–53. http://www.wwwords.co.uk/eerj/.

Hopkin, M., and J. Blyth. 2004. Worlds of welfare, hybrid systems, and political choice: Do welfare regimes constrain anti-inequality programmes? How many varieties of capitalism? Paper presented at the annual meeting of the American Political Science Association.

Hoxby, C. 2000. Does competition among public schools benefit students and taxpayers? *American Economic Review* 90: 1209–38.

————. 2003a. *The economics of school choice*. Chicago: University of Chicago Press.

————. 2003b. School choice and school competition: Evidence from the United States. *Swedish Economic Policy Review* 10: 9–66.

Hursh, D. 2002. Neoliberalism and the control of teachers, students, and learning: The rise of standards, standardization, and accountability. *Cultural Logic* 4, no. 1. http://www.eserver.org/clogic/4–1/hursh.html.

Hursh, D., and C. Martina. 2003. *Neoliberalism and schooling in the U.S: How state and federal government education policies perpetuate inequality.* http://www. jceps.com/index.php?pageID=article&articleID=12.

International Finance Corporation. 2001. IFC and education. Washington, D.C.: International Finance Corporation. http://www.ifc.org/ar2001briefs/IFC_and_Education.pdf.

Johnson, P. and F. Lynch. 2004. Sponging off the poor. *The Guardian.* March 10. London. http://www.guardian.co.uk/analysis/story/0,3604,1165918,00.html.

Kelsh, D. (1998) Desire and Class: The Knowledge Industry in the Wake of Poststructuralism. Cultural Logic-an electronic journal of Marxist Theory and Practice, 1 (2). Online at http://clogic.eserver.org/1-2/kelsh.html.

Kelsh, D., and D. Hill. 2006. The culturalization of class and the occluding of class consciousness: The knowledge industry in/of education. *Journal for Critical Education Policy Studies* 4, no 1.

Kelsh, D., Hill, D. and Macrine, S. (eds.) (2009) *Teaching Class: Knowledge, Pedagogy, Subjectivity.* London: Routledge.

Kimbell, R., and D. Perry. 2001. *Design and technology in a knowledge economy.* London: Engineering Council.

Kumar, R. 2006. State, class and critical framework of praxis: The missing link in Indian educational debates. *Journal of Critical Education Policy Studies* 4, no. 2. http://www.jceps.com/index.php?pageID=article&articleID=68.

———. 2008. Against neoliberal assault on education in India: a counternarrative of resistance. *Journal of Critical Education Policy Studies* 6, no. 1. http://www.jceps. com/index.php?pageID=article&articleID=112.

Laclau, E. 1996. Deconstruction, pragmatism, hegemony. In *Deconstruction and pragmatism*, ed. C. Mouffe, 47–67. London: Routledge.

Laclau, E., and C. Mouffe. 1985. *Hegemony and socialist strategy.* London: NLB.

Luxemburg, R. 1899/1970. *Reform or revolution: Rosa Luxemburg speaks.* New York: Pathfinder.

Machin, S., and A. Vignoles. 2006. *Education policy in the U.K.* London: London School of Economics, Centre for the Economics of Education.

Maisuria, A. 2005. The turbulent times of creativity in the national curriculum. *Policy Futures in Education* 3, no. 2. http://www.wwwords.co.uk/pdf/viewpdf.asp?j=pfie&vol=3&issue=2&year=2005&article=3_Maisuria_PFIE_3_2_web&id=86.132.99.96.

Marshall, G. 1990. *In praise of sociology.* London: Unwin Hyman.

Marx, K. 1867/1977. *Capital: A critique of political economy.* Vol. 1. London: Lawrence & Wishart.

———.1932/1968. The German Ideology. Marxist Internet Archive, May 7. http:// www.marxists.org/archive/marx/works/1845/german-ideology/index.htm.

———. 1933. *Wage-labour and capital.* New York: International Publishers.

———. 1977. *Selected writings.* Ed. D. McLellan. Oxford: Oxford University Press.

Marx, K., and F. Engels. 1985. *The communist manifesto.* New York: Penguin Books.

McLaren, P. 2000. *Che Guevara, Paulo Freire, and the pedagogy of revolution.* Lanham MD: Rowman & Littlefield.

———. 2005a. *Capitalists and conquerors: Critical pedagogy against empire.* Lanham, MD: Rowman & Littlefield.

———. 2005b. *Red seminars: Radical excursions into educational theory, cultural politics and pedagogy.* Cresskill, NJ: Hampton Press.

McLaren, P., and R. Farahmandpur. 2005. *Teaching against global capitalism and the new imperialism: A critical pedagogy.* Lanham, MD: Rowman & Littlefield.

McLaren, P., and V. Scatamburlo d'Annibale. 2004. Class dismissed? Historical materialism and the politics of "difference." *Educational Philosophy and Theory* 36, no. 2: 183–99.

McNeil, L. 2000. *Contradictions of school reform: Educational costs of standardized testing*. New York: Routledge.

Michell, K. 2006. School chief predicts end of state education. *Education Guardian*. April 10. http://politics.guardian.co.uk/publicservices/story/0,,1750886,00.html.

Neary, M. 1997. *Youth, training and the training state*. Basingstoke: Macmillan.

Ollman, B. 2001. *How to take and exam . . . and remake the world*. Montreal: Black Rose Books.

Pakulski, J., and M. Waters. 1996. *The death of class*. London: Sage.

Paraskeva, J. 2006. Continuities, discontinuities and silences: A Marxist literary reading of Michael Apple's lines of thought. Paper delivered at the American Educational Research Association Annual Meeting, San Francisco. Also forthcoming in the *Journal for Critical Education Policy Studies* 4, no. 2.

Reimers, F. 2000. *Unequal schools, unequal chances: The challenges to equal opportunity in the America*. Cambridge, MA: Harvard University Press.

Rikowski, G. 2001. *After the manuscript broke off: Thoughts on Marx, social class and education*. http://www.leeds.ac.uk/educol/documents/00001931.htm.

———. 2002. *Globalisation and education*. Paper prepared for the House of Lords Select Committee on Economic Affairs, Report on "Globalisation," HL Paper 5–1, November 18 (on House of Lords CD-ROM). http://education.portal.dk3.com/article.php?sid=21 and at www.ieps.org.uk.

———. 2003. Schools and the GATS enigma. *Journal for Critical Education Policy Studies* 1, no. 1.

———. 2005. Silence on the wolves: What is absent in New Labour's five year strategy for education. Occasional paper. University of Brighton Education Research Centre.

———. 2008. Schools and the GATS Enigma. *Firgoa*. Universidade Publica. Online at http://firgoa.usc.es/drupal/node/4249.

Rikowski, R. 2002. *The WTO/GATS agenda for libraries*. http://www.ieps.org.uk.cwc.net/rikowski2002a.pdf.

Rose, R., ed. 1960. *Must labour lose?* Harmondsworth: Penguin.

Rosskam, E., ed. 2006. *Winners or losers? Liberalizing public services*. Geneva: International Labour Organisation.

Saltman, K. 2005. *The Edison schools: Corporate schooling and the assault on public education*. London: Routledge Falmer.

Saltman, K., and D. Gabbard. 2003. *Education as enforcement: The militarization and corporatization of schools*. London: Routledge Falmer.

Sarup, M. 1978. *Marxism and education*. London: Routledge & Kegan Paul.

Sarup, M. 1984. *Marxism/structuralism/education*. London: Falmer Press.

Schugurensky, D., and A. Davidson-Harden. 2003. From Cordoba to Washington: WTO/GATS and Latin American education. *Globalisation, Societies and Education* 1, no. 3: 321–57.

Shor, I. 1992. *Empowering education: Critical teaching for social change*. Chicago: University of Chicago Press.

Shor, I., & P. Freire, P. 1987. *A pedagogy for liberation: Dialogues on transforming education*. South Hadley, MA: Bergin & Garvey.

Strass, G., and B. Hansen. 2006. CEO pay soars in 2005 as select group break the $100 mark. *USA Today*, April 11.

Tomasevski, K. 2006a. *Six reasons why the World Bank should be debarred from education*. http://www.brettonwoodsproject.org/art.shtml?x=542516.

———. 2006b. Both arsonist and fire-fighter: the World Bank on school fees. http://www.brettonwoodsproject.org/art.shtml?x=507705.

Toynbee, P. 2003. *Hard work: Life in low paid Britain*. London: Bloomsbury.

Whitty, G., S. Power, and D. Halpin. 1998. *Devolution and choice in education: The school, the state and the market*. Buckingham, UK: Open University Press.

Willis, P. 1977. *Learning to labour: How working class kids get working class jobs*. Farnborough: Saxon House.

7 Brazilian Education, Dependent Capitalism, and the World Bank

Roberto Leher

INTRODUCTION

Since the 1982 World Debt Crisis[1] a quarter of a century has passed, and it can be stated that this crisis is still one of the most important political markers in twentieth-century Latin America. The dramatic events of the subsequent years have provoked transformations in all spheres and dimensions. The composition of the dominant classes that led the managerial-military dictatorships in much of Latin America—represented by the national industrial bourgeoisie, state companies, and multinational corporations—has been profoundly modified, comprising a new power bloc consisting of multinational corporations, financial capital, and various sectors related to agribusiness, mineral exploration, and commodities exports. In retrospect, it can be stated that the dominant coalition of Latin American countries has made the Washington Consensus agenda its own (Williamson, 1990; Dezalay and Garth, 1998), so that it is almost impossible to distinguish between the policies of the Bretton Woods institutions[2] from those led by local dominant factions, and vice versa.

In the 1990s the United States, reorganized for a new cycle of expansion, established a new project for Latin America's introduction into the world economy in the form of a group of policies called the Washington Consensus. At this time, the World Bank (WB) and International Monetary Fund (IMF) assumed new goals to establish general macroeconomic and social policies. Never, until then, had these organizations had so much influence. In fact, the 1982 Debt Crisis was only negotiated with the international board because these organizations were disposed to concede guarantees to those countries that were willing to make "courageous structural reforms"—today characterized as the Washington Consensus. In brief, the specific set of economic policy recommendations included fiscal discipline; redirection of public expenditure priorities toward fields offering both high economic returns and the potential to improve income distribution (such as primary health care, primary education, and infrastructure); tax reform; competitive exchange rates; liberalization of inflows of foreign direct investment; privatization; deregulation (to abolish entry and exit barriers); and secure property rights. In all Latin American countries the Consensus's agenda has included flexible labor laws and weakened unions. Without these prescriptions, country risk (measured by financial institutions!) could be increased and drive away foreign investors. Structural adjustments have changed Latin American macroeconomic architecture. Protectionism has been dissolved in favor of commercial and financial liberalization, producing severe national crises including those in Mexico (1995), Brazil (1999), and Argentina (2001).

The largest contrast between the accumulation pattern in the years 1930–1970 and the current pattern of accumulation by dispossession[3] (Harvey, 2005) is due to the question of what place Latin America should occupy in the world economy according to the dominant power bloc. Formerly, the Economic Commission for Latin America and the Caribbean (ECLAC) and every critical debate over modernization theories declared that import substitution industrialization[4] would force the consolidation of Newly Industrialized Countries, among them Argentina, Brazil, and Mexico.[5] Nowadays, international organs, finance agencies, important local bourgeois factions, and the governments that represent them have converged in evaluating that the goals of the Bandung Conference[6] belong to an impossible past.

Those different expectations have a direct impact on the area of education. The industrialization process and the constitution of state companies characteristic of the post–World-War-II period demanded highly qualified personnel and, for that, required public universities with research development, but which were not critical of conservative modernization.[7] Nowadays, dominant sectors have no expectations concerning the strategic character of public universities. The reprimarization (Arceo and Basualdo, 2006) and spread of maquilas (low-skill, low technology factory) industries makes even technology and technological innovation of little relevance, contrary to common sense, confirming Florestan Fernandes' necessary diagnosis (1974) that the worsening of capitalism's dependent condition would still increase cultural heteronomy.

In fact, the World Bank's structural adjustment policies contributed to deepening educational, scientific, and technological apartheid. One of the indicators used for international comparisons is the percentage of scientists and engineers in the economically active population and the investments made with science, technology, and research and development (R&D). Developing, or peripheral, countries now have three-fourths of the world's population but only 10 percent of the world's engineers and scientists: 7 percent in Asia, 1.8 percent in Latin America, 0.9 percent in Arab countries and 0.3 percent in Africa. Also, those countries have only 3 percent of the world's computers and they invest over US$3 billion in R&D. Central countries, with one-quarter of the world's population, have 90 percent of the world's scientists and engineers: 90 percent in the United States, the European Union, and Japan, and they invest approximately US$220 billion in R&D every year. It is important to register that this amount does not include academic research financed with its own university budgets or with public budgets (Leher, 2005).

In this way, the gulf that separates central and peripheral countries is getting wider. The demand for high-technology manufactured products is increasing at a rate of 15 percent per year, while demand for low-technology manufactures is increasing 5 percent per year and the demand for raw materials is increasing only 2.5 percent (Leher, 2005).

Countries that have achieved relative success in industrialization and have an apparatus for science and technology, like Brazil, India, and Mexico, suffer intense pressure from the World Bank, which considers that investments in these areas are not appropriate to the way these countries should be integrated into the world economy. The World Bank's study on economic returns on educational expenses, based on human capital theory, could not be more convenient for central countries. In the case of Latin America, Africa, and South Asia, the best economic returns should come from basic education (World Bank, 1995a). Free higher education based on a Humboldtian European model was considered not pertinent to Latin America's reality (World Bank, 1995b) because the offer of free education means, in this case, "subsidizing the wrong people," and research is seen as an unacceptable luxury. As Nobel prize winner Gary Becker said, original knowledge is not produced in those areas.

Latin America was repositioned in the world economy so that the European university model—based on a Humboltian tradition (public, free, with unity between teaching and research and self government)—was no longer a goal, and was turned into an obstacle to the modernization of higher education.[8] In terms of dominant ideology, university was not congruent to the so-called scientific-technological revolution that would be driving the "globalization". The alternative, according to that system of thought, is to reduce the university's relations with the state and to aim at a larger opening towards society or, according to Bourdieu and Wacquant (2001), towards the market.

Many Latin American countries have instituted constitutional reforms restricting the human right to education, including Argentina, Brazil, Chile, and Mexico. In the Mexican case, the modification of the 3rd Article of the Constitution (1993) and the new Educational Law (1994) redefined the right to education and the state's duty in providing it to all citizens, in favor of a new conceptualization that views education as a service to be negotiated in the market. In Brazil, the concept that education is a service is expressed in the master plan of the State Reform, initiated in the government of Fernando Henrique Cardoso (1995–2002) and further developed in that of Luiz Inácio Lula da Silva (2003–present) with a public-private partnership (PPP) that extols the greater effectiveness of the private sector concerning popular educational attendance. The absence of free education for postgraduate courses in Argentina, as well as the end of free education in Chilean public institutions, are all expressions of neoliberal policies.

Brazilian and Latin American universities have been altered in all areas, from teaching to research, from financing to evaluation, from curriculum matters to academic careers. The boundary between public and private has shifted with respect to educational offerings and to daily institutional events: public spaces where national problems could be discussed have been invaded by the private sphere, restricting the public to a few niches, many of which are of high academic quality but which lack resources and adequate infrastructure for their level of development.

These changes amount to the abandonment of national problems and the redefining of the form of research, teaching and investigation through the diffusion of the "myth of the method" so important to the neopositivist tradition.

Under neoliberal hegemony, the matter of access to higher education has become more dramatic than in 1968, the year of major student demonstrations. At the turn of the twenty-first century a dizzying increase in secondary education enrollment has occurred in several countries in Latin America, in a context of stagnating public higher education expansion. Paradoxically, however, youth's current struggles are not so massive as they were at the end of the 1960s, in spite of the new mobilization of youth in Chile, for instance, with the "revolt of the penguins" in 2006. Among the factors that explain in part this reduced activism, are the absorption of middle-class youth by private institutions and the creation of private vacancies for lower classes by the state.

A subtle game of words conceals the modern opposition between public and private, through the extending of public subsidies to private institutions and through their redesignation as institutions that contribute to the public interest. This argument is based on the premise that education is a "public good," defined as all that contributes to public interest, irrespective of whether the nature of the institution is public or private. Public interest is measured by scientific methods of standardized evaluation. In that sense, all institutions that have a certain evaluation pattern contribute to public interest and, therefore, deserve public funding. With the spread of public-private partnerships new concessions of public resources—many of them with tributary exemptions—have increased government support for considering higher education to be an enterprise, popularizing the idea that since there is no possibility of significantly expanding public universities, "democratization" should be accomplished by the acquisition of vacancies in private institutions, even if they are (and often they are) of very low quality.[9] Those programs are addressed to the poor who, in the government's point of view, don't need an academic education but a technical education. With these partnerships entrepreneurs no longer need to hide in an aura of philanthropy; they can act entrepreneurially as providers of services. Therefore, the privatized segment is the one increasingly growing in Latin American education.

The expansion of the private sector in Latin America has been constant, starting with the 1982 Crisis. In 1960, 15 percent of institutions were private; in 1985, 46 percent; in 1995, 54 percent; and in 2002, 65 percent, corresponding to more than a half of student enrollments,[10] The Brazilian case is still more serious: in 2005, 88 percent of all institutions were private and 75 percent of enrollments were in private institutions. Of a total of two thousand private institutions, 1520 are privatized institutions.

This boom is due to the enormous market for "educational" services and has been stimulated by the victories of capital in Uruguay's Round/ General Agreement on Tariffs and Trade (GATT),[11] expressed in the creation of World Trade Organization (WTO) and in the definition of the General Agreement of Trade of Services (GATS). The liberalization of educational services is part of the international organ's agenda, not just in the WTO, but also in free trade agreements such as Free Trade Area of the Americas (FTAA), the North American Free Trade Agreement (NAFTA), and the Dominican Republic–Central America Free Trade Agreement (CAFTA), among others. The terms of the agenda stipulate that peripheral countries must open their markets in strategic areas (services, investments, intellectual property, and industrial products), and that central countries will reduce the exchange rate, among other things, to extend peripheral countries' access to agribusiness products and major export commodities. Capital seems to prefer to operate through a kind of "guerrilla" campaign of national commercial agreements, bilateral or multilateral, due to the complexity of compensations offered by generic Free Trade Agreement (FTAs) such as NAFTA or GATT/WTO.

One of the managerial strategies that is becoming pre-eminent is the one that makes possible transnational trade in "educational" services. In Brazil, just to mention an example, big multinational educational companies (Laureate, Fenix/Apollo) have made joint ventures with national institutions aiming to offer postgraduate distance courses. The biggest obstacle that the managerial strategy has had has been the requirement for accreditation, which had always been granted by public universities. To remove that obstacle the federal government amended the rules to allow all undergraduate and postgraduate courses *stricto sensu* to offer distance education courses, including, in addition, master's- and doctoral-level "professional" (i.e., nonthesis) courses.[12] The same project also allows private institutions to recognize and accredit distance education courses offered by foreign companies. Thus, for instance, the Apollo Institute and its world branches can sell distance education courses and they will be accredited by an associated Brazilian company (in this case, the Pitágoras Institute). It is possible, then, to conduct transnational trade without the need to regulate the complex compensations of a free trade agreement. The opening of the market is unilateral.

Resistance to the neoliberal agenda was marked in the 1980s, but the 1990s saw a retrenchment in the struggle due to high unemployment and a precarious labor market, which weakened labor unions. After the election of president Lula da Silva in 2002, even the Central Única dos Trabalhadores (CUT)[13] started to defend private-owned education as a priority.

The struggles have continued, but have been weak. Only since 2006 have new alliances been established among social movements in the countryside and in the cities, unions and parties on the left, making possible a new starting point for the battle to defend public education. As there are no local dominant factions interested in the universalization of quality public education at all levels, the accomplishment of that task will be the workers' legacy. Educators are integrating their efforts with social movements and the agendas of autonomous union movements mobilized in battling the system. Thus, a present challenge is to understand and interact with the experiences of social movements that seek self-education as part of their political strategy (Leher and Setúbal, 2005).

It is in this direction that extraordinary initiatives are being carried out all over Latin America. The Movimento dos Trabalhadores Rurais Sem Terra (MST)[14] created the germ of the first popular Brazilian university, the National School Florestan Fernandes, which offers several degree programs in political education along with several other Brazilian public universities. In Ecuador, indigenous people have created the Intercultural University of Indigenous People, which liases with almost three thousand schools; the Zapatistas have created "committees for good government" which allow self-education in dialog with academic knowledge; Cuba is determined to universalize higher education for all the people, through municipalization. These experiences can create entirely new conditions so that public education can be revolutionized in Latin America.

However, the alliance between educators and several sectors of the working class will have to face hegemonic policies that are being implemented, unifying dominant sectors and part of the forces that formerly combated neoliberal policies that nowadays are the operators of those same policies. In terms of the method of the study, it is important to investigate the policies of international organizations *vis-à-vis* those of local dominant sectors: without knowing how the control domination is carried out, it is impossible to establish clear and objective antisystem strategies that allow overcoming dependent capitalism.

INTERNATIONAL ORGANS AND NATIONAL POWER BLOCS

The decisive role of the Bretton Woods institutions in implementing the framework of the Washington Consensus—which is devastating the economy of the peripheral countries[15]—is a fact that is now hardly questioned, since the contradictions of the structural crisis of capitalism no longer allow these activities to remain hidden. The surprising fact is that those same governments that were elected with the promise of bringing profound changes to neoliberal policies maintain not only the neoliberal agenda, but also the guidelines and recommendations of the IMF and the World Bank. As emphasized previously, the priorities of the coalition of classes in the government and the agenda of those organizations almost always get confused, attesting to the growing internationalization of local bourgeois factions and the the forces of neoliberal hegemony in society as a whole (Anderson, 2004).

Luís Inácio Lula da Silva, Brazilian president (2003–2006 and 2007–present) is an illustrative case (Gonçalves, 2003; Leher, 2003a; Paulani, 2003). Elected in opposition to the neoliberal government of Fernando Henrique Cardoso (1995–2002), he signed a new agreement with the IMF, incorporating their "conditionalities"[16] for structural adjustments in his government's plans: these include maintenance of the primary surplus (equivalent to 4.25 percent of gross domestic product) throughout his period in office; an extremely elevated tax rate, the highest in the world, elevating the debt expenses to the point of allocating 36.7 percent of the federal government's General Budget (2006) for debt payment;[17] and social welfare reforms in the public sector based on a regime of capitalization. No less disconcerting, Lula da Silva asked the World Bank for advice on Brazilian university reform, in spite of its well-known anti-university position and its favoring of monthly fees for students (Leher, 2003b). He is determined to implement a broad economic plan that promotes reprimarization (i.e. a transition in the national economy towards agribusiness and minerals) of the country and export of natural resources, known as the Growth Acceleration Program.

The significance of the influence of these bodies on the configuration of peripheral countries' education has provoked divergent readings. This chapter argues that the redefinition of educational systems is at the center of the structural reforms proposed by the World Bank, and is intimately related to issues of governance-security. In a context of profound structural crisis and, consequently, the escalation of social anticapitalist actions and the crisis of the dominant power bloc, the sectors that have assumed leadership of the dominant classes, in particular the finance sector and commodities export sector, have placed at the top of their political priorities maintaining the order of capital and, because of that, governance is crucial. This preoccupation, as will be seen, guides the action of the World Bank which, verifying the ruinous effects of structural adjustment policies in most of the world, affirms that the "relief of poverty" must be an urgent task of peripheral countries' governments faced with the risk of the return of nationalist and socialist policies. It is in this context that education becomes a priority. Marx's observation, in *Capital*, takes on a worrying relevance: "the more a dominant class is able to receive in its ranks the most valuable men from the dominated classes, the more solid and dangerous is its domain" (Marx, 1985, p. 112).

Not accidentally, the dominant sectors, especially the financial sector and agribusiness, resolutely supported the election of Lula da Silva convinced that, in a crisis situation, a government coming from the opposition could better carry out the Washington Consensus agenda. Social welfare reforms affecting pension funds in public service (part of Brazil's Agreement with the IMF since 1998) had not previously been successful, due to the resistance of the unions and the *Partido dos Trabalhadores* (PT; Workers' Party). Lula da Silva, however, introduced a proposal even more restrictive of social rights than had Cardoso, and in just seven months achieved its approval in parliament (Leher, 2003a).

The assimilation of the agendas of the IMF and World Bank agenda by Lula da Silva's government has been raising intense internal debate in the PT, and, as a result, there were parliamentarians' expulsions, accusations of corruption, removal of almost all of the national direction board of PT due to those accusations and the weakness of political and ideological discussion, motivated by the government's independence from the party (Leher, 2003a), a process that has been increased in the second mandate, initiated in 2007. The unions are also divided about what to do in the face of neoliberal orthodoxy. The majority sectors of (CUT) maintain that it is necessary to support the IMF reforms; however, several unions have cancelled their memberhip in CUT and formed INTERSINDICAL and CONLUTAS,[18] today important protagonists in the fight against neoliberalism.

EDUCATION AS IDEOLOGY

The specific character of the ideologies that guide education reform becomes clearer when we examine how these ideologies are carried out in institutional practice. To comprehend the ideologies throwing education into disarray in Latin America, Africa, and parts of Asia, it is necessary to examine the World Bank's orientations, since the World Bank is, in effect, the world education ministry for peripheral countries.

To understand the institution and the reforms that it imposes, it is necessary to consider the relation between education and security doctrines. Unfortunately, with the childish belief in the end of ideologies, this connection is considered increasingly rare in educational debates. Research on educational agreements between Brazil and the United States, and on the actions of the World Bank and the United Nations Educational, Scientific and Cultural Organization (UNESCO) (Archibald, 1993), makes it evident how security remains a constant preoccupation. This concern is at the very core of the Alliance for Progress doctrine of Kennedy, Johnson, and Bristow, as well as at the heart of the ideology of globalization (Hirst and Thompson, 1998), as defined by the World Bank and by the theoreticians of the knowledge society (Mattelart, 2002). By considering only the instrumental dimension of education (the required abilities and qualifications) in relation to the dynamics of capital, critical thought does not break through the frontiers of "economicism," contributing to hypertrophy the belief in technological determinism, with significantly demobilizing consequences (Holloway and Peláez, 1998).

The thesis that education could be an important instrument for security is present in Washington doctrine since the Cold War, especially in the formulation of the counterinsurgency doctrine. Instead of the traditional concentration of forces and armaments to advance against identified enemy lines, this doctrine praises localized military operations, directly or indirectly operated by the Central Intelligence Agency and the Green Berets, along with intense ideological propaganda. The doctrines and methods of propaganda were developed by the United States Agency for International Development (USAID). According to this conception, support from the local population is an important factor, as the unsuccessful U.S. invasion of the Bay of Pigs in Cuba (on April 17, 1961) has shown. This explains the emphasis on educational actions and, in the case of indigenous populations, the relevance of religious missions like those developed in several peripheral countries by the International Society of Linguistics and by the Wycliffe Bible Translators. The educational program and, more specifically, the propaganda actions of the Alliance for Progress, had this goal. As asserted by Adolf A. Berle, one of the closest of Nelson Rockefeller's collaborators and an important adviser of Kennedy and Johnson, "in Latin America the battlefield is for the control of the minds of the small nucleus of intellectuals, educated and semi-educated people. The strategy is to dominate through educational processes" (Colby and Dennett, 1998, p. 425). Concerning public universities, with what they conveniently proclaimed as the risk of proliferation "of the Marxist doctrine in the educational system and in the economic thought of Latin America" (Scheman, 1988), the control, stated Berle, would have to be clandestine, via private institutions (the Ford Foundation, Rockefeller, Olin etc.) and via exchange programs with American universities, especially Georgetown University, the University of California at Los Angeles and Berkeley, Columbia University, and Stanford University. The aim of all this social engineering is to minimize communist influence and the emergence of a new Cuba in the region. McGeorge Bundy, president of the Ford Foundation in the 1950s and 1960s, was proud that Ford was more agile than the government in the identification and solution of U.S. problems.

The glory days of the counterinsurgency[19] became more opaque at the end of the 1960s. On the one hand, the imminent disaster in Vietnam, along with changes in peripheral countries, such as the process of decolonization and the invigoration of the movement of nonaligned countries, demanded changes in U.S. foreign policy in response to the demands of Cold War. The increasing anti-American feeling in peripheral countries was taken as a threat to U.S. supremacy, putting at risk the strategic goals of the economic and political establishment. On the other hand, the manifestations of the structural crisis of capitalism became clearer in the 1970s (Duménil and Lévy, 1996), a situation that soon would increase social tension within peripheral countries and in their relations with Washington. Consideration of all these factors caused changes in the tactical orientation of the State Department. The preference was now for indirect actions, mediated by multilateral organs such as the Word Bank. In this context, Robert S. McNamara left the Defense Department to become President of the World Bank. Education, then, became a high priority for the Bank. To analyze the reasons for these changes and the purposes of the World Bank's education policies, it is necessary to pose the following questions:

1. What intentions does the World Bank have in determining the guidelines of education policies for peripheral countries?
2. What does the Bank do to determine these guidelines?
3. How is the ideology of security being transposed to those countries?

To answer these questions it is necessary to analyze some aspects of the history of the Bank, which initially was an agency for the reconstruction of Europe and, then, became transformed into the "Lords of the World" (Chomsky and Dietrich, 1995). It is imperative to examine the economic and ideological contexts that motivated the reforms, with emphasis on the ideology of globalization.

POVERTY AND SECURITY

With the discrediting of the counterinsurgency doctrine centered on the use of military force, especially starting with the defeat of the United States in Vietnam, international agencies proceeded to intervene more strongly in the internal policies of the peripheral countries, following Robert McNamara's proposals. In fact, in 1968, the new World Bank president—who had been U.S. Defense Secretary (1961–1968) and, as such, one of the mentors of Vietnam intervention—promoted changes in the orientation of the institution that need to be further researched, given their significant consequences.

Undoubtedly, decolonization and the Cold War underlie the new orientation. Faced with a situation of fast transformation—a quarter of the world's population recently had revolted against colonialism and obtained independence—McNamara reaffirmed, in 1972, the purpose of "protecting the stability of the western world. "In this perspective, during his mandate (1968–1981), McNamara and other directors of the Bank gradually abandoned the policies of development and import-substitution, placing poverty and security at the center of the Bank's concerns. It is in this context that the institution truly began to act in education, with its action becoming more direct and specific. The Bank prioritized programs that targeted directly populations that might be more susceptible to "communism" by making use of technical schools and health and birth-control programs, at the same time as promoting structural changes in the economy of those countries, such as the transposition of the "green revolution" to the so-called Third World.

As it is possible to verify, the focus on the poverty problem has important nuances in relation to the counterinsurgency thesis of Rostow, who proposed the use of more directly coercive means. The support from part of the establishment for McNamara's position can be explained by the U.S. difficulties in Vietnam and by the new features of the Cold War. In his self-critical work *In Retrospect: the Tragedy and Lessons of Vietnam* (1996, p. 311), McNamara affirms that he was in "profound" disagreement with Walt Bristow's and Johnson's analyses concerning the prolongation of the military force in Vietnam. He recalls this in his speech in the American Association of Newspapers (1966), when he said: "there is amongst us a tendency to think our security problem as an exclusively military problem," however, "a nation can reach a point at which it cannot buy more security by just buying military equipment, and we have reached this point." Therefore, "we should assist the underdeveloped countries which genuinely need and require our help and, as an essential precondition, which are willing to help themselves" (p. 311).

The financial aid granted to the Bank during McNamara's administration indicates that he was not just talking for himself. In the twenty-two years prior to his World Bank presidency the Bank had approved 708 projects, with a total cost of US$10.7 billion. However, in the first period of his administration alone (1968–1973), 760 projects were approved with a total cost of US$13.4 billion (George and Sabelli, 1994, p. 43). In this period, the Bank became the world's biggest nonsovereign collector of financial resources.

The analysis of the way the Bank carries out its new guidelines contributes to an understanding of how this institution obtains the capacity to define the direction of peripheral countries' policies. The Bank made important organizational changes, enlarging its technical staff and transforming itself into the largest world information center on development. Based on that information, the World Bank extended control over the countries that took loans from it. Thus, the Bank modified the scope of the projects by changing them to programs (much more complex and inclusive, covering vast sectors such as education), imposing more severe conditions through the recommendation that the countries should modify their national constitutions to assist the precepts of Washington Consensus.

This reorientation of the Bank was successful, not so much in terms of sectoral policies, which failed economically as well as socially, but in terms of a wider policy. Furthermore, it enlarged the number of member nations, maintaining its presence in 179 countries in 1995.

Many factors contributed to the relative exhaustion of the strategy focusing on the security-poverty connection. The main one, without doubt, was the structural crisis of capitalism that could be seen in the early 1970s

(Duménil and Lévy, 1996). In this crisis, the debts of peripheral countries increased with rising taxes and with the falling values of the main commodities. It is necessary to emphasize, as well, the fact that the World Bank lent and guaranteed loans with strategic purposes, allowing debts which were higher than the countries' repayment capacity. Many governments friendly to the "West" (for example, those of Mobutu Sese Seko of the Democratic Republic of the Congo, formerly Zaire, 1965–1997; Ferdinand Marcos of the Philippines, 1965–1986; and Anastásio Somoza of Nicaragua, 1967–1972 and 1974–1979) embezzled considerable amounts of these loans for their own particular purposes.

In this new context, peripheral countries lost some of their pressure power. Reagan used military force for specific actions to weaken socialist countries in their own territory, creating the "contras" in Nicaragua, UNITA in Angola, and so forth. The Bank embraced neoliberal social and economic ideas and, with the vulnerability of the indebted countries, imposed drastic structural adjustment reforms such as the liberalization of entrance and exit of capitals. This crisis presented new challenges for the World Bank, providing exceptional conditions for the exercise of power. In the structural crisis, as stated before, the Bank had unprecedented scope to impose its conditions.

The countries that at the beginning of the 1980s resisted interventionism and the imposition of neoliberalism, sustaining neostructuralist policies,[20] soon submitted to the rules of the "New Lords of the World". This is what happened to Brazil, especially in the governments of Fernando Collor de Mello (1990–1992) and Fernando Henrique Cardoso (1995–2002).

The structural adjustment that dismantled the precarious social state was done in the name of globalization, a process presented as relentless and irresistible, against which nothing could be done, except fitting in, even though it could result in exponential increases in unemployment and privatization, exchange crises, increasing taxes, and destruction of labor rights.

The idea that the economic crisis of the 1970s and 1980s were the start of a new "era" of globalization is shared not only by the followers of neoliberalism (especially those of the knowledge society or intellectual capitalism) who adopted globalization as a fact, but also by some of the critics of neoliberalism, notably those who support the scientific-technological revolution thesis (and the end of labor):[21]

> The changes that surround us are not passing phenomena but the product of powerful and headstrong forces: globalization, which has opened immense new markets with its relentless corollary, an enormous amount of competition; diffusion of information technology and the disordered growth of computer sciences nets (Stewart, 1998, p. 33)

According to the president of the World Bank, James Wolfensohn[22] the transformation of economic policies underway in underdeveloped countries would be configuring the "era of the market" or "globalization." When situating the recent context in which the Bank works, Wolfensohn said, "we are operating in a very different context from ten or even five years ago. The post–Cold War era marks the largest moment of change in history: country after country has moved to an economy guided by the market . . . which has been accelerating global integration."

In this "new era" Thomas A. Stewart (1998, pp. 9–26 75–87), publisher of *Fortune* magazine, said that "knowledge was converted into the most important factor of production" of a rather imprecise "intellectual capitalism" that would have succeeded industrial capitalism. In this "new era of capitalism, the main capital is intellectual capital" and, because of this, education, as a condition of capital, became a matter for managers and no longer for educators. Underlying the glamour, the ideological (and not even original) character of this formulation stands out. In this renewed version of the human capital theory, knowledge does not belong anymore to a person, neither is it conceived by him or her: "it is the company that must try to acquire all the human capital that it can use." The company needs "to use efficiently its employees' brains" who should be trustees of useful knowledge for capital.

Hayek (1998, p. 58) sums up the importance of education in liberal society: "it is by using his own means and own knowledge that defines a free man who is able to contribute to spontaneous order." This connection between knowledge and order constitutes the "solid nucleus" of the World Bank's propositions for education in the 1990s.

THE EDUCATIONAL ORIENTATIONS THAT SUIT CAPITAL

> Education is the biggest instrument for economic and social development. It is central for the World Bank's strategy to help countries reduce poverty and promote standards of living for sustainable growth and investment in people. This double strategy requires the promotion of the productive use of work (the main good of the poor) and provide basic social services for the poor. (World Bank, 1990)

The centrality acquired by education in the World Bank's discourse in the 1990s is recent. In the 1960s, a vice president of the Bank, Robert Gardner, declared, "we cannot lend for education and health. We are a bank!" (Caufield, 1996, p. 64). This situation started to change in George Woods's administration (1963–1968) and, more strongly, in that of Robert McNamara (1968–1981), when the emphasis on the problem of poverty made education stand out among the priorities of the Bank. In the 1970s, this institution considered financing primary and general secondary schools, and defended technical and vocational teaching as more adequate to the presumed needs of underdeveloped countries. In the neoliberal turn of the

1980s, the Bank's educational orientation changed towards primary education. The former orientation was then severely attacked as voluntarist and
wasteful (World Bank, 1995b). In the 1990s, the neoliberal inflection not
only remained valid but was radicalized.

In the Bank's more recent documents and in the pronouncements of its
leaders, the frequent occurrence of the poverty issue and dread regarding
security is visible. Education is conceived as being a relief instrument to
poverty and, therefore, as important for security. In Wolfensohn's terms,
"the poor people of the World should be helped, otherwise they will be
angry" (Caufield, 1996, p. 315). That is, poverty can generate an unfavorable climate for business. And the problem is that global exclusion does not
stop growing. The United Nations Development Program Studies (1998)
and, more recently, Chossudovsky's work (2002), which developed an inclusive study of globalization of poverty in the world, attests that peripheral
countries have suffered seriously in their economic and social situation in
the last thirty years. In maintaining a policy of free trade, efforts to contain
the tensions produced by unemployment will have to be increased. In Brazil
between 1985 and 1998 the number of industrial jobs fell by 43 percent,
while industrial production grew just 2.7 percent (Pochmann, 1999). For
dominant ideologies, the best antidote to the current maladies of unemployment, in Brazil, for example, is primary education (the first four years,
mostly the responsibility of the municipal districts) and vocational education (which may be separated from formal education or accompanying three
years of upper secondary school, after eight years of fundamental education).
This explains, largely, the World Bank's guidelines for higher education. For
a long time countries that insisted on universalizing twentieth-century technologies in their territories were criticized by the Bank. However, never was
the Bank so explicit and determined in its nonuniversity policy, in its focus
on elementary and pre-university vocational education.[23]

According to Amin's analysis (1996), the markets of peripheral countries,
unlike those of central countries, are not integrated in a three-dimensional
way (capital, merchandise, and labor), but only in two dimensions (capital and
merchandise)—labor, in the peripheries, is excluded from the labor market
based on advanced scientific knowledge, being confined by national barriers
that separate central countries from peripheries. The work in these countries is in accordance with the way these nations are inserted into the world
economy: in a subordinate form, peripheral, restricted to low-aggregate-value
goods.[24] The basic economic premise is that a free global market decides better which jobs are located in which country (Caufield, 1996, p. 294).

Thus, the guidelines for higher education are coherent with the economic propositions of the Bank. If a country submitting to the Bank's orientations abdicates responsibility for constructing an independent nation,
then a higher education system with relative autonomy from private institutions does seem anachronistic. The Brazilian Minister of Education, Paulo
Renato de Sousa (1995–2002), does not see any sense in new knowledge

production in public universities because, in his conception, the productive system "can" get technological packages in the free market. Moved by this reasoning, since the end of the 1980s the Bank has not financed any academic activity in sub-Saharan Africa (World Bank, 1974, 1980). According to the Bank's analysis, Latin America is going in the same direction (World Bank, 1995a). This does not mean that the Bank suggests that all research should be eradicated: even a functional university needs institutionalized research. Despite the fact that the logic of the process indicates that new knowledge production and research and development should be produced in the more advanced centers, notably in the United States, countries like Brazil, besides the breadth of its productive base, would have to have a few centers of excellence able to adapt technological packages to local reality and also to be part of the leading elite to produce necessary knowledge for social control, which is already happening in some universities.

Although published more than a decade ago, the document *Higher Education: the Lessons of Experience* (World Bank, 1994), still contains the main direction for the sector. It explains the crisis of public higher education firstly as a result of the fiscal crisis. However, through the document, the political purposes become explicit, overriding the fiscal ones. This document is a paradigm, constituting the matrix of the main propositions of the federal government of Brazil over the last decade. The document proposes a wider differentiation in higher education, demanding the suppression of the association between teaching and research, in the terms of the General Law of National Education (Law 9394/96)—which distinguishes public higher education institutions from academic centers—a euphemism to legitimate universities that do not carry out research. The Bank indicates the instruments for this policy implementation, emphasizing the importance of redefining the university's autonomy in neoliberal form, an autonomy that means the expulsion of the state from the life of institutions. The Bank searches for the implementation of a certain autonomy model, in neoliberal molds, so that the power of the market can, itself, determine all the dimensions of the university: courses, periods, work, teaching, research, and so forth. In Hayek's formulation, autonomy is always thought as autonomy vis-à-vis the State. This conception of autonomy deinstitutionalizes the universities, transforming them in social organizations that cannot deserve to be called universities (Leher, 2001).

> A wider institutional autonomy is the key for the success of the reform in public higher education, especially in order to diversify and to use resources more efficiently. An indicative goal could be that of state higher education institutions generating enough resources to finance about 30% of their total resources needs. (World Bank, 1995a, p. 7)

At the center of this discourse lies the opposition between primary education (meant for the general population, and admitted as a nonexclusive duty of the state) and higher education (destined for privileged elites that, although not needing public education, enjoy the largest part of the educational budget). Once the discourse has been defined, the document focuses on the political orientation: "it is necessary to break this mold" through actions undertaken with much caution. The reform underway is carried out with the minimum possible ostentation.

In the words of Paulo Renato de Souza, former Minister of Education in Cardoso's government, "Brazilian society does not want to give more resources to public universities;" echoes Becker, "the governments who keep free higher education are subsidizing the wrong people."[25] Still, in the minister's interpretation, "the emphasis on university education was characteristic of a self-supported development model that demanded developing research and its own technologies . . . today this model is in terminal agony."[26] The ideology of globalization supplies arguments so the minister may maintain that

> the access to knowledge is facilitated, the associations and joint ventures take care of providing know-how to the companies of the countries that need it, such as Brazil. The subcontracting of universities, as Korea did, does make much more sense from an economic point of view.[27]

The same evaluation has been made by Lula da Silva's government. A recent "package" that has been negotiated between the Bank and the Brazilian government has as a condition put an end to free higher education,[28] a position that, as exposed in the former Minister of Education's speech in UNESCO, Cristóvam Buarque (2003), can count on his full sympathy.[29] Larger enthusiasm for the end of free education can be observed in the economic area, considering its neoliberal orthodoxy, as it is evident in the documents of the Brazilian Department of Treasury and, in particular, in the document *Social Expenditure of the Central Government: 2001 and 2002*.[30] This document, in conformity with the Chicago School theoretician Gary Becker, postulates that free higher education is the main obstacle to achieving social justice in the country, recommending loans to students so that they study at private schools, cheaper for the state.

Due to the exclusion of public universities from the priority policies, the public secondary school also remains without a place in education policies. The expansion of the public secondary school would contradict the privatization policy for the university, and it would bring evidence, even more, of the segregationist character of the current policies. For the responsibility of primary education to remain with the state the Brazilian government has been undertaking important changes at this level. The creation of a new financing form for primary school is redrawing the allocations of the state and municipal districts. The curriculum reform is molding schools to the "imperative of globalization." The National Curriculum Parameters don't aim to guarantee a unitary education, simultaneously scientific, technological, artistic, and cultural and, at the secondary level, the scientific and technological foundations of the labor world. The official discourse affirms that curriculum should be "for life" diffusing appropriate ideological dispositions with the deregulation and flexibilization of the labor rights (Kuenzer, 2000; Hill, 2003). A centralized evaluation guarantees state control of teaching activity and "technological packages" guarantee the standardization of teacher education (Barreto and Leher, 2003). Formally, all of them can enjoy the benefits of globalization and the conditions of governability would be assured. This is the map of ideas that constitutes a true planetary educational apartheid, led by the World Bank.

AN EFFORT TO CONCLUDE

The education–security–poverty connection forms the substratum of the educational reforms underway in Latin America that has been deepened since the Debt Crisis of 1982, when the IMF and World Bank, in consonance with the dominant power bloc, undertook a deep neoliberal process of structural adjustment. With the unprecedented deepening of the polarization in the 1990s, the Bank dedicates increasing attention to the construction of institutions adapted to the era of the market (World Bank, 2000), so that it has institutional resources to "manage" the contradictions of the system. Education is radically modified, becoming less and less polytechnic (in the sense of Marx) and more and more instrumental: the contents are strongly filled with paeans to capital and the educational debate is ruled largely by "businessmen" and political strategists.

It is left to education to operate the contradictions of segregation, providing openings for the future. The presupposition here is that all people who have made the correct educational choices will have limitless possibilities. The individuals (and countries) which prioritize education correctly will have a glorious future ahead, proving, thus, the validity of the system. Current capitalism is fair to those who qualify themselves correctly. It is enough not to insist on the wrong priorities. It is no use spending money on public higher education and research, because, according to the comparative advantage thesis, the developing countries should pursue market niches where it is possible to sell low-aggregate-value goods.

Critique of that legitimization process of structural exclusion are complicated by the increasing adherence of leftist parties and unions to the ideology of globalization[31] and to technological determinism (World Bank, 2003). In this sense, problems of unemployment and the precariousness/insecurity of labour are explained by workers' qualifications. It is as if the exclusion insecurity was due to the individuals' mistaken educational options. In that case, the only realistic alternative is professional education. The majority of Brazilian unions, independent of affiliation to CUT or Força Sindical, the two main Brazilian workers' unions, are determined to make agreements with the government in order to obtain qualifications and training courses for their associates. Also, governments elected in opposition to neoliberalism, like Lula da Silva's, incorporated the belief that public and free higher education is not socially just and that the state is not a good education manager, summoning the so called "third sector" to lead education policies and even to propose buying educational services from private establishments.

A fundamental prerequisite for confronting the dismantling of public education is to criticize the presuppositions on which current government policies are based. This study contributes to the construction of this critique, as it is not possible to comprehend the sense and the meaning of current reforms without considering their conceptual matrix, formulated by the World Bank.

NOTES

1. In 1982, Mexico, Brazil and Argentina defaulted on their debt payments, threatening the international credit system. The IMF and World Bank stepped into these nations prescribing their loans and structural adjustment policies to ensure debt repayment.
2. In July of 1944, representatives of the nations allied against the Fascist axis (including Brazil) met in Bretton Woods, in the northeast of the United States, to undertake one of the most audacious initiatives in social engineering tried before or since. The goal was to create rules and formal institutions of ordination of an international monetary system capable of overcoming the enormous limitations that the systems known, the gold standard and the system of competitive exchange depreciations, had not just imposed to the international trade but also to the operation of their own domestic savings. . . . The institutions created in Bretton Woods—the International Monetary Fund and the World Bank—are far away from receiving world approval that would be anticipated if the intentions of the conference had come true (Carvalho, F. 2004 Bretton Woods to the 60 Years. *Novos Estudos Cebrap*, 70, pp. 51–63).
3. The new capital expansion courses are ramifying and reaching new territories and domains of life, such as water and biodiversity control. At the same time, means of labor exploitation are being intensified in very similar forms, as described by Marx, in primitive accumulation. Assuming that it seems wrong to denominate as primitive an ongoing process, Harvey substitutes these terms for "accumulation by dispossession." In this accumulation mode it is possible to find mercantilization of the land and privatization, forced expulsion of farmers, and destruction of common property rights in favor of corporate property rights and appropriation of natural resources.
4. With the crisis of 1929 and World War II, Latin American countries undertook a very intense industrialization process by the substitution of the imports (especially Argentina, Brazil, Chile, and Mexico). The Latin American, African and Asian gross domestic product (GDP) all together increased approximately 4.2 percent per year, in the 1953–1990 period, a higher index than that of European countries during the origins of industrialization in the nineteenth century (1.9 percent annually), although GDP per capita has been significantly smaller (2oercent annually) due to the population growth.

5. Newly Industrialized Countries (NIC) of Latin America are just shades of the past, remaining an incomplete industrialization where the links of the productive chain of larger technological sophistication are placed at the central countries. Distinctly, Asian East countries (South Korea, Taiwan, Singapore) didn't follow orthodox neoliberal policies applied in Latin America and protected their companies fortifying state industrial policies, maintaining strong public companies and sustaining a great apparatus of scientific, technological, and development research.

6. The efforts of the peripheries in favor of the development after World War II produced a broad movement that gathered several governments in order to fight for a New International Economical Order, culminating in the Conference of Bandung (1955). Latin America soon joined that movement, led by former revolutionaries and colonial radicals—Nehru from India, Sukarno from Indonesia, Colonel Gamel Nasser from Egypt, and a dissident communist, president Tito from Yugoslavia—and by idealizers of the United Nations Conference on Trade and Development (UNCTAD), directed in its first years (1964–1969) by Prebisch, which reiterated the "unequal trade" theme. The Cuban Revolution was the most radical and symbolic expression of the criticism towards subdevelopment worsened by dependent capitalism outside the marks of the modernization theory.

7. While the World Bank mantained a conservative modernization harnessed by managerial-military dictatorships, ECLAC was addressing strong criticism to the liberal model and to the subordination of the Latin American economy to international labor division. Among the main critics it is necessary to mention Raúl Prebisch (Argentina) and Celso Furtado (Brazil) and, later on, several authors that debated the dependence theory.

8. Countries that have achieved relative success in industrialization and that have an apparatus for science and technology, like Brazil, India, and Mexico, suffer heavy pressure from the World Bank, which maintains that the investments in the area are not appropriate with the way those countries should be inserted into the world economy. The World Bank's study on economical return of educational expenses based on Human Capital Theory could not be more convenient to the central countries. In the case of Latin America, Africa, and south Asia, the best economic return would be in basic education (World Bank, 1995a, 1995b).

9. The *Programa Universidade para Todos* (University for All Program), created by the Brazilian Federal Government in 2004, is an example of public-private partnership. In exchange for tributary exemptions that achieve 25 percent of the gain of these institutions, the same institutions must make available a percentage of vacancies as scholarships. Originally, the MEC (Brazilian Ministry of Education) foresaw 20 percent of integral scholarship, but after the pressure from entrepreneurs, this percentage was reduced to 4.25 percent. Now, more than 50 percent of private institutions that join the Program have been criticized by the MEC itself for not achieving the minimum required quality.

10. Global University Network for Innovation (GUNI). 2005. *La educación superior en el mundo 2006: la financiación de las universidades*. Madrid: Ediciones Mundi-Prensa.

11. The expected Uruguay Round of General Agreement on Tariffs and Trade (GATT) (1986–1994), which promised to recover hopes deposited in the Conference of Bandung, was an elucidative demonstration of the political weakness of peripheral countries. Not only was the issue of unequal commercial exchange terms not discussed, but more sectors became subject to the rules of free trade agreements—such as education, health, social welfare, and the environment.

12. For more information see Brasil, Ministério da Educação, Decreto n. 5.622, December 19, 2005, on regulation of distance education.
13. The Unique Worker's Center (Central Única dos Trabalhadores—CUT) formed in 1983, is the chief union federation in Brazil, along with the Worker's Party (Partido dos Trabalhadores—PT) and the Landless Worker's Movement (Movimento dos Trabalhadores Rurais Sem Terra—MST). Today it is the largest and most important labor federation in Brazil. CUT is close to the Worker's Party. In March 2004, dissidents opposed to the government of Luiz Inácio Lula da Silva and formed the National Coordination of Struggles (Coordenação Nacional de Lutas—CONLUTAS) and INTERSINDICAL. Both are close to the Socialism and Freedom Party (Partido do Socialismo e da Liberdade—PSOL) and Unified Socialist Worker's Party (Partido Socialista dos Trabalhadores Unificados—PSTU).
14. Brazil's Landless Workers Movement, or in Portuguese Movimento dos Trabalhadores Rurais Sem Terra (MST), is the largest social movement in Latin America, with an estimated 1.5 million landless members organized in twenty-three out of twenty-seven states. The MST carries out long-overdue land reform in a country mired in unjust land distribution. In Brazil, 1.6 percent of landowners control roughly half (46.8 percent) of arable land. A mere 3 percent of the population owns two-thirds of all arable land. The MST has won land titles for more than 350,000 families in 2,000 settlements as a result of MST actions, and 180,000 encamped families currently await government recognition. Land occupations are rooted in the Brazilian Constitution, which says that land that remains unproductive should be used for a "larger social function." The MST's success lies in its ability to organize and educate. Members have not only managed to secure land, and thereby food security for their families, but also continue to develop a sustainable socioeconomic model that offers a concrete alternative to today's globalization that puts profits before people and humanity. http://www.mstbrazil.org.
15. See Caufield (1996), Chomsky and Dietrich (1995), and Chossudovsky (2002).
16. Conditions for the loans demanded by the IMF and World Bank: the obtaining of loans started to depend on the customer's country's disposition in committing not just to certain parameters of macroeconomic policies, but also to more or less profound changes in their institutional structures (Carvalho, 2004).
17. For a study of the debt and its political and social implications see *ABC da Dívida: sabe quanto você está pagando?* Rede Jubileu Sul/ Brasil. Auditoria Cidadã da Dívida, 2nd reviewed and updated edition, April 2007. www.divida-auditoriacidada.org.br.
18. In April 2006, the Assembléia Nacional Popular e de Esquerda—ANPE, with about four hundred participants that determined the creation of a new INTERSINDICAL (accomplished in June 2006), gathered unions that had formerly joined CUT and that comprised part of the left wing of that union. In May 2006 the Congresso Nacional dos Trabalhadores da Coordenação Nacional de Lutas (CONLUTAS) took place, with more than 3,500 participants. In this Congress, the coordination of struggles was formalized in a national entity that has as an objective to join unions, social movements, students, and formal and informal workers, urban and rural.
19. Counterinsurgency: military, paramilitary, political, economic, psychological, and civic actions taken by a government to defeat insurgency. The most notable such actions include the French-Indochinese War (1946–1954), the Vietnam War (1965–1973) and Malasia (1948–1960).
20. Neostructuralism can be associated with the Chilean economist Osvaldo Sunkel's work which, in 1991, organized the book *El desarrollo desde dentro: un enfoque neoestruturalista para la América Latina*, considered a mark

of that conception. The author argues that the issue of Latin American debt in the 1980s must be at the core of the analysis of economic reality and alternative proposals. Seeking a transition towards a development model that guarantees and strengthen democracy and could be sustainable in the medium and long terms, Sunkel defends a development strategy and industrialization from inside.

21. Among the most outstanding are André Gorz, Claus Offe, Alain Torraine, and Adam Schaff. For a criticism of these authors see Ricardo Antunes. 1995. *Adeus ao Trabalho? Ensaio sobre as metaforfoses e a centralidade do mundo do trabalho.* São Paulo: Cortez Editora/ Campinas, São Paulo: Editora da Universidade Estadual de Campinas.

22. .Wolfensohn, James D. 1995. Opening address by the president of the World Bank group. In *Annual Meeting 1995,* pp.17–28. http://www.imf.org/external/pubs/ft/summary/50/pdf/part01.pdf.

23. *Higher Education in Developing Countries: Peril and Promise* (2000) was produced by the *Task Force on Higher Education in Developing Countries,* convened by the World Bank and UNESCO, to deepen the previous "lessons." *Peril and promise* indicate there is no doubt about what, when, where and how the "solution" is to be applied efficiently, between "longstanding problems and new realities": *expansion* ("a result of the tremendous increase in the number of students"), *differentiation* ("a process whereby new types of institutions are born and new providers enter the sector") and *the knowledge revolution* ("a revolution has occurred in people's ability to access knowledge quickly and from increasingly distant locations") (See Barreto, R. G. 2008. *Journal for Critical Education Policy Studies,* 6(1). Retrieved May 5, 2008 from http://www.jceps.com/?pageID=article&article10=117

24. Basualdo (2002) asserts that in the 1990s, in Argentina, distinctly during the period of import substitution (1958–1976), and even during the 1980s, the industrial sector stopped being the dynamic nucleus of economy, and the most important managerial sectors, in particular, in benefit of commercial companies and holdings (Basualdo, 2002a, p. 142). Between 1973 and 1993, 15 thousand establishments disappeared (15 percent of the total) and 320 thousand people were expelled from the sector (24 percent of employees).

25. Netz, Clayton. 1996. Investimento sem risco. *Revista Exame,* July 17. http://portalexame.abril.com.br/revista/exame/edicoes/0614/m0051334.html.

26. Ibid.

27. Ibid.

28. Solomon, Marta. 2003. Gratuitousness in federal universities still provokes debate. *Folha de São Paulo,* August 3, p. C4. On the other hand, for the possible loan of US$8 billion (to be distributed in the next four years), the Bank awaits revision of the gratuitousness principle.

29. In UNESCO, Lula's former minister of education, Cristóvam Buarque, defended a differentiated tax proposal for those who graduated from public institutions that would, then, pay for their courses, a measure that would demand modification of Article 206 of the Federal Constitution, which establishes the gratuitousness in official establishments.

30. BRASIL, Ministério da Fazenda, Secretaria de Política Econômica. 2003. *Gasto Social do Governo Central: 2001 e 2002.* Brasília, D.F. http://www.fazenda.gov.br/portugues/documentos/2003/Gasto%20Social%20do%20Governo%20Central%202001–2002.pdf.

31. These are the cases of Partido dos Trabalhadores and Central Única dos Trabalhadores that, starting from the election of Lula da Silva in 2002, are sustaining the government's neoliberal agenda, especially the illegitimate debt

payment policies, high primary superavits, increased flexibility of labor laws, public-private partnerships, a capitalization regime in social welfare, transfers of public resources to private higher education institutions and, in the external plan, the sending of the armed forces troops to Haiti.

REFERENCES

Amin, S. 1996. *Les défi s de la mondialisation*. Paris: L'Harmattan.
Anderson, P. 2004. El papel de las ideas en la construcción de alternativas. In *Nueva hegemonía mundial: Alternativas de cambio y movimientos sociales*, ed. A. Borón, 37–52. Buenos Aires: Consejo Latinoamericano de Ciencias Sociales.
Arceo, E., and E. M. Basualdo. 2006. Los cambios de los sectores dominantes en América Latina bajo el neoliberalismo: La problemática propuesta. In *Neoliberalismo y sectores dominantes: tendencias globales y experiencias nacionales*, ed. E. Arceo and E. Basualdo, 15–26. Buenos Aires: Consejo Latinoamericano de Ciencias Sociales.
Archibald, G. 1993. *Les États-Unis et L'Unesco*. Paris: Publ. de la Sorbonne.
Barreto, R. G., and R. Leher. 2003. Trabalho docente e as reformas neoliberais. In *Reformas educacionais na América Latina e os trabalhadores docentes*, ed. D. Oliveira, 39–60. Belo Horizonte: Autêntica.
Basualdo, E. M. 2002a. La crisis actual en Argentina: Entre la dolarización, la devaluación y la redistribución del ingreso. *Chiapas* 13: 7–41.
Basualdo, E. M. 2002b. *Concentracion y centralizacion del capital en la Argentina durante la década del noventa*. Bs.As: Universidad Nacional de Quilmes Ed.
Bourdieu, P., and L. Wacquant. 2001. NewLiberalSpeak: notes on the new planetary vulgate. *Radical Philosophy* 105: 2–5. http://www.radicalphilosophy.com/default.asp.
Buarque, C. 2003. *A universidade numa encruzilhada*. http://www.ufv.br/reforma/doc_ru/CristovaoBuarque.pdf.
Carvalho, F. J. C. 2004. Bretton Woods aos 60 anos. *Novos Estudos Cebrap* 70: 51–63.
Caufield, C. 1996. *Masters of illusion: The World Bank and the poverty of nations*. New York: Henry Holt.
Chomsky, N., and H. Dietrich. 1995. *La sociedad global*. México City: Joaquín Moriz.
Chossudovsky, M. 2002. *Globalización de la pobreza y nuevo orden mundial*. México City: Siglo XXI.
Colby, G., and C. Dennett. 1998. *Seja feita a vossa vontade*. Rio de Janeiro: Record.
Dezalay, Y., and B. G. Garth. 1998. Le "Washington consensus": Contribution à une sociologie de l'hégémonie du néolibéralisme. *Actes de la recherche en science sociales* 121/122: 3–22.
Duménil, G., and D. Lévy. 1996. *La dynamique du capital: Un siécle d'économie américaine*. Paris: Presses Universitaires de France.
Fernandes, F. 1974. *A revolução burguesa no Brasil. Um ensaio de interpretação sociológica*. Rio de Janeiro: Zahar.
George, S., and F. Sabelli. 1994. *Faith e credit: The World Bank's secular empire*. Boulder: Westview Press.
Gonçalves, R. 2003. Lula: Aposta perdida. http://www.outrobrasil.net (accessed December 20, 2003).
Harvey, D. 2005. El "nuevo" imperialismo: Acumulación por desposesión. In *El nuevo desafío imperial*, ed. L. Panitch and C. Leys. Buenos Aires: Consejo Latinoamericano de Ciencias Sociales.

Hayek, F. A. 1998. Os princípios de uma ordem social liberal. In *Ideologias políticas*, ed. A. Crespigny and J. Cronin, 43–64. Brasília: Editora da Universidade de Brasília (UnB).

Hill, D. 2003. O neoliberalismo global, a resistência e a deformação da educação. *Currículo sem Fronteiras*, 3: 2: 24–59.

Hirst, P., and G. Thompson. 1998. *Globalização em questão*. Petrópolis, RJ: Vozes.

Holloway, J., and E. Peláez. 1998, Aprendendo a curvar-se: Pós-fordismo e determinismo tecnológico. *Outubro* 2: 21–30.

Kuenzer, A. Z. 2000. O ensino médio agora é para a vida: Entre o pretendido, o dito e o feito. *Educação & Sociedade* 70: 15–39. http://www.scielo.br/pdf/es/v21n70/a03v2170.pdf.

Lahóz, A. 2000. Educação: como o Brasil está fazendo a lição de casa. *Revista Exame*, São Paulo: Editora Abril Edição 711, 34, n7: 34–39.

Leher, R. 2001. Projetos e modelos de autonomia e privatização das universidades públicas. In *Universidades na penumbra: Neoliberalismo e reestruturação universitária*, ed. P. Gentili, 151–181. São Paulo: Cortez.

———. 2003a. O governo Lula e os confl itos sociais no Brasil. *Revista del Observatório Social de América Latina* 10: 81–96.

———. 2003b. Reforma universitária do governo Lula: Protagonismo do Banco Mundial e das lutas antineoliberais. *Folha Dirigid*. http://www.consciencia.net/2003/12/12/leher.html. December 12, 2003.

———. 2005. Für eine emanzipierte gesellschaft. *Denken+Glauben* 138/139: 28–31.

Leher, R., and M. Setúbal, eds. 2005. *Pensamento crítico e movimentos sociais: Diálogos para uma nova práxis*. São Paulo: Cortez.

Marx, K. 1985. *O capital*, vol. 3, t. 2: 112. São Paulo: Abril Cultural.

Mattelart, A. 2002. *História da sociedade da informação*. São Paulo: Loyola.

McNamara, R. S. 1996. *In retrospect: The tragedy and lessons of Vietnam*. New York: Vintage Books.

Paulani, L. M. 2003. Brasil delivery: Razões, contradições e limites da política econômica nos primeiros seis meses do governo Lula. *Revista de Economia Política* 23, no. 4 (92): 58–73.

Pochmann, M. 1999. *O trabalho sob fogo cruzado: exclusão, desemprego e precarização no final do século*. São Paulo: Contexto.

Rostow, W. W. 1964. *As etapas do desenvolvimento econômico*. Rio de Janeiro: Zahar.

Scheman, L. R. ed. 1988. *The alliance for progress*. New York: Praeger.

Stewart, T. A. 1998. *La nueva riqueza de las organizaciones: El capital intelectual*. Buenos Aires: Granica.

Sunkel, O. 1991. *El desarrollo desde dentro: un enfoque neoestruturalista para la América Latina*, Mexico: Fondo de Cultura Económica.

United Nations Development Programme. 1998. Human Development Report. http://hdr.undp.org/en/reports/global/hdr1998.

Williamson, J. 1990. *What Washington means by policy reform. Latin American adjustment: how much has happened?* Washington, D.C.: Institute for International Economics.

World Bank. 1974. *Education: Sector working paper*. Washington, D.C.: Banque Internationale pour la Reconstruction et le Développement /World Bank.

———. 1980. *Education: Sector working paper*. Washington, D.C.: Banque Internationale pour la Reconstruction et le Développement /World Bank.

———. 1990. *World development report*. Washington, D.C.: Banque Internationale pour la Reconstruction et le Développement /World Bank.

———. 1994. Higher education: The lessons of experience. http://web. worldbank. org/WBSITE/EXTERNAL/TOPICS/EXTEDUCATION/0,contentMDK:205

28436~menuPK:617592~pagePK:148956~piPK:216618~theSitePK:282386,00
.html (accessed July 11, 1997).

————. 1995a. *Proceedings of the World Bank: Annual Conference on Development Economics, 1994, 19.* Washington D.C.: Banque Internationale pour la Reconstruction et le Développement /World Bank.

————. 1995b. *World Bank: Priorities and strategies for education: a World Bank review.* Washington, D.C.: Banque Internationale pour la Reconstruction et le Développement /World Bank.

————. 2000. *Higher education in developing countries: Peril and promise.* Washington, D.C: World Bank.

————. 2003. *Lifelong learning in the global knowledge economy: Challenges for developing countries.* http://web.worldbank.org/WBSITE/EXTERNAL/TOPICS/ EXTEDUCATION/ 0,contentMDK:20283504~menuPK:617592~pagePK:148956 ~piPK:216618~theSitePK:282386,00.html

8 World Bank Discourse and Policy on Education and Cultural Diversity for Latin America[1]

*Eduardo Domenech and
Carlos Mora-Ninci*

INTRODUCTION

After several decades of implementing neoliberal policies in Latin America, neoliberalism shows clear signs of decay, mainly on cultural, political and ideological grounds (Boron, 2003). There is increasing evidence of the failures of neoliberal policies and analysis carried out by mainstream international agencies. However, institutions that respond to the neoliberal orthodoxy are far from retreating.[2] In the field of education, specifically, the World Bank (WB) shows a renewed willingness to continue with those reforms initiated during the 1990s, forcing the implementation of a new political agenda in the current decade. This fact merits an analysis of the role that this international credit organization plays in the building of global neoliberal policies and discourse.

These organizations argue that problems of education are mainly due to poor management, dilapidation of resources, lack of freedom of choice, outdated curricula, and ill-prepared teachers. These themes have often been highlighted by the WB[3] as central issues. Consequently, they blatantly prescribe the need to adopt rigorous structural adjustment policies and the opening of markets of peripheral nations. In particular, the education sector has been the target of privatization schemes, massive dismissals of teachers, lowering of real incomes, decentralizing of services, changes in the curriculum towards more accountability, and higher standards in the direction of unreachable student achievements, accompanied by the sordid involvement of banks and private enterprises in the public affairs of education, all with the exclusive purpose of optimizing profits. Throughout recent decades, the consequences of implementing such policies have produced a general widening gap between, on the one hand, an education system for the private schools and elite universities of the very rich; and on the other, the growth of a ripped-off public school system for the poor, working, and middle classes.

Even though there is a large number of current academic articles which analyze the educational policies of the WB, it is not as frequent that they specifically address the issue of cultural diversity in examining the topics, priorities, and recommendations of the Bank. Our analysis suggests that the WB discourse and policy with regard to diversity and inequality are supported by a technocratic and pragmatic logic founded on a conservative vision of society; at the same time they adhere to (neo)liberal postulates in a combination that has been called *conservative modernization*. It also shows that in the educational sector, the basic principles and strategies of the neoliberal program, as articulated by the WB, have not been yet displaced in spite of the Bank's new post–Washington Consensus rhetoric.[4] For that purpose, we examine several WB documents on education, in particular *Educational Change in Latin America and the Caribbean* (World Bank, 1999a) due to its impact on the current decade of the 2000s (its first publication was in 1999 and a Spanish version appeared as late as 2004). In addition, we also examine the first WB documents with a worldwide scope on education such as *Prioridades y estrategias para la educación* (*Priorities and Strategies for Education;* World Bank, 1996); *Education Sector Strategy* (World Bank, 1999b); and others on topics of ethnicity, indigenous communities, and migration.[5]

The WB is of particular importance because, among other things, it is one of the principal promoters of the *exclusive thought,* a main actor in the implementation of neoliberal ideologies, as well as in the construction of its political agenda.[6] As such, it tries to construct a rigid political ideology, "an ideology which does not refer exclusively to the economy but to the global representation of a reality that asserts, in essence, *that the market is what governs and the Government who administers what is dictated by the market*" (Estefanía, 1998, p. 26; italics in the original). On the other hand, the WB is one of the neoliberal institutions with vast powers for influencing public policy and education, powers that were previously reserved to national governments. As Bonal (2002, p. 4) stated, the use of conditioned loans as mechanisms for financing education presupposes a form of governing that goes beyond the space of the nation-state, and gives a supranational institution the ability to rule without a government. On those grounds, the focus of this study is to analyze the WB political discourse on educational policy as a major player within the global neoliberal project. Thus, this chapter examines the discourse and policy of the WB in the field of education regarding cultural diversity, and its relationship with social inequality since the late 1990s, that is, during the time when a discourse was produced that contributed to shape the policies for the current decade.

THE NEOLIBERAL ADVANCE: THE WASHINGTON CONSENSUS AND BEYOND

As a response to the Latin American crisis of the mid-1970s, international lending agencies prepared a set of measures based on demand-side economics that would be broadly known in the early 1990s as the Washington Consensus. This set of proposals was implicitly adopted by such institutions as the International Monetary Fund (IMF), the WB, the Inter-American Development Bank (IDB), the World Trade Organization (WTO), and the U. S. Department of the Treasury. This neoliberal recipe book consisted of guidelines for the adjustment and stabilization of programs as the only solution for tackling the economic problems of the region, noting that its points of view should not be questioned because they were regarded as optimal. The guidelines were expected to be consistently adopted by the national governments of most Latin American countries. The mode and pace of its implementation varied from country to country according to the particular forms taken by the local dominant sectors, as well as by their relationship with the State apparatus and its subordinate social strata (Castellani, 2002, p. 91).

The neoliberal program is strongly critical of the welfare state, which is blamed for having a high degree of inefficiency, bureaucratization, and centralism, alongside promoting an unfair system. Therefore, the WB has taken a strong position arguing for the reduction of the state and for the strengthening of the markets. From this perspective, the educational systems of Latin America are perceived as experiencing a crisis of efficacy, efficiency, and productivity (Gentili, 1998a). Likewise, the Washington Consensus with respect to the field of education assumes the principle that in order to overcome the current educational crisis the markets must be strong while the state sector should weaken. Therefore, decentralization and privatization of services are promoted as fundamental policy measures for the education sector. According to this view, the problems of education would be solved by tackling the inefficiencies of the sector, such as implementing budgetary constraints and limiting the role of the state; in a similar vein, the field of education should be let loose in the wilderness of free enterprise of private businesses. In this regard, the WB closely follows the recommendations of neoliberal ideologue Milton Friedman, who advocated the elimination of federal- and state-supported higher education programs and the privatization of schools, on the principle that educational finance must focus on the individual and not on the system in order to best respond to the needs of parents and the family.

By the end of the 1990s, some significant changes had been made to the early versions of the Washington Consensus, mainly relating to the role and organization of the state.[7] In this regard, Stiglitz claimed that "the government should be complementary to the market, taking actions to make its functioning better and correcting its flaws" (Stiglitz, 1998, p. 713). The role of the state is still circumscribed within specific modes and social sectors, while the private and nongovernmental organizations have a strategic place in its decision-making processes. That is why Stiglitz suggested placing the discussion on the role played by the State, its activities and methods, instead of focusing on the reduction of the size of the state or on whether the government should be involved in these processes (Stiglitz, 1998, p. 712). Castellani affirms that according to the central recommendations of the post–Washington Consensus period, the state should a) respect, foment, and accept private initiative and the formation of competitive markets; b) in the abence of a high level of institutional capacity, try to provide the goods and public services that cannot be satisfactorily obtained through the market or the voluntary civil society; c) guarantee that its institutions will not act in an arbitrary manner; d) only take on more complex intervention programs when the institutional capacity is highly competitive; e) reinforce its own capacity. States need norms and limitations in society and within their own state apparatuses; they need to promote greater efficiency in the public and private spheres, to facilitate the free exchange of opinions and associations within and beyond their borders, to mainain an independent judiciary system, to promote free association with external agents such as the business and civil society sectors, and to promote internal associations (Castellani, 2002).[8]

According to WB's policies for the first decade of the millennium, the state should increase

> "the efficiency of public finances and the essential services provided by the government, limiting the involvement of governments in those activities that cannot be effectively performed by the private sector, making service providers be more responsive to their clients, and promoting equity and participation of stakeholders in all aspects of the management of social services" (World Bank, 1999a, p. 18).

Thus, the state should support those processes towards decentralization of the economy and the administration, promote the growth of the private sector in financing and implementing educational services, and assure the betterment of quality and efficiency in education and the management of evaluation in education. The WB expects that states would not be the sole agents to deliver educational services. According to this view educational services should be in the hands of local governments, communities, families, individuals, and the private sector. The state should mainly procure educational services to those social sectors that cannot acquire it in the educational market. Following this principle, the WB proposes to raise the pedagogical quality and strengthen public schools for those poor students (World Bank, 1999a). In this sense, the role of the state should be to correct the *imperfections* of the market.

In spite of the rejection of state intervention on the side of the neoliberal current, the truth of the matter is that to be able to provide a continuity of policies and programs, the WB needs official organizations as leading actors. In fact, the WB recommends strengthening the functions of the state with a sturdy but flexible leadership that can provide a continuity within Ministries of Education at the same time that it limits and redefines its tasks at the national level, always targeting what can be best accomplished with loans from international financial agencies.

> Education ministries must have the capacity to formulate, communicate, and implement policy; evaluate schools and programs; and provide technical assistance to local governments, schools and teachers . . . This implies the need for the education ministry to be a learning organization that continually identifies problems, formulates solutions and evaluates results. (World Bank, 1999a, pp. 59–60)

THE WORLD BANK BEHIND THE SCENES

In the WB documents one can observe its hegemonic vocation and strategic interest in carrying out a political project through the dexterous use of the power it enjoys as provider of credit, through the production and systematization of knowledge and experience on a global scale, as well as its use of an extensive network of academic institutions and research centers, civil society and private sector organizations, and the mass media. The WB documents show this strategic interest in order to carry out a political project that uses all the power arising from its participation in transnational relations and networks.[9] For that, the Bank proposals and recommendations are not reduced to, nor should be seen as, mere economic recipes.

> This skill mix, diverse knowledge base, and a broad geographic experience contribute to the analytic rigor of Bank research, project design, and policy advice. These attributes will help the Bank bring neutrality and objectivity to studies, policy advice, and monitoring and evaluation of work in development of the education sector in LAC. The World Bank supports the critical role of monitoring and evaluation in lending operations which contributes to the development of accountability and transparency in the management of the education sector." (World Bank, 1999a, p.70)

In order to legitimize its role as a global leader, one of the central tasks of the WB in educational policies is to organize, select, and prepare knowledge and experience at the worldwide level, especially towards the affairs of developing nations. One way of carrying this out is by studying "good practices" of development in specific case studies that can show its clients how efficiently public policy can be implemented in a sustainable manner. Educational researchers and policy analysts are crucial at this stage as providers of guidelines and examples about how to proceed.

Furthermore, although the partnership of the WB with international agencies like the International Monetary Fund, the World Trade Organization and the U.S. Department of the Treasure is well known, its strategic alliances with other organizations of the United Nations, such as UNESCO and UNICEF, as well as with others at the regional level like the Inter-American Development Bank, is vital to understanding its advance in the field of education and culture.

Without ignoring the important differences amongst these organizations, because in the UN organizations it is common to attribute to the state an active role with its own goals and with a determinate idea of citizenship (Rivero, 1999), the critics seem to be agreed in that the former organizations accept as inevitable the new neoliberal order without questioning, while only procuring a more humane face to the model. At the national level, the WB considers the national ministers of education, as well as other local government agents, private businesses, or nongovernmental associations, to be their natural partners and allies in the implementation of its policy recommendations. It is eloquent that the WB considers the functionaries of the ministries of education "the Bank's education partner" and ministries of finance "the Bank's chief interlocutor" (World Bank, 1999a, p. 70).

The WB, together with international agencies and national governments, seeks to gather together public officials, academics, designers and beneficiaries of nongovernmental programs, with the aim of revising its strategies and policies in search of new agreements and political support for its economic and social reforms.[10] In this process, the WB procures the involvement of all public, private and nongovernmental agencies that are seen as complementary to the optimization of the programs to reduce government expenditures. It is also important to note that the relationship between the WB and these international, governmental and nongovernmental organizations is not linear or unilateral., Also undeniable is the powerful position of the United States over the WB as well as the influence of other such powerful nations in the redesigning of the thought and practice of the Bank, such as in the culture sector where the Bank has had less experience.

The WB was compelled to modify its discourse during the 1990s due to heavy criticism and opposition from various social and political entities, especially the so-called new social movements. As a by-product of those criticisms the WB sought more credibility and legitimacy by associating its policies with successful cases of "good practice" that resulted in sophisticated research and statistical analyses, as well as empirical and theoretical arguments. In addition to the traditional target audience of technicians and specialists, the WB's new audience includes all individuals occupied in social affairs.

The Bank's discourse has become an odd mixture of decontextualization, generalization, distortion, and omission. For instance, it has concealed the real effects of the stabilization policies and economic liberalization implemented in Latin America and made local governments completely responsible for the consequences of these policies—in spite of the fact that the WB is itself a *regulatory* and *proactive* loan agency (Torres, 2002) that fosters the reforms and establishes the conditions for granting credit—thus denying its own role and blaming economic globalization, the invisible hand of our times, as if the WB itself were not one of the key international actors that has engineered the so-called new international order.

WORLD BANK EDUCATION: CULTURAL DIVERSITY AND SOCIAL INEQUALITY IN LATIN AMERICA

The WB has increased its intervention in the field of education to the point of now being the main source of external financing of education in many dependent economies, reaching the level of about one-fourth of all external funds. Since 1980, the total volume of loans for education has tripled, and the proportion of its loans has doubled (World Bank, 1996, p. 162). Its activities are not limited to those of a mere financial agency. After over forty years of action it has become one of the main sources of advice in education, and an important agency that promotes educational research (especially after 1980 when the WB published its first educational policy document) in a field that traditionally belonged to UNESCO.

The WB policy analysts have argued that education is crucial to create economic growth and reduce poverty levels because it enhances the development of human capital through quality investments and specific outreach to the most needy sectors of society, which should in turn help to achieve sustainable benefits for its investments (World Bank, 1999a). Some of the excluded sectors in need of urgent attention are certain ethnic minorities who should be the immediate target of investment according to the Bank's vision of education for human capital (World Bank, 1999a). The Bank's guiding principle is that the betterment of educational achievement of the poor, women, and indigenous populations would increase the chances of economic wealth and reduction of poverty levels.

According to the theory of human capital, education is seen as an investment to improve the individual's personal productivity, and consequently lift their occupational status and income. This approach relies on an individualist perspective that promotes personal challenge through acquiring higher levels of education over structural social conditions of inequality, making each individual person solely responsible for his or her own successes and failures. According to Verena Stolcke this is a liberal illusion that assumes that through mere will, and with a lot of efforts and time, most social obstacles can be overcome, but that in fact this is an ideology that hides the underlying causes of inequality in a system of exploitation of the majority by a small powerful minority (Stolcke, 1998, p. 321).

Likewise, the principles and strategic goals of the WB do not change in the context of the post–Washington Consensus period. Its policy recommendations continue to be based on cost-benefit models of education that seek high returns on educational investments and are linked to the principles that constitute the hard core of neoliberal thought: equity, efficiency, efficacy, and quality. The WB's goals still include the achievement of equity by improving efficiency, efficacy, and quality through compensatory, focused, and decentralized policies (World Bank 1999a, 1999b).

Compensatory and focused policies substitute the idea of equality for that of equity.[11] The supporters of equity elaborate this concept on both the unfinished project of modernity and its ideals, and have altered the meaning of equality on the wrong supposition that equality is the same as homogeneity; in fact, equality means universality, while equity is concerned with particularity. The notion of equality is grounded on the universal request that can start from the singular in what can be called (González Casanova, 1994) a *particularistic universalism;* on the other hand, equity can be projected from its *universalistic particularism.* That is to say, equality implies the notion of common welfare or general interest, while equity implies paying attention to particular interest, which is rooted in individualism. Even though neoliberalism shares with classical liberalism its adherence to individualism,[11] in the neoliberal version it loses the social component that is present in the liberal tradition. Individualism, according to Gentili (1998b), supports itself in an ethics of gain which rejects any relationship between common good and equality. In this sense, neoliberalism is founded on a "thesis of incompatibility" between individual and social interests, where the search for the well-being of society contradicts the individual search of maximization of profits in the market.

Friedrich von Hayek, one of the founding fathers of the neoliberal doctrine, maintained that the only way to put people in an equal position was to treat them as different, thus opposing egalitarianism as a threat to individual liberties (DiPol, 1987, p. 44). Thus, following this view in the field of education, educational supply should be diversified and rely on the notion of equity. However, what actually occurs is that diversity in the educational supply-side model ends up reinforcing and legitimizing the unequal distribution of knowledge and produces educational circuits that are differential in terms of the social and cultural backgrounds of the actors. This gives grounds to what Díaz and Alonso (2004) have called a *pedagogy for the poor* or a *pedagogy for the excluded.*

Compensatory policies help consolidate the segmentation and fragmentation of educational circuits. The WB does not only seek to facilitate access and provide education for these social sectors and cultural groups, but also to satisfy their basic needs, such as nutrition, health, and so forth. It is common that these subaltern sectors receive a public-service type of education. As it has been broadly accepted, the problem is that within contexts of poverty, assistentialism is the substitute rather than the complement to the pedagogical function, a process that Achilli (1996) calls *neutralization of the educational function.* It evokes the deterioration of the pedagogical practice at the level of elaboration of pertinent strategies, as well as at the level of representations and expectations that allows generating actual learning in children. That is, within this context, the school only plays an assistentialist function that displaces other pedagogical responsibilities. It is to note that from the WB perspective, the detection and satisfaction of basic needs are not based upon arguments linked to liberal principles, such as human rights, but based on criteria of efficiency, efficacy, and profitability.

> There is by now substantial evidence that poor health and an inadequate early learning environment lead to handicaps that are difficult to reverse later in life, beginning with difficulties in school that result in the high probability of school repetition and early drop out . . . Thus, these handicaps lower the return to both private and public investment in education. Early childhood programs may both increase the efficiency of investments in schooling and promote equity in the population they serve. (World Bank, 1999a, p. 53)

The idea of focused policies is derived from, and complementary to, the concept of equity. For the WB the "disadvantaged groups" that are the target of focused and compensatory programs should be clearly identified, and its policies concentrated on those representing higher risks. In this way, indigenous communities and ethnic and linguistic minorities are reduced to the category of *disadvantaged* groups,[13] and therefore are the object of analysis and intervention of the WB's focused and compensatory programs. The interest of the WB in these communities is framed within the relationship between poverty, culture, and development, and as a framework of analysis and action, they are subject to restrictions under the principles of economic pragmatism. The WB is interested in studying and monitoring these ethnic and cultural minorities with the purpose that they might be of help to economic development.[14] This focus on indigenous communities should be understood as a way to deal with issues of development with the purpose of furthering capital expansion and opportunities. These communities have traditionally been outside the outskirts of the market and its emphasis is precisely to bring them inside the realm of capital. Furthermore, the focus on these communities is also due to their anticapitalist nature as they provide further motives for attention.[15]

The WB recommends the implementation of special measures on the financial front directed towards the "disadvantaged groups," with the goal of raising enrollment and retention levels in schooling.[16] These measures are to provide bilingual education in those countries with multiple linguistic communities (World Bank, 1999a). Bilingual education is understood as an instrument to reach equity levels in terms of efficiency and efficacy. Good practices in this area are those schools where there is a high degree of linguistic flexibility in instruction, parental support, and no prescriptive application in the curriculum. The recent WB policy recommendations do not emphasize the provision of bilingual education at the elementary level and it is justified only as belonging to basic education. It seems that beyond certain basic years of schooling, bilingual education ceases to be profitable.[17] As stated by Kincheloe and Steinberg (1999) in relation to what Peter McLaren (1995) calls *conservative multiculturalism,* the educational, social, and political precepts formulated by the New Right seek to protect the market economy, which is allowed to damage the people in the name of a more efficient economy. The WB policy recommendations in regard to bilingual education are not based on liberal ideals, as might be those of collective rights or the peoples' rights, or cultural recognition, but on technocratic concepts of quality of education defined in neoliberal terms as more efficient educational services where the training for the labor market is the top priority.

> Learning is more efficient and it can save time if in the first grades instruction is given in the children's native language . . . Once a solid knowledge has been acquired in the native language, the national, regional or metropolitan language can be learnt in the upper grades of primary school as a preparation for High School. *However, the production of textbooks in the native language can increase the costs of education.* (World Bank, 1996, pp. 86–87, emphasis added)

> The fact of not knowing the dominant language can limit the opportunities of learning and employment mobility and thus reduce people's income and opportunities to escape poverty. Therefore, there is an incentive based on the labor market for learning the dominant language. (World Bank, 1996, pp. 87–88)

Within the "disadvantaged groups" the WB also includes the subcategories of nomads, as well as those who live in isolated regions, street children, and refugees. For each group a different strategy should be applied, for example for the "disadvantaged" nonformal methods are more appropriate than formal schooling. The policy of the WB is not to include these sectors in the formal school system, which in general is the only system financed and controlled by the state. Thus, the Bank does not actually intend to include all the excluded people but only those whose inclusion is profitable, or whose exclusion would be a threat to social order. In fact, for the WB strategists, the idea of socioeconomic inclusion is not one of full or equal citizenship rights. The poverty of these sectors is treated as an anomaly of the free will of the markets, not assuming at any level a redistribution of socioeconomic resources and income[18] (Bonal, 2002, p. 26).

It is also interesting to observe in WB documents the description of how indigenous peoples have been subject to domination and exploitation during the colonial period and the role attributed to the nation-state in the process of cultural homogenization, in opposition to its open posture on cultural diversity and participative strategies. It seems that oppression, inequality, and assimilation solely function within the milieu of personal circumstances (Kincheloe and Steinberg, 1999, p. 38). Likewise, the WB describes the material and symbolic circumstances under which ethnic minorities participate in the educational system, where unequal conditions are believed to be due to the cultural conflict between school and community. Thus, the Bank overlooks the complex mechanisms and social actors behind the construction of inequality related to socioeconomic order. In the same way, it limits its recommendations to the understanding and acknowledgement of ethnic differences, aligning with a tendency that is also promoted by other agents of capital which minimize or deny the classist character of social inequality. As evidence, the Bank attributes the low levels of school achievement and high dropout rates to differences of culture and language and of cultural and family environment. This naturalization and concealing of unequal social conditions through cultural or ethnic differences can also be found in other WB documents: "Indigenous peoples are *different* as a group because they *share* a history of colonial repression and are viewed as *different* by external power structures" (Roper, Frechione and DeWalt, 1996, p. 3, emphasis added).

This is precisely what has been denounced as *conservative multiculturalism,* which regards "diversity" as uncovering the ideology of assimilation (McLaren, 1995). Once cultural diversity is understood merely as a harmonic and horizontal coexistence of different cultures (that is, as a nonconflictual or unhierarchical relationship between cultural groups), then the actual structures of power and domination that are the cause of social and ethnic violence are reinforced by the defense of difference (Grüner, 2002). In the terrain of education, the perspective of diversity is doubly problematic when it is limited to a proclamation of diversity without a pedagogy centered on the political critique of identity and difference (Silva, 2000, p. 73).

Neoliberalism's interpretation and appropriation of cultural diversity can by generalized under the liberal rubric of the necessary, the possible and the indicated: to increase respect and tolerance (Díaz and Alonso, 1997). In this sense, the new processes of social and cultural integration molded as *essentialist multiculturalism* (Bauman, 2001), and based on a liberal discourse of respect and tolerance to diversity and difference, would not be encouraging emancipatory practices or assuming a model or proposal for change or an alternative to the classic assimilationist integration. On the contrary, this practice can serve to cover up mechanisms and processes of devaluation, segregation, discrimination, and inequality in the struggle of ethnic minorities for public space.

Related to policies of decentralization is the issue of *partnership.* The negotiations that the WB has established with indigenous organizations show this approach. Far from any idea of communitarianism, this strategy is promoted by the WB as a criterion of efficacy and efficiency, as well as to seek a consensus that would assure legitimacy and reduce the tone of its critics (Bonal, 2002, p. 27). One of the main problems with programs promoting decentralization and participation in "developing" nations, and the reason why most such programs do not work in the long term, is that they represent societies as being for the most part homogeneous, without considering their great social variety, such as class differences within local communities.[19]

A clear demonstration is the approach toward indigenous communities in Latin America with the purpose of promoting self-development and ethnodevelopment. In the above-mentioned report by Roper, Frechione and DeWalt (1996), even though the WB takes account of indigenous involvement throughout the different stages of development with the purpose of ensuring local priorities, what commands most attention is the internalization of the projects on the part of its participants.[20] That is, the presence or the formation of indigenous organizations is encouraged and supported only when they serve the organs of representation (vis-à-vis the Bank) in the processes of development and when they carry out local initiatives. Likewise, as already discussed on the issue of bilingual education, the use or construction of indigenous knowledge is only justified in order to guarantee the success of the project. On the other hand, even though the authors highlight the importance of a legal framework that accounts for indigenous rights, the WB documents suggest that land and other natural resources can be considered a prerequisite or a condition for the success of development, but it cannot assure its accomplishment. Following traditional neoliberal doctrine, this position suggests that the WB is more ready to accept legal egalitarianism before social and economic egalitarianism, given that the latter puts economic freedom under risk of socioeconomic turmoil. These thoughts and liberal practices seek to reconcile their proclamation of formal equality before the law, together with the support of ideas of inequality facing the material conditions of life.

In another document of the WB (Partridge and Uquillas, 1996, p. 31) dedicated to ethnodevelopment and which seeks to plan future strategies, neoliberalism again postulates the need for approaches based on decentralized processes of development that would also include (in addition to indigenous peoples) representatives from governments and nongovernmental organizations in recognition of social and cultural diversity. These changes are due to proven impacts of bleak strategies that have been implemented before. They conclude that the only manner of assuring an efficient focused policy and distributing development projects is to assign them directly to the indigenous governments and leaders. In the projects financed by the Bank, it covers up the real effects of participation of indigenous organizations with a discourse on *partnership*. In fact, the WB disguises through a discourse on partnership the actual effects of the participation of indigenous organizations in the financed projects. It forces the indigenous organizations to lose autonomy through their involvement in monitoring, evaluating, and claims for accountability, at the same time that these communities internalize the criteria of the Bank.

The fact that the Bank seeks to assist "the great masses of indigenous population" to overcome their poverty by strengthening their participation in the development process, makes one think that the Bank's interest is to include these groups from the market economy as a way to achieve its purposes of liberalization, deregulation, and privatization, as well as to control those who might challenge its objectives.

Last but not the least is the WB interest in what is known as *education in values.* Among the responsibilities that the Bank renders to the State and which justifies its investments, the issues of social cohesion and democracy are emphasized, which should both be promoted through education (to be precise, another issue implicit in most of the documents is the identification of democracy with the market, in spite of the connotations of tension and contradiction in this relation; through simple logic, the WB states that democracy equals freedom, freedom equals the market; therefore democracy is equivalent to the market). This role of education complements the social conflicts and violent confrontations that paradoxically have taken place in the Latin American region precisely due to the brutal implementation of neoliberal reforms.

> Three interrelated social goals drive government investment in education in LAC countries: providing a skilled and flexible workforce in the interest of economic growth, fostering social cohesion and promoting democracy, and reducing social inequalities and poverty. (World Bank, 1999a, p. 9)

> Policies of inclusion are essential to fostering social cohesion and decreasing the incidence of violence and social unrest. (World Bank, 1999a, p. 51)

> Social cohesion and democratic participation cannot be achieved unless all citizens are educated and taught "a spirit of cooperation and integrity" (Summit of the Americas II, 1998, cited in World Bank, 1999a, p. 20)

The WB discourse denotes a degree of disciplining under the democratic regimes even though it adheres to the liberal idea of developing "educational strategies for both inside and outside the classroom that foster democratic principles, human rights, gender equity, peace, tolerance, and respect for the environment and natural resources" (World Bank, 1999a, p. 75). Indeed, its call for social cohesion and democracy might indicate a call for discipline since neoliberal thought "tries to enunciate a practical 'utility' of the democratic system as a form of government that assures and protects . . . economic freedom, the right to choose; in short: the implementation and expansion of property rights" (Gentili, 1998b, p. 59).

THE WORLD EDUCATION FORUM OF PORTO ALEGRE: A RESPONSE TO NEOLIBERAL AND NEOCONSERVATIVE POLICIES

As we have seen in this chapter, the WB promotes educational strategies and policies based on (neo)liberal principles which adhere to a pragmatic, technocratic, and conservative vision of society. That is the reason why many progressive social movements linked to the World Education Forum (started in Porto Alegre, Brazil, in 2001) are an alternative and a legitimate response to neoliberal and neoconservative policies in the fields of education and culture opposed to other organizations, that intend to provide these policies a human face. The creation of the World Education Forum is seen as a new space to fight neoliberal hegemony with a proposal directed towards the search for universality in public, secular, free, quality education that is socially distinct.

As it is claimed in its founding declaration, its purpose is to create a collective social movement that will mobilize educators, students, unions, social movements, governments, nongovernmental organizations, universities, and schools, to advance the debate to motivate the citizenry on the difficulties and successes in carrying out an education for freedom, all-inclusive, capable of motivating an active citizenry, inter/multicultural, and planetary.[21]

The consensus among the different social sectors involved in this forum against neoliberalism seems to have been reached through the common commitment to public education as an exclusive social right. The World Education Forum appears at this historical moment not by accident when the agencies of the United Nations and other international organizations such as the WB, the WTO, the IMF, etc., are being heavily questioned and are in need of legitimation. International events such as the World Conference on Education for All in Jomtien (Thailand, 1990) and the World Education Forum in Dakar (Senegal, 2000)[22] contributed to the distrust of the likelihood of these mega-events helping the development of policies and strategies directed at overcoming the great issues of inequality within education and access to quality education. The World Education Forum of Porto Alegre asserted the importance of public education in renewing the expectations surrounding emancipatory education, and of suggesting critical alternatives in order to build the idea that *Another World is Possible*—as claimed by the World Education Forum slogan—moving away from the technocratic concepts and proposals that proliferate in other international meetings.

The political goals of the World Education Forum are based on democratic and participatory principles. Its organizational structure seeks to democratize the decision-making process by implementing mechanisms of collective elaboration. This Forum seeks to avoid the establishment of a centralized power structure away from democratic criteria that were common in the international events of Jomtien and Dakar. It is expected that the World Education Forum will articulate the international and local struggles for public, free, democratic, and quality education as a right for all citizens, as well as a state obligation constructed on behalf of organized society.

Given the wide variety of events called by representatives of national governments, nongovernmental organizations, and international agencies, one feature distinguishes the World Education Forum from the rest: the participation of diverse social sectors, from educators and individual researchers to diverse social actors and unions. It is interesting to note the absence from the World Education Forum of international development organizations, even though their participation in education is growing and ever more frequent. As we have already seen, the WB is amongst the top sponsors of the international meetings of education that took place in Jomtien and Dakar. On the other hand, the World Education Forum of Porto Alegre also fights for the universalization of education and for the reduction of illiteracy, but it explicitly defends the public, secular, and free, emancipatory, and popular nature of education, fully funded by the state, guaranteed at primary and secondary levels, for all social sectors. Instead, the role of education supported by Jomtien, and specially by Dakar, leaves grounds for a technocratic perspective based on some of the neoliberal axioms such as efficiency and focused policies.

In short, the fundamental difference between the Jomtien and Dakar meetings organized by UNESCO (amongst other UN agencies) together with the WB, on the one hand, and on the other the World Educational Forum of Porto Alegre, is the formulation of two opposite projects for world society. The World Education Forum must transcend its own claims in order to develop a space from which to articulate critical and emancipatory proposals and actions for social and educational change, with the purpose to influence in public affairs and to develop its full potential to intervene at the national and international stages.

NOTES

1. An earlier version of this chapter was presented in the 2004 meeting of the Working Group on Culture and Power of CLACSO, the Latin American Council for the Social Sciences. We would like to thank Prof. Ignacio Marcial Candioti for his assessment of the translation of the English version of this chapter.
2. See Sader and Gentili (1999) for a discussion on the scope of neoliberalism and its alternatives in the fields of culture, politics, and the economy in Latin America.
3. The World Bank Group is integrated with the International Bank for Reconstruction and Development (IBRD), the International Development Association (IDA) and three affiliated institutions: the International Finance Corporation (IFC), the Multilateral Investment Guarantee Agency (MIGA)

and the International Centre for Settlement of Investment Disputes (ICSID). The World Bank started with the Bretton Woods agreements that took place in New Hampshire, United States in 1944 within the framework of the International Monetary and Financial Conference of the United Nations.

4. We regard here the dominant institutional vision of the WB, which does not mean that its discourse and policies might not have fissures and contradictions, or that tensions and conflicts still exist inside this organization as has been shown by official documents of the Bank (Torres, 1997) or by the formation of internal associations with the purpose of promoting and defending the interests of its functionaries, following their own ethnic or national identification (Ribeiro, 2002).

5. See Bates (1999); Clark, Hatton, and Williamson (2004); Collier (1999); Davis (1993); Partridge and Uquillas (1996); Psacharopoulos (1992); Psacharopoulos and Patrinos (1994); Roper, Frechione, and DeWalt (1996); Russell (1995); and Schiff (1996).

6. It should be noted that in this study we deal with an international organization which is clearly identified with neoliberal ideas, but as Daniel Mato has pointed out, it is important to analyze social actors who do not necessarily perceive themselves as neoliberals (social and political leaders, professionals of diverse disciplines and traditions, and opinion builders, among others) as well as those with roots in the commonsense neoliberal types of local functionaries, especially those who participate of decision-making processes facing organizations such as the IMF and the WB which put into question the unilateral idea of this relationship. On the other hand, the importance of certain institutions on the development of professional networks and research centers dedicated to the creation, diffusion, and promotion of neoliberal thought and policies should not be ignored

7. Such change is promoted by intellectuals like Joseph Stiglitz, who was vice president and chief economist of the WB during the last years of the 1990s. In general terms, he advanced a critique of certain technical aspects of the Washington Consensus, which even though it proposes broadening the Consensus's aims and further changing its neoliberal rhetoric, nevertheless does not question the paradigm of development or its objectives. That is, Stiglitz's analysis questions and reviews the Washington Consensus regarding its main outcome, to help markets function better.

8. Whether it was the Keynesian paradigm of the enhanced role of the state or whether it was a phase of the new doctrine on "Another World is Possible," none of these ideas tackle the inherent flaws underlying capitalism itself. Many intellectuals propagate the idea that capitalism can have a more "human face," whereas the ideology about the so-called withdrawal of the state and the current shifts towards commercialization of education might emerge from this odd idea of humanitarian capitalism. We thank Ravi Kumar for this comment.

9. See Mato (2001, 2004) for a discussion about transnational relations and networks in the Latin American context.

10. In effect, the elaboration of the main World Bank document that we discuss here was produced under the auspices of such a conference (2004). For example, James Wolfensohn, the President of the World Bank at the time, called national ministers of education and leaders of the private sector in Latin America and the Caribbean to meet in Washington D.C. in 1998 to reinforce the basic agreements of the Summit of the Americas II that had taken place a few months before in Santiago, Chile. The objective of this meeting was to give policy support for the principles outlined in the Summit of the Americas for 2010: focused policies, evaluation of the quality of education, teachers' professional training, decentralization, and training for the labor market.

11. Even though the WB document *Educational Change in Latin America and the Caribbean* (1999) refers to the terms inequality, social inequality, and extreme inequality, setting it apart from previous documents which did not use them, the issue of poverty continues to be understood in terms of equity, which is seen in one of the priority reforms established for the following decade: its attention to equity.

12. Eric Hobsbawm, in a conference delivered at the Institute of Education of London in 1996, recalls the division that exists between the left and the politics of identity. He postulated that while the political project of the left is universalistic, the politics of identity is directed only to members of an specific group. The only form of politics of identity based on a common cause, at least within the limits of the state, would be that of civic nationalism (Hobsbawm, 2000).

13. For the WB, this category mainly includes "indigenous populations, poor children in rural and urban areas, the physically handicapped and, in many instances, girls. Policies of inclusion are essential to fostering social cohesion and decreasing the incidence of violence and civil unrest" (World Bank, 1999a, p. 51). Another denomination used by the neoliberal discourse that refers to the excluded, oppressed, and exploited population is "vulnerable groups" (See Briones et al., 2007).

14. This coincides with the international concern for the Balkan conflicts and its potential extension to other regions of the world. For instance, in the mid-1990s, the International Labor Organization included issues related to indigenous peoples in its negotiations with Argentina because of fears that new foci of conflict might be propagated. On the other hand, the resurgence of a perspective that is founded on the management of cultural and ethnic conflicts should be noted. Actions such as Program MOST of UNESCO, which promotes from its project Multicultural and Multiethnic Societies a harmonic and enriched vision of ethnic and cultural relations, reassured by the respect of individual human rights under the banner of tolerance and liberal democracy, show the degree of involvement with the logic of neoliberalism within diverse international organizations. This logic comes to displace policies of management of multiculturalism, migration, and cultural diversity.

15. We appreciate the comments on this paragraph made by Ravi Kumar.

16. The WB points out that the lowering turnout of ethnic minority students at schools is due to the fact that students are "generally poor and also to the normative on languages" (World Bank, 1996, p. 49).

17. For example, in the year 1990 the WB sponsors together with UNESCO the world conference on Education for All in Jomtien and ten years later participates in the World Educational Forum that took place in Dakar (it should not be confused with the homonymous meeting of Porto Alegre). It is not a minor fact that even though the WB is one of the sponsors, it distances itself from the idea of expanded/extended education that came out of the Jomtien event and sustains its defense for basic education. During the same period, ten years later the WB imposed its perspective in the World Educational Forum in Dakar in 2000. It reduced what in Jomtien was agreed as education for all, there was a focalization on poverty (the poor among the poorest) combined with a focalization on infancy, especially on girls. Furthermore, the notion of basic education was constrained to elementary education (while in Jomtien the possibility of including secondary education was contemplated; Torres, 2000).

18. In this sense, the WB's own slogan, "Our Dream is a World Without Poverty," is misleading, since it claim a reduction of poverty—it never refers to

elimination—without altering the mechanisms of social and cultural reproduction which are intrinsic to a model of capitalist accumulation.
19. We would like to thank Ravi Kumar for his important comment on this issue.
20. See Briones et al. (2007) for an interesting discussion on the role carried out
by some indigenous individuals and anthropologist as consultants, experts,
and managers in the implementation of plans and programs by national and
international organizations.
21. More information about the World Social Forum and the World Education
Forum can be found at http://www.forumsocialmundial.org.br.
22. In 1990, delegates from 155 countries as well as representatives from some 150
organizations agreed at the World Conference on Education for All (Jomtien,
Thailand, March 5–9, 1990) to universalize primary education and massively
reduce illiteracy before the end of the decade. The World Education Forum
(Dakar, Senegal, April 2000) was the first event in education at the dawn of the
new century. By adopting the Dakar Framework for Action, the eleven hundred
participants of the Forum reaffirmed their commitment to achieving education
for all by the year 2015. More information about these events can be found at
http://www.unesco.org/education/efa/ed_for_all/background/world_confer-
ence_jomtien.shtml and http://www.unesco.org/education/efa/wef_2000/.

REFERENCES

Achilli, E. 1996. *Práctica docente y diversidad sociocultural. Los desafíos de la igualdad educativa frente a la desigualdad social.* Rosario: Universidad Nacional de Rosario/Homo Sapiens.
Bates, R. 1999. Ethnicity, capital formation, and conflict. Working paper no. 22838. Washington, D.C.: World Bank.
Bauman, G. 2001. *El enigma multicultural. Un replanteamiento de las identidades nacionales, étnicas y religiosas.* Barcelona: Paidós.
Bonal, X. 2002. Globalización y política educativa: Un análisis crítico de la agenda del Banco Mundial para América Latina. *Revista Mexicana de Sociología* 64, no. 3: 3–35.
Boron, A. 2003. Prefacio a la segunda edición en lengua castellana. In *La trama del neoliberalismo: Mercado, crisis y exclusión* social, ed. E. Sader and P. Gentili, 7–16. Buenos Aires: Eudeba/Consejo Latinoamericano de Ciencias Sociales.
Briones, C., L. Cañuqueo, L. Kropff, and M. Leudan. 2007. Assessing the effects of multicultural neoliberalism. A perspective from the south of the south (Patagonia, Argentina). *Latin American and Caribbean Ethnic Studies* 2, no. 1: 69–91.
Castellani, A. G. 2002. Implementación del modelo neoliberal y restricciones al desarrollo en la Argentina contemporánea. In *Mas allá del pensamiento único*, ed. M. Schorr, A.G. Castellani, M. Duarte, and D. Debrott Sánchez. Buenos Aires: Consejo Latinoamericano de Ciencias Sociales.
Clark, X., T. Hatton, and J. Williamson. 2004. Explaining U.S. immigration 1971–1998. World Bank Policy Research Working Paper No. 3252. Washington, D.C.: World Bank.
Collier, P. 1999. *Implications of ethnic diversity.* Washington, D.C.: World Bank.
Davis, S. 1993. The World Bank and indigenous peoples. World Bank Working Paper No. 27205. Washington, D.C.: World Bank.
Díaz, R., and G. Alonso. 2004. *Construcción de espacios interculturales.* Buenos Aires: Miño y Dávila.
———. 1997. Cultura, pedagogia y politica. Algunos cruces entre educación popular e intercultural. In *Cuadernos de Pedagogia*, No 2.

DiPol, R. S. 1987. Educación, libertad y eficiencia en el pensamiento y en los programas del neoliberalismo. *Revista de Educación* 288: 37–62.

Estefanía, J. 1998. *Contra el pensamiento único*. Madrid: Taurus.

Gentili, P. 1998a. El consenso de Washington y la crisis de la educación en América Latina. In *Neoliberalismo versus democracia*, ed. F. Álvarez-Uría, A. García Santesmases, J. Muguerza, J. Pastor, G. Rendueles, and J. Varela, 102–129. Madrid: La Piqueta.

———. 1998b. *Retórica de la desigualdad. Los fundamentos doctrinarios de la reforma educativa neoliberal*. Doctoral thesis. Buenos Aires: Universidad de Buenos Aires.

González Casanova, P. 1994. Lo universal y lo particular a fines del siglo XX. *Nueva Sociedad* 134: 42–57.

Grüner, E. 2002. *El fin de las pequeñas historias. De los estudios culturales al retorno (imposible) de lo trágico*. Buenos Aires: Paidós.

Hobsbawm, E. 2000. La izquierda y la política de la identidad. *New Left Review (Spanish Edition)* 0: 114–25.

Kincheloe, J., and S. Steinberg. 1999. *Repensar el multiculturalismo*. Barcelona: Octaedro.

Mato, D. 2001. Producción transnacional de representaciones sociales y transformaciones sociales en tiempos de globalización. In *Estudios latinoamericanos sobre cultura y transformaciones sociales en tiempos de globalización*, ed. D. Mato, 127–159. Buenos Aires: Consejo Latinoamericano de Ciencias Sociales.

———. 2004. Redes transnacionales de actores globales y locales en la producción de representaciones de ideas de sociedad civil. In *Políticas de ciudadanía y sociedad civil en tiempos de globalización*, ed. D. Mato, 68–93. Caracas: Facultad de Ciencias Economicas y Sociales (FACES)/Universidad Central de Venezuela.

McLaren, P. 1995. *Critical pedagogy and predatory culture: Oppositional politics in a postmodern era*. New York and London: Routledge.

Partridge, W., and J. Uquillas. 1996. Including the excluded: Ethnodevelopment in Latin America. World Bank Working Paper No. 27202. Washington, D.C.: World Bank.

Psacharopoulos, G. 1992. Ethnicity, education, and earnings in Bolivia and Guatemala. World Bank Working Paper No. 1014. Washington, D.C: World Bank.

Psacharopoulos, G., and H. Patrinos, eds. 1994. *Indigenous people and poverty in Latin America. An empirical analysis*. Washington, D.C.: World Bank.

Ribeiro, G. 2002. Diversidad étnica en el planeta Banco. Cosmopolitismo y transnacionalismo en el Banco Mundial. *Nueva Sociedad* 178: 70–88.

Rivero, J. 1999. *Educación y exclusión en América Latina*. Buenos Aires: Miño y Dávila.

Roper, M., J. Frechione, and B. DeWalt. 1996. Indigenous people and development in Latin America: A literature survey and recommendations. World Bank Working Paper No. 27203. Washington, D.C.: World Bank.

Russell, S. S. 1995. International migration: Implications for the World Bank. World Bank Human Capital Development and Operations Policy Working Paper No. 54. Washington, D.C.: World Bank.

Sader, E., and P. Gentili, eds. 1999. *La trama del neoliberalismo. Mercado, crisis y exclusión social*. Buenos Aires: Consejo Latinoamericano de Ciencias Sociales.

Schiff, M. 1996. South–North Migration and Trade. A Survey. World Bank Working Paper No. 1696. Washington, D.C.: World Bank.

Silva, T. T. da. 2000. A produçao social da identidade e da diferença. In *Identidade e diferença. A perspectiva dos Estudos Culturais*, ed. T. T. da Silva, 73–102. Petrópolis, RJ: Vozes.

Stiglitz, J. 1998. Más instrumentos y metas más amplias para el desarrollo. Hacia el consenso post-Washington. *Desarrollo Económico* 38, no. 151: 691–722.

Stolcke, V. 1998. ¿Es el sexo para el género como la raza para la etnicidad? In *Neo-liberalismo versus democracia,* ed. F. Álvarez-Uría, A. García Santesmases, J. Muguerza, J. Pastor, G. Rendueles, and J. Varela, 292–327. Madrid: La Piqueta.

Torres, C. A. 2002. The state, privatization and educational policy: A critique of neo-liberalism in Latin America and some ethical and political implications. *Comparative Education* 38, no. 4: 365–85.

Torres, R. M. 1997. ¿Mejorar la calidad de la educación básica? La estrategia del Banco Mundial. In *La educación según el Banco Mundial. Un análisis de sus propuestas y métodos,* ed. J. L. Coraggio and R. M. Torres, 73–164. Buenos Aires: Miño y Dávila.

———. 2000. ¿Qué pasó en el Foro Mundial de la Educación? http://www.frone-sis.org/documentos/quepasoenelforodedakar (accessed November 30, 2005).

———. 1996. *Prioridades y estrategias para la educación: Examen del Banco Mundial.* Washington, D.C.: World Bank.

———. 1999a. *Educational change in Latin America and the Caribbean: A World Bank strategy paper.* Washington, D.C.: World Bank.

———. 1999b. *Education sector strategy.* Washington, D.C.: World Bank.

9 The News Media and the Conservative Heritage Foundation
Promoting Education Advocacy at the Expense of Authority

Eric Haas

INTRODUCTION

Almost every U.S. household owns a television and a radio (Croteau and Hoynes, 2000); on a typical day over half of American adults read a newspaper (Newspaper Association of America, 2000); and the average American adult spends over two hours a day watching, reading, or listening to the news (National Science Foundation, 2000 p. A-579). While Americans are often skeptical about news reports on education, they nevertheless want the news media to cover education more than it currently does (Farkas, 1997). Therefore, when the news media select a source on education, they position it to play a prominent role in shaping the education debate (Cuban, 1998; Farkas, 1997; Moses, 2007).

Since Americans rely on mass media news as an important source of information on education issues, they indirectly vest news sources with the power to help define the terms of the debate. It is not that, through the selection of its sources, the news media tell Americans *what* to think, so much as frame what to think *about* (Cuban, 1998). In other words, those education issues defined by the public and policy makers as problems and the types of solutions needed to address them are, to a large extent, influenced by the sources selected by the news media (Davis and Owen, 1998; van Dijk, 2001; Fairclough, 1995; Herman and Chomsky, 1988; Lawrence, 2000; McChesney, 1999; Page, Shapiro, and Dempsey, 1987).

The number of think tanks and their use by the news media as expert commentators has grown steadily, if not dramatically, in the last twenty years (Abelson, 2002; Dolny, 1996, 1997, 1998, 2000, 2001, 2002; Rich and Weaver, 2000; Smith, 1991). Analyses of the news media's use of think tank experts can be categorized into three main groups: descriptions of social change apparatuses, mostly conservative, of which think tanks and the media are integral and interconnected parts (see, e.g., Abelson, 2002; Blumenthal, 1986; Callahan, 1999; Diamond, 1995; Ricci, 1993; Rich and Weaver, 1998; Smith, 1991); descriptions of specific public policy campaigns, mostly conservative (see, e.g., Lieberman, 2000; Messer-Davidow,

1993); and statistics on the news media's use or description of all types of think tanks (see, e.g., Dolny 1996, 1997, 1998, 2000, 2001, 2002; Rich and Weaver, 2000; Solomon, 1996; Steele, 1995). Though education has been a consistent subject of think tank publications from the Heritage Foundation's seminal booklet *A New Agenda for Education* (Gardiner, 1985) to the present day (see, e.g., RAND Corporation's book *Rhetoric versus Reality* [Gill, Timpane, Ross, and Brewer 2002]; the Heritage Foundation's booklet *School Choice 2003* [Kafer, 2003]; and the Economic Policy Institute's book *Class and Schools* [Rothstein, 2004]), no analysis of the think tank–media relationship has focused extensively on K–12 education.

This chapter presents data on the scope and presentation of the education-related documents and spokespersons from the Heritage Foundation by the news media during 2001.[1] The Heritage Foundation is the subject of this chapter because it is one of the largest, most cited, and most influential think tanks of a conservative movement that dominates public policy debate and formation (Abelson, 2002; Diamond, 1995; Ricci, 1993; Scatamburlo, 1998). It is intended that this chapter will contribute to the larger understanding of how the news media use and present information about education.

This chapter shows that news media outlets across the country regularly included the Heritage Foundation as an expert source of information on education in their presentation of education issues despite their general consensus that they are an advocacy think tank rather than an academic research think tank (Rich, 2004; Weaver and McGann, 2000). This use and presentation likely increased their influence in promoting conservative education policies like school choice, reductions in education spending, and high-stakes standardized testing (Anderson, 2007; van Dijk, 2001; Page, Shapiro, and Dempsey, 1987). Before presenting the results of this examination, the literature on the news media use and presentation of think tanks will be reviewed, highlighting aspects of the literature that discuss the Heritage Foundation. Then the methodology and the results of the content analysis will be presented, along with a brief overview of the Heritage Foundation and the results of the content analysis, followed by a discussion of the findings.

THE RISE OF THINK TANKS

Think tanks are defined here as organizations that have significant autonomy from governmental interests and that synthesize, create and/or disseminate information, ideas and/or advice to the public, policy makers, other organizations (both private and governmental), and/or the press (Rich, 2004; Ricci, 1993; Smith, J., 1991; Weaver and McGann, 2000; Weaver and Stares, 2001). The first think tanks appeared in the first half of the 1900s (for example, the Hoover Institution, 1919; the Council on Foreign Relations, 1921; and the Brookings Institution, 1927). More appeared in the 1940s and 1950s (for example, the American Enterprise Institute, 1943 and RAND, 1948). They further proliferated during the 1970s and 1980s (for example, the Heritage Foundation, 1973; the Cato Institute, 1977; the Manhattan Institute, 1978; the Economic Policy Institute, 1986; and the Progressive Policy Institute, 1989). Today, more than one thousand think tanks operate in the United States (Abelson and Lindquist, 2000; Rich, 2004; Smith, 1991).

The largest, best funded and best organized of the think tanks are conservative. As a group, they have deliberately spent hundreds of millions of dollars to move U.S. public policy to the right (Abelson, 2002; Diamond, 1995; Spring, 2002; Stefancic and Delgado, 1996). Soon, this group, sometimes referred to as "movement conservatism," expects its expenditures to exceed $1 billion (Kuttner, 2002).

Education is one area of public policy that conservative think tanks are attempting to change, and the Heritage Foundation is an industry leader. The Heritage Foundation began the efforts of conservative think tanks to move education policy to the right with the publication of its booklet *A New Agenda for Education* (Gardiner, 1985), a collection of policy analyses and recommended actions for the Reagan administration. The Heritage Foundation has promoted its education agenda with a simultaneous four-part public relations delivery system designed to both create and satisfy the demand for conservative ideas. The delivery system simultaneously disseminates ideological messages, policy recommendations, and studies to (a) the media and the public; (b) Congress, the White House, and government agencies; (c) universities and other research institutions; and (d) businesses and corporations (Messer-Davidow, 1993). "Every Heritage study goes out with a synopsis to those who might be interested; every study is turned into an op-ed piece, distributed by the Heritage Features Syndicate to newspapers that publish them" (Blumenthal, 1986, p. 49).

The Heritage Foundation has been using and improving this system for over 20 years. Covington and Parachini (1995) describe part of this strategic alliance of conservative public policy institutes (or think tanks) and the key role played by the Heritage Foundation:

> Today, over 100 conservative public policy institutes exist. They are closely linked through extensive support and communication networks. The Heritage Foundation, with an annual budget in 1994 of $25 million, has actively worked to create or support a group of 60 state-level public policy institutes and think tanks while the [conservative] Madison Group networks with a similar number of activist public policy and other organizations across the country. These networks facilitate the exchange of conservative policy ideas, public relations campaigns, and political strategies ultimately aimed at shaping public opinion, gaining office, and winning desired legislation. (p. 28)

Some researchers credit the public relations system developed by the Heritage Foundation and now used by numerous conservative think tanks with being able to manufacture education crises and then resolve them with conservative policies (Berliner and Biddle, 1995; Messer-Davidow, 1993; Spring, 2002).

Conservative think tanks take great pride in what "movement conservativism" has accomplished. Robert Kuttner, a self-described liberal and invitee to a 2002 national conference of conservative foundations entitled "Philanthropy, Think Tanks, and the Importance of Ideas," reported the remarks from the speeches delivered by several conservative think tank presidents. Christopher DeMuth, President of the American Enterprise Institute, described how conservative think tanks as a group had "reframed the national debate by investing in and then promoting idea-mongers for the long term" (Kuttner, 2002, par. 7). Ed Crane, head of the conservative/libertarian Cato Institute, "complimented his [conservative] patrons in the audience for recognizing that these battles of ideas take two or three decades" (Kuttner, 2002, par. 5). And Edwin Feulner, president of the Heritage Foundation, described "his institution's strategic planning in building a conservative movement. He emphasized 'the four M's: mission, money, management, and marketing' (Kuttner, 2002, par. 6).

Media relations, not research, is a cornerstone of this coordinated conservative think tank strategy to influence public opinion and public policy (Callahan, 1999; Covington, 1997; Covington and Parachini, 1995; Ricci, 1993; Smith, 1991). According to Stefancic and Delgado (1996), conservative think tanks "deployed a series of shrewd moves, orchestrating one campaign after another with the aid of money and brains" to make America's social agenda more conservative (p. 139). Lieberman (2000) describes the media work of conservative think tanks as a continuous series of campaigns that focus on courting the press; attacking the press as too "liberal," including specific reporters and outlets; marketing their messages often, in a variety of media-friendly formats and from multiple, coordinated sources; and silencing their critics by responding quickly and fiercely to any opposing ideas or organizations that arise in the media.

Conservative think tanks use a variety of specific short- and long-term strategies to change the way news is reported and to get their information and opinions included. Short-term strategies include producing and disseminating countless media-ready op-eds, news articles and information packets; promoting think tank fellows available for news program appearances and personal interviews for print journalists; and funding symposia, press conferences and speaking tours for the press and the public to hear in-house scholars speak on policy issues. Specific long-term strategies include targeting specific journalists who they believe are receptive to conservative ideas and who might be swayed by a letter or telephone campaign and establishing programs to train conservative students to enter print and broadcast media (Brock, 2004; Lieberman, 2000; Messer-Davidow, 1993; Ricci, 1993; Smith, 1991; Stefancic and Delgado, 1996).

Despite the emphasis of marketing over research, Ricci (1993) contends that, in general, think tank researchers are devoted to "scientific tenets of proof and disproof" (p. 220) and that "we can expect most of those men and women to work honestly" (p. 227). Singling out the Heritage Foundation, Ricci continues, "Washingtonians know that the advocacy thrust of Heritage's research is paramount. Even so, they may say that because such research is technically proficient, it deserves some respect for its qualitative excellence" (p. 220).

Ricci (1993) appears to represent the minority view. While many laud the marketing abilities of conservative think tanks, the substance of what they market has received sharp criticism. Public Citizen (1996), Ralph Nader's social advocacy organization, described attacks by conservative think tank, including the Heritage Foundation, on the Food and Drug Administration in the early 1990s as follows:

> For the past several years, a group of conservative think tanks with close ties to congressional Republicans has waged an aggressive public relations and lobbying campaign against the federal Food and Drug Administration. The campaign relies on misinformation and distortion of the F.D.A.'s record. Between 1992 and 1995, seven of the think tanks [including the Heritage Foundation] received at least $3.5 million dollars in contributions from the industries with the most to gain from the anti-F.D.A. campaign—pharmaceutical, medical device, biotechnology and tobacco manufacturers. (par. 1)

Lieberman (2000) described the conservative/libertarian Cato Institute's Policy Analysis No. 187 criticizing Head Start as "intellectually dishonest" (p. 102) . . ."but emblematic of the strategy used not only by Cato but by other right-wing think tanks that dress up ideology as objective evaluation" (p. 101). Soley (1992) set forth the weak scholarly credentials of Heritage Foundation personnel: "Of its 34 permanent 'fellows, scholars, and staff' members, only 7 have Ph.D.'s. None are renowned scholars in their fields" (p. 60).

Similar criticisms exist regarding conservative think tank research on education. Spring (2002) describes the conservative Manhattan Institute's research on education vouchers as "not a search for truth but a search for justifications for its political program . . . the goal of the institute's support of research is not to prove vouchers are effective but to create arguments supporting voucher plans" (pp. 31–32). Spring's conclusion appears consistent with two recent analyses of the Manhattan Institute's *An Evaluation of the Florida A-Plus Accountability and School Choice Program* (Greene, 2001). Camilli and Bulkley (2001) concluded that the Manhattan Institute's report was a "generous and simplistic reading of the evidence" and they "raised serious questions regarding the validity of Greene's empirical results and conclusions" (2001, "Conclusion," par. 1) Examining the same Manhattan Institute report as well as public statements by its author, Kupermintz wrote in a generous tone that "Greene might have over-stated the case for the simple explanation he promoted in his report and in the press" which Kupermintz concluded had the effect that "the reader of the Manhattan Institute laudatory report is offered a false sense of a dramatic success" (2001, "Conclusion," par. 3).

THINK TANKS AND MEDIA INFLUENCE

Studies show that the news media extensively use the writings and spokespersons of think tanks, especially conservative think tanks. Fairness and Accuracy in Reporting (FAIR), a liberal media watch group, regularly reports on how the media utilizes think tanks in their presentation of news. Michael Dolny, in annual reports for FAIR (1996, 1997, 1998, 2000, 2001, 2002), searched Nexis, an extensive database of newspaper, television and radio news pieces, to count think tank citations in the media by ideology: conservative/libertarian, centrist, or left/progressive. Dolny reported that in 1995, the news media cited think tanks over 15,000 times. By 2001, the number of citations had increased to almost 26,000. Each year, conservative/libertarian think tanks were cited most often and were, depending on the year, cited two to five times as often as progressive/liberal think tanks.

Examining network television news programs, Soley (1992) and Steele (1995) found that these "expert" commentators were often spokespersons from conservative think tanks. Soley (1992) examined the analysts selected by network television news organizations during two six-week periods in 1979–1980 and 1987–1988. He found that the vast majority of these "experts" were East Coast, white males who were former public officials or associated with conservative think tanks. Steele (1995) conducted an extensive examination of "unofficial sources" presented during eight months of regularly scheduled network news about the Persian Gulf War. She found that think tanks, often conservative, were the largest group of experts, accounting for almost 30 percent of the total.

Only two researchers have described the extent to which think tanks have been utilized by the news media in its coverage of K–12 education. Spring (2002) writes briefly about conservative think tanks. He notes the "frequent appearance of their [Manhattan Institute] experts' names in newspaper stories" (p. 32), and further states that, with the support of conservative think tanks, Chester Finn (Hudson Institute) and Diane Ravitch (Manhattan Institute) have "flooded the market with neoconservative opinions about education," publishing literally hundreds of articles in the professional and popular press as well as numerous books (p. 48). Spring, however, does not provide systemic documentation of this influence.

In an unpublished presentation at the national conference of the American Educational Research Association, Alex Molnar, who directs the "progressive/liberal" Education Policy Studies Laboratory at Arizona State University, examined both the extent and presentation of the news coverage of the conservative Manhattan Institute's evaluation of the Florida A-Plus education program that was authored by Jay Greene. The Manhattan Institute report was not subject to peer review; however, two independent follow-up reports were done by Camilli and Bulkley (2001) and Kupermintz (2001), discussed briefly above, and both were highly critical.

Molnar (2001) found that the Manhattan Institute promoted their study in a nationally distributed press release and that the news media, including *USA Today* and *The New York Times,* picked it up, citing or discussing it in thirty news stories and commentaries. Of these pieces, Molnar found that seventeen were printed without authoritative comment on the quality of the findings, ten were printed with balanced comments on the study's findings including criticisms, and three consisted of mostly comments or arguments questioning the study. In contrast, the follow-up critiques, published in the education journal, *Education Policy Analysis Archives,* within one month of the Manhattan Institute report, were not cited or covered in the mainstream press, but only once in *Education Week.* Molnar found the lack of critical reporting disturbing and commented that "the distribution of [think tank] policy reports not subject to a peer review process carries with it a risk that sound [education] policy may be subverted" (2001, "Introduction," par. 8).

The findings of Molnar (2001) support the conclusions reached by Dolny, Soley and Steele—that the news media utilize conservative think tank writings and materials on education quite readily. Molnar's findings also point to the conclusion that the news media most often present conservative think tanks in a manner that overstates their academic expertise and understates their political leanings and motives.

MEDIA PRESENTATION OF THINK TANK REPORTS AND SPOKESPERSONS

The study by Molnar (2001) is the only study that has focused specifically on the news media presentation of think tank materials and spokespersons on education; however, several general media studies appear to agree with his findings and conclusions.

The FAIR report on the news media utilization of think tanks during 1997 also examined how the top four most cited think tanks—Brookings Institute (centrist), Heritage Foundation (conservative), American Enterprise Institute (conservative), and Cato Institute (conservative/libertarian)—were identified in the press. Since none of these top four most cited think tanks were liberal/progressive, Dolny also examined the labels of the top most cited liberal/progressive think tank, the Economic Policy Institute (EPI). Dolny calculated that Brookings and the three conservative think tanks did not receive any descriptive ideological label about three-fourths of the time. EPI, on the other hand, did not receive a descriptive label just over one-half of the time. At the same time, when descriptive labels identifying ideological orientation or funding sources were given, the liberal/progressive EPI received a higher percentage of these descriptive labels, than Brookings and the three conservative think tanks. Dolny (1998) concluded that the news media not only use liberal think tanks less often than conservative think tanks, they also present them more critically:

> The fact that [liberal] EPI was the group most often identified ideologi-cally—and the only one scrutinized in terms of its funding sources—suggests that even when progressive think tanks are allowed to take part in the usually center-right debate, the playing field is still not level. ("Missing Labels," par. 8)

FAIR also published short articles on the news media and think tanks that provided examples of how the news media uncritically utilized and gen-erously presented conservative think tanks. These included an examina-tion of the widespread reporting of poverty and welfare advocacy pieces promulgated by Robert Reed of the Heritage Foundation as "research" (Ackerman, 1999), examples of when the news media failed to describe Heritage Foundation funding sources in news reports where it might affect the objectivity of their expert commentary (Solomon, 1996), and survey results from news journalists, noting that more than half "often" or "nearly always" contacted think tanks as sources on economic policy issues (Cro-teau, 1998).

In a study of four right-wing policy campaigns entitled *Slanting the Story* (2000), Trudy Lieberman also concluded that the news media uncritically utilized and generously presented the work of conservative think tanks. As noted previously, Lieberman concluded that the Cato Institute's Policy Analysis No. 187, which it presented as research noting the failures of Head Start, was not even remotely close to social science research. Rather, Policy Analysis No. 187, entitled "Caveat Emptor: The Head Start Scam," used a "rhetorical style of unbridled scorn" (2000, p. 102) backed mostly by news reports and numerous out-of-context quotes and mischaracterizations of research studies that turned the words of Head Start supporters into criticisms. According to Lieberman, the Cato Institute then used these "criticisms" to support No. 187's conclu-sions that Head Start should be eliminated or replaced with a preschool voucher program.

In addition, Lieberman notes that No. 187's author, John Hood, was not qualified to evaluate Head Start. At the time of the report, he was research director for the John Locke Foundation, a conservative state-policy think tank in North Carolina that worked "mostly on state fiscal matters" (2000,

p. 107). He did not have expertise or experience in investigative reporting, child development or the evaluation of education programs.

Nevertheless, both No. 187 and John Hood received extensive, supportive coverage in the news media. According to Lieberman, the news media, through numerous hard news and syndicated opinion columns in newspapers across the country, presented No. 187 as "research" and John Hood as a "researcher," "expert," and "academic" (2000, pp. 108–109). Further, the Cato Institute itself was also given quite favorable coverage for it was presented as either having "expertise" in child development (2000, p. 110) or with such lackluster descriptors like "Cato Institute" or "Washington-based research organization" from which readers could not discern Cato's ideological orientation (2000, p. 110). Taking all this together, Lieberman concludes,

> Cato's attack also exemplified the media's gullibility, intellectual laziness, and eagerness to run with a story without searching what was behind it. The media gave a massive amount of attention to Cato's one-sided analysis, failed to do its own digging to verify its claims, and allowed Cato to portray Head Start in a way that was both incomplete and misleading. (2000, p. 102)

EXPLAINING THE THINK TANK–NEW MEDIA RELATIONSHIP

Despite her strong language, Lieberman's final thoughts on why the media uncritically utilize—and even misrepresent—conservative think tank writings and spokespersons is much more subdued. Lieberman shies away from the possible conclusion that journalists consciously alter the news and characterizes journalists as having *"unwittingly* [emphasis added] helped advance the right wing's agenda" (2000, p. 157). This appears to fit into the most accepted description of news production. According to Allan (2000), "journalists are not propagandists" (p. 60) who intentionally misrepresent the news; rather "it is the culture of routine, day-to-day interactions within specific news institutions" (p. 61) which determine how and what news is produced. In this vein, Lieberman (2000) gives four related explanations for why conservative think tanks receive extensive and favorable news coverage despite the criticisms of their work and credentials.

First, today's journalists are now more predisposed to accept right-wing explanations as valid because, on economic matters, journalists are more conservative than the public at large. Second, large corporate media owners subtly steer reporters away from stories that might affect their bottom-line economic interests. Learning the "master narrative" of their media organization, journalists who get ahead in their careers know what stories are off-limits. Third, a journalistic culture that craves conflict and balanced reporting has shied away from "connecting the dots" and instead publishes "he said, she said" accounts of events while limiting their comments on the consequences of what is being advocated (pp. 158–59). According to Lieberman, journalists perceive that there is a lack of media-savvy, liberal experts, an overabundance of well-marketed conservative experts, and that no experts can meet their tests of "objectivity and neutrality" (p. 160).[2] In the end, they fall back on the "'he said, she said' model and hope that somehow the public will understand what is at stake" (p. 160). The end result, according to one unnamed reporter, is that journalists will choose conservatives most often because what drives expert selection are "angles" and "interesting ideas" and the right wing is currently "an interesting group to talk to" (p. 161).

Finally, Lieberman faults an uninvolved public. Given the previous three explanations for the use of right-wing think tanks as sources of information—conservative journalist predisposition, corporate media economic interests, and journalistic culture favoring conflict and balance—Lieberman concludes that the media will continue to utilize right-wing think tanks until the public makes it economically unfeasible or ethically untenable to do so.

Soley (1992) provides a similar explanation. He suggests that well-known journalists (and most likely media owners) "ceaselessly" turn to the same sources, often conservative think tanks, because they feel comfortable with them. Conservative think tank personnel and journalists are part of "the power elite's political, economic, and social networks," while "labor union spokespersons, members of grassroots political organizations, or minorities" are not (1992, p. 43).

Another explanation is that conservative think tanks have "new" expertise desired by the current news culture. Interviewing a number of prominent television news producers, Steele (1995) finds that their expert selection results from some basic general criteria which are "unusual" (p. 805) and completely different from scholarly or "ordinary standards" (p. 806) of expertise. One criterion is "operational bias," the extent to which an expert can make "predictions, [and comment on] players, and policies" (p. 809) and whether they are "good on television" (p. 802). Another criterion can best be described as credibility. These are characteristics that include whether the expert has "already been quoted in the *New York Times* or *Washington Post*" (p. 801), whether the current expert being used can vouch for the possible next expert, and whether the expert has "real world experience" (p. 807) as opposed to book knowledge. Another criterion is convenience, including whether the producers have developed a "working relationship" with the expert's organization (p. 802), and the "proximity of an expert to a network studio" (p. 803). Conservative think tanks, with their emphasis on marketing ideas through media campaigns, appear to have positioned themselves to take advantage of the need for this new expertise.

Such a conclusion is consistent with the findings of Davis and Owen (1998) in their research on *new media outlets*. According to Davis and Owen, new media outlets are talk radio and television, electronic town meetings, television news magazines, MTV, print and electronic tabloids, and computer networks, including the Internet (1998, p. vii; see also Croteau and Hoynes, 2000). They contend that new media outlets have small staffs and little research support and therefore intentionally rely on external interest groups to meet their information needs. These interest groups, they contend, "are well aware of this dependency and have proactively moved to meet it" (1998, p. 247).

As an interest group example, Davis and Owen note that the Heritage Foundation provides space for talk show broadcasts, sponsors conferences for the talk radio industry, and freely distributes position papers and press releases to talk radio shows. In turn, talk radio producers specifically contact the Heritage Foundation for information to help fill the long blocks of time that their hosts must fill. Davis and Owen do not provide any specific information on the extent or presentation of the Heritage Foundation materials by the "new media outlets" except to say that one radio host "routinely cites" Heritage Foundation reports on his program (1998, p. 247).

Davis and Owen conclude that new media outlets present the "research" or "facts" disseminated by conservative think tanks knowing that it is thinly veiled ideology because such materials provide inexpensive entertainment which means greater profits than producing their own materials. Since "new media outlets" are without an "agreed-upon code of ethics" or "code of public service imperatives" (1998, p. 254), audiences should not expect anything more than entertainment. Still, because the idea that entertainment trumps veracity is not made explicit, sometimes audience members "feel they've been conned because they thought it was purely public service" (Davis and Owen, 1998, p. 252, quoting Victoria Jones of WRC radio in Washington, D.C.). If the new media have any truly populist bent or democratic influence, Davis and Owen argue, it is "accidental" (1998, p. 253).

Ricci (1993) is a notable exception to this line of explanation. As discussed above, Ricci finds think tank research to be of high quality, and he seems to imply that it is "objectively" disseminated by an unbiased media interested only in public service.

> Sometimes these institutes [think tanks] deliver knowledge to the city directly, in books, special reports, journals, conferences, and newsletters. At other times, information is conveyed by the mass media where, as we have seen, the constant demand for news about a host of policy issues ensures that reporters and newscasters will cite think-tank fellows. With respect to amassing the facts, then . . . the capital seems well equipped. (p. 210)

Ricci (1993) goes on to contend that think tank research is likely to be more helpful to public policy construction than academic research. Singling out the Heritage Foundation, Ricci writes,

> think-tankers contribute to the great conversation because both pro-fessionally and politically, they tend to take principles seriously . . . [C]ommitment can make a positive contribution to the great conversa-tion, for it can encourage fellows to restate the same conclusions in publication after publication, as the Heritage Foundation and the In-stitute for Policy Studies certainly do. Academic scholars, who may also study policy issues, are driven by a pursuit of scientific novelty, which does not permit them to repeat their findings again and again, as if they had nothing "new" to say. Yet in the larger scheme of things, where political decisions must be worked out in an open marketplace of ideas, such repetition can be crucial for inspiring and fortifying pub-lic opinion. (p. 225)

Despite Ricci's (1993) conclusions that think tanks and the news media operate in a climate of openness and public service, his book finds that the vast majority of think tank production comes from conservative think tanks. Asking rhetorically why the stories of conservative think tanks appear to "stand alone" (p. 235) in Washington's great conversation, Ricci appears to place the blame solely on the liberals—for he has no explana-tion. Instead he "leave[s] others to wonder" why liberal think tanks have not added their stories to this conversation in order to achieve a balanced ordering of public policy facts and theories (p. 235).

Little has been written about why the news media utilize think tanks, and specifically conservative think tanks, in their education reporting. Berliner and Biddle (1995) argue that the public perception that education is in crisis is manufactured by conservative think tanks and others who deliberately misuse and misrepresent research and who use the "compli-ant" press (p. 54) to disseminate that misinformation. Berliner and Biddle describe the education press as "ignorant [and] highly critical" (p. 11), possibly "brainwashed by the critics" of public schools (p. 62), "gullible" (p. 162), and "irresponsible" (p. 168). Berliner and Biddle do not examine why the press might cover education so inaccurately other than to say in passing that it might be due to "cupidity, bias, or desires to pander to readers" (p. 170).

In 1998, Berliner and Biddle continued their criticisms of press report-ing on education by listing and then giving examples to support "defi-ciencies" they found in the press coverage of education. They concluded then that "the press seems either too scared, too controlled, or too uninformed to raise what we consider the most basic issue confronting education in the United States—achieving a fair distribution of oppor-tunities to succeed" (p. 30). Instead, they contend, the press chooses to publish stories that criticize and ridicule public schools, following the "if it bleeds, it leads" rule of news journalism (p. 27). As a result, "the newspapers have become a *natural ally* [emphasis added] of those who believe that public schools have failed" (p. 27). Like Lieberman (2000), Berliner and Biddle (1998) strongly criticize the news media, but if they believe that the media are active, conscious partners with think tanks or others in manufacturing the perception of crisis in education, they stop just short of saying so.

Denis Doyle, associated at times with various think tanks including the Brookings Institution, the American Enterprise Institute, the Heritage Foundation, and the Hudson Institute, disagrees. He directly attacks the remarks of Berliner and Biddle (1995), interpreting them as charging that there is a media conspiracy against the education establishment and calling it "errant nonsense" (1998, p. 52) Doyle posits instead that media coverage of schools is "weak" because "the schools themselves are obdurate; they neither report on themselves nor provide opportunities for third parties—in this case the press and its readers—to dip beneath the surface . . . [leaving] not much of substance to report" (p. 55). Doyle limits his remarks to general media coverage of education and does not address the role of think tanks in this process.

Taken together, the research discussed point to the following conclusions. It appears that the news media utilize conservative think tanks' works and spokespersons despite questions about their rigor and expertise, respectively, because it is convenient and profitable to do so. It also appears that the news media unintentionally present conservative think tanks' works and spokespersons in a generous manner by omission of their clear political leanings and their emphasis on advocacy as well as by accepting the scientific descriptions think tank present of their work and spokespersons without verifying whether this is accurate. The specific presentation of conservative think tank works and spokespersons on education appear to follow this general pattern of utilization and presentation by the news media. In the end, the news, including education reporting, appears to be more of a spectacle, more like infotainment, than a source of accurate and complete information (Anderson, 2007; Killeen, 2007; Moses, 2007).

If these conclusions are correct, then one would expect to find repeated and generous citations of the works and spokespersons of the Heritage Foundation on education, including citations of criticized works and spokespersons without experience or expertise in education.

THE PRESENT ANALYSIS

This chapter aims to determine (a) the scope and (b) the presentation of the Heritage Foundation by the news media by examining the news media's coverage of the foundation's education-related documents and spokespersons during 2001.

The Nexis database at www.nexis.com was searched for news entries that concerned education and included references to the Heritage Foundation. The search was conducted for the period January 1–December 31, 2001.[3] This period was chosen because it was the beginning of the presidential term of George W. Bush, who had made education reform a key component of his agenda. The entries returned by Nexis were then reviewed for relevance to eliminate any "false positives."[4] One hundred fifty-nine relevant entries were found. These entries are every media citation to the Heritage Foundation as a source on education contained in the Nexis database.[5]

A content analysis was conducted by coding the relevant entries.[6] The general coding categories included types of news media (e.g., general news newspapers, education publications, television news), specific news outlets (e.g., *New York Times, Business Week, Fox News Live*), topic (e.g., curriculum and school governance, school choice, Heritage Foundation activities), and Heritage Foundation source (e.g., names of specific personnel, publications, Heritage Foundation as an entity). In total, over 150 different codes were used. In addition, the Heritage Foundation web site (www.heritage.org) was searched for information on the foundation's media practices, publications, and personnel and organizational structure.

THE HERITAGE FOUNDATION

Marketing Values

"Education" is listed as one of the Heritage Foundation's 29 "key issue" subject areas (Heritage Foundation, 2002, on-line). During 2001, twenty-six different authors wrote forty-three education-related publications. The Heritage Foundation listed seven of these authors—Krista Kafer, Megan Farnsworth, Stuart Butler, Robert Moffitt, Mike Franc, Kirk Johnson, and Tom Hinton—as "Experts on Education." Education-related publications represented about 5 percent of the total papers, studies and books produced by the Heritage Foundation during 2001. Nevertheless, education-related citations accounted for approximately 8 percent of its news citations.

The Heritage Foundation's strategy for marketing conservative ideas on education appears to be paying dividends in the mass media news. The Heritage Foundation had its first news media citation related to education in 1979. In that year, it was cited once in the *Washington Post*.[7] In 2001, 159 news items related to education drew on the Heritage Foundation as a source.[8] In total during 2001, it received over two thousand news media citations (Dolny, 2002).

RESULTS

Media Presence of the Heritage Foundation

Often and Everywhere

During 2001, the Heritage Foundation blanketed the United States with its views on education. As Tables 9.1 and 9.2 illustrate, the Heritage Foundation was cited by 81 media sources in 159 news items. It was cited in the print, television, and radio media on a variety of education topics in both general news and opinion formats. Excluding news wire services, which do not publish directly to the public, the Heritage Foundation was present in the media debate on education on average more than once every three days.

Table 9.1.   Heritage Foundation Media Presence Related to Education, 2001.

News Item	No. of citations	Media Sources	No. of citations
General news	75	General news newspapers	39
Op-ed	71	Television programs	13
Personnel	11	Policy publications	9
Event calendar	2	News wire services	7
Total	*159*	Business publications	6
		Radio programs	4
		Education publications	3
		Total	*81*

Table 9.2.   Number of Heritage Foundation News Entries by Main Topic, 2001 [9]

Curriculum and school governance	54
School choice	22
Education spending	21
Heritage Foundation activities	21
Role of government in education	14
Education legislation (ESEA)	16
Testing	11
Other education issues	5

During 2001, the Heritage Foundation received the greatest attention from the east coast national newspapers. This supports Steele's contention that geography—location near a national news broadcast center like Washington, D.C. or New York—is a key criterion in determining whether a group is included as an expertise news source. Table 9.3 shows that *The Washington Times* cited the Heritage Foundation 17 times during 2001, more than the combined totals of the next two highest concentrations, the *New York Times* (8) and the *Washington Post* (7). On the other coast, the *Los Angeles Times* cited the Heritage Foundation only once. The next two concentrations of citations were in the *Chattanooga Times/Free Press* (7) and the *Dallas Morning News* (6), both regional newspapers.

Other national news outlets that included the heritage foundation on education included *business week, cnn today* (cable), and "all things considered" of *national public radio* (npr). In addition, local newspapers from florida (*florida times union, the ledger*) to california (*daily news of los angeles, modesto bee, san diego union-tribune*) also cited the heritage foundation, though mostly only once or twice.

Heritage Foundation personnel were granted fifteen opinion bylines and were television or radio guests on seventeen occasions. Of the fifteen bylines, eight were in the *Washington Times*, while the remaining seven bylines occurred once each in seven different newspapers.

In its citations, the Heritage Foundation presented its views on eight general topics (see Table 9.2) encompassing 42 subtopics. The topics included such commonly debated issues as school choice (yes), testing (more), and education spending (too much already), as well as less-debated issues like the relationship between marriage and educational achievement of children (it helps) and private-public partnerships in school construction (they are needed). Almost half (44 percent) of the citations were in editorial and opinion formats (See Table 9.1).

Table 9.3.   Top Citations of the Heritage Foundation by Media Source, 2001

Media Sources	No. of citations
Washington Times	17
New York Times	8
Washington Post	7
Chattanooga Times/Free Press	7
Dallas Morning News	6
United Press International	5
Gannett News Service	4
Fox News Live	4

Opinions and Syndicated Columns—News as Stenography

On several occasions, different newspapers across the country repeated the same Heritage Foundation statement to tens of thousands and even hundreds of thousands of readers. The three most extensive examples are shown in Tables 9.4 and 9.5.

The first example, set forth in Table 9.4, began as a Heritage Foundation opinion piece entitled "Look Who's Supporting School Choice Now." In this opinion piece, the Heritage Foundation's Jennifer Garrett argued that many members of Congress were hypocrites on vouchers because they were sending their own children to private schools while opposing voucher legislation and thus denying many parents this same opportunity. It was released by the Heritage Foundation on April 25, 2001.

As listed in Table 9.4 below, this Garrett opinion piece was distributed nationally by Scripps-Howard News Wire on April 26, 2001, as "Hypocrisy on Vouchers." Over the next two weeks, Garrett's opinion piece appeared virtually unchanged as "Hypocrisy on School Choice" in the *The Deseret News* (Salt Lake City, UT) on April 27, as "Hypocrisy Rife on School Choice" in *The Chattanooga Times/Free Press* on April 29, and as "Hypocrisy on School Vouchers" in the *Washington Times* on May 8. In addition, Garrett's opinion piece in the *Washington Times* was later cited by name on May 27 in a *Washington Times* opinion column entitled "Children yes, Unions no."

In three of the articles, Jennifer Garrett was described as "a domestic policy researcher for the Heritage Foundation" and one article did not tell who she was. The Heritage Foundation was only listed as the "Heritage Foundation," without description.

The second and third examples, set forth in Table 9.5, are quotes from Heritage Foundation spokespersons that were used to support the opinions expressed in two syndicated columns. In April 2001, syndicated columnists Michael Kelly and Cal Thomas wrote about the problems of U.S. public schools and claimed that the recently released National Assessment of Educational Progress (NAEP) scores demonstrated that federal

Table 9.4. References to Jennifer Garrett's "Look Who's Supporting School Choice Now," Heritage Foundation, April 25, 2001

Title	Date	News Organization
"Hypocrisy on Vouchers"	4/26/01	Scripps-Howard News Service
"Hypocrisy on School Choice"	4/27/01	Deseret News (Salt Lake City)
"Hypocrisy Rife on School Vouchers"	4/29/01	Chattanooga Times/Free Press
"Hypocrisy on School Vouchers"	5/8/01	The Washington Times

Table 9.5.   Publication of the Opinions of Heritage Foundation Spokespersons

From Michael Kelly's Syndicated Column "And, as Krista Kafer of the Heritage Foundation has noted, $80 billion of this sum [on Title 1] was spent in the past decade, largely in the Clinton years."		*From Cal Thomas's Syndicated Column "The Heritage Foundation's Dr. Stuart Butler says that serious studies of major federal education programs either don't exist or suggest that the programs are unsuccessful."*	
Date	News Outlet	Date	News Outlet
4/11/01	*Times Union* (Albany, NY)	4/11/01	*Washington Times*
4/11/01	*The Washington Post*	4/11/01	*Milwaukee Journal Sentinel*
4/12/01	*Dayton Daily News*	4/11/01	*Chattanooga Times/ Free Press*
4/15/01	*South Bend Tribune*	4/12/01	*South Bend Tribune*
4/16/01	*Milwaukee Journal Sentinel*	4/13/01	*Augusta Chronicle*

education programs were generally a failure, that federal money targeted for the education of poor children (Title 1) specifically had not produced results, and that Title 1 expenditures were another example of Clinton and Democrat spending that hurt, not helped, the poor. They quoted the Heritage Foundation's Krista Kafer and Stuart Butler to support, or arguably, to make, these contentions.

During a one-week period, these Heritage Foundation statements were repeated ten times (Table 9.5). Readers of the *Milwaukee Journal Sentinel* and *South Bend Tribune* saw both statements. In these articles, both Krista Kafer and Stuart Butler were named without description other than being from the Heritage Foundation. The Heritage Foundation also was only named, but not described.

The reach of the Heritage Foundation's influence appears to be extensive. From an office in Washington, DC, the Heritage Foundation put the three opinions of Garrett, Kafer and Butler, discussed above, before millions of readers across the United States.

Table 9.6 sets forth the average daily circulations for the newspapers that published the three Heritage Foundation opinions. Combining the newspaper circulations, the Heritage Foundation's Jennifer Garrett, Krista Kafer and Stuart Butler had their opinions presented to 236,000; 1,347,500; and 573,600 news readers, respectively. These three Heritage Foundation staff members, during the height of the Congressional and White House debates on education spending and the place of vouchers in U.S. public education, told 2,157,500 news readers, including members of Congress and the White House who read the *Washington Post* and *Washington Times,* that Title I, federal money targeted to support the education of poor children,

Table 9.6. Average Daily Circulations of Newspapers that Published Opinions of the Heritage Foundation's Garrett, Kafer and Butler[10]

Name of Media Source	Circulation
Augusta Chronicle	54,600
Chattanooga Times/Free Press	65,000
Dayton Daily News	135,000
Deseret News (Salt Lake City)	68,000
Milwaukee Journal Sentinel	278,000
South Bend Tribune	73,000
Times Union (Albany, N.Y.)	99,500
Washington Post	762,000
Washington Times	103,000

is a failure and that Americans should have vouchers. At the same time, these articles provided virtually no information for the reader to discern the quality of these statements or the expertise of these spokespersons. The reader would never know from the descriptions of Jennifer Garrett[11], Krista Kafer, and Stuart Butler that none have ever studied or worked in education. This aspect of the news media presentation of Heritage Foundation sources—generous omissions—will be discussed further in the section on Media Presentation below.

Heritage Foundation as News

At times, the Heritage Foundation itself was education news. Table 9.2 shows that the Heritage Foundation was the topic of twenty-one education news items. Six of these news items headlined the Heritage Foundation. For example, the two news articles from the *Education Technology News* were discussions of the Heritage Foundation's online school report cards ("Heritage Foundation Puts School Report Cards in One Place Online," vol. 18, no. 17, August 15, 2001; "Schools Can Improve, Parents Get Informed When School Data Is Accessible Online," vol. 18, no. 23, November 7, 2001). Both articles described how the Heritage Foundation's Report Card Report site would improve school performance by providing parents and policy makers with data for comparing the differences between high-performing and low-performing schools.[12]

Table 9.1 shows that eleven news reports featured personnel changes at the Heritage Foundation related to education. The *Washington Post* article,

"Appointments," E7, April 2, 2001, is typical. Located in the financial section, this article announced the hiring of Krista Kafer as a policy analyst for the Heritage Foundation.

Media Presentation of the Heritage Foundation

The news media, with rare exception, generously presented the Heritage Foundation's work and spokespersons on education. As shown below, it did not matter whether the source was a spokesperson or a document—almost none of the news media presentations described the Heritage Foundation in a manner more critical than the Heritage Foundation's own descriptions of its people and its work.

For example, only four news items, or 2.5 percent, of the total 159 news items on education that referenced the Heritage Foundation included any criticism of the Heritage Foundation. They appeared three times in the education press's *Phi Delta Kappan* and once in the *New York Times*. Thus, three of the seven items in the education press, or 43 percent, included criticisms of the Heritage Foundation. This was a much higher percentage than in the popular or general interest press, in which only one of the 152 news items, or less than 1 percent, contained criticisms of the Heritage Foundation. Interestingly, the education press was much more critical of the Heritage Foundation's work on education than was the general interest press. The seven news items in the education press were 4 percent of the total 159 news items, yet they contained 75 percent of the total news items with criticisms of the Heritage Foundation.

Spokespersons: Experts Without Expertise

Generous media characterizations of their expertise were certainly the norm for Heritage Foundation personnel. During 2001, Krista Kafer was the Heritage Foundation's most cited source on education. She was cited in forty-even news items, more than twice as often as the next most cited source. On the Heritage Foundation web page, Krista Kafer is presented as an "expert on education" and a "senior policy analyst, education" with "expertise [in] school choice, education standards and testing, charter schools, [and] federal education programs (Heritage Foundation Kafer Bio, 2002). In the news media during 2001, she was presented most often in the same terms, as an "education analyst" (14), a "policy analyst" (9) or "of the Heritage Foundation" (19). Whatever title the media gave her, not one of the news entries explained the derivation of this title or Krista Kafer's qualifications.[13]

According to her Heritage Foundation biography[14] and an article in *Roll Call* (April 28, 1997), Krista Kafer graduated from the University of Colorado with a B.A. in history in 1994. She then worked for the Colorado chapter of the National Right to Life Committee, Rep. Dave McIntosh

(R-IN) and Rep. Bob Schaffer (R-CO) as well as Sen. Bob Dole's 1996 presidential campaign. According to the *Washington Post* (April 2, 2001), she joined the Heritage Foundation in the spring of 2001. It appears that Krista Kafer has never studied or worked in education.

A lack of relevant expertise is consistent across the Heritage Foundation's seven "experts in education." Reviewing the staff biographies on the Heritage Foundation website, it appears that like Krista Kafer, Stuart Butler, Robert Moffitt, Michael Franc, and Kirk Johnson have never studied or worked in education.[15] One "expert in education," Thomas Hinton, has a B.A. in political science and Christian education and no work experience in education.[16]

Megan Farnsworth appears to be the Heritage Foundation's most qualified "expert in education." According to her Heritage Foundation biography, she has worked as a teacher, curriculum specialist and school evaluator, and she holds a master's degree in education from UCLA and an unspecified degree from Harvard's Graduate School of Education.[17]

Documents: Media Conferred Social Science Legitimacy

During 2001, the news media presented Heritage Foundation publications as sound social science research conducted by qualified experts, characterizations more generous than the Heritage Foundation's own characterizations of its work. For example, fifteen Heritage Foundation publications were cited by the news media. Ten of these were "Backgrounders." Neither the "Backgrounders" themselves nor the Heritage Foundation website describes what the Heritage Foundation intends a "Backgrounder" to be. Ricci (1993) describes them as "essays, thoroughly researched and fully footnoted, [that] were usually written in six to eight weeks but could be produced if necessary within days" (p. 161). A representative of the Heritage Foundation described a "Backgrounder" as a "general recommendation" publication (D. Hunter, personal communication[18]).

The news media, in contrast, described a "Backgrounder" most often as a "report" (eight) or "study" (five), a description that would lead one to conclude that they are more scientific and "objective" than either "essay" or "general recommendation." Seven of the twenty news media descriptions, "backgrounder" (one), "analysis" (two), "survey" (two), "document" (one), and "paper" (one), were generally synonymous with those provided by Ricci (1993) and the Heritage Foundation.

Documents and Spokespersons: Unquestioned authority

As set forth above, less than 3 percent of the news items that cited the Heritage Foundation on education voiced any criticism of the Heritage Foundation or its work. Thus, during 2001, 155 of the 159, or 97 percent, of the news items presented the Heritage Foundation in a manner similar to or in a more generous manner than it presented itself.

No Excuses was the only Heritage Foundation source to receive a negative presentation in the news items. No Excuses was initially released on April 18, 2000. Since then, it has gone through several editions and is now the focal point of a national "No Excuses" campaign.[19] *No Excuses* or its author, Samuel Casey Carter, were cited in eighteen news items in twelve news media outlets from January through November 2001. Four of those citations, or 22 percent, included critical comments. A review of these critical articles is instructive.

On January 1, *Phi Delta Kappan* published its first of three lengthy criticisms of *No Excuses* during 2001. In this edition, author Gerald Bracey, a research psychologist with a Ph.D. from Stanford University, criticized the methodology, analysis, and conclusions of No Excuses and the subsequent claims of Heritage Foundation "education expert" Megan Farnsworth.[20] In a *New York Times* article dated January 3, Richard Rothstein presented several criticisms of the research and conclusions in *No Excuses*.[21] Rothstein also made positive comments, but the overall thrust of his article was that *No Excuses* was inspired by "ideology, not evidence." In the March edition of *Phi Delta Kappan*, Bracey presented additional examples for why he believed that No Excuses was poor research that presented inaccurate and misleading conclusions.[22] In this article, Bracey cited extensively from Rothstein's January 3 article in the *New York Times*. In November, *Phi Delta Kappan* published an article entitled, "Point of View—No Excuse for *No Excuses*."[23] In this article, George Schmidt, editor of *Substance*, an independent newspaper devoted to public education in Chicago,[24] presented numerous examples of what he believed were errors in the *No Excuses* research in the Chicago area. George Schmidt concluded his article with these words, "For more than 20 years, the Heritage Foundation has been promoting myths . . . Now, in *No Excuses*, Heritage rehashes discredited nonsense. The sad thing is that these claims and the shoddy numbers that underpin them are still widely publicized" (2001, p. 194).

None of these criticisms—either of *No Excuses* specifically or the Heritage Foundation generally—found its way into any of the other 155 education news items that referenced the Heritage Foundation. No hint of the *New York Times* critique of *No Excuses* and by implication of the Heritage Foundation on January 3 ever emerged in the subsequent six *New York Times* citations to the Heritage Foundation during 2001.[25] Interestingly, Rothstein's article appeared the day after another *New York Times* article citing *No Excuses*. In that article, published on January 2nd, the *New York Times* gave a supportive citation to *No Excuses* and a glowing report on a Harlem school featured therein. Criticism of the Heritage Foundation's work on education, it appears, did not reach across a single newsroom.

PUTTING IT ALL TOGETHER

During 2001, the Heritage Foundation was cited

1. regularly and often;
2. in print, television and radio news sources across the country;
3. through Krista Kafer, who was presented as an education expert without disclosing her lack of expertise; and
4. almost without criticism.

This resulted in a news image that often enhanced the Heritage Foundation's presentation of itself as a think tank that produced "objective," scientific research.

One further example illustrates the character and extent of the Heritage Foundation's presence in the news media as an expert source on education during 2001. The Elementary and Secondary Education Act (ESEA), enacted in Congressional bills H.R.1 and S.1 and titled the "No Child Left Behind Act" dominated the political debate on education for much of 2001.[26] In its coverage, the news media utilized the Heritage Foundation as a source for commentary and information on ESEA. The Heritage Foundation was cited in twenty-eight news items, of which twenty were general news items and seven were opinions or editorials. The Heritage Foundation appeared most often in the *Dallas Morning News* (five), followed by the *New York Times* (four) and the *Washington Times* (two). Krista Kafer or her work was cited in twenty-five of the twenty-eight news items. Each news item presented the Heritage Foundation as a knowledgeable source of "objective" research information and analysis.

Of further note is the comparison of Heritage Foundation citations to other unofficial or nongovernmental source citations (Steele, 1995) in the twenty general news items on ESEA. The Heritage Foundation was cited twenty-four times (sometimes different Heritage Foundation sources in the same news item) while the other nongovernmental sources received many fewer citations: other think tanks (fourteen—the Brookings Institution was the most cited think tank [four]), university professors (four), union and labor groups (four), business leaders and organizations (four), and other news publications (two). As this research focused on the Heritage Foundation, an examination of all the articles on ESEA might find that the other nongovernmental sources were cited in articles that did not cite the Heritage Foundation, so that there is balance in the overall coverage of this issue over a period of several months. But the finding that the Heritage Foundation can dominate a series of twenty general news articles contradicts the idea that journalists consistently promote a balanced, "he said, she said" approach to news. More study is necessary, however, before firm conclusions can be made.

DISCUSSION

The Heritage Foundation was created to promote conservative values and ideas. Emphasizing marketing over research, it has aggressively promoted publications and "experts" with little apparent expertise to policy makers and the news media.

This research suggests that the news media, at least in the area of education, uncritically uses and presents the Heritage Foundation's work. During 2001, the news media presented a Heritage Foundation statement on education more than once every three days. Moreover, almost every news item presented the Heritage Foundation in a favorable light. Scientific words such as "study" and "analyst" appeared in almost every citation. Words such as "marketer"—a Heritage Foundation self-description—never did (Smith, 1991).[27] It is hard to imagine a more generous presentation.

How, then, does it happen that the news media present the Heritage Foundation as education experts when their self-professed mission is the marketing of conservative ideas, their assertion of "expert" in education could be determined as exaggerated with only a cursory examination of its website and news articles, and its publication *No Excuses* has been criticized as poor social science research? This question is especially provocative given that the Heritage Foundation has been described as a driving force in a conservative movement that has been the focus of the exact same criticisms—its lack of public policy expertise and poor social science research methods.

Part of the explanation appears to be the process by which the news media select experts. Experts are an integral part of news coverage. They add credibility and authority to news stories in which journalists aim to present an objective and balanced picture of events (Steele, 1995). The key, then, is the selection criteria. Taken together, Soley, Steele, and Lieberman describe the selection criteria as influenced by the conservative economic outlook of journalists, bottom-line profit motive of the media organizations, and a focus on predictions, players, and policies that emphasizes media savvy and real-world experience over in-depth, contextual knowledge. This is in accord with general media studies (Allan, 2000).

This research study supports these conclusions. One could argue that the news media utilized the Heritage Foundation during 2001 because the Heritage Foundation (a) promotes conservative social and economic policies for education, (b) is a free and eagerly convenient source of media-friendly resources, and (c) will format its materials to meet the requirements of the news media, emphasizing marketing over subject knowledge. It does not have ordinary or scholarly expertise, but it has media expertise.

An additional question then is, why does the news media consistently present the Heritage Foundation in a manner that overstates its expertise and understates its conservative advocacy? One explanation appears to be the need or desire of journalists to meet conflicting demands—the professional need to present objective, balanced news reports (Steele, 1995; Allan, 2000) and the economic need to present news at a profit (McChesney, 1999). Having utilized the Heritage Foundation to meet the economic need, a journalist or news organization must now justify its use to a consuming public that expects experts to have more scholarly qualifications—namely, in-depth, long-term knowledge of the subject area (Steele, 1995). Caught in this irreconcilable bind, journalists might emphasize descriptions of Heritage Foundation expertise that the public will find acceptable and downplay or omit those that are unfavorable.

This research supports such a conclusion. The noneducation press—from the *New York Times* and the *Washington Post* to CNN and Fox News—presented the Heritage Foundation quite generously as a source on education. The noneducation press, with one exception amounting to less than 1 percent of the news articles citing the Heritage Foundation on education during 2001, never presented the Heritage Foundation, its writings, or its spokespersons' statements on education as conservative advocacy or possibly questionable expertise or research. Rather, they were depicted as objective and scientific. In so doing, the noneducation news media were able to enhance the credibility of their news reports while minimizing their costs.

This is not to say that the news media were not or should not have been aware of the Heritage Foundation's objectives and lack of expertise concerning education. In fact, it would likely defy reason to assert that the news media are not aware that the Heritage Foundation's experts on education are ideological wolves dressed in the sheep's clothing of scientific expertise. For more than fifteen years, it has been an open secret that the Heritage Foundation, first and foremost, is a marketer of conservative ideas and that,at least some of its experts and research publications are suspect. This is borne out by researchers, information, and documents available on the Heritage Foundation Web site, and by public statements made by foundation personnel. Many are discussed in this chapter.

Thus, it appears well known that Heritage Foundation spokespersons are not experts in their subject areas. The quote from Soley (1992) bears repeating and expansion:

> Among [Washington, D.C.] beltway think tanks, Heritage [Foundation] associates have the weakest scholarly credentials . . . Of its 34 permanent 'fellows, scholars, and staff' members, only 7 have Ph.D.'s. None are renowned scholars in their fields. (p. 60)

An examination of the Heritage Foundation biography of their most cited "education expert" during 2001, Krista Kafer, demonstrates unequivocally that her credentials fall well short of expert. Soley's assessment continues to be dead on.

It appears equally well known that the Heritage Foundation is first and foremost a conservative advocacy organization (Rich, 2004; Weaver and McGann, 2000). In 1986, President Reagan addressed a room full of conservative donors who had gathered to celebrate the conclusion of a Heritage Foundation fundraising campaign. In his remarks, "the president commended the foundation's promotion of ideas through seminars, conferences, publications, and 'its buttonholing of congressmen—for informational purposes only, of course' [which caused] a titter of knowing laughter [to] spread through the ballroom . . ." (Smith, 1991, p. 19).

The Heritage Foundation, itself, is not so subtle. As Edwin Fuelner, president of the Heritage Foundation, wrote at the beginning of the second Bush administration,

> conservative opportunity and liberal opposition are about to collide like warm and cold fronts on a summer's day, and the probability of thunderstorms is 100 percent. This will be a take-no-prisoners war, and there are going to be winners and losers. Make no mistake about that. (Berkowitz, 2002, par.3)

In this "war" of public policy, Reagan knew what Feulner boasts, expertise in promotion and fundraising, not the social issues themselves, is the Heritage Foundation's clear weapon of choice. Nevertheless, one would have to read countless newspapers extremely carefully to find even a hint of this information in the news media's use and presentation of the Heritage Foundation on education issues during 2001. Taken together, it is hard to conceive that the inaccurately generous news media presentations of the Heritage Foundation on education were anything less than the result of a reckless or even knowing disregard for the truth.

Examining the coverage of education issues, the results of this present analysis supports the media criticisms presented by Davis and Owen, Berliner and Biddle, and the strongest statements by Lieberman. Davis and Owen (1998) provide the strongest condemnation of the media use of think tanks in news coverage. They contend that segments of the news media—the new media outlets—consciously manipulate the news by selecting bits of pre-packaged news disseminated by advocacy groups like conservative think tanks that they can use to create news-like populist entertainment. The new media outlets utilize conservative think tanks for their populist entertainment because they provide free, ready-to-use, and engaging material on social and political issues. Whether it is accurate is less important than whether it is entertaining.

Davis and Owen's analysis of new media outlets does not include network television news and newspapers. Lieberman and Berliner and Biddle, whose examination focused on network television news and newspapers, might agree that the media is reckless in its reporting on education, but they stop short of stating that the press consciously or knowingly manipulates the news. The results presented in this chapter suggest that the positions of Davis and Owens, Lieberman, and Berliner and Biddle are now the *best* that one can conclude about the news media's use and presentation of conservative think tanks. The present analysis further suggests that it is likely that the entire news media—both the new media outlets as well as network television news, radio news, and newspapers—now act in a manner that goes beyond the criticisms of Lieberman and Berliner and Biddle to knowingly, or with reckless disregard for readily available information, misrepresenting the conservative think tanks that they include in their news reports.

What appears most evident is that the news media's use of balanced "he said, she said" reporting as a means to achieve the professional standard of objective journalism plays into the hands of advocacy think tanks like the Heritage Foundation. Judis (2001) contends that there is a direct link between the rise of conservative think tanks and the news media's defensive use of balanced reporting:

> The new think tanks and policy groups created by conservatives and their business allies began to overshadow their rivals. The press, on the defensive itself, began treating the products of the AEI [American Enterprise Institute], Heritage [Foundation], and the American Center [for the Study of Business] with the same respect as those of Brookings [Institute], NBER [National Bureau of Economic Research], or a university economics department. They accepted the canard that different views simply reflected different ideologies and that to be fair, both left and right, liberal and conservative, had to be represented. Once this concession was made, the conservatives triumphed, because in the late 1970s and 1980s they had for more money than their rivals with which to broadcast, publish, and promote their opinions. (p. 172)

According to Parenti (1993, 1996) and Altschull (1984, 1990), among others, news objectivity is a dangerous myth that balanced reporting will perpetuate, but never reach; in countless daily news decisions, "selectivity and subjectivity are unavoidable" (Parenti, 1993, p. 54). Taking "he said, she said" reporting and journalistic objectivity together, Parenti (1993) finds that the news media's use of balance is inconsistent in a manner that promotes social inequality by favoring members of the corporate business class, like the Heritage Foundation:

> If reporters play "dumb and more innocent" than they are, it is in selective ways. They may obligingly report whatever politico-economic elites pronounce, be it truth, half-truths, or lies, but they instantly resuscitate their critical faculties when dealing with dissenters. (p. 54)

Parenti argues that the news media must neither accept biases and distortions as inevitable nor strive for unrealistic objectivity. Instead, they should pursue a type of investigative reporting that

> strive[s] for standards of fairness and accuracy—which are best achieved by questioning the self-serving assumptions of policy, by unearthing revealing background material, and by giving exposure to a wide range of dissident critics along with the usual establishment commentators. (1993, p. 54)

With respect to the Heritage Foundation, this type of reporting is not happening.

In the end, this chapter presents a poor, and possibly damning, picture of the news media's role in the public debate on education. If parents and policy makers who look to the media for news about schools and education need information for judging its quality, this chapter shows that they did not receive it in the news media use of Heritage Foundation sources. If sound public policy decisions depend, in part, on a citizenry informed by news that provides a rigorous examination of the issues and a wide range of informed opinions, the findings presented here suggest that the news media have fallen well short of the mark.

NOTES

1. I would like to thank the Education Policy Studies Laboratory at Arizona State University for their support much of the research of this chapter.
2. The entire notion of objectivity in news reporting is quite controversial. Many media scholars argue that true objectivity is impossible and that the media's attempt to achieve it through presenting both sides of an issue reproduces conservative ideologies (see e.g. Altschull, 1984, 1990; Herman and Chomsky, 1988; Parenti, 1993, 1996). These arguments are addressed in the "Discussion" section.
3. The destruction of the World Trade Center buildings on September 11, 2001, impacted the news media coverage of events during the last quarter of the year. It is not clear how this might have affected the news coverage of education issues, but it mostly likely diminished it to some degree.
4. False positives were news entry references to "Heritage Foundation" or to names of individuals that did not refer to both the Washington-based think tank and education.
5. To the best available knowledge, the entries examined in this study are the vast majority of the education-related items published in the United States during 2001 that referenced the Heritage Foundation. It is likely that some media pieces are not present because the Nexis database does not contain every media source. The Nexis database does provide access to over 30,000 information sources and 2.8 billion documents; however, it does not contain, for example, *The Arizona Republic* or *The Detroit News*. In addition, since the Supreme Court decision in *The New York Times Company v. Jonathan Tasini*, 533 U.S. 483 (2001), Nexis has eliminated many freelance articles published in the sources that it does contain.

6. The 159 news entries retrieved from the Nexis database were coded using the following codes.

By Types of News Media
1.   General News Newspapers
2.   Education Publications
3.   Business Publications
4.   Policy Publications
5.   Television Programs
6.   Radio Programs
7.   News Wire Services

By Types of News Media Sources

1. General News Newspapers
    a.   *Arkansas Democrat-Gazette*
    b.   *Atlanta Journal and Constitution*
    c.   *Augusta Chronicle* (Augusta, Ga.)
    d.   *Baltimore Sun*
    e.   *Boston Globe*
    f.   *Capital* (Annapolis, Md.)
    g.   *Chattanooga Times/Chattanooga Free Press*
    h.   *Chicago Independent Bulletin*
    i.   *Commercial Appeal* (Memphis, Tenn.)
    j.   *Daily News of Los Angeles*
    k.   *Dallas Morning News*
    l.   *Dayton Daily News* (Dayton, Ohio)
    m.   *Denver Rocky Mountain News*
    n.   *Deseret News* (Salt Lake City, Utah)
    o.   *El Nuevo Herald* (Spanish language)
    p.   *Florida Times Union* (Jacksonville, FL)
    q.   *Houston Chronicle*
    r.   *Insight on the News* (published by *The Washington Times*)
    s.   *Ledger* (Lakeland, FL)
    t.   *Los Angeles Times*
    u.   *Milwaukee Journal Sentinel*
    v.   *Modesto Bee* (Modesto, Calif.)
    w.   *Morning Call* (Allentown, Pa.)
    x.   *New York Post*
    y.   *New York Times*
    z.   *Pittsburgh Post-Gazette*
    aa. *Plain Dealer* (Cleveland, Ohio)
    bb. *Roanoke Times and World News* (Roanoke, Va.)
    cc. *San Diego Union-Tribune*
    dd. *Saturday Oklahoman*
    ee. *South Bend Tribune*
    ff. *Sunday Gazette-Mail* (Charleston, N.C.)
    gg. *Times Picayune* (New Orleans, La.)
    hh. *Times Union* (Albany, N.Y.)
    ii. *Topeka Capital Journal*
    jj. *Union Leader* (Manchester, N.H.)

      kk.   Washington Post
      ll.   Washington Times
      mm. World and I (published by *The Washington Times*)
  2. Education Publications
      a. Leadership (official magazine of the Association of California School Administrators)
      b. Phi Delta Kappan
      c. Education Technology News
  3. Business Publications
      a. The Bond Buyer
      b. Business Week
      c. The Chronicle of Philanthropy
      d. Forbes
      e. Government Executive
      f. The National Tax Journal
  4. Politics and Policy Publications
      a. Federal News Service (FNS) Daybook
      b. First Things: A Monthly Journal of Religion and Public Life
      c. The Hill (Washington, D.C.)
      d. National Journal
      e. National Journal's Congress Daily
      f. National Journal's Technology Daily
      g. The Public Interest
      h. Washington Internet Daily
      i. The Women's Quarterly
  5. Television Programs
    a. Television News
      i. 9 Eyewitness News at 9:00, WUSA-TV
      ii. Channel 9 News Weekend Report, WCPO-TV
      iii. Fox News Live (Cable)
      iv. KOVR 13 News Tonight
      v. News 3 Nightside, KVBC-TV
      vi. News at Sunrise, KVBC-TV
      vii.   The Patrick Report, KTBU-TV
    b. Television Talk Shows
      i. Barnicle, MSNBC Cable Programming
      ii. Book TV, CSPAN-2
      iii. CNN Talkback Live (Cable)
      iv. CNN Today (Cable)
      v. Softball, MSNBC Cable Programming
      vi. WB2Day
  6. Radio Programs
    a. Radio News
      i. All Things Considered, National Public Radio
    b. Radio Talk Shows
      i. Diane Rehm Show, WAMU-FM
      ii. Public Interest, WAMU-FM
      iii. The Connection, WBUR-FM
  7. News Wire Services
    a. Copley News Service
    b. Cox News Service

      c. Gannett News Service
      d. Newhouse News Service
      e. Scripps Howard News Service
      f. United Press International
      g. U.S. Newswire

By Topics of Media Entries

1. Curriculum and School Governance
    a. Reading
    b. Zero tolerance policies
    c. Technology in schools
    d. Teacher certification
    e. General criticism of failing public schools
    f. General statements on the need for education reform
    g. Food served in schools
    h. Gender equity activities
    i. Grove City College
    j. Sex education classes
    k. High-performing schools
    l. Internet report cards on school performance
    m. Grade inflation
    n. High school marriage classes
    o. Merit pay for teachers
    p. Prison classes
    q. Racial preferences in university admissions
    r. School to work programs
    s. Lack of free speech on college campuses
    t. General statements on need for educational reform

2. Education Legislation

3. Education Spending
    a. Federal education spending and grants to states
    b. Public-private school partnerships relating to construction bonds
    c. Spending on public schools
    d. Spending and educational achievement

4. Heritage Foundation Activities
    a. Publications itself as a topic
    b. Publicized or media events
    c. Personnel highlights

5. Role of Federal Government in education
    a. Job Corps critique
    b. US Department of Education use of student information
    c. Head Start critique

6. School Choice
    a. School Choice generally
    b. Vouchers
    c. Tax credits for ed-tech partnerships
    d. Charter schools
    e. School choice opponents

7. Testing

8. Other

      a. Washington's Birthday
      b. Marriage and educational achievement

By Heritage Foundation Sources

  1. Specific Heritage Foundation Personnel
      a. Bill Bennett (not named as a Heritage Foundation source)
      b. Stuart Butler
      c. Samuel Casey Carter
      d. Thomas Dawson
      e. Patrick Fagan
      f. Megan Farnsworth
      g. Al Felzenberg
      h. Edwin Feulner
      i. Michael Franc
      j. Jennifer Garrett
      k. Todd Goziano
      l. Eugene Hickock
      m. Tom Hinton
      n. Scott Jeffrey
      o. Kirk Johnson
      p. Krista Kafer
      q. Daniel McGroarty
      r. Adam Meyerson
      s. Virginia Miller
      t. Robert Moffitt
      u. Nina Shokaii Rees
      v. Robert Rector
      w. Janice Smith
      x. Virginia Thomas
      y. Ron Utt
      z. Mark Wilson

  2. Publications
      a. *New Tax Law Boosts School Construction with Public-Private Partnerships*
      b. *No Excuses: Lessons from 21 High-Performing, High Poverty Schools*
      c. *School Choice 2001: What's Happening in the States*
      d. *Still Leaving Children Behind: The House and Senate Education Bills*
      e. *The Report Card Report: America's Best Web Sites for School Profiles*
      f. *Trinnietta Gets a Chance: Six Families and Their School Choice Experience*
      g. *Why More Money Will Not Solve America's Education Crisis*

  3. Heritage Foundation cited as an entity
      a. Heritage Foundation study
      b. Heritage Foundation speaking as an entity
      c. Heritage Foundation study
      d. Heritage Foundation report
      e. Heritage Foundation researchers, nonspecific

7. According to a search of the Lexis/Nexis Database with the terms "Heritage Foundation and (educat! or school!)," the first article relating to education that cited the Heritage Foundation was "'New Right' Figure Sees McCarthyism

in NEA's Conference on Conservatives," *Washington Post*, A2, February 24, 1979. It was the only article relating to education that referenced the Heritage Foundation during 1979.

8. See the section "Media Presence of the Heritage Foundation."
9. Some news entries concerned more than one topic.
10. The newspaper circulations for these newspapers were gathered from the following sources:

   Augusta Chronicle
   SRDS Circulation 2002: The Complete Source for Newspaper Circulation Information, Des Plaines, Ill: Standard Rate and Data Service

   Chattanooga Times/Free Press
   2001 Working Press of the Nation, vol. 1, Newspaper Directory, pp. 2–212

   Dayton Daily News
   http://uspolitics.about.com/gi/dynamic/offsite.htm?site=http%3A%2F%2Fwww.infoplease.com%2Fipea%2FA0004420.html

   Deseret News (Utah)
   2001 Working Press of the Nation, vol. 1, Newspaper Directory, pp. 2–231

   Milwaukee Journal Sentinel
   http://www.geocities.com/newspaperstats/

   South Bend Tribune
   http://www.geocities.com/newspaperstats/

   Times Union (Albany, N.Y.)
   2001 Working Press of the Nation, vol. 1, Newspaper Directory, pp. 2–147

   Washington Post
   http://www.naa.org/info/facts01/18_top20circ/index.html

   Washington Times
   http://www.geocities.com/newspaperstats/

11. Jennifer Garrett's Heritage Foundation biography can be found at http://www.heritage.org/About/Staff/JenniferGarrett.cfm.
12. The Heritage Foundation's "The Report Card Report: America's Best Web Sites for School Profiles" is located online at http://www.heritage.org/report-cards/welcome.html.
13. The only descriptions of her qualifications came in three appointment announcements, "People for March 24, 2001," *National Journal*, vol. 905, no. 33, p. 12, March 24, 2001; "Movers & Shakers," *Washington Times*, D14, March 26, 2001; and "Appointments," *Washington Post*, E7, April 2, 2001.
14. Krista Kafer's Heritage Foundation biography is available at http://www.heritage.org/staff/kafer.html.
15. These Heritage Foundation biographies are located at the following locations:

   Stuart Butler
   http://www.heritage.org/staff/butler.htm

   Robert Moffitt
   http://www.heritage.org/staff/moffit.htm

   Michael Franc
   http://www.heritage.org/staff/franc.html

   Kirk Johnson
   http://www.heritage.org/staff/kirk_johnson.html

16. The Heritage Foundation biography for Thomas Hinton is located at http://www.heritage.org/staff/hinton.html.
17. The Heritage Foundation biography for Megan Farnsworth is located at http://www.heritage.org/staff/farnsworth.html.
18. Telephone call to the Heritage Foundation's publications department, April 26, 2001.
19. The Heritage Foundation operates a website for the No Excuses campaign at http://www.noexcuses.org/.
20. "Backtalk: Response to a Criticism," *Phi Delta Kappan*, no. 5, vol. 82, p. 419, January 1, 2001.
21. "Poverty and Achievement, and Great Misconceptions," *New York Times*, B8, January 3, 2001.
22. "Research—At the Beep, Pay Attention; influence of social factors on academic achievement and learning process," *Phi Delta Kappan*, no. 7, vol. 82, p. 555, March 1, 2001
23. "Point of View—No Excuses for *No Excuses, Phi Delta Kappan*, vol. 83, no. 3, p. 194, November 1, 2001.
24. Information on *Substance* can be found at their website at http://www.substancenews.com/.
25. The following *New York Times* articles cited the Heritage Foundation on education during 2001:
    "A New Model For Learning in a Harlem School; Tough Standards and High Scores," *New York Times*, B1, January 2, 2001.
    "Poverty and Achievement, and Great Misconceptions," *New York Times*, B8, January 3, 2001.
    "Cheney Assembles Formidable Team," *New York Times*, A1, February 3, 2001.
    "On Way to Passage, Bush's Education Plan Gets a Makeover," *New York Times*, A16, May 4, 2001.
    "House Votes for New Testing to Hold Schools Accountable," *New York Times*, A1, May 24, 2001.
    "Bush Seems to Ease His Stance on the Accountability of Schools," *New York Times*, A1, July 10, 2001.
    "Inmate Education Is Found to Lower Risk of New Arrest," *New York Times*, A22, November 16, 2001.
    "Congress Reaches Compromise on Education Bill," *New York Times*, A1, December 12, 2001.
    Six of the eight citations came after Richard Rothstein's article on January 3, 2001.
26. The No Child Left Behind Act was passed into law in 2002.
27. "Marketer" comes from the Heritage Foundation's descriptions of itself. For example, James Smith quotes Edwin Feulner, the president of the Heritage Foundation, saying, "We specialize in the area of quick-response public policy research and in marketing the academic works for public policy consumption" (1991, p. 201). Smith also quotes Feulner characterizing the Heritage Foundation as a "secondhand dealer of ideas" (1991, p. 201).

REFERENCES

Abelson, D. 2002. *Do think tanks matter? Assessing the impact of public policy institutes*. Montreal: McGill-Queen's University Press.

Abelson, D., and E. Lindquist. 2000. Think tanks in North America. In *Think tanks & civil societies: Catalysts for ideas and actions*, ed. J. McGann and R. K. Weaver, 37–66. New Brunswick, N.J.: Transaction Publishers.

Ackerman, S. 1999. Think tank monitor: The ever-present yet non-existent poor [Electronic version]. *Extra!*, January/February. http://www.fair.org/extra/9901/rector.html.

Allan, S. 2000. *News culture*. Philadelphia: Open University Press.

Altschull, J. H. 1984. *Agents of power: The role of the news media in human affairs*. New York: Longman.

———. 1990. *From Milton to McLuhan: The ideas behind American journalism*. New York: Longman.

Anderson, G. L. 2007. Media's impact on educational policies and practices: Political spectacle and social control. *Peabody Journal of Education* 82, no. 1: 103–120.

Berkowitz, B. 2002. The Heritage Foundation soars. *Zmag*, July 19. www.zmag.org/ZMag/articles/june01berkowitz.htm.

Berliner, D., and B. Biddle. 1995. *The manufactured crisis: Myths, fraud, and the attack of America's public schools*. Reading, Mass: Addison-Wesley.

———. 1998. The lamentable alliance between the media and school critics. In *Imaging education: The media and schools in* America, ed. G. Maeroff, 26–45. New York: Teachers College Press.

Blumenthal, S. 1986. *The rise of the conservative establishment: From conservative ideology to political power*. New York: Times Books.

Brock, D. 2004. *The Republican noise machine: Right-wing media and how it corrupts democracy*. New York: Crown Publishers.

Callahan, D. 1999. *$1 billion for ideas: Conservative think tanks in the 1990s*. Washington, D.C.: National Committee for Responsive Philanthropy.

Camilli, G., and K. Bulkley. 2001. Critique of *An evaluation of the Florida A-Plus accountability and school choice program*. *Education Policy Analysis Archives* 9, no. 7. http://epaa.asu.edu/epaa/v9n7/.

Covington, S. 1997. *Moving a public policy agenda: The strategic philanthropy of conservative foundations*. Washington, D.C.: National Committee for Responsive Philanthropy.

Covington, S., and L. Parachini. 1995. *Foundations in the Newt era*. Washington, D.C.: National Committee for Responsive Philanthropy.

Croteau, D. 1998. *Examining the "liberal media" bias*. Washington, D.C.: Fairness and Accuracy in Reporting.

Croteau, D., and W. Hoynes. 2000. *Media/society: Industries, images, and audiences*. Thousand Oaks, Calif: Pine Forge Press.

Cuban, L. 1998. The media and polls on education—Over the years. In *Imaging education: The media and schools in* America, ed. G. Maeroff, 69–84. New York: Teachers College Press.

Davis, R., and D. Owen. 1998. *New media and American politics*. New York: Oxford University Press.

Diamond, S. 1995. *Roads to dominion: Right-wing movements and political power in the United States*. New York: Guilford Press.

Dolny, M. 1996. The think tank spectrum: For the media, some thinkers are more equal than others. *Extra!*, May/June. http://www.fair.org/extra/9605/tank.html.

———. 1997. New survey on think tanks: Media favored conservative institution in 1996. *Extra!*, July/August. http://www.fair.org/extra/9707/new_think_tanks.html.

———. 1998. What's in a label? Right-wing think tanks often quoted, rarely labeled. *Extra!*, May/June. http://www.fair.org/extra/9805/think-tanks.html.

———. 2000. Think tank: The rich get richer. *Extra!*, May/June. http://www.fair.org/extra/0005/think-tanks-survey.html.

———. 2001. Think tank Y2K. *Extra!*, July/August. http://www.fair.org/extra/0108/think_tanks_y2k.html.

———. 2002. Think tanks in a time of crisis: FAIR's 2001 survey of the media's institutional experts. *Extra!*, March/April: 28–29.

Doyle, D. 1998. Education and the press: Ignorance is bliss. In *Imaging education: The media and schools in America*, ed. G. Maeroff, 46–56. New York: Teachers College Press.

Fairclough, N. 1995. *Media discourse*. New York: St. Martin's Press.

Farkas, S. 1997. *Good news, bad news: What people really think about the education press*. New York: Public Agenda.

Gardiner, E., ed. 1985. *A new agenda for education*. Washington, D.C.: Heritage Foundation.

Gill, B., M. Timpane, K. Ross, and D. Brewer. 2002. *Rhetoric versus reality: What we know and what we need to know about vouchers and charter schools*. Santa Monica, CA.: RAND Corporation.

Greene, J. P. 2001. *An evaluation of the Florida A-Plus accountability and school choice program*. New York: The Manhattan Institute.

Heritage Foundation. 2002. *Issues*. http://www.heritage.org/research/.

Herman, E., and N. Chomsky. 1988. *Manufacturing consent: The political economy of the mass media*. New York: Pantheon Books.

Judis, J. B. 2001. *The paradox of American democracy: Elites, special interests, and the betrayal of public trust*. New York: Routledge.

Kafer, K. 2003. *School choice 2003: How states are providing greater opportunity in education*. Washington, D.C.: Heritage Foundation.

Killeen, K. 2007. How the media misleads the story of school consumerism: A perspective from school finance. *Peabody Journal of Education* 82, no. 1: 32–62.

Kupermintz, H. 2001. The effects of vouchers on school improvement: Another look at the Florida data. *Education Policy Analysis Archives* 9, no. 8. http://epaa.asu.edu/epaa/v9n8/.

Kuttner, R. 2002. Philanthropy and movements [Electronic version]. *American Prospect*, July 15. http://www.prospect.org/web/page/ww?section=root&name=ViewPrint&articleId=6365.

———. 2000. *The politics of force: Media and the construction of police brutality*. Los Angeles, Calif: University of California Press.

Lieberman, T. 2000. *Slanting the story: The forces that shape the news*. New York: The New Press.

McChesney, R. 1999. *Rich media, poor democracy: Communications politics in dubious times*. New York: The New Press.

Messer-Davidow, E. 1993. Manufacturing the attack on liberalized higher education. *Social Text*, 36, Autumn: 40–80.

Molnar, A. 2001. The media and educational research: What we know versus what the public hears. Paper presented at the American Educational Research Association annual meeting, Seattle, Washington. http://www.asu.edu/educ/epsl/EPRU/documents/cerai-01–14.htm.

Moses, M. 2007. The media as educators, educational research, and autonomous deliberation. *Peabody Journal of Education*, 82, no. 1: 150–165.

National Science Foundation. 2000. *Science and engineering indicators, 2000*. Washington D.C.: U.S. Government Printing Office. http://www.nsf.gov/sbe/srs/seind00/start.htm.

Newspaper Association of America. 2000. Facts about newspapers: A statistical summary of the newspaper industry published in the year 2000. http://

uspolitics.about.com/gi/dynamic/offsite.htm?site=http%3A%F%2Fwww.
naa.org%Finfo%Ffacts00%2Findex.html.

Page, B., R. Shapiro, and G. Dempsey. 1987. What moves public opinion? In *Media Power in Politics*, ed. Doris Graber, 112–27. Washington, D.C.: Congressional Quarterly Press.

Parenti, M. 1993. *Inventing reality: The politics of news media reality* 2nd ed. New York: St. Martin's Press.

———. 1996. *Dirty truths: Reflections on politics, media, ideology, conspiracy, ethnic life and class power.* San Francisco: City Lights Books.

Public Citizen. 1996. Executive summary: Drug, medical device, biotech and tobacco companies gave at least $3.5 million for deceptive anti-FDA campaign. In *A million for your thoughts: The industry-funded campaign against the FDA by conservative think tanks.* Washington, D.C.: Public Citizen. http://www.citizen.org/congress/regulations/archives/fdarollback/articles.cfm?ID=844.

Ricci, D. 1993. *The transformation of American Politics: The new Washington and the rise of think tanks.* New Haven, Conn.: Yale University Press.

Rich, A. 2004. *Think tanks, public policy, and the politics of expertise.* Cambridge, England: Cambridge University Press.

Rich, A., and R. K. Weaver. 1998. Advocates and analysts: Think tanks and the politicization of expertise. In *Interest group politics*, 5th ed., ed. A. Cigler and B. Loomis, 235–53. Washington, D.C.: Congressional Quarterly.

———. 2000. Think tanks in the U.S. media. *Press/Politics* 5, no. 4: 81–103.

Rothstein, R. 2004. *Class and schools—Using social, economic, and educational reform to close the black-white achievement gap.* Washington, D.C.: Economic Policy Institute.

Scatamburlo, V. 1998. *Soldiers of misfortune: The New Right's culture war and the politics of political correctness.* New York: Peter Lang.

Schmidt, G. 2001. Point of view: No excuses for no excuses. *Phi Delta Kappan* 83, no. 3: 194–95.

Smith, J. 1991. *The idea brokers: Think tanks and the rise of the new policy elite.* New York: The Free Press.

Soley, L. 1992. *The news shapers: The sources who explain the news.* New York: Praeger Publishers.

Solomon, N. 1996. The media's favorite think tank. *Extra!*, July/August. http://www.fair.org/extra/9607/heritage.html.

Spring, J. 2002. *Political agendas for education: From the religious right to the green party.* 2nd ed. Mahwah, N.J.: Lawrence Erlbaum Associates.

Steele, J. 1995. Experts and opinion bias of the Persian Gulf War. *Journalism and Mass Communication Quarterly* 72, no. 4: 799–812.

Stefancic, J., and R. Delgado. 1996. *No mercy: How conservative think tanks and foundations changed America's social agenda.* Philadelphia: Temple University Press.

van Dijk, T. 2001. Critical discourse analysis. In *The handbook of discourse analysis*, ed. D. Schiffrin, D. Tannen, and H. Hamilton, 352–71. Oxford: Blackwell.

Weaver, R. K., and J. McGann. 2000. Think tanks and civil societies in a time of change. In *Think tanks & civil societies: Catalysts for ideas and actions*, ed. J. McGann and R. K. Weaver, 1–35. New Brunswick, N.J.: Transaction Publishers.

Weaver, R. K., and P. Stares, eds. 2001. *Guidance for governors: Comparing alternative sources of public policy advice.* New York: Japan Center for International Exchange.

10 Markets and Education in the Era of Globalized Capitalism[1]

Nico Hirtt

INTRODUCTION

Does capitalism need education? To many, this question may seem strange. Don't we live in the age of the "knowledge economy"? Are not Organisation for Economic Co-operation and Development (OECD) experts, those heralds of the free market and growth, going around the world, telling us that "the most effective modern economies will be those that produce the most information and knowledge—and make that information and knowledge easily accessible to the greatest number of individuals and enterprises [and that] countries and continents that invest heavily in education and skills benefit economically and socially from that choice" (Schleicher, 2006)?

Andreas Schleicher, who published these comments in an alarmist report for the *Lisbon Council,* supports his statements by arguing that investments in higher education (whether private or public) yield substantial benefits for the individual in terms of future income and job stability. Nobody really questions that. However, do these advantages come from higher education itself or, on the contrary, from its relative scarcity? In other words, would these benefits increase or decrease if we were able to increase substantially the number of degrees? Or indeed, is the benefit for the individual also a benefit for society or for the economy? Or is it rather an indication of a power struggle in the labor market, or in the distribution of a limited number of available jobs?

Schleicher has difficulty producing any convincing correlation, among OECD countries, between investments in education and economic growth. Even if such a correlation did exist, what does it prove? That education stimulates the economy? Perhaps. Maybe we should consider the opposite hypothesis: that a flourishing economy will boost participation in education, while providing a sine qua non for investment in education.

The mountains of studies and reports published since the early 1990s by national and international agencies, think tanks and commissions proclaim their faith in education as the new miracle cure for the world economy; they do not convince us. Does the system really need a broad dissemination of science and culture, a massive expansion of education, universal access to the understanding of our material and social world? Such a proposition incites us to a prudent scepticism, drawing on our understanding of history and of current education policies. Over the past two hundred years of anti-capitalist struggle, we have learned to detect the ideology behind capitalist rhetoric, and its "imaginary relations to the real conditions of existence" (Althusser, 1972).

THE CAPITALIST SCHOOL: FAITH AND FUNCTIONS

What is the true purpose of education and, in particular, of compulsory education? This is indeed an interesting question which raises many others. What is the official position on the role of schools? What is expected of them by society, by families, employers, teachers, and pupils? What are the real functions and objectives of the educational system? And how do so many different positions, expectations, and functions fit together?

The institutional attitude towards education can more or less be summarized in four fundamental statements:

- school education ensures the full development of the person and unleashes his or her full potential;
- school trains people to be free and responsible citizens, capable of playing their role in a democratic society;
- education for all guarantees equal opportunities for social advancement;
- a general and professional education provides the key which opens the door to the labor market.

The dishonest, or at the very least biased, basis for these four claims should be obvious. Is it possible to create free and responsible citizens when half of them are locked into a technico-professional education that almost completely deprives them of whole areas of essential general knowledge? Can you turn people into thinking citizens when you indoctrinate them with the dogma that a world dominated by capital and profit is democratic? And what about those equal opportunities? The selection process within the schools has never been as harsh and arbitrary as it is today! For every "gifted" student who manages to climb out of social misery thanks to an education, how many others, no less "gifted," are mercilessly rejected by the system? Access to jobs for all? But in a world of persistently high unemployment levels, what impact can education have? And how on earth can schools "unleash the potential" of those left behind by our unjust society? In fact, there is only one way: by giving them the weapons of knowledge and organizational capacity which will then allow them to revolt. But is this really what we expect from the school?

So here we have four ideological claims, which are in fact four dishonest statements. Still, they remain four ideological statements, which can have a basis in reality and offer a reflection on that underlying reality. Behind each lies one of the four objective functions[2] of education in a capitalist world:

- the socialization function;
- the ideological function;
- the social reproduction function; and
- the economic function.

The first of the four claims—"the development of the person and his or her potential"—formulates, in an obscure language and with a touch of Christian "personalism" (though there are other versions), the idea that a pupil has to become what is expected of him: a social being with the necessary knowledge, skills, norms and attitudes for its future life. This "socialization" function is probably the least obscure in the ideological rhetoric.

The second claim—"to create free and responsible citizens"—barely conceals its deeper meaning: education has the function of ensuring the ideological cohesion of society by explicitly defending its economic and political organization and by justifying social inequalities through selection mechanisms.

The "equal opportunities" dogma is designed to legitimize true inequality: hierarchical social selection constitutes the third "function" of the capitalist school system. Given that "opportunities" for social advancement are believed to be equal, inequality in social achievement is perceived as the logical outcome of differences in merit or individual talents.

Finally, behind all those promises of access to employment lies the necessity of providing the economy with sufficient numbers of workers and consumers to meet current requirements.

These functions are not necessarily kept hermetically separate; they often become intertwined. To give but one example, the "reproduction" function integrates aspects of socialization (education offered in a "public school" is not the same as that offered in a school in a poor neighborhood), of politics (educating citizens who respect the institutions is one thing, educating the leaders of these institutions is another), and obviously of economics.

THE CAPITALIST SCHOOL FROM A
MATERIALIST HISTORICAL PERSPECTIVE

The four functions of education have a history. They have been present for as long as schools and capitalism have existed, albeit to different and changing degrees. An understanding of this history is necessary, because it helps us to understand the present situation.

Before the first industrial revolution, educational institutions essentially fulfilled the role of reproducing the elite. Higher education institutions and the more "prestigious" private schools still play this role today.

In those days, the main role of education was to provide children of the higher social classes with the knowledge and culture that would allow them to identify with their own class, assume power, and prepare themselves for leadership.

At the end of the eighteenth century, and especially at the beginning of the nineteenth century, we see an almost simultaneous development in all capitalist countries: a primary school system for the socialization of children of the lower orders. Why? The fragmentation and "de-skilling" of manual labour brought on by industrialization had gradually dismantled the master-apprentice system inherited from the Middle Ages. Yet the traditional apprenticeship was not just a way of obtaining professional qualifications: the young apprentice learned much more than just his skills, he was also taught, disciplined, and instructed in the knowledge required for everyday life and life in society. In the countryside, the socialization of children began very early in extended rural families where several generations lived together and the child took his or her place in productive activities, and hence in social life.

With the emergence of industrialization and urbanization, the extended family was inexorably replaced by the urban nuclear family, consisting of a single couple of adults, both forced to sell their labor to survive, and a limited number of children. Once, too soon, the children reached a "working age," they were recruited into a fragmented, mind-numbing production process, which hardly contributed to their intellectual or moral upbringing.

In large urban centers, where social and religious control were not as strong as in the countryside, where there were more temptations, and where, above all, exploitation, misery, and glaring social inequalities tended to legitimize any way of gleaning a scrap of happiness, some of the proletariat fell into a life of vice and crime.

The dominating classes therefore began to worry about these "instigators of social disorder," these "seeds of hooliganism," these "young bandits," which they had nevertheless done everything to create. Since neither the family nor work on the farm or in the workshop could now play a role in educating working-class children, off to school with them! In 1841, King Leopold I of Belgium argued in favor of education, saying: "It's a question of social order" (De Clerck, 1975). "Opening a school means closing a prison," concurred Victor Hugo. At about the same time in the United States, Horace Mann inaugurated common public schools, while, in England, the Grant Act (1833) and Forster's Education Act (1870) established the role of government in primary education.

Progress, however, remained slow. Torn between their hunger for profits, which led them to reject instinctively restrictive and costly regulations, and their disgust for, or fear of, the wanton lifestyle of the working classes, the middle classes were in two minds about the introduction of universal education. Certainly they encouraged families to send their children to school, but they still balked at the idea of making education compulsory.

Some probably thought that sending children to the coalface or the mill for their socialization would be more profitable.

Soon, however, new arguments in favor of education emerged. The middle classes watched with mounting anxiety the organization of the proletariat they had created. As a result, they imbued the school with a new ideological mission: to ensure a minimum of political cohesion. In France, Jules Ferry founded the École républicaine to counter "proletarian education," the dangers of which the Commune de Paris had made abundantly explicit. Ferry remarked: "We ascribe to the State the only role it can take in education: that of maintaining a certain moral concept of the State, a certain doctrine of the State that is important for its preservation."[3] Patriotism was, of course, prominent on this agenda: the struggles among the great powers were intensifying, France wanted to recuperate Alsace-Lorraine, and possession of colonies had become crucially important for the economy. In short, the time had come for preparing cannon fodder for the Great War.

In the United States, following the War of Independence, Charles Dudley Warner (2004) wrote in *Education of the Negro,*

> A growing ignorant mass in our body politic, inevitably cherishing bitterness of feeling, is an increasing peril to the public. In order to remove this peril, by transforming the Negro into an industrial, law-abiding citizen, . . . the opportunity of the common school must be universal, and attendance in it compulsory.

From the beginning of the twentieth century, the development of mechanical and chemical industries, together with the expansion of the public administration and of the commercial job market, created new demands for qualified human resources. For the majority of workers, basic socialization was still sufficient, but a growing number of them were expected to learn a profession and technical skills. Recourse to apprenticeships would not suffice. The education system had to be opened to "modern" subjects which would provide technical or professional opportunities for the "best" children from the working classes, based explicitly on merit. This led to a new emphasis on the economic role of education. But, given the nature of the beast, the school soon evolved into a selection machine.

In the aftermath of World War II, a period of strong and sustained economic growth and extensive long-term technological innovation (electrification of railroads, construction of port and airport infrastructures, motorways, nuclear plants, telephones, and the petrochemical industry) led to the preeminence of the school's economic mission. Now was the time for improving the level of education for workers and consumers. This was provided through the rapid massification of secondary education and, to a lesser extent, of higher education. All this was accomplished with the state footing the bill, at a time when this was still possible.

But massification also resulted in reviving the education system's role as a machine for reproducing social stratification. Now that everybody had access to a secondary education, social selection could no longer take place "spontaneously" at the end of primary school, but was now exercised at the secondary school. In the olden days, with a few rare exceptions, only children of the elite studied the classics as a preparation for higher education. Middle-class children were offered general or "modern" secondary studies. Children of the lower classes left school after primary school or, in rare cases, obtained a few years of technical or professional secondary training.

The period of massification from the 1950s to the 1980s dramatically changed this "natural" balance. From then on, greater numbers of children went on to secondary schools and colleges; many took their chances and obtained a general education because the demand for a qualified labor force, in services or government administration for example, offered opportunities for social promotion. As a result, the process of selection now took place during secondary school. Indirectly, massification of education led to massification of poor results and of repeated years, thus creating a new form of hierarchical selection. Moreover, as if by some remarkable pedagogical miracle, this selection still turns out to be a selection by social class. Now everybody goes to secondary school and follows the same educational programs, but the difference today, as in the past, is that it is usually the children from the upper classes who "succeed," enter the "more noble" study programs, and are accepted for university studies in prestigious and respected faculties. The school has thus become, in the words of French sociologist Pierre Bourdieu, "a machine for reproducing class inequalities."

TOWARDS A GLOBAL EDUCATION POLICY

So what is the situation today? The great theories on educational matters are no longer advanced by the likes of Ferry or Dewey, but rather by OECD, the World Bank, WTO and the European Commission. Their priority in education is no longer the "formatting" of citizens, since this is now carried out much more effectively by the mass media than by the school system, but rather the preparation of producers and consumers for their role in the new economy. "Education is vital," says the World Bank, "those who can best engage in competition (with more advanced literacy, numeracy and other skills) have an enormous advantage over their less prepared rivals in a changing economic environment" (World Bank, 1999). For the OECD, "it is now obvious that the level of education is not only essential for the economic well-being of individuals, but also for that of nations. Access to education, linked to academic success, is a key factor in the accumulation of human capital and economic growth" (Organisation For Economic Co-operation and Development, 2002). For its part, the European Commission calls for "a widespread homogenization of school systems . . . to meet the needs of companies, in order to reap all the benefits of the abolition of borders and offer strong competition with the United States and Japan" (Kaufmann, 2000).

In a little over a century, the school has been transformed: it is no longer an instrument of state ideology, but a machine serving global and international economic competition. In industrialized countries, this mutation has taken place progressively since the beginning of the twentieth century, with first the creation, followed by the expansion, of technical and professional education, and later more rapidly with the massification of secondary education. These changes, however, were merely transformations of the "old" education system, inherited from the nineteenth century. But the upheavals caused by the economic crises of the 1970s and the acceleration of technological change led to much more radical reforms, beginning in the 1980s, with the approbation of powerful supranational organizations of modern capitalism. In third world countries, the newborn education systems barely had the time to mature: they were immediately caught up in the quagmire of national debt and the neoliberal offensive.

It is no longer a question of applying homeopathic remedies to an education system diagnosed as sclerotic, or of grafting greater interest in the business sector: now is the time for "in-depth reforms." We are entering the era of the merchandization of schools, where they will be expected to conform more closely to the needs of the market, and subsequently to initiate their own transformation into a new market.

When considering the evolution of compulsory education in industrialized capitalist countries, especially in Europe, we can see several important common trends. The first, and in my opinion the most obvious, of these trends is decentralization and deregulation. The former state-run centralized education systems have been transformed into networks of flexible, competitive schools, often managed by local authorities or nongovernmental groups. Their ability to influence the local development of customized programs and teaching methods has been greatly enhanced. In a report published eight years ago, the European Research Institute on Education, Eurydice, noted already that "reforms in European education systems can be summarized as a progressive movement towards decentralization and reduction of the central power of the State" (Eurydice, 1997). This evolution is strongly supported by industrial lobbies, such as the European Round Table of Industrialists (ERT): "We must encourage training systems that are less institutional, more informal . . . As industrialists, we believe that educators themselves should be free to conduct similar internal research for efficiency without interference or undue pressures exerted from the outside" (European Round Table of Industrialists, 1995). But, as we will see later, decentralization and deregulation in the field of management often goes hand in hand with more centralized state control over certain specific achievements and the definition of educational objectives (skills, work-related learning, and preparation for lifelong learning).

The second trend is the dramatic slowdown, during the 1980s and the 1990s, of the rapid increases in educational spending that had characterized the 1950s, 1960s, and 1970s. In the European Union, public expenditure on education stagnated for more than ten years at around 5 percent of GDP (with the notable exception of Scandinavian countries, where expenditure remains high at about 7 percent of GDP; Eurydice, 2005). In some countries, such as Belgium, spending has been severely reduced, even though the number of students in higher education continues to increase.

Thirdly, when we look at school programs, and more precisely at the objectives of education, we see that the emphasis is no longer on knowledge or "general culture," but increasingly on skills aimed at "lifelong learning": professional skills (mastering a second language, or information and communications technology skills), and vague transversal skills (problem-solving), or so-called "social skills" (adaptability). (European Commission, 1995, 1996; European Round Table of Industrialists, 1995, 1997; Organisation For Economic Co-Operation and Development 1994, 2001a; Reiffers, 1996).

The fourth common trend, observed over a period of fifteen years, is growing social inequality in schools. Both national and international studies show that the educational gap between higher-class and lower-class children is again widening in many countries (Thélot and Vallet, 2000; Groupe Européen de Recherche sur l'Equité des Systèmes Educatifs [GERESE], 2003; Nicaise, Van den Brande, and Groenez, 2003; Albouy and Wanecq, 2003). The process of massification in comprehensive education that marked the 1960s and 1970s has been halted. We notice a return to a more rigorous and earlier selection, which often leads to social discrimination. The objective of democratizing access to a general secondary education has often been abandoned in favor of the so-called "second chance" education, usually involving work-oriented vocational training.

This brings us to the fifth trend, a more work-oriented form of education. Greater emphasis is placed on vocational training, work-related teaching, development of partnerships between schools and private companies, and promotion of "entrepreneurship" in education (European Commission, 1995, 1997, 2000c, 2001b; Organisation For Economic Co-operation and Development, 2001a)

Not only do schools seek contacts with business, but business now comes into the school. We have observed a tremendous growth of miscellaneous forms of commercial presence in the schools: advertisements posted on school walls or printed on teaching material, sponsoring of activities by private companies (GMV-Conseil, 1998), or even the use of education to sustain the market in ICT technologies, as was decided by the European Union in Lisbon five years ago (European Commission 1996, 1997, 2000a, 2000b, 2000c, 2001a).

And so we come to the last common trend, where education itself becomes a new and profitable market: private teaching, private schools, private management of schools, online learning, in a word: the Education Business. The U.S. consulting group Eduventures writes that

> the 1990s will be remembered as a time when the education-for-profit industry came of age. The foundations for a vibrant 21st century education industry—entrepreneurship, technology innovations and market opportunities—began to coalesce and achieve critical mass. (Newman, 2000)

Merrill Lynch's analysis is that "the situation is ripe for a vast privatization-for-profit of education." Although this statement may seem somewhat exaggerated in most European countries, where this extreme form of merchandization applies at the moment almost exclusively to higher education and lifelong learning, in other parts of the world the evolution towards privatization is moving noticeably more rapidly (Johnstone, 1998; Patrinos, 1999; International Finance Corporation, 1999; Robertson, Bonal, and Dale, 2001; World Bank, 1999). This is especially true in the Far East and Southeast Asia. In South Korea, private spending on education recently surpassed government spending (Bray, 2004).

ECONOMIC DETERMINATION OF
SCHOOL MERCHANDIZATION

The trends described above go hand in hand with the process of economic globalization and the emergence of the so-called "information society of knowledge," It seems likely, therefore—and according to Marxist analytical framework, it is now almost inevitable—that developments in the field of education will be linked to the evolution of the economic environment. To develop this point further, we must identify certain aspects and contradictions of economic globalization.

Since the mid-1980s, the economies of advanced capitalist countries have faced two major challenges. First, economic competition has intensified, resulting initially from the economic crisis of the late 1970s. This has led to a high level of instability, high unemployment rates, heavy pressure on public spending and the relentless pursuit of competitiveness. Second, industry and services have entered into the era of new technologies, especially in the field of information and communication. These technologies have given rise to new forms of labor organization, with more flexibility, just-in-time production and rapid internationalization of production and trade, but have also created greater unpredictability, instability, and unequal development, which in turn further intensify economic competition (European Commission, 1997; Field, 1997).

So while technological development is stimulated by investors, companies, and governments as a way of solving the problem of competitiveness at the local or national level, it is also a key element in maintaining an exacerbated economic environment which can compete at the international level. Now we have, on the one hand, the global economy and, on the other, a global evolution of education systems. But how does the one lead to the other?

An exacerbated economic competition has one indirect and three direct consequences for education systems. Let us begin with the indirect consequence. To improve the competitiveness of national or local industries and services, governments are urged to diminish fiscal pressure. "Lower taxes" is one of the principal demands made by national companies. And lower taxes means less spending on public services, especially the most costly: education. This is, obviously, the first and principal explanation for the relative decline in public spending on education noted above. This link is considered an "indirect" consequence because most of the organizations representing business and capitalists are not actually demanding a reduction in education budgets: the ERT has even called for increased education spending (European Round Table, 1989). Yet at the same time, their members ask their national governments to reduce taxes. This is a characteristic contradiction between the global and individual interests of capitalism. We will see later why the individual interest (cutting taxes to improve competitiveness) wins.

Let us now turn to the direct consequences of globalized competition: what are the three main axes of "merchandization" of schools? First, intense economic competition forces investors to search constantly for new profitable markets. As, of course, many public services in advanced capitalist countries have now been privatized, the $2,000 billion world education market is seen as a New Eldorado (Patrinos and Ariasingam, 1997; Larsen and Vincent-Lancrin, 2003). It follows, therefore, that companies will try to use the vast commercial opportunities offered by hundreds of millions of students and pupils to reinforce their presence in schools. For sectors that governments see as "strategic," such as information and communications technology markets, we see the European Commission itself plead the cause of education as a way of stimulating these markets:

> It is doubtful if our continent will keep hold of the industrial position that it has achieved in this new market of multimedia if our systems of education and training do not rapidly step up their efforts. The development of these technologies, in a context of strong international competition, requires that the effects of scale play their full role. If the world of education and training does not make use of them, the European market will become too small a mass market, too late." (European Commission, 1996.)

Finally, strong economic competition puts pressure on governments to adapt swiftly and to tighten educational programs and structures so that they can respond more rapidly to changing demands for skills in the workforce. All this helps explain, of course, the move towards a more labor-oriented education system. But other factors also have a role to play.

FLEXIBILITY AND ADAPTABILITY

As we have already seen, globalization is more than just international competition. It also involves a new organization of labor and the constant emergence of new, and the disappearance of older, markets in a rapidly changing technological and industrial environment. All of this demands greater flexibility and conversely produces a less predictable environment.

The intensification of the struggle for competitivenes is forcing industrialists and service providers to accelerate the development and launch of new production and mass market technologies. It took fifty-four years for civil aviation to capture 25 percent of its market; the telephone needed thirty-five years, television, twenty-six. The personal computer captured a quarter of its potential market in fifteen years, the cell phone needed twenty-three years and Internet only seven years (World Bank, 1995). The economic, industrial, and technological environment has thus become more unstable, more volatile, and more chaotic than ever. The window of economic predictability continues to shrink. In this context, it is increasingly difficult to predict which specific qualifications will be needed in ten or fifteen years' time. As the OECD has pointed out: "The acceleration of the rhythm of change implies that learning and qualifications are increasingly exposed to the risks of intellectual depreciation" (Organisation For Economic Co-Operation And Development, 2001b).

Therefore, education is required to give less importance to knowledge, which "is nowadays, in our fast-moving societies and economies, a perishable product" (Cresson, 1998), and more emphasis on skills that guarantee flexibility and adaptability in the workforce. An OECD report states this very clearly:

> It is more important to aim at educational objectives of a general character than to learn things which are too specific. In the working world, there exists a set of basic competences—relationship qualities, linguistic aptitudes, creativity, the capacity to work in a team and to solve problems, a good understanding of new technologies—which have today become essential to possess to be able to obtain a job and to adapt rapidly to the evolving demands of working life. (Organisation For Economic Co-Operation And Development, 1998)

Workers are being asked to find their way in a constantly changing environment because technologies evolve, because products keep changing, because restructuring and reorganizing lead to job mobility, and because competition leads to job insecurity. Continual retraining is costly in both time and money. To teach a worker the specifics of a new production environment is an expensive investment in time and money, and slows down or delays the launch of new ventures. The multiplication of such costs, because of rapid turnover in labor and technologies, soon becomes prohibitive. Yet the very nature of these technologies and their increasing complexity make the acquisition of knowledge, and consequently of education, more crucial than ever.

From now on, the most important activity at school is no longer learning, but "learning to learn," the ability to adapt quickly to a fast changing technological environment and to a rapid rotation of the labor force in industry and services. "The advocacy for lifelong learning rests on the idea that preparation for active life may not be considered as definitive and that workers must [follow] training during their professional life to remain productive and employable" (Organisation For Economic Co-Operation And Development, 1997).

Basic education methods and programs must therefore be reexamined in order to develop workers' capacity to face an extremely varied range of professional situations. As recommended by the European Council meeting in Amsterdam in 1997, it is a question of "giving priority to the development of professional and social skills for a better adaptation of workers to the evolution of the labour market" (European Commission, 1997).

General knowledge, as a resource for understanding our common world culture, has never been considered particularly important in terms of the economy. General secondary education programs, which are nowadays thought to be "too heavily oriented" towards the acquisition of knowledge, are reminiscent of an era in which this type of education was reserved for children of the upper classes, to prepare for their role as future leaders. They had to be provided with the weapons of knowledge, the cultural characteristics of their class and the legitimacy of power. These programs, despite their unsuitability to the ambitious target of raising levels of professional training among the masses, have nevertheless largely survived the introduction of education massification. This was due in part no doubt to considerations of quantity (increases in the average length of schooling), which for a time attracted considerable attention, to the detriment of qualitative factors (adaptation of content and of structures to the needs of the economy).

In an economic context where attention is directed towards content and the quest for employability, this "piling up" of general knowledge is now under attack from all sides. As always, the real hypertrophy of certain programs becomes the pretext that justifies abandonment of the very objective of education: to pass on knowledge. The promotion of certain pedagogical doctrines, such as the so-called "skills approach," serves to confirm this tendency. These doctrines favor skills—"an integrated and functional ensemble of knowledge (know-how, personal behaviour, personal development), which allows the individual to adapt, solve problems and carry out projects in a variety of situations" (Bernaerdt, et al. 2001)—as opposed to pure knowledge. It is less important to accumulate general knowledge than to know how to access new knowledge and use it in unforeseen situations. The apparent generosity of the concept should not blind us to its real objective: without an adequate knowledge base, the "new knowledge" acquired by future citizens "throughout their life" will remain confined to elementary sectors, such as mastering new software, using a new machine, adapting to a new working environment. The goal of turning education into a tool for economic competition dominates all thinking on educational issues.

Among the qualifications so vigorously demanded by employers, it is worth mentioning diplomas in information and communication (ICT) technologies, as indicated in the European Commission's concept paper on the objectives of education:

> It is the opinion of all Member States that the basic skills acquired by young people at the end of their education or professional training should be reviewed and be broadened to include information and communication technologies. (European Commission, 2001b)

It is absolutely essential that all future workers are taught to find their way in an environment dominated by ICT technologies, to be familiar with the man-machine dialogue via a keyboard and a mouse, to respond to orders appearing on a computer screen, and to adapt rapidly, almost intuitively, to various ever-changing software.

Flexibility and unpredictability also mean that education systems themselves must develop their capacity to adapt by becoming more autonomous, more competitive, and less dependent on central regulation. In 1993, the ERT pointed out that "We must encourage training methods that are less institutional, more informal" (European Round Table, 1993). Two years later, the European Commission showed that it had understood this lesson: "The most decentralized [education] systems are also the most flexible, the quickest to adapt and hence have the greatest propensity to develop new forms of partnership" (European Commission, 1995). For the OECD as well,

> the school system should strive to shorten its response time, by using more flexible formulas than those established by the public administration, in order to be able to open—or close—technical and professional sections, use competent personnel, and have all necessary equipment at their disposal. (Organisation For Economic Co-Operation And Development, 1998)

Increasing school autonomy offers greater scope for adapting to the expectations of the business community, but also, perhaps, to those of society and of parents. Indeed, in a world where competition for the most prestigious jobs increases dramatically every day, the expectations of parents (expressed by parent-teacher associations, for example) very often reflect those of their employers. In this regard, it is worth noting that the fact that schools are under pressure to introduce a few hours of English or computer studies in the first years of basic education is particularly significant.

Among other possibilities, autonomy allows the creation of partner-ships with business; in fact, it provides an incentive, since, in periods of budget restrictions, they will thus have access to potential sponsors. And so, according to the European Commission report on the "concrete objec-tives" of education systems, "it is recommended that they tighten their links with the local environment and, more specifically, with companies and employers, in order to better their understanding of the latter's needs and thereby increase the employability of the pupils" (European Commis-sion, 2001b).

Finally, the call for deregulation also encompasses the distribution of diplomas. In a context of rapid turnover in the workforce, employers are, as we have seen, particularly keen that the labor market should become as flexible as possible. Today, the labor market is strongly regulated by the qualification and diplomas system, particularly during collective bargain-ing negotiations on salaries, working conditions, and social protection. In order to destroy this "rigid" system, the business community is calling for the introduction of "modular" qualifications. This has the dual advan-tage of allowing a more flexible system of recruitment (thereby putting more pressure on workers' rights) and of inciting "pupils" to include in their *cursus* everything that contributes (or appears to contribute) to their employability.

WHEN SOCIAL DUALITY OVERCOMES CONTRADICTIONS

Of course, there remains a great danger in the evolution we have just described. The emphasis on work-oriented skills rather than on general knowledge, fewer regulatory barriers, and, above all, cuts in education budgets can quickly lead to inequality in education. Here again, we find the contradiction mentioned earlier: how can education be more effective in producing the workforce needed by the knowledge society if it has less financial resources and if it continues to evolve towards a social polar-ization which leaves a large number of future workers without high-level qualifications? Some people on the left believe that the growing demand for a highly skilled workforce will be sufficient to force governments to invest more in education and to push education systems towards social democra-tization in the long term.

Unfortunately, this may well turn out to be excessively optimistic. In fact, we totally misunderstand the concept of the "knowledge society" if we believe that all the future economy needs is a highly skilled workforce. On the con-trary, in all advanced countries where statistics are available, we can observe a polarized evolution of the labor market. In the United States, for instance, of the thirty occupations with the greatest rate of job creation, 22 percent do indeed require a very high level of education (a bachelor's or doctoral degree) but, on the other hand, almost 70 percent of these jobs require only short- to medium-term on-the-job training: cashiers, cleaners, waiters, truck drivers, security guards, home care aides, and so forth (Braddock, 1999).

We can see the same evolution in France, where the number of unskilled jobs has risen from 4.3 million to 5 million in the last ten years, compared to a constant decrease over previous decades (Chardon, 2001). The Thélot Commission's report suggested that

> The proportion of "low skilled" jobs, or jobs necessitating "behavioural" or "relational" qualifications, will remain significant in the future: a large number of jobs will probably be created in certain sectors (sales, personal services etc.); in sectors with a concentration of low-skilled employees and workers, the loss of jobs will be more than compensated by the necessity of replacing the huge numbers of workers going into retirement (Thelot, 2004).

This is the reality of the so-called knowledge society in industrialized countries. It allows us to understand how knowledge societies will deal with social polarization, deregulation, and budgetary cuts in their education systems. It also explains how the European Commission can make proposals that, twenty years ago, would have been unacceptable: "Education could be rationalized by providing a shorter period of general education, better tailored to market needs" (European Commission, 1993).

For decades, the general slide towards highly qualified jobs had justified the massification of access to education (first in secondary, later in higher education). It had also permitted the emergence of a rhetoric advocating the democratization of education. Some went so far as to imagine that unskilled jobs would disappear in the medium term. The present evolution is burying these myths.

> The notion of success for all should not be misunderstood. It does certainly not mean that the school must do its utmost to ensure that all pupils will reach the highest levels of education. This would create both an illusion for the individual pupil and a social absurdity, since educational qualifications would no longer be linked, even vaguely, to job structures (Thélot, 2004).

THE EDUCATION BUSINESS

The different aspects of this new education policy are strongly interconnected and all contribute to stimulating the rapid development of the education business. Less regulation opens the door to private investments in education; emphasis on skills and labor-oriented teaching, together with the reluctance of public education systems to adapt to this demand, makes private education more attractive; social polarization and budget cuts in education also contribute to making investments in private education profitable. As the European Commission pointed out in its White Paper on Education and Training,

There are many today who think that the time for education outside the school has arrived, and that the liberation of the education process which it would make possible will result in the control of education by providers who would be more innovative than the traditional structures. (European Commission, 1995)

By allowing new forms of "distance learning systems," and hence new niches that are beyond state control, ICT is another very important catalyst for the education business.

The development of different sources of information and knowledge is going to bring about a rapid decline in the monopoly of educational institutions in the domain of information and knowledge." (European Commission, 1997)

The OECD concludes that

The multiple evolutions rendered necessary by economic and technological change will no longer allow education systems, or governments, to have sole responsibility for initial training and continuing education of the workforce . .[It is therefore necessary] . . . to define the sharing of responsibility which, according to the specific requirements in each country, would guarantee both the quality and the flexibility of education and training.[4]

CONCLUSION

The above analysis demonstrates that the present evolution of educational systems in advanced capitalist countries is not just the result of political choices. The neoliberal agenda in education is also, and more importantly, a product of objective and material considerations in the capitalist economy. In my opinion, these mutations offer a new identity for school and business, namely, a transition from the historical era of "massification" of education to that of the "marketization" of education.

The alignment of education to the new aspirations of industrial and financial powers will have two dramatic consequences: it will instrumentalize schools and require them to serve the needs of economic competition, and it will exacerbate social inequalities in terms of access to knowledge. The school was "massified" by giving working-class children access—albeit partially and timidly—to the wealth of knowledge until then reserved to the sons and daughters of the middle classes. Now that massification has achieved its goal, the teacher is required to bring education back to a role that (in some people's eyes) it should never have forsaken: teaching how to produce and consume and, by the same process, ensure respect for the existing institutions. No more, no less.

The present evolution in the education system is taking place at the cost of reduced access to the knowledge and skills required to understand and play a role in today's world. It is precisely those who are most exploited who are being deprived of the intellectual weapons they need to fight for their collective emancipation.

Today more than ever, this School for Production will become an agency for social reproduction. In the name of the struggle against failure (and this is the height of hypocrisy), the level of requirements is divided, selected, and lowered for some (those who will enter the low-skilled workforce required by the "new" economy), while at the same time others will be encouraged to look towards "more innovative education providers" for the knowledge which will place them at the forefront of international competition. The deregulation of programs and structures, together with the explosion of diverse forms of paid education, will provide the breeding ground for class inequalities which will be transformed, even more effectively than now, into inequalities in the access to knowledge.

Unless a radical and worldwide movement emerges to stop this development and to defend a public and democratic school for all, education will quickly evolve towards a polarized system, whereby "public authorities will only have to ensure access to education for those who will never constitute a profitable market, and whose exclusion from the society will grow, while others will continue to progress" (Organisation For Economic Co-operation and Development, 1996).

NOTES

1. Translated from the French by Andrée Durand, Silke Reichrath and Caroline Mackenzie.
2. The term 'function' should not be understood in the sense of intentionality, but rather in a 'biological' sense: our eyes have the function to see, even though nobody has ever intended to give us this function. Vision is an outcome of biological evolution, just like the functions of education are an outcome of social evolution.
3. Quoted by Edwy Pénel, *Le Monde*, September 14, 1980.
4. l'Observateur de l'OCDE, no.193, April–May 1995.

REFERENCES

Albouy, V., and T. Wanecq. 2003. Les inégalités sociales d'accès aux grandes écoles. *Économie et Statistique* 361, 27–52.
Althusser, L. 1972. *Lénine et la philosophie. Suivi de Marx et Lénine devant Hegel.* Paris: F. Maspero.

Bernaerdt, G., C. Delory, A. Genard, A. Leroy, L. Paquay, B. Rey, M. Romainville, J-L Wolfs. 2001. *À ceux qui s'interrogent sur les compétences et leur évaluation*, Le Point sur la Recherche en Education—no. 2.

Braddock, D. 1999. Occupational employment projections to 2008. *Monthly Labor review* 122, no. 11.

Bray, M. 2004. *The shadow education system*. Paper presented at the Séminaire préparatoire à la CIE, Genève.

Chardon, O. 2001. Les transformations de l'emploi non qualifi é depuis vingt ans. *INSEE Première* 796.

Cresson, E. 1998. Putting our knowledge to work: a second chance for young people. Speech delivered at Harrogate, March 5, 1998.

De Clerck, K. 1975. *Momenten uit de geschiedenis van het Belgisch onderwijs*. Antwerpen: De Sikkel.

European Commission. 1993. Employment. In *White Paper on growth, competitiveness, and employment: The challenges and ways forward into the 21st century*. COM (93) 700 final. Brussels.

———. 1995. White paper on education and training, teaching and learning towards the learning society. COM (95) 590. Brussels.

———. 1996. Learning in the information society: Action plan for a European education initiative (1996–1998). Communication to the European Parliament, the Council, the Economic and Social Committee and the Committee of the Regions. Brussels.

———. 1997. Towards a Europe of knowledge. Communication from the Commission COM (97) 563 final. Brussels.

———. 2000a. eEurope: An information society for all. Progress report for the Special European Council on Employment, Economic Reforms and Social Cohesion: Towards a Europe based on innovation and knowledge. COM (2000) 130 final. Brussels.

———. 2000b. e-Learning: Designing tomorrow's education. COM (2000) 318 final. Brussels.

———. 2000c. A memorandum on lifelong learning. SEC (2000) 1832. Brussels.

———. 2001a. The concrete future objectives of education systems. Com (2001) 59 Final. Brussels.

———. 2001b. The eLearning action plan: Designing tomorrow's education. COM (2001)172 final. Brussels.

European Round Table of Industrialists. 1989. Education et compétence en Europe. Etude la Table Ronde Européenne sur l'éducation et la formation en Europe. Brussels: ERT.

———. 1993. Les marchés du travail en Europe: Les perspectives de création d'emplois dans la deuxième moitié des années 90. Brussels: ERT.

———. 1995. Education for Europeans: Towards the learning society. Brussels: ERT.

———. 1997. Investing in knowledge: The integration of technology in European education. Brussels: ERT.

Eurydice. 1997. Dix années de réformes au niveau de l'enseignement obligatoire dans l'union européenne (1984–1994). Brussels: Eurydice.

———. 2005. *Chiffres-clés de l'éducation en Europe, 2005*.

Field, J. 1997. The European Union and the learning society: Contested sovereignty in an age of globalisation. . In *A national strategy for lifelong learning*, ed. F. Coffield, Department of Education, Newcastle University, 95–11

GMV-Conseil. 1998. Le marketing à l'école, étude sur les pratiques commerciales dans les écoles réalisée à la demande de la Commission européenne. Brussels: European Commission.

Groupe Européen de Recherche sur l'Equité des Systèmes Educatifs (GERESE). 2003. L'équité des systèmes éducatifs européens. Un ensemble d'indicateurs. Service de pédagogie expérimentale, Université de Liège. http://europa.eu.int/comm/education/programmes/socrates/observation/equality_fr.pdf.

International Finance Corporation. 1999. *Investir dans l'enseignement privé dans les pays en développement.* Washington DC: IFC.

Johnstone, D. 1998. The financing and management of higher education: A status report on worldwide reforms. Washington DC: World Bank.

Kaufmann, C. 2000. L'enseignement supérieur en Europe: État des lieux. Paper presented at the Colloquium "l'Université dans la tourmente," Brussels, February 25.

Larsen, K., and S. Vincent-Lancrin. 2003. Le commerce de l'éducation, un nouvel enjeu international? *L'observateur de l'OCDE,* February 25.

Lynch, M. 1999. *The book of knowledge: Investing in the growing education and training industry.* Merrill Lynch Research and Economics Group.

Newman, A. 2000. What is the education-industry? http://www.eduventures.com/pdf/whatiseduindstry.pdf.

Nicaise, I., I. Van den Brande, and S. Groenez. 2003. Cijferboek social ongelijkheid in het Vlaamse onderwijs, Een verkennend onderzoek op de Panelstudie van Belgische Huishoudens. *LOA-rapport* 10. Steunpunt LOA.

Organisation for Economic Co-operation and Development. 1994. *Redéfinir le curriculum: Un enseignement pour le XXIe siècle.* OCDE. Paris: OECD.

———. 1996. *Adult learning and technology in OECD countries.* Paris: OECD.

———.1997. *Politiques du marché du travail: Nouveaux défi s. Apprendre a tout âge pour rester employable durant toute la vie.* Paper presented at the Réunion du comité de l'emploi, du travail et des affaires sociales, au niveau ministériel, Château de la Muette, Paris, October 14–15.

———. 1998. *Analyse des politiques d'éducation.* Paris: OECD.

———. 2001a. *Investing in competencies for all.* Communiqué. Paper presented at the meeting of the OECD Education Ministers, Paris, April 3–4.

———. 2001b. *What future for our schools (six scenarios).* Paris: OECD.

———. 2002. Mechanisms for the co-finance of lifelong learning. Paper presented at the Second International Seminar: Taking Stock of Experience with Cofinance Mechanisms, London.

Patrinos, H. 1999. Market forces in education. Paper presented at the seminar "Education: The Point of View of the Economists," Donostia-San Sebastián, Spain, July 22–24.

Patrinos, H., and Ariasingam, D. 1997. *Decentralization of Education: Demandside financing.* Washington DC: World Bank.

Reiffers, J.-L. 1996. Accomplishing Europe through education and training. Report of the Study Group on Education and Training. Brussels: European Commission.

Robertson, S., X. Bonal, and R. Dale. 2001. GATS and the education service industry: The politics of scale and global re-territorialization. *Comparative Education Review* 46, no. 4: 472–496.

Schleicher, A. 2006. *The economics of knowledge: Why education is key for Europe's success.* Brussels: The Lisbon Council.

Thélot, C. 2004. Vers la réussite de tous les élèves. Rapport de la Commission du débat national sur l'avenir de l'école, 4. Paris.

Thélot, C., and L.-A.Vallet. 2000. La réduction des inégalités sociales devant l'école depuis le début du siècle. *Économie et Statistique* 334.

Warner, C. D. 2004. *Education of the negro.* Project Gutenberg.

World Bank. (1995). *Priorities and strategies for education: A World Bank review.* Washington, D.C.: World Bank.

———. (1999). Education sector strategy. Report prepared July 1999, by World Bank, Washington, D.C.

11 Education in Cuba
Socialism and the Encroachment of Capitalism

Curry Malott

INTRODUCTION

Many people laboring for the interests of profiteers as value-producing commodity dissatisfied with the exploitive and alienating nature of capitalist society, a direct attack on our "species being" (Marx, 1884/1978), have turned to the enemy of capitalism, that is, Marxism, anarchism, and the movements and nations that claim to follow their texts in the form of socialism and communism. If the longing gaze of those critically conscious laborers, alienated by private capital, has more than once been fixated upon socialist nations, then what is it that we see and hope to see in countries such as post-1959 Cuba, which has been described as an island of socialism in a sea of capitalism? Put another way, what can we learn from Cuba about resisting capitalism? In the following essay it is my attempt to begin to answer this question, taking cues from some of the most insightful scholars in the struggle.

Given their ability to thwart nearly fifty years of U.S. terrorism (Blum, 1995; Chávez, 2005; Chomsky, 1999), many on the international left view Cuba as evidence that U.S. imperialism can be successfully resisted, and therefore be a source of hope for a global future without capitalism. At the same time many capitalist cheerleaders point to Cuba's restrictions on civil liberties and the country's relatively low standard of living as evidence against not only a "dying" Cuba, but against socialism in general and Marxism in particular as "outdated" or simply "wrong." Marxists and socialists, most notably Castro and the Cuban government in general (Báez, 2004), on the other hand, tend to point to the United States's trade sanctions and terrorism against the little-big nation as explaining the revolution's militant policy toward counterrevolutionaries and the poverty and lack of basic necessities rampant among Cuba's population. One of the most common examples put forth by pro-Cuban radicals making the case for the humanitarian nature of the revolution is that as a result of the social reforms implemented the Cuban people are more educated and healthier than before 1959. That is, Cuba went from having one of the highest illiteracy rates in the so-called third world to having one of the most highly educated citizenries in the world. According to Fidel Castro (1999),

In 1961, only two years after the triumph, with the support of young students working as teachers, about 1 million people learned how to read and write. They went to the countryside, to the mountains, the remotest places and there they taught people that were even 80 years old how to read and write. Later on, there were follow-up courses and the necessary steps were taken in a constant effort to attain what we have today. A revolution can only be born from culture and ideas. (p. 5)

It is the magnitude of such humanitarian achievements, realized under the constant threat of U.S. aggression (outlined below) that has earned Cuba the respect of almost the entire international community. In this chapter, in the spirit of maximizing what can be learned about resisting capital, I take a critical approach to the legacy of revolutionary Cuba, homing in on both strengths and weaknesses situated in a larger context of neoliberal global capitalism. Comprehending this larger capitalist context is crucial because it provides the explanatory insight necessary to fully understand Cuba's resistance to capital and the lack thereof, and the dual role the island's system of education plays. On one hand, Cuban education serves as an egalitarian leveler, and on the other, is implicated in socially reproducing labor power, upon which the Cuban system draws life.

What follows is an outline of the events that have led to Cuba's current engagement with global capitalism and the implications for Cuban education. After looking at neoliberalism and the fall of Soviet communism, I examine Cuba's internationally renowned education system and why it remains sheltered from the direct forces of neoliberal privatization when other areas of the economy have been opened up for international private investment. Finally, I reflect on the lessons we can discern from Cuba about resisting capitalism.

CONTEXTUALIZING CUBA

Why has the U.S. government waged an illegal campaign of economic and social warfare against Fidel Castro's Cuba? For decades, Washington claimed that socialist Cuba, acting as a communist tentacle of Russia, posed a threat to U.S. national security and therefore must be strangled at all costs. Responding to the presidential administration of John Kennedy, Fidel Castro (1961/1969), in a speech made in 1961 in Havana, positioned the United States as the real aggressor, therefore rejecting the claim that Cuba's socialism and its trading deals with the Soviet Union threatened a passive United States:

The U.S. government says that a socialist regime here threatens U.S. security. But what threatens the security of the North American people is the aggressive policy of the warmongers of the United States.

What threatens the security of the North American family and people is the violence, that aggressive policy that ignores the sovereignty and the rights of other people . . . That aggressive policy can give rise to a world war; and that world war can cost the lives of tens of millions of North Americans. Therefore, the one who threatens the security of the United States is not the Cuban Revolutionary Government but the aggressor, the aggressive government of the United States. (p. 80)

After the fall of Soviet Russia in 1989, and with it the "threat of Soviet communism," such that it was, Washington claimed that Fidel's socialist Cuba was antidemocratic and to engage the country in business would prolong its "democratization." However, while Cuba's human-rights violations have intensified in recent years (Amnesty International, 2003), they pale in comparison to the human-rights violations in comparable Latin American countries who have received the full support of the United States despite their apparent disdain for freedom and democracy, as evidenced by the suffering inflicted upon their respective populations.

For example, since the 1950s Washington has supported and helped into office a series of increasingly brutal Guatemalan governments with the effect of squashing the popular movement for human rights and liberties and leading to the eventual slaughter of hundreds of thousands of Guatemalans (Blum, 1995; Chomsky, 1999). It is not surprising that Castro (2002, 1999, 1959/2004) has consistently spoken out against those very regimes supported by the U.S. military and corporate interests, and has supported anticolonialist/anti-imperialist struggles throughout the world (discussed below). It should not come as a surprise that the Cuban revolution has provided an example and model for other oppressed, impoverished Latin American and Caribbean countries suffering similar conditions, such as Guatemala, in their struggle for independence. Henry Kissinger of the U.S. State Department understood that the revolutionary spirit of Cuba could (and has) spread like a "virus" empowering other regions to follow suit, an intolerable proposition.

According to Stephen Lendman (2006), "before the Castro revolution, the Cuban people had only known decades of exploitation, repression and no attention paid to the most basic of human social needs. But since Fidel Castro came to power they've gotten them . . ." (p. 11). Describing their revolution, on May 21, 1959, in a televised speech to the Cuban people, Castro announced to the world that the new Cuba was neither capitalist nor communist, but was finding what amounted to its own social democratic way. Even during the height of Russia's support for Cuba, Castro maintained political independence from the Soviets as evidenced by its support of anti-imperialist, revolutionary movements and governments (Báez, 2004). What is more, Castro is one of the only, if not *the* only, national leaders who has consistently and openly expressed solidarity for not only revolutionary democratic governments, but the contemporary movement against the intensification of the globalization of capital (Báez,

2004; Castro, 1999). Castro and the Cuban governments' public speech tends to also " . . . promote an alternative form of globalization, one that is based on the cooperation of states in material development and fair trade among the nations instead of competition" (Báez, 2004, p. 8).

In practice, Castro's globalization resembles a form of state capitalism engaged in the process of value production to serve the interests of the public good rather than private interests. When we look at the social conditions of prerevolutionary Cuba and compare them to the conditions of present-revolutionary Cuba, it can be argued that Castro and Cuba's form of state capitalism has had a democratizing effect. For example, the number of physicians per capita is often associated with human social progress. Since the revolution Cuba's number of physicians per capita, according to the World Bank, has gone from 1,038 in 1960, to 219 in 1980, down to 136 in 1989 (Báez, 2004). As a result, other indicators of human progress and democratization have improved, such as Cuba's infant mortality rate (see Báez, 2004; Castro, 1999, 2002). Cuba extracts value from its labor power to fund internal social programs such as education, health care, and food distribution, and externally as aid to popular revolutions and developing countries in need. Arguing in support of the Cuban government as the will of the people and their revolution Castro (2002) asks,

> Has this power, this enormous prestige, this strength and unity of the people, achieved through the revolution, served to satisfy personal vanity, or greed for power or material goods? No, it has served to withstand the assault launched by the empire at one of the most dangerous and difficult moments in the history of our country . . . Today our country is first among all countries in the world, both developed and underdeveloped, in terms of the number of professors and teachers, doctors, and high-level physical education and sports instructors . . . We are sharing this immense *human capital* with our sister nations of the Third World, without charging a cent [*emphasis added*]. (pp. 89–91)

Indeed, Cuba's independence has allowed it to offer aid to other governments attempting to serve the interests of their own populations rather than those of private capital, which tend to be the administrations the United States actively works to undermine, such as the Sandinista government of Nicaragua mentioned above. However, with the fall of the Soviet Union and the end of Russian aid, coupled with an intensified U.S. blockade, prerevolutionary desperation has begun to return to Cuba:

> [The US has not been] trying to influence the revolution but to destroy it. Just as in Hannibal's times when the Senate in ancient Rome proclaimed the destruction of Carthage, the obsessively pursued motto of U.S. administrations has been: Cuba must be destroyed. (Castro, 2002, p. 6)

The twisted logic informing the United States's war against the Cuban people and their revolution is represented in the trade embargo (Blum, 1995; Chomsky, 1999); the Cuban government, drawing on the United Nations Universal Declaration of Human Rights of 1948, has consistently reminded the world that an embargo is an act of economic war and can therefore only be internationally recognized as legal between countries at war with each other. According to international law, only one conclusion can be drawn: the U.S embargo against Cuba is an act of U.S. terrorism. Not only is the embargo internationally illegal, it has been revised throughout the course of ten U.S. presidential administrations, consistently intensifying its levels of brutality. For example, in 1992 the United States passed the Torricelli Act, after Cuba lost 85 percent of its foreign trade after the fall of the Soviet Union, which further restricted Cuba's ability to purchase food and medicine from U.S. subsidiaries in third countries.

The effect of the embargo on the Cuban people has been severe. For example, in a groundbreaking analysis of Cuba's resistance to the pressure to privatize from neoliberal global capital, Báez (2004) notes that the US$41 billion Cuba lost between 1962 and 1996 has had a real impact on the Cuban people's standard of living. Báez (2004) notes that "the written object of the law was to punish any businesses that were investing in Cuba, in addition to prohibiting the IMF and World Bank from facilitating business transactions on the Island" (p. 111). In the aforementioned Cuban report published in *Granma* (2005), the devastating manifestations of the consistently intensifying U.S. embargo, supported and added to by Democratic and Republican presidential administrations alike, are laid out in detail, highlighting the implications on Cuba's "food sector," "health sector," "education sector," "tourism sector," "finances," transportation sector," "civil aviation," and "oil," among other areas such as the "sports sector." The Cuban report pulls no punches concerning the seriousness of the embargo and its combined effect on the various sectors of Cuban economic and social life:

> This policy . . . amounts to an act of genocide under the provisions of paragraph (c) of article II of the Geneva Convention for the Prevention and Punishment of the Crime of Genocide of 9 December 1948 and therefore constitutes a violation of International Law. This Convention defines this as '(. . .) acts perpetrated with the intention to totally or partially destroy a national, ethnic, racial or religious group,' and in these cases provides for 'the intentional subjugation of the group to conditions that result in their total or partial physical destruction.' (pp. 3–4)

Again, the Cuban government—noting that the U.S. embargo *has* in fact been designed to "totally . . . destroy" their nation, constituting an act of genocide—has repeatedly garnered the overwhelming support of the international community in the call for its immediate termination. Despite the real devastation the embargo and other forms of U.S. terrorism have had on Cubans, Báez (2004) argues that they cannot alone explain all of Cuba's problems. Báez (2004) points to the fall of the Soviet Union has having perhaps the most (or equally) dire effects on Cuba, paving the way for the opening up of certain areas of the "Cuban market" to foreign investors.

THE END OF SOVIET COMMUNISM: NEOLIBERALISM AND THE CUBAN ECONOMY

> They took to the former Soviet Union their neo-liberal and market recipes, causing destruction . . . They brought about the economic and political dismantling of federations of republics reducing life expectancy in some cases by 14 and 15 years, multiplying infant mortality by three to four times and generating social and economic problems which not even a resurrected Dante would dare to imagine. (Castro, 1999, p. 22)

Indeed, the fall of the Soviet Union has had a tremendously negative impact on not only the people of Eastern Europe, but, of particular importance here, the people of Cuba (Báez, 2004). Because the Cuban revolution was "built within" and thus "depended on" this "economic international order" (Chomsky, Carr, and Smorkaloff, 2004, p. 595), many analysts predicted that with Soviet communism, so too would end Cuban socialism. In other words, it was assumed that the Cuban economy would not survive without the aid they received from the Soviet Union, which almost immediately dried up after "the fall." Summarizing the effect the end of European socialism has had on Cubans Castro (2002) argues that

> In economic terms, Cuba sustained terrible damage. The price we had been paid for our sugar was not that prevailing in the unfair world market. We had obtained a preferential price, in the same way the United States grants preferences to Europe for their imports of this commodity. Supplies of fuel, food, raw materials and parts for machinery and factories were abruptly and almost completely cut off. The daily intake of calories dropped from 3,000 to 1,900 and that of protein from 80 to 50 grams. Some people could not put up with the difficulties, but the immense majority confronted the hardships with remarkable courage, honor and determination. (p. 6)

It can hardly be denied that Cuba's achievements, most notably in the areas of education and health care, have been a fundamental source of the Cuban people's "courage, honor and determination" in supporting their government, despite the rampant poverty. What is more, it is widely believed by Cubans that privatization would almost instantly lead to illiteracy and a spike in infant mortality rates (Báez, 2004). Báez (2004) and other activist scholars are watching closely to see whether the pride of the revolution will eventually attract investment offers too good to turn down, given the economic hardships endured by the Cuban people as a result of U.S. economic warfare/terrorism coupled with the end of Soviet aid. Indeed, it has been noted on more than one occasion that the Cuban people comprise the best-educated and healthiest populations in Latin America, increasing their value as a commodity on the international market.

Castro (1999) takes special care to note that even during Cuba's most financially desperate times, funding for their education and health care programs was never cut, and gains in the health of the population were even realized. However, the government had to work hard to make its corporations more profitable to fund these programs, which have required more financial compensation for their workers to compete with the lucrative tourism industry. According to Gasperini,

> In March 1999, teachers received a 30 percent salary increase . . . Teacher motivation and retention are also threatened by decreases in the purchasing power of salaries and the attractiveness of new professional activities, especially in tourism and in foreign firms, as evidenced by teacher attrition of 4 to 8 percent per year in the eastern oriental provinces, where tourism is more developed. (Gasperini, 2000. p. 16)

Because the state maintains high levels of education as a basic right, and because the economy is set up around an externally controlled global market system based on the manufacture of scarcity, the level of education among the population tends to exceed that which is needed in employment. It is within this context of real material desperation that we can begin to understand Cuba's economic reform policies that have reprivatized certain segments of the Cuban economy, which are now competing with the very social programs they were intended to support.

Despite Cuba's economic hardships and the states' attempts at rectification, unlike their eastern European counterparts the Cuban people did not respond with demonstrations and riots, but maintained, for the most part, their support of their government, as argued above (Báez, 2004, p. 142). As a result, Cuba has been able to achieve a number of remarkable gains outlined below. In the following narrative I attempt to formulate an understanding of Cuba's system of education, situated within the complexities and contradictions of constructing a social order based on socialist principles in a sea of hostile capitalist profiteers.

EDUCATION IN CUBA: "SPECIES BEING" AND "THE NEW MAN" VERSUS VALUE PRODUCTION

> The work of education is perhaps the most important thing the country should do. (Castro 1997, pp. 4–5)

Cuba's ability to overcome an almost institutionalized illiteracy rate virtually overnight has been one of their major claims to fame. At the time of the revolution, stemming from decades of abuse and neglect, more than half of all Cuban children did not attend school, that is, " . . . 72 percent of 13 to 19 year olds failed to reach intermediate levels of schooling . . ." (Gasperini, 2000, p. 14) contributing to the over one million Cubans classified as illiterate. Within a few years after the revolution Cuba's chronic illiteracy rate was virtually abolished, and, with every passing year, fades further and further into the past. To this day, after over forty years of regionally unusual political stability and therefore sustained high levels of funding, Cuba, according to UNESCO reports, appears to have maintained a 100 percent rate of literacy despite the severe shortages in school supplies and facilities directly attributable to the increasingly restrictive U.S. embargo (*Granma*, 2005).

Compensating for shortages of every sort imaginable, Cuba allocates from 10 to 11 percent of their gross domestic product to education, which, compared to other Latin American and Caribbean countries, is high and 4 to 5 percent higher than recommended by UNESCO. Cuban educational success is also attributable to their strong teacher education and lifelong teacher training programs, which are considered among the finest in the world and in which collectives of teachers meet every two weeks to discuss strategies, problems, and the general climate of the learning environment. What is more, through their teacher-training programs, teachers learn to conduct action research, and are expected to employ those skills in the classroom to improve and develop new learning and teaching strategies. According to Lavinia Gasperini (2000) in "The Cuban Education System: Lessons and Dilemmas,"

> The record of Cuban education is outstanding: universal school enrollment and attendance; nearly universal adult literacy; proportional female representation at all levels, including higher education; a strong scientific training base, particularly in chemistry and medicine; consistent pedagogical quality across widely dispersed classrooms; equality of basic educational opportunity, even in impoverished areas, both rural and urban. In a recent regional study of Latin America and the Caribbean, Cuba ranked first in math and science achievement, at all grade levels, among both males and females. In many ways, Cuba's schools are the equals of schools in OECD countries, despite the fact that Cuba's economy is that of a developing country. (p. 10)

Not only is the Cuban system of education applauded for its ability to consistently produce the highest math and science scores in the region, contributing to their world-class cadre of doctors and scientists, it is also exalted for less traditional advances in education. For example, furthering her analysis of the Cuban system of education, Gasperini (2000) praises Cuba for the egalitarian nature of its schooling practices. For Gasperini (2000), the fact that Cubans have been able to sustain the level of education they have under the enormous pressures they are under from neoliberal market mechanisms is nothing short of remarkable. In the following passage Gasperini (2000) situates the social justice nature of education in Cuba in the context of an increasingly globalized system of capitalism:

> Cuba's schools have been remarkably successful in achieving gender equity, reaching rural and disadvantaged populations, and fostering community participation, even in the context of rapidly dwindling resources. Cuba is a poor country, and the past decade has been particularly difficult economically. Yet the success of its schools flaunts conventional wisdom: Education in Cuba is entirely public, centrally planned, and free, in a global reform environment of privatization, downscaling of the state role, and cost recovery. (p. 14)

These internationally renowned achievements gained as a result of Cuba's intense focus on education is in no small part a direct result of Fidel Castro who, according to Peter McLaren (2000) " . . . attended the best Jesuit schools in Cuba, instilling in him a legendary passion for learning . . ." (p. 43). After the 1959 revolution a reformed compulsory system of education became one of the programs successfully put into practice, as described above. However, because it has already been established that the Cuban government performs the role of a state corporation that has begrudgingly begun placing Cuban labor power on the international market through the opening of a select few areas of the economy to foreign investors, such as tourism, resulting in the partial erosion of the revolutionary sense of cooperation as Cubans are pitted against Cubans in a racially mediated competition for access to dollars, we must examine closely the dual role that Cuba's system of education seems to assume. That is, the egalitarian leveler and the social reproducer of labor power summarize the two roles of Cuba's system of education.

For example, in addition to what has already been laid out above, contributing to the fulfillment of the role of egalitarian leveler is the institutionalized links teachers make with the communities in which they serve. It has been reported that teachers spend 80 percent of their time at work in the classroom and 20 percent in the homes of their students assisting in parental education and organizing study groups in targeted homes. Teachers also participate in community organizations. As a result, teachers acquire an understanding of students' lives, their problems, and possible solutions, which is precisely why Freire (2005) argued that it is indispensable for teachers to understand their students in the contexts in which they live. Summarizing this position Freire (2005) argues that

> . . . Our relationship with learners demands that we respect them and demands equally that we be aware of the concrete conditions of their

world, the conditions that shape them . . . Without this, we have no access to the way they think, so only with great difficulty can we perceive what and how they know. (p. 58)

Freire (2005) goes on to suggest that the ways teachers approach literacy can either facilitate or hinder the student/teacher relationship and the process of liberation. That is, because the form which literacy takes can either be indoctrinating, implicated in the social reproduction of labor power, or empowering, as an egalitarian leveler, we must deepen our analysis and analyze Cuba drawing on Freire's conceptions of literacy. For example, based on a lifetime of work on literacy, we know from Freire (2005) that we can learn to read passively, where reading is viewed as " . . . a mechanical exercise in the memorization of certain parts of a text," commonly referred to as the banking model of education, or actively, where the " . . . reading of the word enables us to read a previous reading of the world" (p. 34). What Freire (2005) refers to as the dialectical reading of the word and the world, that is, critical literacy, has served as the primary model, internationally, for revolutionary education since the 1970s because it is designed to foster critical consciousness where educators and learners actively engage in a process of discovery with the intention to not only understand the world, but to transform it. Henry Giroux (1987) describes the way in which Paulo Freire has approached literacy as a tool to be put into practice by

> . . . Movements designed to provide Third-World people with the conditions for criticism and social action either for overthrowing fascist dictatorships or for use in postrevolutionary situations where people are engaged in the process of national reconstruction. In each case, literacy becomes a hallmark of liberation and transformation designed to throw off the colonial voice and further develop the collective voice of suffering and affirmation silenced beneath the terror and brutality of despotic regimes. (p. 8)

Giroux's understanding of literacy as a central component of political struggle seems to coalesce with Castro's (1999) idea that "a revolution can only be born from culture and ideas" (p. 5). It should therefore be expected that the system of education built under Cuba's revolutionary government be focused on not only making a conscious connection between school and the community, as outlined above, but it should also follow a revolutionary model of active engagement when it comes to literacy. In other words, are Cuban students taught to dialectically read the word and the world in the spirit of a never-ending revolution? I believe the correct answer is "it depends. " Absolutely, when engaging with issues external to Cuba, such as U.S. terrorism and foreign corporations externally controlling productive capacities, extracting wealth, that is, potential capital, as abstract or dead Cuban labor embedded within commodities, leaving behind the misery and social decay of abject poverty. In other words, when it comes to resisting the external imposition of globalized capitalism, education serves as a leveler providing students with a critical analysis of international capitalism and the role played by the United States, and the rightness of laboring for the benefit of their own social programs, rather than a foreign corporation. For example, the following excerpt comes from Cuba's elementary curriculum:

THEME 1: IMPERIALISM

Imperialism is a common phenomenon of our age. Imperialists are those countries that, having well-developed economies, concentrate a large percentage of capital in the hands of a few. They then use that capital to exploit other countries' economies, forcing them to export natural resources and import value-added goods. They thus deform these economies, robbing them of their independence. An imperialist country doesn't necessarily have colonies. Any country that exploits another is imperialistic.

Exercise 1: Once, the Yankees attacked us. They sent many bad people. They wanted to do away with Free Cuba. The populace defeated them. Fidel led the fight.
Question: What does this say about Fidel?

While this example challenges students to think critically about the external threat of U.S. imperialism, it does so steeped in patriotic overtones. Internally, these very real external factors are used by Castro in his speeches and in school curricula to explain why the system is set up the way it is. That is, the economic decisions that have been made have been done so because they truly benefit the Cuban people, however unequally—compared to fully privatized areas in the region. For example, in the name of the revolution, Cubans expend their labor hours creating products such as sugar, which the government then sells on the international market realizing the potential value, which is used to fund social programs, which benefit the people. The U.S. trade sanctions and the fall of the former Soviet Union, as demonstrated above, make it increasingly difficult for the government to sell and purchase commodities from other countries to keep the nation afloat. Desperate for the hard currency (i.e., dollars) needed to sustain the revolution, as outlined above, the Cuban government has engaged in economic reform policies opening Cuban labor power to foreign investment (Báez, 2004; Gasperini, 2000; Lutjens, 1998; Mtonga, 1993).

Not only has Cuba partially opened its doors to foreign investment, it has intensified its efforts to create state-run corporations, as explored above, which require trained managers to operate with a return, that is, to accumulate surplus value. Managers must go to school, the training for which begins quite early as students are tracked for various career paths based on test scores. To accommodate this need the government has dedicated more resources to training better managers to run businesses (Báez, 2004, p. 124). However, Cuba has not completely dissolved pre-1959 systems of racialized privilege, which can be seen in elite pre-university schools designed to train managers such as The Centro Vocational Lenin en Ciencias Exactas outside of Havana. These schools offer a high level of education marked by greater student autonomy where teachers act more as learning facilitators, rather than depositors of predetermined facts. It has been reported that the director of the Vocational Lenin School, when asked about why there were so few Afro-Cubans at the center, responded that change takes time (Gasperini, 2000). However, the primary role of Cuba's system of education is the creation of a productive working class.

As a result, when it comes to critiquing the Cuban government's role as a capitalist engaged in the process of creating value through the external control of Cuban labor power (Báez, 2004; Gasperini, 2000; Lutjens, 1998; Mtonga, 1993; Roucek, 1964), critical inquiry seems to diminish. This state-run economy requires that the state decide what is to be produced, how it is produced, whose labor produces it, what wages will be, and how the wealth generated shall be used. As a result, labor power is externally controlled, not for private enrichment, but for the benefit of the people. However, because the external control of one's creative capacities is dehumanizing, regardless of whose interests it serves, consent must be manufactured. The Cuban system, to my knowledge, never questions this. That is, the external control of labor power is treated as normal and natural. Cuba's system of education is designed to create this consent focusing on the development of attitudes and dispositions through Values Education (outlined below) two hours a week, similar to the civics education of their U.S. counterparts (Allman, McLaren, and Rikowski, 2005). In other words, Cubans are expected to allow their labor power to be externally controlled to thwart the increasing external pressures to privatize, which ultimately is for the benefit of the revolution. For example, outlining Cuba's Labor Education program Gasperini (2000) notes,

> The primary curriculum includes 480 hours of "labor education" over six years . . . By participating in simple agricultural activities, students are expected to develop a positive attitude toward work along with attitudes of solidarity with workers. School gardens size range from one to more than 20 hectares. When schools do not have their own garden, students work in "collective gardens" in the provincial capitals . . . In secondary school (grades 7 to 9), labor education represent 280 hours . . . a less significant share than in primary school but still equivalent to half the time devoted to History . . . Work, when appropriate to children's age, appears to have become an instrument of intellectual and social development and a sharing of responsibilities. The danger is that compulsory work may lead to . . . an aversion to work. (p. 16)

Expanding on the argument just laid out, let us proceed, further answering the question, how do we know that education serves this indoctrinating function? Our first clue resides in the fact that schooling in Cuba, until the age of sixteen, is compulsory, that is, mandatory/required. Because it has been widely argued by Marxist educators within capitalist nations such as the United States that " . . . the ritual of compulsory schooling serves to assist the state in the enforcement of a market society" (Gabbard, 2003. p. 71), we must look critically at the significance of the compulsory nature of Cuban education. In the following analysis I demonstrate that when labor power is externally controlled, and thus human creativity diminished, as it is in not only in private capitalist nations such as the United States but in state-run-market societies like Cuba, humans will naturally resist and thus must be controlled by either force or the manipulation of ideas. In countries such as Cuba whose popular support is, in part, guaranteed by the freedoms and liberties won in the revolution, the capacity for force as a means of social control is diminished, although not completely. Schooling, in part, serves this indoctrinating function, and therefore must be compulsory. In the following paragraphs I proceed with my analysis drawing on Marx's (1844/1978) conception of "species being" because it provides the framework through which we can begin to understand why humans naturally resist the external control of their labor power. In so doing I draw connections to what Ernesto " Ché" Guevara termed "the New Man," which was to be engendered after the revolution, in part, through Values Education.

In the *Economic and Philosophic Manuscripts of 1844* Marx (1844/1978) demonstrates, in great detail, what it is that makes humans beings in and of themselves distinct from all other species making the point that in capitalist societies—societies marked by " . . . two classes—the property-*owners* and propertyless *workers*—. . . the relationship of the *worker* to production" (pp. 70–73) is a direct attack on what it is that makes humans human, that is, the ability to use our labor power to re-create the world in our own image. Marx begins his discussion explaining how workers are alienated not only from, but *by* the very products of their labor, arguing that "the worker becomes an ever cheaper commodity the more commodities he creates. With the *increasing value* of the world of things proceeds in direct proportion the *devaluation* of the world of men" (p. 71). If the products of one's labor has an alienating effect, then the process of production must also be alienating, reasons Marx. In other words, " . . . the fact that labour is *external* to the worker, i.e., it does not belong to his essential being; that in his work, therefore, he does not affirm himself but denies himself . . ." (p. 74).

What this implies then is that when at work, when engaged in transforming the natural world from which humans " . . . must remain in continuous intercourse . . ." (Marx, 1844/1978, p. 75) if we are to survive, the labor of workers belongs not to those who toil, but to someone else, and therefore the individual worker does not belong to herself but to the class of property owners. As a result, workers tend to only feel freely human as creative beings when engaged in animal functions, that is, when eating, fornicating, defecating, dressing, and when at home in general, to the extent that animal functions become human and vice versa. In short, when our labor is externally controlled, our very human-specific creative capacities, our species being, are suppressed and we become alienated from ourselves, that which we produce, and the natural world, upon which life is dependent.

Marx (1844/1978) envisions communism as the solution to this contradiction, involving not only the seizure of state power, like that achieved in Cuba, but also the process of resocialization whereby men and women become humanized by taking control of their individual creative capacities for the common good. During and immediately after the Cuban Revolution, Guevara (1965/1995), interpreting Marx's work, called for the emergence of the "New Man," which he described as being motivated not by individualistic materialism, but by self-sacrifice and the moral incentives embedded therein. Because the external control over one's labor power interferes with our "species being," regardless of whose interests the value generated benefits, Cuba must therefore manufacture consent through cultural institutions such as education. Today in Cuba Values Education assumes this role through the implementation of a curriculum focused on promoting " . . . social cohesion by preventing internal disruption from violence, drugs, and criminality . . . They teach values and attitudes aiming at consolidating internationalism, national identity and patriotism, a morality of work, solidarity and defense against external threat" (Gasperini, 2000. p. 28).

In effect, Cuba's educational system socializes students to be willing to sell their labor power as a commodity for the valorization of state capital, that is, to socially reproduce labor power (Báez, 2004; Gasperini, 2000; Lutjens, 1998; Mtonga, 1993; Roucek, 1964). However, because Values Education tends to have an indoctrinating taste to it, in times of heightened crisis, while maintaining their dedication to an independent Cuba, the Cuban people have been known to abandon the spirit of cooperation and engage in extralegal individualistic measures to meet their basic necessities, as argued above. The Cuban system, as noted above, has nevertheless been quite successful at maintaining legitimacy, which, in my estimation, can largely be attributed to the righteousness of their just cause of maintaining political and economic independence for the benefit of the Cuban people, as well as gains in health and education.

The Cuban state is quite aware that private interests cannot be trusted to uphold the social programs of the revolution because corporations, by design, and in some nations such as the United States, by law, must put the economic interests of their shareholders before those of their stakeholders, such as employees and the communities in which they function. It is therefore not surprising that the state has maintained control over this major achievement in human progress. Indeed, it has been widely publicized that in capitalist countries such as the United States, the effect of neoliberal capitalism on education has been grave. The move to privatize education has resulted in the defunding of education and therefore an increase in illiteracy. Cuba, in an attempt to not betray the people and their revolution, has therefore resisted the privatization of its social programs. However, the fact that education in Cuba is mandatory and follows a predetermined curriculum, it is expected that most students, with the possible exception of those who attend the elite schools, will graduate not completely satisfied as a species being. One area that we can return to is the existence of an overt patriotism within the curriculum that has tended to dominate discussions of ethnicity, avoiding one of the real social concerns of many Cubans. According to Annelise Wunderlich (2005) in "Hip Hop Pushes the Limits," referring to a young Cuban rap artist:

> Police harassment and discrimination are everyday experiences for many black Cubans . . . For years, Castro positioned racism as a problem outside of the country. But a growing number of Afro Cubans wonder if that was just a way of displacing the racial question at home . . . In school when Sarrias tried to talk about his African Ancestry, teachers called him unpatriotic for thinking of himself as something other than Cuban . . ."In school they taught him about slavery, but they didn't go into depth," his mother says. (p. 69)

Wunderlich (2005) goes on to discuss the informal teachers Sarrias and other Afro-Cuban rappers have sought out in their efforts to satisfy their human creative impulses, that is, their species being, and ultimately, the fulfillment of the revolutionary call to transform and engage. Young Cubans are not only looking to national heroes such as El Ché and José Martí, but ironically, to the United States for a discourse and praxis of liberation in figures such as Malcom X and Mumia Abu-Jamal, as well as politically conscious African-American rappers such as Public Enemy and Dead Prez. It is the militant Black identity in songs such as Dead Prez' "I'm a African" and "They Schools," that attracts Afro-Cubans who live in a context they deem is falsely described by Castro as "color-blind." What is more, according to Wunderlich (2005), young Cubans have been taking advantage of the extraordinary privilege of learning from Black Liberationist Assata Shakur, who was granted political asylum by Cuba after being liberated from incarceration behind enemy lines in New Jersey, United States, about Black history and global politics.

LESSONS ON FIGHTING CAPITAL FROM CUBA: SOLIDARITY AND MARXIST MULTICULTURALISM

> I believe in the unity of all the countries in the world, in the unity of all the peoples in the world and in a free unity, a truly free unity. I am not thinking of a fusion but of a free unity of all cultures in a truly just

> world, in a truly democratic world, in a world where it would be pos-
> sible to apply the kind of globalization that Karl Marx talked about in
> his time . . . (Castro, 1999, p. 85)

What is it then that we can decipher from studying the Cuban system about resisting capitalism in the twenty-first century? One of the most obvious lessons we can learn, alluded to throughout this essay, and reiterated in the above quote by Castro in his concluding address to the first International Congress on Culture and Development held in Havana in June 1999, is the power of unity and international solidarity. Throughout this paper I have made the case that Cuba's internal humanitarian achievements have garnered international admiration and support. However, perhaps equally important has been their unwavering dedication to other oppressed peoples throughout the world that has earned them not only the respect, but also the watchful eye of the international community, which, it can be argued, has contributed to their longevity. While Castro has consistently been portrayed as a despotic dictator in the United States, his public speeches and his national and international policies have reflected a man driven by revolutionary love genuinely searching for a more just, egalitarian future beyond the destructive tendencies of capitalism.

The example of Castro's unwavering militant dedication to the People's Revolution, and the Cuban populace's relentless push forward in the areas of human social progress, stand as a glaring example of the magnitude of what can be accomplished against the neoliberal push to privatize public services with a continuously diminishing supply of resources in an increasingly hostile environment. In other words, Cuba should be a source of inspiration to those of us who understand the urgency of creating a life informed by values of cooperation and mutual aid, rather than a world structured around competition and manufactured scarcity. At the same time, however, Cuba makes clear that participating in the global market, even when done as a means of providing for the people, makes them vulnerable to the inherent crises built into the capitalist system of value production. What is more, such engagement has pushed back gains in antiracism as Cubans are pitted against Cubans in a desperate scramble for dollars. It is obvious that the external investment of foreign capital motivated by private gain is steeped in divisiveness and crises. Even Cuba's state-run businesses, informed by values of cooperation and equality, while producing many benefits when accompanied by a strong trading partner such as the former Soviet Union, depend on the external control of labor power, and are therefore somewhat dehumanizing. The diagnosis: Capitalism is not good for humanity regardless of whether it is state- or privately run. We can therefore conclude that while the Cuban experiment has made progress toward humanization, it is still hindered by the dehumanizing nature of value production.

Finally, and to reiterate, Cuba's forty-plus years of international solidarity reminds those of us paying attention that there is little room in today's crisis-ridden global environment for inter-left squabbling. Open and healthy debate of course should be encouraged for tactical and philosophical reasons, but in the spirit of solidarity. The future truly is undetermined: there is no guarantee, for example, that humanity will overcome the institutionalization of authoritarianism and the process of value production, whether state-sponsored, privately controlled, or more commonly, a mixed system of state and private domination. Marx spoke of strength within diversity providing people with a better opportunity to meet each other's needs in a socialist context. Marx was referring to a diversity of skills. Peter McLaren and Ramin Farahmandpur (2005) and Paula Allman (2001) have extended his analysis to include a diversity of ethnic and cultural backgrounds. Similarly, I would add that a diversity of ideas, Marxist and anarchist to name just two, should not only be tolerated, but encouraged as evidence of an open and free movement against all forms of oppression. As we forge ahead into the unforeseeable future, whoever and wherever we are, acting as international solidarity workers, let us image and practice increasingly just, egalitarian, antiracist, antisexist, antihomophobic, and anticapitalist creative ways to regain control of our labor power in the spirit of our species being and for the betterment of all life on this planet.

REFERENCES

Allman, P. 2001. *Critical education against global capitalism: Karl Marx and revolutionary critical education.* London: Bergin & Garvey.

Allman, P., P. McLaren, and G. Rikowski. 2005. After the Box People: The labour-capital relation as class constitution and its consequences for Marxist educational theory and human resistance. In *Capitalists and conquerors: A critical pedagogy against empire*, Peter McLaren. New York: Roman & Littlefield.

Amnesty International 2003. Cuba. http://web.amnesty.org/web/web.nsf/print/425C41E3DC6E6F0080256E7F0037A61D (accessed January 2006).

Báez, A. 2004. *State resistance to globalization in Cuba.* London: Pluto Press.

Blum, W. 1995. *Killing hope: US military and CIA interventions since World War II.* Monroe, Maine: Common Courage Press.

Castro, F. 1959/2004. Castro calls on Cubans to resist the counterrevolution. In *The Cuba reader: History, culture, politics*, ed. Aviva Chomsky, Barry Carr, and Pamela Maria Smorkaloff. London: Duke University Press.

———. 1961/1969. Turn toward socialism: Cuba's socialism proclaimed. In *Fidel Castro speaks*, ed. Martin Kenner and James Petras, 80. New York: Grove Press.

———. 1997. Editorial, *Granma*. September 4.

———. 1999. *On imperialist globalization: Two speeches.* New York: Zed Books.

———. 2002. *War, racism and economic injustice: The global ravages of capitalism.* New York: Ocean Press.

Chávez, L. 2005. Adrift: An introduction to contemporary Cuba. In *Capitalism, God and a good cigar: Cuba enters the twenty-first century*, ed. Lydia Chávez and Mimi Chakarova. London: Duke University Press.

Chomsky, A., B. Carr, and P. Smorkaloff. 2004. The "Período Especial" and the future of the revolution. In *The Cuba reader: History, culture, politics*, ed.

Aviva Chomsky, Barry Carr, and Pamela Maria Smorkaloff. London: Duke University press.

Chomsky, N. 1999. *Profit over people: Neo-liberalism and global order.* New York: Seven Stories Press.

Freire, P. 2005. *Teachers as cultural workers: Letters to those who dare teach.* Boulder, Colo.: Westview Press.

Gabbard, D. 2003. Education IS enforcement: The centrality of compulsory schooling in market societies. In *Education as enforcement: The militarization and corporatization of schools,* ed. Kenneth Saltman and David Gabbard, 71. New York: Routledge.

Gasperini, L. 2000. The Cuban education system: Lessons and dilemmas. *Country Studies: Education and Management Publication Series* 1, no. 5: 16.

Giroux, H. 1987. Introduction: Literacy and the pedagogy of political empowerment. In *Literacy: Reading the word and the world,* ed. Paulo Freire and Donaldo Mecedo, 8. London: Bergin & Garvey.

Granma. 2005. Report by Cuba on Resolution 59/11 of the United Nations General Assembly. August 15.

Guevara, Ernest. 1965/1995. *Che Guevara speaks: Selected speeches and writings.* New York: Pathfinder.

Lendman, S. 2006. *Cuba under Fidel Castro.* A Review article. http://www.globalresearch.ca/index.php?content=va&aid=3084.

Lutjens, S. 1998. Education and the Cuban revolution: A selected bibliography. *Comparative Education Review* 42, no. 2: 197–224.

Marx, K. 1844/1978. Economic and philosophic manuscripts of 1844. In *The Marx-Engels reader:* 2nd ed., ed. Robert C. Tucker, 70–75. New York: W.W. Norton & Company.

McLaren, P. 2000. *Che Guevara, Paulo Freire and the pedagogy of revolution.* New York: Routledge.

McLaren, P., and R. Farahmandpur. 2005. *Teaching against global capitalism and the new imperialism: A critical pedagogy.* New York: Rowman & Littlefield.

Mtonga, H. 1993. Comparing the role of education in serving socioeconomic and political development in Tanzania and Cuba. *Journal of Black Studies* 23, no. 3: 382–402.

Roucek, J. 1964. Pro-communist revolution in Cuban education. *Journal of Inter-American Studies* 6, no. 3: 323–335.

Wunderlich, A. 2005. Hip hop pushes the limits. In *Capitalism, God and a good cigar: Cuba enters the twenty-first century,* ed. Lydia Chávez and Mimi Chakarova, 69. London: Duke University Press.

Contributors

Pierrick Devidal holds a Maîtrise (international law) and a Master's degree (DESS- international policy) from the Université Jean Moulin, Lyon, France; a Master's degree (LL.M.- International Law) from the Dean Rusk Center, University of Georgia School of Law, United States; and a Certificate from the Hague Academy of International Law, The Netherlands. He is an international humanitarian rights worker currently working for an international humanitarian organization in Colombia.

Eduardo Domenech coordinates the Program on Multiculturalism, Migrations and Inequality in Latin America at the Center of Advanced Studies of the National University of Córdoba, Argentina. He has pursued graduate studies in political science and postgraduate studies in demography, education and sociology. He is a member of the Working Group on "Migration and Culture" of the Latin American Council on Social Sciences (CLACSO). He has edited *Migraciones internacionales y diversidad cultural en la Argentina* (CEA-UNC, 2005).

Henry A. Giroux holds the Global TV Network Chair in English and Cultural Studies at McMaster University in Canada. His most recent books include *America on the Edge* (2006); *The Giroux Reader* (2006); *Beyond the Spectacle of Terrorism* (2006), *Stormy Weather: Katrina and the Politics of Disposability* (2006), and *The University in Chains: Confronting the Military-Industrial-Academic Complex* (2007).

Nick Grant works at Cardinal Wiseman High School, Ealing, West London, is secretary of the Ealing branch of the National Union of Teachers, and is active in the U.K. Socialist Teachers Alliance.

Nigel M. Greaves was recently awarded a PhD for his work on Antonio Gramsci's political philosophy at the University of Northampton, United Kingdom. He has lectured at University College Northampton on the phenomenon of Italian fascism, at the University of Bristol on the history of political thought from Plato to Marx, and at Thames Valley University on the classical ideologies and their implication for welfare policies. His research interests are in the area of hegemonic formations and the state in capitalist systems.

Eric Haas is a Senior Fellow at the Rockridge Institute in Berkeley, California. He is also a lawyer and a former assistant professor of educational policy at the University of Connecticut. His research interests include education law and the media's framing of school issues.

Dave Hill is Professor of education policy, University of Northampton, United Kingdom. For twenty years he was a local and regional political and labor union leader in England. He cofounded the Hillcole Group of Radical Left Educators in Britain and, inter alia, coedited a trilogy on schooling and inequality for Cassell and Kogan Page. He is Routledge Series Editor for *Education and Neoliberalism* and also Routledge Series Editor for *Education and Marxism*. He is Chief Editor of the international refereed academic journal, the *Journal for Critical Education Policy Studies*.

Nico Hirtt is an independent researcher on education policy working for the Belgian movement «Appel pour une école démocratique» (www.ecoledemocratique.org). He has published several books on Belgian and European education policy.

Ravi Kumar teaches in the Department of Sociology, Jamia Millia Islamia University, New Delhi, India. He has done extensive fieldwork on identity politics, caste-based mobilizations, educational inequality, and social movements in North India. His publications include *The Politics of Imperialism and Counterstrategies* (coedited, Delhi: Aakar Books, 2004) and *The Crisis of Elementary Education in India* (edited, Sage, 2006).

Roberto Leher is a Professor at the Universidade Federal do Rio de Janeiro, Brazil; Coordinator of the Working Group "University and Society" of the Latin American Board of Social Sciences (CLACSO); and conducts research that investigates the World Bank's and the World Trade Organization's policies for higher education in peripheral countries.

Alpesh Maisuria is a Lecturer at the University of Wolverhampton, England. He completed a B.A. (Hons) in education studies at University College Northampton. He then went on to complete a Masters' degree with distinction in education studies: culture, language and identity at Goldsmiths College, University of London. Alpesh is involved with various political and social movements vis-à-vis "race" and social class in Europe.

Curry Malott is a Professor in the social and philosophical foundations of education at D'Youville College in Buffalo, New York. His most recent books include *A Call to Action: An Introduction to Education, Philosophy and Native North America* (2008) and *An International Examination of Urban Education: The Destructive Path of Neoliberalism* (forthcoming) coedited with Brad Porfilio.

Tristan McCowan is Senior Lecturer in education at Roehampton University, London. His research interests include citizenship education, curriculum theory, and higher education policy. From 2002–2003 he was Coordinator of the Observatory of Latin American Education Policy in Rio de Janeiro, Brazil. Recent publications have appeared in the journals *Higher Education*, the *Journal of Education Policy*, the *International Journal of Educational Development* and the *Journal for Critical Education Policy Studies*.

Carlos Mora-Ninci has a PhD in Social Sciences and Comparative Education from the University of California, Los Angeles (UCLA) and is author of *Latinos in the West: The Student Movement and Academic Labor in Los Angeles* (Rowman and Littlefield, 2007). His interests include the social and cognitive foundations of bilingual and multicultural education, and the sociopolitical economy of education. Dr. Mora-Ninci can be reached through his book webpage: www.latinosinthewest.org. He is at the University of Córdoba, Argentina.

Index

A

academic freedom 81
access to education 39, 118, 119
accountability 16, 17–18, 45
accreditation 131
Acts of Resistance 36
Africa 57–8, 128, 134
Afro-Cubans 238, 241
Agamben, Giorgio 32
agency
    challenge to corporatization of education 42; devaluing of political 46; education for social reproduction 224; superstructure as, of economic base 108
Alliance for Progress 134, 135
Althusser, Louis 111–12
American Association of University Professors 42
American Council of Education 42
American Enterprise Institute 174, 177, 183
anti-democratization 17
anti-egalitarianism 1, 16
anti-radicalization 116
Apollo Group 57, 60, 67, 70, 131
Apple, Michael W. 104, 105
apprenticeship 211
Argentina 128, 129
Argosy Education Group 59
Aronowitz, Stanley 39
Article 2 (ICESCR) 81
Article 13 (ICESCR) 78–9, 81
Ashburn, Elyse 43
Asia 57, 58, 128, 134
assimilation 160, 161
assistentialism 158–9
Association of Teachers and Lecturers 117

atomization 31
autonomy
    ethnodevelopment partnerships and loss of 162; in teacher education/ training 62, *see also* institutional autonomy; student autonomy
availability, right to education 96

B

balanced reporting 180, 197–8
Bandung Conference 128
barbarism 15
Barnhizer, D. 85
basic needs, WB policy on 159
The Battle In Seattle 19
Bauman, Zygmunt 30, 32
Becker, Gary 129, 142
Belgium 215
Bentham, Jeremy 109
Berkeley University 67, 135
Berle, Adolf A. 135
Berliner, D. 182–3, 196, 197
best practice, research-based 64
Biddle, B. 182–3, 196, 197
bilingual education 159–60
binary class relations 103–4, 106, 108, 110
Birkbeck University 68
Blair, Tony 115
BMW 44
Bond University (Australia) 58
Bourdieu, Pierre 36, 47, 49
bourgeois class 107
bourgeois democracy 110
Bowles, S. 112
Bracey 192
brain drain 82
branding 38, 63–4
Brazil 128

education
    as antidote to unemployment 140;
        assimilation of WB and IMF
        agenda 133–4; higher 140–1;
        primary 142–3; private sector
        expansion 131; as a service 129;
        transnational trade in services 131
    for-profit higher education 58
        dubious quality control 61;
        efficiency 67; expenditure on
        advertising 63; lack of research
        64–5; part-time staff 66
    structural adjustment 133, 138; uni-
        versities 130, 132, 142
Bretton Woods institutions 127, 132
Bristow, Walt 137
Britain *see* United Kingdom
Brookings Institute 177, 183, 193
Buarque, Cristóvam 142
Bundy, McGeorge 135
Bush administration 16, 34–5, 39–40,
    47, 57, 184
business agendas, for education 2,
    21–2, 215
Butler, Stuart 189, 191

C
California State University 62
Campaign for the Future of Higher
    Education 20–1
Capital 107, 109, 133
capital
    class, education and 19–20; encroach-
        ment into state/public education
        114; need for interventionist state
        3, *see also* human capital; intel-
        lectual capital
capital accumulation 2, 14, 115, 121,
    128
capitalism
    and education
        empirical analysis 112–20;
            inevitable increase in inequality
            120–1; Marxist analysis 103–12;
            need for 208–9; orientations that
            suit 139–43
        fundamental principle 2; structural
            crisis, early 1970s 135–6, 137–8,
            see also global capitalism;
            national capitalism; neoliberal-
            ism; state capitalism
capitalist agenda
    international 22–4; for schools 21–2;
        in schools 22

capitalist class 2, 103, 104, 106, 111
capitalist education 115, 116, 210
capitalist institutions 106
capitalization 12, 119, 121
Cardoso, Fernando Henrique 129, 133,
    138.
career choices 40, 59
Career Education 59, 63
Castro, Fidel 227, 228, 229, 230, 232,
    233, 235, 241–2, 242
Cato Institute 173, 174, 175, 177, 178,
    179
CDI Education Corporation 59
Central America Free Trade Agreement
    (CAFTA) 131
Central Intelligence Agency 39, 135
Central Única dos Trabalhadores (CUT)
    132, 134
centralization 115–17
Centre for Economics of Education 118
Centre for Racial Equality 19
charter schools 17
Chavez, Hugh 121
chief executive officers (CEOs) 14, 38,
    67–8, 113–14
child poverty 35
children, structuralized by education
    111–12
Chile 129, 130
China 113, 121
choice, and inequality 117–20
Christian 'personalism' 210
Christian right 35, 36
Chronicle of Higher Education 39, 43
citizenship 50, 111, 160
City Technology Colleges 15
civic engagement/participation 69, 85
civil society 85
civilization, education as tool for 111
class consciousness 111, 121
class struggle 35, 106, 113, 117, 121
class(es)
    anxieties, projected onto youth 36;
        education and capital 19–20;
        racialized and gendered 12, 16,
        115; rejection as binary relation
        103–4; relations of production
        105–6; selection by 213; upward
        mobility between 110, 115;
        Weberian formulations 103–4,
        see also capitalist class; middle
        classes; working class
Clemson university 44
The Coca-Cola Kids 22

Cold War 79–80, 135, 136, 137
collective resistance, university corpora-
    tization 48–50
college presidents 38
Collor de Mello, Fernando 138
Columbia University 135
commercial presence, supply of services
    77
commitment schedules (GATS) 77–8
Committee for Economic, Social and
    Cultural Rights 87
'committees for good government' 132
commodification 20–1, 36, 84–5
The Communist Manifesto 2, 109
communism 136, 240
community participation 18
compensatory policies (WB) 158–9
competition
    from lower-wage economies 113;
        for jobs 109, *see also* economic
        competition; free competition;
        market competition
competitiveness
    in education 15, 16, 117; in industry
        217, 218
comprehensive education 1, 16, 115,
    215
compulsory education 214, 235, 239
conditioned loans (WB) 152
conditioning 108
conflict, free trade and education 87–93
CONLUTAS 134
conservative modernization 152
conservative multiculturalism 160, 161
conservative think tanks 173–6
    educational research 175–6; market-
        ing 174–5, 184; media relations
        174; movement conservatism
        174; news media use of 176–7;
        reasons for favourable news
        coverage 179–80; rise of 197;
        strategies to change news
        reporting 174, *see also* Heritage
        Foundation
Conservatives
    United Kingdom
        broad appeal 110; education poli-
            cies 15–16, 117
    United States, backlash against higher
        education 46–7
consumer practices 48
consumer satisfaction, as surrogate for
    learning 38
consumerism 113

consumers, students as 21, 37, 41, 43,
    44
consumption abroad, of services 77
    in education 82
contract labor 42–3
contradictions
    educational effectiveness and finan-
        cial cutbacks 221; free market
        and loss of civil liberties 36;
        relations of production 106;
        social democratic resistance to
        capital 121
control 13, 34, 36, 104, 109, 110, 116
convenience, conservative think tank
    news coverage 180
cooperation, in right to education 81
Corinthian Colleges 59
corporate state 36
corporate university 37–45
    future for 45–50
cost-effectiveness 67–8
cost-efficiency 43
counterinsurgency doctrine 135, 136,
    137
Covington, S. 173
Crane, Ed 174
creativity 116
credibility, conservative think tank news
    coverage 180
credit crisis 14
critical educators 19, 46
critical literacy 236
critical thought, loss of 18–19, 116
cross-border supply, of services 77
    in education 82
cross-subsidization, universities 67
Crow, Michael 39
Cuba 227–43
    economic reform policies 233, 237;
    education 233–41
        abolition of illiteracy 234; egalitar-
            ian schooling practices 234–5;
            GDP allocated to 234; higher
            132; imperialism in the cur-
            riculum 237–41; indoctrinat-
            ing function 238–9; patriotism
            within the curriculum 241;
            privatization 240–1; racialized
            privilege 238; social produc-
            tion of labor power 228, 235–6,
            238–9, 240; success 234
        human rights violations 229;
            humanitarian achievements 228,
            242; illiteracy rate 234; negative

impact of fall of the Soviet Union
232–3; perceived as threat to US
security 228–9;
resistance
to capitalism 241–2; to US imperialism 227
social conditions 230; state-run corporations 237–8, 242; US trade
embargo against 230–2
Cuban Education System: Lessons and
Dilemmas 234
cultural diversity, WB policy 152,
157–65
cultural privatization 37
cultural reproduction 210–11
cynicism 33, 36, 45

D
Davis, R. 196, 197
'death of class' 104, 107
decentralization 18, 153, 154, 161,
214, 220
decolonization 135, 136
Dell Inc. 43
demand, and quality of education 61,
62
democracy 33, 36, 37, 42, 46, 49, 50,
85, 163
'democracy to come' 34
democratic education 46
democratization 33, 130, 222, 230
DeMuth Christopher 174
deontological approach, human rights
92
Department of the Treasure (US) 155
deradicalisation 110, 111
deregulation 31, 87–9, 214, 221
Derrida, Jacques 34
developing world
class war 113; education companies
in 60; privatization conditions
attached to development finance
119, *see also* peripheral countries
Dewey, John 49
dialectical reading 236
dialectics 106
Dickens, Charles 108
differentiation 118
disadvantaged groups, WB focus on
159–63
disinvestment 31, 45
disposability, politics of 33–7
dispute settlements, GATS 76–7, 91
distance learning 56, 131, 223

diversity
strength within 243, *see also* cultural
diversity
Doha Conference (2001) 75
Dolny, Michael 176, 177
Doyle, Denis 183

E
ECLAC *see* Economic Commission for
Latin America and the Caribbean
École républicaine 212
economic base 106, 108
Economic Commission for Latin
America and the Caribbean
(ECLAC) 128
economic competition 214, 216, 217,
220
economic depression, 1970s 113
economic growth 33, 157, 212, 213
*Economic and Philosophic Manuscripts
of 1844* 239
Economic Policy Institute (EPI) 173,
177, 178
economic pragmatism 159
Ecuador 132
Edison 56
education
Brazil *see* Brazil;
and capitalism
economic need for 208–9; empirical analysis 112–20; inevitable
increase in inequality 120–1;
international agenda 22–4;
Marxist analysis 19–20, 103–12;
orientations that suit 139–43,
see also global capitalism
centralization 115–17; commodification 20–1, 84–5; comprehensive
1, 16, 115, 215; compulsory 214,
235, 239; conditioned loans 152;
conflict between free trade 87–93;
contexts of change 1–2; Cuba *see*
Cuba; debate, news media 171;
dual market structures 82; economic competition 217, 220;
and GATS
ambiguous relationship 83–4; economic approach to 84–5; opacity
of negotiations between 85–6;
privatization 22–4; reform and
protection of human rights 86–7
ideological claims of 209–10; as
ideology 134–6; in liberal society

139; markets in 1–2, 14–17, 20–1, 54, 215–16; poverty and security 143;
press coverage 182–3
see also think tank-news media relationship
privatization see privatization; public expenditure 215, 217; social stratification 213; standardization 64, 115–17; universal 119–20, 211–12; use value 107–8; in values 163, see also bilingual education; higher education; primary education; right to education; secondary education
Education Bill (2006) 115, 117
Education Management Corporation (EDMC) 59
Education of the Negro 212
education policy
global 213–16; instrumental rationality 20;
United Kingdom
Conservative 15–16; New Labour 16, 22, 117
World Bank see World Bank
Education Reform Act (1988) 15, 16
Educational Change in Latin America and the Caribbean 152
educational inequality 102–21, 128–9
choice 117–20; ethnic minorities 161; markets and 14–17; Marxist perspective 102–3; neoliberalism and increase in 120–1; social strata 105; WB policies 128–9
educational research
conservative think tanks 175–6; renaissance of Marxist 103–5
educational services
definitions under GATS 84; privatization 113; suppliers, international movement of 82;
trade in
development of 73–4; liberalization of 82, 94, 131; opposition to 74; transnational 131
World Bank view on 154
educational strategy, need for 80
Educor 58, 60
EduTrek International 59
Eduventures 216
efficacy 157, 159, 161
efficiency 92, 157, 159, 161
efficiency model, trade law 91

egalitarianism, Cuban education 235–7
elite
education and reproduction of 210–11, see also ruling classes
elite educational institutions 16, 18, 68, 118, 238
embezzlement, WB loans 138
embourgeoisement 110
employment
education and promise of 210; FPIs' concern for future 68–9, see also job-oriented education; unskilled jobs
empowerment right, right to education as 79
Engels 105, 108, 111
entertainment, conservative news media coverage 181
entrepreneurship 215
equal treatment 80
equality 1, 158
see also inequality
equality of opportunity 15, 68, 210
equiphobia 16
equity 119, 158, 159
equivalence of exploitation 105
essentialist multiculturalism 161
Estácio de Sá 58, 61, 64–5
ethnic minorities 160–1
ethnicity 241
ethnodevelopment 162
European Commission 21, 213–14, 217, 220, 221, 222, 223
European Round Table (ERT) 21–2, 214, 217
European Union (EU) 3, 128
European university model 129
An Evaluation of the Florida A-Plus Accountability and School Choice Programme 175–6, 177
exceptions, to GATS 76–7, 83, 88–9
necessity test 91–2
exchange value 109
exclusion 30, 160
exclusive thought 152
experts/expertise (news media) 176, 186, 194
exploitation 30
capitalist 2, 106, 107; equivalence model 105; in higher education 47; rising rate of 113

F
Failing Schools 15, 117

Fairness and Accuracy in Reporting
(FAIR) 176, 177, 178
FAO *see* Food and Agricultural Organization
Farnsworth, Megan 191, 192
'fat cats' 114
fear 31, 32, 34, 35, 36, 44
Ferry, Jules 212
Feulner, Edwin 174, 196
film, representations of youth 34
Finn, Chester 176
fiscal inequality 112–14
Flores, Antonio 69
focused policies (WB) 159–63
Food and Agricultural Organization
(FAO) 13
food prices, global 13
*For-Profit Higher Education: Develop-
ing a World-Class Workforce* 57
for-profit institutions, higher education
54–70
bankruptcies and failures 63; branding 63–4; concern for student
destinations 68–9; desire for
expansion 58–60; enrollment in
55, 57; European resistance to
57; growth of 55–8; investment
and cost-effectiveness 67–8;
large-scale takeovers 59; litigation by students 62; part-time
educators 66; proper reward
and utilisation of teachers 65–6;
quality control 60–3; research
and development 64–5; teacher
education 62
Forbes magazine 14
forces of production 105–6, 112
foreign direct investment, in education 82
FPIs *see* for-profit institutions
France
École républicaine 212; unskilled jobs
222
free competition, GATS rationale for 90
free economy 16
free education 129, 142
free trade
agreements 131; conflict between
education and 87–93; principle
of non-discrimination 75
Free Trade Area of the Americas
(FTAA) 131
free-market model 2–3, 31, 35
free-riders, MFN clause and 76
freedom 109

Freire, P. 235–6
Fresh Start Schools 15, 117
Friedman, Milton 153
fulfillment, right to education 81
funding, educational 15, 19, 35, 40,
233, 234

G
Gardner, Robert 139
Garrett, Jennifer 187, 189
Gasperini, L. 233, 234–5, 238
GATS *see* General Agreement on Trade
in Services
Geiger, Jack 50, 69
gender, and inequality 104, 105
gendered social class 12, 115
General Agreement on Trade in Services
(GATS) 73–95
anti-democratization 17; bottom-up
approach 77–8; commitment
schedules 77–8; criticisms of
75–6;
and education
ambiguous relationship between
83–4; as a commodity 84–5;
inclusion of higher 93; opacity
of negotiations between 85–6;
privatization 22–4; reform and
protection of human rights 86–7
exceptions 76–7, 83, 88–9
necessity test 91–2
liberalization of trade 87–8; main
rules and obligations 76–7;
nature, aims and objectives
75–6; negotiating process 78;
non-discrimination principle
90; origins and evolution 74–5;
subsidies 91; threat to success of
75; top-down approach 76–7;
transfer of governmental authority to WTO 89
general knowledge 219
General Law of National Education
(Law 9394/96) 141
Genio, João di 65
geography, expert news sources 186
Georgetown University 135
The German Ideology 105, 106
Germany
dual track system of education 115;
for-profit higher education 57
Gintis, H. 112
Giroux, Henry 236
global capitalism

Cuba
  education as a leveller against
    235–7; movement against inten-
    sification of 229
cuts in public expenditure 2;
and education
  business agenda for 2, 21–2, 215;
    consequences of 223–4; flex-
    ibility and adaptability 218–21;
    functions of 209–10; materialist
    historical perspective 210–13;
    school merchandization 216–17
  education policy 213–16
  development of education business
    222–3
  expansion 1; neoliberalism 2–3,
    30, 50
global corporate market 3
The global education industry 68
global inequalities, growth of 12–17
globalization 2, 12, 19, 82, 138–9, 142,
    230
Gould, Eric 46
governance security 133
Gramsci, Antonio 111
Grant Maintained schools 15
Green Berets 135
green revolution 137
Greenberg, Milton 41–2
Growth Acceleration Program 133
Guatemala 229
Guevara, Ernesto (Ché) 239, 240

H
Hanley, Larry 41
Hanseatic University 57
Hartridge, David 23
Hayek, Friedrich von 3, 139, 141, 158
health care 31, 38, 233
hedge fund managers, pay 14
hegemonic policies 132
hegemonic vocation, of WB 155
hegemony 110, 111, 130, 133
Heritage Foundation 172, 173, 177,
    178, 183
  conservative movement 174; market-
    ing values 184; media presence
    185–93, 194–5; media presenta-
    tion 190–3; news media outlets
    172, 181; public relations system
    173–4; research 175
Hickey, T. 105
hidden curriculum 41, 112
hierarchicalization, educational 16, 118

*Higher Education: The Lessons of
    Experience* 141
higher education
  access to, Latin America 130; com-
    modification 20–1;
  corporatization of 37–45
    solutions to 45–50
  democratic 34, 46; differentiation
    118; for-profit institutions *see*
    for-profit institutions; inclusion
    in GATS 93; need for defence
    of 45–6; right-wing reforms 42;
    WB orientations 140–2, *see also*
    universities
Hinton, Thomas 191
Hood, John 178–9
Hudson Institute 183
Hugo, Victor 108, 211
human capital 157, 213, 230
Human Development Report (UNDP,
    2005) 13
human rights
  functionalist vision adopted by WTO
    91; justification of 92; non-
    discrimination principle 90, 91;
    right to education 73, 78–81;
    transfer of governmental author-
    ity to WTO 89; transforming into
    services 83–7; violations 229
human rights law, conflict between
    trade and 82–95
Hurricane Katrina 33

I
IBM 44
ICESCR *see* International Covenant on
    Economic, Social and Cultural
    Rights
identities
  learning about 45, *see also* market
    identities; social identities
ideological claims, of education 209–10
ideological reproduction, education
    and 21
ideological state apparatuses 113
ideology
  challenge for university faculties 48;
    class hegemony 111; educa-
    tional reform 134–6; liberal 3,
    109, 115, 157; market funda-
    mentalism 30, 36, 37, 42, 44,
    46; neoliberal *see* neoliberalism;
    relations of production 108;
    WB political 152

ideology critique 110
IFC *see* International Finance
    Corporation
Illinois, University of 43
illiteracy 36, 234
imagination 116
IMF *see* International Monetary Fund
imperialism 35, 227, 237–41
import substitution 128, 136
In Retrospect: the Tragedy and Lessons
    of Vietnam 137
inclusion 37, 163
income inequality 13–14
incompatibility, thesis of 158
India 1, 13, 17, 18, 57, 113, 129
indigenous peoples
    creation of intercultural university
        132; WB policy 159–63
individualism 31, 113, 158
indoctrination 238–9, 240
industrialization 128, 129, 211
inequality
    domestic trade policy formation
        85; economic 32; resistance
        to 121; scientific and techno-
        logical 128–9; WB discourse and
        policy 152, *see also* educational
        inequality; equiphobia; fiscal
        inequality; income inequality;
        social inequality
information and communication (ICT)
    220
infrastructure, productive 106
inmiseration of workers 109, 113
insecurity 31, 32, 33, 44
    see also security
insitutionalization 108
Institute of Economic Affairs 54
institutional autonomy 81, 141, 220–1
intellectual capital 139
Intercultural University of Indigenous
    People 132
interest groups, news media outlets 181
international capitalist agenda, educa-
    tion 22–4
International Covenant on Economic,
    Social and Cultural Rights
    (ICESCR)
    Article 2 81; Article 13 78–9, 81
International Finance Corporation
    (IFC) 54, 58, 119
International Monetary Fund (IMF) 3,
    17, 113, 118, 127, 133, 134, 155
INTERSINDICAL 134

interventionist state 3
investigative reporting 198
investment, for-profit higher education
    67–8
'invisible hand' 87
ITT Educational Services 60

J
job-oriented education 18
joint ventures, postgraduate distance
    courses 131
Jones, Victoria 181
journalists, conservative think tank
    news coverage 179–80
Judis, J.B. 197

K
K-12 schools 17, 35
Kafer, Krista 188, 189, 190–1, 195
Kant 92
Karle, Dr Hans 62
Kelly, Michael 187–8
Kennedy, John 228
Keynesian welfare state 12
Kissinger, Henry 229
knowledge acquisition 219–20
knowledge economy 115
knowledge society 221, 222
Kurfess, Thomas 44
Kuttner, Robert 174

L
labor 19, 42–3, 109–10, 140
Labor Education Programme (Cuba)
    238
labor market 132, 140, 160, 221–2
labor power, social production 224
    capitalist business agenda for 2; cru-
        cial to capitalism 3; Cuba 228,
        235–6, 238–9, 240; state need to
        control 116; teachers as danger-
        ous 19–20
laissez-faire (classic) liberalism 3
Latin America
    education, private sector expansion
        130, 131
    enrollment in secondary education
        130; for-profit higher educa-
        tion 57, 58; managerial-military
        dictatorships 127; right to
        education 129; universities 130;
        Washington Consensus 127–8;
        WB education policy 157–65,
        see also individual countries

law graduates, student debt 40
learning 38, 42, 215, 219
'learning to learn' 219
left postmodernism *see* postmodernism
Lenin 106
liberal think tanks 178
liberalism 3, 109, 115, 157
liberalization, financial 128
liberalization of trade 75, 87–8, 131
   impact on educational services 82,
      94; and the 'race to the bottom'
      113
Lieberman, Trudy 178, 179–80, 196,
   197
life, neoliberal impact on 32
lifelong learning 215, 219
Lipman, P. 16
literacy, as component of political
   struggle 236
literature, representations of youth 34
LMICs *see* low-income and middle-
   income countries
Locke 92
low income families, non-enrollment of
   qualified students 41
low-income and middle-income countries (LMICs), for-profit higher
   education 57, 58, 60
Lula da Silva, Luiz Inácio 129, 132,
   133, 134, 142, 144
Lynch, Merril 216

M
McNamara, Robert S. 136, 137, 139
Madhusudan, C.N. 66
management training, Cuba 237–8
managerial-military dictatorships, Latin
   America 127
managerialism 20, 43, 131
Manhattan Institute 173, 175, 177
market access, GATS commitments 77
market competition 109–10
market fundamentalism 30, 36, 37, 42,
   44, 46
market identities 48
market imperfections 154
market model 2–3
market values 36
markets, in education 1–2, 14–17,
   20–1, 54, 215–16
Marx, Karl 14, 104, 105, 106, 108,
   109, 110, 111, 239, 240, 243
Marxism, capitalism and education
   19–20, 103–12

Marxist humanism 109
Marxist multiculturalism 241–3
massification 213, 215, 222, 223
materialism 32
medical schools 62
Mehra, M. 85
Mexico 128, 129
Microsoft Corporation 43
middle classes 130, 211–12, 213
middle-income countries *see* low-
   income and middle-income
   countries
militarization 33, 48, 50
Mill, James 109
Millennium Round 75
mode of production 106
modular qualifications 221
Molnar, Alex 176–7
*Mortgaging our future: How financial
   barriers to college undercut
   America's global competitiveness* 41
'most-favoured nation' clause 75, 76
Movimento dos Trabalhadores Rurais
   Sem Terra (MST) 132
Mulderrig, J. 20
multiculturalism 17, 160, 161, 241–3
'myth of the method' 130

N
Nader, Ralph 175
national capitalism, cuts in public
   expenditure 2
national inequalities, growth of 12–17
National Institute for Information
   Technology (NIIT) 57, 60, 62,
   65, 66, 67
National School Florestan Fernandes
   132
'national treatment' principle 75, 77
National Youth Sports Program 35
necessity test, exceptions to GATS 91–2
negotiation process (GATS) 78, 85–6
neo-Marxists 103
neoconservatism 16, 35
neoliberalism
   demands of 3–4; fiscal inequality
      112–14; of global capitalism
      2–3;
   impacts of
   growth of national and global
      inequalities 12–17; growth of
      undemocratic (un)accountability
      17–18; increase in educational

inequality 120–1; loss of critical thought 18–19
scourge of 30–3;
WB education policy 152, 153–5
    Latin America 157–65; response to 164–5
youth and the politics of disposability 33–7
Neue Rheinische Zeitung 109
'neutralization of the education function' 158
New Labour 15, 16, 22, 114, 117, 121
'New Lords of the World' 138
New Man 239, 240
new public managerialism 20
New Right 112, 160
A New Agenda for Education 172, 173
news media 171–98
    experts/expertise 176, 186, 194; shaping of educational debate 171;
    and think tanks
    presentation of reports and spokespersons 177–9; use of 171–2, 176–7, *see also* think tank-news media relationship
news media outlets, conservative think tank news coverage 181
Nicaragua 121, 138
No Child Left Behind 16, 115, 117, 193
No Excuses 192, 194
non-discrimination 75, 80–1, 90, 91
non-university policy 140
nonprofit internationalization 94
nontarrif barriers 88
Nord Anglia 23
normative arguments, protection of human rights 92
norms (conflicting) trade and education 90–1, 92
North American Free Trade Agreement (NAFTA) 131

O

Old Labour 114
Open University 68
operational bias, conservative think tank news coverage 180
oppression 104, 105, 160
Organisation for Economic Co-operation and Development (OECD) 21, 60, 208, 213, 218, 223
Owen, D. 196, 197

P

Palattela, John 42
Parachini, L. 173
'parallelist' model, exploitation 105
parental choice 1–2, 15, 117
Parenti, M. 197–8
part-time educators 42–3, 47, 66
particularistic universalism 158
Partido dos Trabalhadores (PT) 134
partnerships 130, 161–2, 221
'pathologization of the market model' 2
patriotism 241
pedagogy 20, 46, 111, 116
'pedagogy for the poor/for the excluded' 158
Pell Grants 39–40
peripheral countries
    growing inequality between central countries and 129; increasing debt 138; influence of IMF and WB 133; labor 140; liberalization of trade in services 131; percentage of scientists and engineers 128; poverty 133, 140; US relations 135–6
personalism 210
Peru 58
Phi Delta Kappan 192
Philippines 58, 66, 69
Phoenix, University of 57, 59, 61, 64, 66, 67, 68
Pitágoras Group 60, 131
pluralism 104
Policy Analysis No. 187 (Cato Institute) 175, 178, 179
politics, neoliberal 32, 45
poor students, access to education 39, 118, 119
Portugal, for-profit higher education 57
postgraduate education 129, 131
postmodernism 17, 104, 107
postsecondary education *see* higher education
poverty 36, 37
    assistentialism 158; education as relief instrument to 140; and security 133, 136–9, 143, *see also* child poverty; poor students
precaution, duty concerning right to education 81
Preface 106, 108
'preferential commitments' 76
presence of a natural person, supply of services 77

primary education 96, 140, 141–2, 142–3, 211
private education 68, 119
privatization
  conditions attached to development finance 119; Cuba 232–3; cultural and linguistic 37;
  education 114
    anti-democratization 17; capitalist agenda 22–3; Cuba 240–1; Latin America 130, 131; proponents of 54; under GATS 22–3, 94; WB policy 153
privatized utilities 2
professors, part-time 42–3
profit 2, 106
Progressive Policy Institute 173
Project on Student Debt 40
propaganda 135
protection, right to education 81
PT *see* Partido dos Trabalhadores
public, conservative think tank news coverage 180
Public Citizen 175
public expenditure 2
  on education 215, 217
public good, education as 130
public interest 130
public morals, derogation from GATS' commitments 88–9
public relations, Heritage Foundation 173–4
public services
  cuts in expenditure 2; privatization 23, 114; subject to rules of the market 31
public-private partnerships 130

Q

quality control, for-profit higher education 60–3

R

race, and inequality 104, 105
'race to the bottom' 113
racial anxieties, projected on to youth 36
racialized privilege, Cuba 238
racialized social class 12, 16, 115
racism 32, 35, 36, 104
Radical Right 16
Ravitch, Diane 176
Reagan administration 113, 138, 173
reality 111

Reed, Robert 178
relations of production 105–6, 112
religious fundamentalism 35
remuneration
  chief executive officers 14, 67–8, 113–14; part-time educators 43, *see also* wages
repressive state apparatuses 12–13, 113
reprimarization 128, 133
reproducing nature, superstructure 111
reproduction function
  of education 210–11, *see also* social production
reproduction theorists 108
'request-offer' process (GATS) 78, 88
research and development, for-profit higher education 64–5
reserve army, of labor 109
resistance
  Cuban
    to capitalism 241–2; to US imperialism 227
  for-profit higher education 57; to inequality 121; to neoliberalism, Latin America 132; to university corporatization 48–50
resistance theorists 108, 110
resocialization 240
respect, right to education 81
revisionist left 104, 121
revolutionary education 236, 238
revolution(s)
  Cuban 227, 232, 237; liberal 109
Ricci, D. 175, 181–2, 191
right to education
  conflict between trade and human rights law 82–3; as fundamental human right 73; Latin America 129; nature and evolution 79–81; origin and sources 78–9; positive obligations 81
Rikowski, Glenn 19–20
Rio Salado College 43
RioLearn 43
rollback rule 88
Rothstein, Richard 192
ruling classes 12, 107, 108, 110
Russia 23, 55–6, 121

S

Sarrias 241
'sausage factory' metaphor 107, 108, 115–17
Schleicher, Andreas 208

Schmidt, George 192
scholarship 39
school autonomy 220–1
school choice 15, 117
School for Production 224
schools
    capitalist agenda for 21–2; capitalist
        agenda in 22; commercial pres-
        ence in 215; elite pre-university,
        Cuba 238; inequalities between
        15, 215; as locus of intellectual
        recruitment 111; as machines
        serving economic competition
        214; media coverage 183; mer-
        chandization 216–17; zero-tol-
        erance in 34, *see also individual
        schools*; state schools
scientific apartheid 128–9
scientific-technological revolution thesis
    138
scientists, and international compari-
        sons 128–9
Seattle negotiations (1999) 75
'second generation' rights 95
secondary education 130, 213, 215,
    219
security
    and education 134–5, 143; poverty
        and 133, 136–9, 143, *see also*
        governance-security; insecurity
selection 15, 16, 117, 213
sexism 35, 104
Shakur, Assata 241
sink schools 15, 117
skill reproduction 21, 215, 218, 219–20
Slanting the Story 178
social change, need for 50
social class *see* class(es)
social cohesion 163, 210, 240
social contract 33, 34, 36
social critics, liberal 109
social democracy 12, 114, 116–17, 121
Social Democrats 121
social engineering 135
*Social Expenditure of the Central Gov-
        ernment: 2001 and 2002* 142
social identities 12
social inequality 37
    alignment of education to industry
        and financial powers 222–3;
        education and preparation for
        acceptance of 111–12; growth
        of national and global 12–17;
        media use of balanced reporting

197–8; in schools 215; social
        democracy 116–17; solutions to
        problem in higher education 49;
        tryptych model 104, 105; WB
        education policy, Latin America
        157–65
social justice 33, 37, 42, 142, 235
social movements, defence of public
        education 132
social order 211
social production
    of elite, role of education 210–11
    labor power *see* labor power
social relations 31–2, 34
social science research, media conferral
        of legitimacy 191
social selection, secondary schools 213
social stratification 213
socialism 104, 109, 227
socialist resistance 121, 227, 241–2
socialization 210, 211, 212, 240
Soley, L. 176, 177, 180, 195
solidarity 241–2
Sousa, Paulo Renata de 140–1, 142
South Africa 57–8, 60
Soviet Union
    impact of fall of, on Cuba 232–3;
        vocational education 108
'species being' 238–9
Sperling, John 57, 67, 69
Spring, J. 175
standardization 64, 115–17
Stanford University 135
state capitalism 230
state companies 128, 237–8, 242
state schools 56, 58–9
state violence 32
state(s)
    demands of neoliberalism 3–4, 31;
    and education
        capacity to control 90; involvement
            in 115; need for control of 20;
            program provision 80; retreat of
            as provider of 1
    need to control social production of
        labor power 116;
    right to education
        dependency on behaviour and
            policies 80; obligations concern-
            ing 81
    voluntary nature of commitments,
        under GATS 88; Washington
        Consensus on role and organiza-
        tion 153–4, *see also* corporate

state; interventionist state; strong state
Steele, J. 176, 177, 186
Stewart, Thomas A. 139
Stiglitz, J. 153
Stolcke, Verena 157
strong state 3, 12–13, 16
Stroup, Sally 57
structural adjustment
  international agency programs 118–19;
  Latin America 128
    Brazil 133, 138
  WB policies 113, 128, 138, 151
structural challenge, for faculties 47–8
structural crisis, capitalism 135–6, 137–8
student autonomy 238
student debt 40
student loans 40
student protests 48
students
  costs of higher education 39–41; as customers 37, 41, 43, 44;
  enrollment
    in FPIs 55, 57; in higher education 59–60, 130; reduction in 41
  for-profit institutions
    concern for future employment 68–9; implications of bankruptcies 63; litigations 62
  waning concern for 44, *see also* teacher-student relationships; youth
subsidies 91
superstructure 108, 110, 111
supply of services, GATS commitments 77
surplus value 3, 19, 107, 113
surveillance 13, 16, 34, 36
Sweden, inequality 116–17
Sylvan Learning Systems 59, 60, 62

T
Tannock, Stuart 49
teacher education 18, 20, 62
teacher educators 18–19
teacher training 18, 20, 234
teacher-student relationships, Cuba 235–6
teachers
  as dangerous 19–20; proper rewards and utilisation of 65–6; waning concern for 44

technological apartheid 128–9
technological development 216–17
Thatcherism 3
Theory of Increasing Misery 14
'thesis of incompatibility' 158
think tank-news media relationship study 179–83
  analysis 183–4; results 185–93; discussion 194–8
think tanks
  defined 172;
  news media
    presentation of reports and spokespersons 177–9; use of 171–2, 176–7
  rise of 172–3, *see also* conservative think tanks
Thomas, Cal 187–8
Thor, Linda 43
Tooley, James 54–5, 59, 60–1, 62, 63, 64, 65, 66, 69
totalitarian power 32
Tothkopf, David 14
trade
  conflict between human rights law and 82–95; in services *see* General Agreement on Trade in Services, *see also* free trade
trade barriers, removing 87–9
trade law, efficiency model 91
transnational trade, educational services 131
transparency rule (GATS) 76
Tucker, Robert 57, 69

U
undemocratic (un)accountability 17–18
underclass 42, 117
unemployment 109
UNIP 58, 65
United Kingdom
  education policy 15–16, 22–3, 56, 117; fiscal inequality 114;
  higher education
    differentiation 118; for-profit 57, 58
United Nations 18
  involvement in trade policy making 86; judicial mechanisms, protection of human rights 92
United Nations Convention on Economic, Social and Cultural Rights 119

United Nations Development Program
  Studies 140
United Nations Educational, Scien-
  tific and Cultural Organization
  (UNESCO) 87, 134, 155, 234
United States
  Cuban resistance to imperialism
    227; Cuban socialism perceived
    as threat to 228–9; education
    policy 16, 115, 117; fiscal
    inequality 113–14; global cor-
    porate market 3;
  higher education
    companies, large-scale takeovers
    59
    corporatization 37–45; for-profit
    55, 56, 70
  income inequality 13–14; marketiza-
    tion of school system 16–17;
    neoliberalism in 33; percentage
    of scientists and engineers 128;
    state violence and totalitarian
    power 32; teacher education
    62; trade embargo against Cuba
    230–2; university fees 118;
    unskilled jobs 221–2
United States Agency for International
  Development (USAID) 135
UniverCidade 61
Universal Declaration of Human Rights
  73, 78, 231
universal education 80, 119–20,
  211–12
universalistic particularism 158
universities
  Brazil and Latin America 130, 132,
    142; cross-subsidization 67;
    cynicism and disinvestment in
    45; European model 129; fees
    16, 118; institutional autonomy
    141; language of the market in
    21; power within 47; racialized
    social class hierarchicalization
    16, *see also* corporate univer-
    sity; higher education; *individ-
    ual universities*; students
university culture 43
university deans 39
university faculties
  protecting full-time jobs 47; as
    sources of contract labor 42–3;
    structural and ideological chal-
    lenge 47–8; threats facing 45
university presidents 38–9

The university in ruins 45
unskilled jobs 221–2
unusual, conservative think tank
  news coverage 180
upward mobility 110, 115
urbanization 211
Uruguay Round 74, 131
use value 107–8

V
value-creating labor 19
values, education in 163
Values Education 238, 240
Van Auken, B. 13
venture capitalists 39
Vietnam 135, 136, 137
vocational training/education 108,
  215

W
Wage-Labour and Capital 104
wages 14, 109, 113, 114
Walden University 59, 64
Warner, C.D. 212
Washington Consensus 127–8, 132,
  134, 152–5
WB *see* World Bank
wealth inequality 13–14
Weber, Max 103
Weber, Samuel 48
*The weight of the world: Social suffer-
  ing in contemporary society* 36
Williams, Jeff 40
Wolfensohn, James 138–9, 140
Wood administration 139
working class
  consciousness 121; education 218,
    220, 238; embourgoisement 110;
    exploitation/oppression 2, 105,
    107, 239; inmiseration 109, 113;
    movements 12, 132; as redeem-
    ing feature of capitalism 106–7;
    tax 114; wages 113
Working Group on Extreme Inequality
  (2008) 13
World Bank 3, 17, 18, 118, 119, 127,
  129
  discourse on diversity and inequality
    152; education, and ideology
    134–6;
  education policy 151–65, 213
    association with 'good practice'
    156; central task 155; hege-
    monic vocation and strategic

interest 155; neoliberalism *see* neoliberalism; role and organization of the state 153–4; strategic alliances 155–6
educational orientation 139–43; for-profit higher education 58, 59; political ideology 152; poverty and security 136–9; structural adjustment policies 113, 128, 133, 138, 151
World Conference on Education for All in Jomtien 164, 165
World Debt Crisis (1982) 127, 131, 143
World Education Forum
Dakar 164, 165; Porto Alegre 164–5

World Trade Organisation (WTO) 3, 23, 73, 74, 75, 76, 85, 86–7, 89, 91, 94, 155
Wunderlich, Annelise 241

Y
Young, Beverly 62
youth
and the politics of disposability 33–7; reduced activism 130, *see also* children; students

Z
Zapatistas 132
Zemsky, Robert 38
zero-tolerance 34